AF215427

The Netherlands

Friesland
(Fryslân)
p218

Northeastern
Netherlands
p238

Haarlem &
North Holland
p122

AMSTERDAM
p46

Utrecht
Province
p150

Central
Netherlands
p258

Rotterdam &
South Holland
p170

Southeastern
Netherlands
p278

**Barbara Woolsey, Abigail Blasi, Mark Elliott, Catherine
Le Nevez, Sara van Geloven**

CONTENTS

Plan Your Trip

The Journey Begins Here 4

The Netherlands Map 6

Our Picks 8

Regions & Cities 20

Itineraries 22

When to Go 30

Get Prepared 32

The Food Scene 34

Cycling Nation 37

The Outdoors 40

The Guide

Amsterdam 46
  Find Your Way 48
  Plan Your Days 50
  Medieval Centre &
  Red Light District 52
  Royal Palace 57
  Oude Kerk 60
  Western Canal Ring,
  Jordaan & the West 63
  Anne Frank Huis 67
  Cycle Houthaven &
  the Western Islands 72
  Southern Canal Ring 78
  Vondelpark,
  Oud-West & Oud-Zuid 86
  Rijksmuseum 90
  Van Gogh Museum 94
  De Pijp & Zuid 98
  Oosterpark &
  East of the Amstel 104
  Nieuwmarkt,
  Plantage & the
  Eastern Islands 108
  Amsterdam Noord 116
  Places to Stay 120

Haarlem &
North Holland 122
  Find Your Way 124
  Plan Your Time 125
  Haarlem 126
  Texel 135
  Zaanse Schans 139
  Places to Stay 149

Utrecht Province 150
  Find Your Way 152
  Plan Your Time 153
  Utrecht City 154
  Places to Stay 169

Rotterdam &
South Holland 170
  Find Your Way 172
  Plan Your Time 174
  Rotterdam 175
  Delfshaven 180
  Centraal Station 187
  Markthal 191
  Depot at
  Museum Boijmans
  van Beuningen 193
  Den Haag 199
  Scheveningen 203
  Mauritshuis 209
  Places to Stay 217

Friesland (Fryslân) 218
  Find Your Way 220
  Plan Your Time 221
  Leeuwarden (Ljouwert) 222
  Frisian Lakes 232
  Places to Stay 237

Rotterdam (p170)

Northeastern
Netherlands 238
  Find Your Way 240
  Plan Your Time 241
  Groningen 242
  Drenthe 252
  Places to Stay 257

Central Netherlands 258
  Find Your Way 260
  Plan Your Time 261
  Arnhem 262
  Giethoorn &
  Weerribben-Wieden
  National Park 271
  Places to Stay 277

Southeastern
Netherlands 278
  Find Your Way 280
  Plan Your Time 281
  Den Bosch 282
  Maastricht 295
  Places to Stay 299

Friesland (Fryslân; p218)

CLOCKWISE FROM TOP LEFT: NANCY PAUWELS/SHUTTERSTOCK, MISTERVLAD/SHUTTERSTOCK, ALLARD ONE/SHUTTERSTOCK

Binnenhof (p202), Den Haag

Toolkit

Arriving 302

Getting Around 303

Money 304

Accommodation 305

Family Travel 306

Health & Safe Travel 307

Food, Drink & Nightlife 308

Responsible Travel 310

LGBTIQ+ Travellers 312

Accessible Travel 313

Sustainable Shopping 314

Nuts & Bolts 315

Language 316

Storybook

A History of the
Netherlands
in 15 Places 320

Meet the Dutch 324

Reclaiming Land
from Water 326

Proud Dutch Rainbows 330

Gedogen: The
Blind-Eye Principle 333

Beyond the Randstad 336

Under the (Dutch)
Influence 338

R. DE BRUIJN, PHOTOGRAPHY/SHUTTERSTOCK

Watertaxi (p176)

THE NETHERLANDS

THE JOURNEY BEGINS HERE

Timeworn windmills and tulip fields are the traditional reasons why everyone visits the Netherlands. And everyone and their mother (literally) does. Consequently, Amsterdam runs an anti-tourism 'stay away' campaign, aimed at discouraging disrespectful visitors. There's also a moratorium on building hotels, a direct, no-nonsense and fittingly Dutch approach to contesting insufferable overtourism. Local officials seek to calm streets and open up a more nuanced perspective on the Netherlands as much more than canals. Bucket lists be 'Dam'ned, your most memorable travel probably won't be in the capital, but exploring the coast and the countryside. Smaller centres outdo Amsterdam's scenic beauty and reveal the easy-going, laid-back nature of Dutch life with authenticity.

Barbara Woolsey

@xo.babxi

Barbara is a Filipina-Canadian writer telling stories about fascinating people, food and culture. When she's not penning guidebooks, find her DJing in Berlin, Amsterdam and beyond.

My favourite experience (also that of my one-year-old daughter) is zipping around Rotterdam (p176) in a watertaxi. I know the captain's showboating – speeding up, crashing into waves – was for her screams of delight, but it's a blast for adults, too..

WHO GOES WHERE

Our writers and experts choose the places which, for them, define the Netherlands.

The Frisian Wadden island of **Vlieland** (p230) is one of my favourite places in the world. The main road in the single village is lined with cosy cafes, restaurants and hotels. Nothing beats a hot cocoa with whipped cream by the fire after a day spent on the blustery beach battered by the North Sea waves or after a bike ride through deserted dunes.

Sara van Geloven

@saravangeloven
Sara is an Amsterdam-based travel writer with a passion for sustainable travel. Originally from the north of the country, she wrote the Friesland (Fryslân) and Northeastern Netherlands chapters.

The canals of Utrecht and Amersfoort are so pretty, and both cities have top pub-cafes, but as a beer lover, my defining experience was finding unexpected corners of Tilburg as I cycled across the city and down the Kanaldijk to Koningshoeven Abbey, grabbing a late slot for a comedy-gold tour of the **La Trappe Brewery** (p291).

Mark Elliott

@markbekaz
Mark has been writing about travel in Europe and Asia since the mid-1990s and is the (co)author of more than 70 guidebooks. He wrote the Utrecht Province and Southeastern Netherlands chapters.

Travelling from Amsterdam Centraal to De Pijp was until recently a meandering tram ride through the backstreets. Now, the three-minute metro trip is virtually instantaneous, but its sense of community is still intact: the kind of place where there are always familiar faces at the shops, markets, cafes and bars. On summer evenings, **Sarphatipark** (p100) feels like a local festival.

Catherine Le Nevez

lonelyplanet.com/authors/catherine-le-nevez
A Lonely Planet author since 2004, Catherine has a Doctorate in Creative Arts in Writing and insatiable wanderlust. She wrote the Amsterdam chapter.

Hoge Veluwe National Park (p267) is nothing like the postcard Netherlands. It's a forested ridge, a knobby backbone running through the Central Netherlands. The landscape is heath, sunlight-splicing trees and, oddly, great drifts of sand. There are treasures dotted across it too: the Kröller-Müller Museum, full of Van Gogh paintings, and the art deco-meets-brutalist Radio Kootwijk.

Abigail Blasi

@abi.where
Abigail is a travel writer specialising in Italy, India, the Netherlands and Denmark, with a focus on art, food and family travel. She wrote the Haarlem & North Holland and Central Netherlands chapters.

5

FROM LEFT, THOMAS ROELL/SHUTTERSTOCK, FROM LEFT, EDWIN BUTTER/SHUTTERSTOCK

Groningen
Bar-hop on a bicycle across student-scene pubs (p242)

Giethoorn
The charming 'Venice of the North' (p271)

Frisian Lakes
Get on the level of lush maritime life (p232)

Texel
Traipse around nature reserves and tranquil beaches (p135)

Amsterdam
Crisscross iconic canals and bucket-list museums (p46)

Haarlem
Bum around beach and 'burbs (p122)

Lisse
The world's largest flower garden (p216)

50 km
25 miles

6

Utrecht
Delight in canal-side cafes and independent boutiques (p154)

Gouda
Relish delicious cheese and hot-off-the-iron *stroopwafel* (caramel-syrup-filled wafers; p196)

Maastricht
Explore Roman architecture with a beer buzz (p295)

Kinderdijk
Iconic windmills, canals and countryside (p197)

Rotterdam
Marvel at mind-boggling buildings and art (p176)

Delft
Historic antiques and Vermeer's footsteps (p211)

Leiden
Suss out hidden urban art (p214)

Den Haag
Swan-dive into world peace history (p199)

7

SPECTACULAR SHORES

With so much water around, as well as famously reclaimed land, the Netherlands can at times feel like an island. Its 450km of coastline stretches across the North Sea and the nearby islands nestled into the Waddenzee, a mesmerising kaleidoscope of gold-sand beaches, rocky outcrops and windswept dunes. Cycling puts it all within a gear shift's reach. Craving seclusion? Off the mainland, hop aboard a ferry and discover shores well off the average traveller's radar.

Dutch Frisia

The West Frisian Islands are an endless bonanza of beautiful barriers. Go island-hopping here for a grab bag of recreational leisure and lounging.

Coastal Cycling Route

The 626km LF Coastal Route reveals a smorgasbord of gorgeous Dutch seasides. Discover sandy stretches, dunes and maritime villages between the Belgian and German borders.

Lonely Beaches

Lounge away from the crowds in the least-populous province of Zeeland. Across this glorious clutch of islands and peninsulas, empty shores abound.

FROM LEFT: TASFOTONL/SHUTTERSTOCK, RUDMER ZWERVER/SHUTTERSTOCK, NANCY PAUWELS/SHUTTERSTOCK.

BEST BEACH EXPERIENCES

Enjoy theatre performances staged on sandy dunes and beaches during the Frisian island Terschelling's summer ❶ **Oerol Festival** (p231).

Head outside of Haarlem, where ❷ **Bloemendaal aan Zee** (p131) is a prime stretch for suntanning and watersports classes.

Surf North Sea waves and stroll along the sands of ❸ **Scheveningen**'s (p203) beach near Den Haag. Cycle around to find stunning dunes.

Hike and explore ❹ **Twente**'s (p276) glorious mixed bag of golden-sand river beaches, marshy wetlands and heather fields.

Sink into the pristine white beaches of Waddenzee's ❺ **Texel** (p135). The island's soft, endless sands are some of the Netherlands' most inviting.

SARAHLOU PHOTOGRAPHY/SHUTTERSTOCK

A'DAM Tower(p116)

GREAT HEIGHTS

Landscapes as flat as *pannenkoeken* (pancakes) promise captivating panoramic views. Take in expansive perspectives, including picking out islands and peninsulas (or vice versa, to the Amsterdam mainland and beyond) when skies are clear. Sprawling tulip fields in full bloom, plus stoic windmills and historic architecture against vibrant sunsets, rival paintings by Dutch Masters any day.

Top Engineering

Innovative architecture rocks the landscape. Towers and bridges offer stunning views and fascinating backstories of bolstering local life via transport and flood protection.

Europe's Greatest Theme Park

Most Dutch people have fond childhood memories of Disneyland rival Efteling. Its roller coasters are perhaps among the craziest you'll ever ride.

BEST PANORAMIC EXPERIENCES

Confront acrophobia while dangling atop Europe's highest swing on ❶ **A'DAM Tower** (p116). The 100m-high observation deck offers divine skyline views.

Climb ❷ **Domtoren**'s (p154) iconic belfry tower – the Netherlands' tallest – for a panoramic perspective over Utrecht's meandering canals, skinny lanes and medieval architecture.

Ascend the 73m-tall spire of Arnhem's ❸ **Eusebiuskerk** (p265) to gape at Europe's biggest carillon and extraordinary vistas from glass balconies.

Zip line on the ❹ **Euromast** (p189) skyscraper or check out the 100m-high observation deck.

Trek 183 steps up the tower of ❺ **Sint Stevenskerk** (p270) in Nijmegen and take in splendid historical architecture below.

SUBTERRANEAN EXPLORATIONS

The Netherlands' subterranean world is a captivating realm of canals, tunnels and catacombs. Subterranean canals like those in Maastricht, coupled with extensive bunker systems from WWII, offer a fascinating glimpse into the country's history and below-ground engineering. Head underground to hidden caves, creaky passages and out-of-sight canals concealing some of the country's neatest anecdotes.

FROM LEFT: KIEVVICTOR/SHUTTERSTOCK, DEFOTOBERG/SHUTTERSTOCK

WWII Remnants

The Dutch Water Line defence system of bunkers and underground fortifications was constructed against possible invasions. Tunnels and cellars coordinated the resistance movement.

Roman Ruins

Uncover buried ancient Roman relics, including military camps and archaeological treasures, shedding light on the era's regional influence and enduring cultural presence.

Underground Waterways

The Netherlands' impressive water management systems include underground storm surge barriers and tunnels passing beneath canals, and ensure efficient urban mobility and safeguard local life.

BEST UNDERGROUND EXPERIENCES

Act like an amateur archaeologist discovering Roman relics in the darkened lair beneath Utrecht's ❶ **DOMunder** (p154).

Uncover a honeycomb of tunnels and underground forts that reveal Roman, Napoleonic and WWII history on a tour with ❷ **Maastricht Underground** (p298).

Sip cocktails at ❸ **Somewhere in the Middle** (p298) in Maastricht, a speakeasy in a cellar beneath the Vrijthof square.

Explore an unexpected subterranean aquarium within Den Helder's humongous hilltop ❹ **Fort Kijkduin** (p138).

Dance to house and techno in Amsterdam's basement nightclub ❺ **Shelter** (p117), ironically, housed in one of Amsterdam's tallest buildings.

FROM LEFT: IVO ANTONIE DE ROOIJ/SHUTTERSTOCK, OLIVERDELAHAYE/SHUTTERSTOCK, ROB ATHERTON/SHUTTERSTOCK

MEANINGFUL HISTORY

Dutch history has its fair share of darkness, but also moving resilience. Napoleonic rule, as well as Nazi occupation, has required a determination to rise from hardship and suffering. Contrastingly, a past on history's other side – as a former colonial empire, or aggressor – creates a complicated legacy. Mementoes of adversity, minorities sharing their stories, and an effort to decolonise tours and building names demonstrate the modern glory of a vibrant, progressive society.

Remembering the Holocaust

The Anne Frank Huis is one of the world's most evocative Holocaust sites. It's a highlight of any Amsterdam itinerary, attracting more than a million visitors annually.

Decolonising Travel

Decolonising tourism initiatives, including sightseeing tours and the renaming of institutions, address the Netherlands' colonial legacy and offer experiential insights into gentrification, immigration and identity.

Queer Heritage

Dutch LGBTIQ+ history shows up in monuments, tours and vibrant community spaces, plus manifold Pride events. Celebrate in the first country to legalise same-sex marriage.

BEST HISTORIC EXPERIENCES

Discover the **❶ National Holocaust Museum** (p113), a still-working synagogue and more in Amsterdam's Jewish Cultural Quarter.

Visit the **❷ Corrie ten Boom House** (p129) in Haarlem, where a family risked their lives hiding hundreds of Jews and Dutch resistors.

Uncover dark WWII history at the **❸ Airborne Museum Hartenstein** (p266) near Arnhem. The 19th-century, primrose-yellow mansion was once a Nazi and Allied base.

Visit the Holocaust memorial at **❹ Nationaal Monument Kamp Vught** (p289) in Noord-Brabant, which once served as a former Nazi labour and transit camp.

Explore how the Netherlands is reckoning with its colonial legacy by visiting the fascinating 'Our Colonial Inheritance' exhibit at **❺ Wereldmuseum Amsterdam** (p104).

OLRAT/SHUTTERSTOCK

De Oude Sluis (p189), Rotterdam

BRUIN CAFÉ CULTURE

The term *gezelligheid* describes the uniquely Dutch state of conviviality, cosiness, warmth and togetherness. It's a hallmark of the country's famous *bruin cafés* (traditional pubs, literally 'brown cafes'), so named for their dimmed lights and smoke-stained, centuries-old interiors. Swig a beer amid flickering candles and chum around with the locals.

Sips & Snacks

Order draught beer on tap or *jenever* (gin), plus plates of *bitterballen* (fried balls filled with ragu) and other *borrelhapjes* (deep-fried snacks).

Buzzy Ambience

Steeped in fascinating tales of patron sailors and intellectuals, *bruin cafés* are lively hangouts. Enjoy live music, pub trivia and more carousing.

BEST BRUIN CAFÉ EXPERIENCES

Cosy up in the 1642-erected ❶ **Café Papeneiland** (p76), a beautifully preserved, atmospheric standout among Amsterdam's hundreds of *bruin cafés*.

Quench your thirst sipping a lager at ❷ **Café Chris** (p76), Amsterdam's oldest *bruin café*.

Dine on classic Dutch fare with a classic windmill view at ❸ **De Oude Sluis** (p198) in Rotterdam's historic quarter of Delftshaven.

Head out for a night of furious dancing at the popular ❹ **De Zwarte Ruiter** (p210). Nightly offerings mix live music and DJs.

Indulge in regional brews and delicacies – most notably, *zuurvlees* (vinegar-stewed beef) at the student-favourite ❺ **Café Sjiek** (p297).

LUMINARY ARTISTRY

Rembrandt, Vermeer, Hals, Steen, Van Gogh, Escher, Mondrian... Some of the world's most revered artists hail from the Netherlands, and their exceptional works fill museums and galleries across the country. Alongside the most high-profile art repositories that brim with masterpieces, countless smaller venues await discovery, including historic premises where the creators themselves lived and worked.

Jam-Packed Capital

Amsterdam's world-class museums draw millions of visitors. The art collections take pride of place – you can't walk a kilometre without bumping into a masterpiece.

Transformative Art

Post-WWII destruction, Rotterdam's hasty concrete constructions disappointed locals. They've since beautified the cityscape with tonnes of urban art, from funky sculptures to colourful murals.

Outdoor Surprises

Museums pack masterpieces, but leave time for stumbling upon outdoor surprises, like installations sprouting from Rotterdam buildings and Leiden's quirky sculptures.

BEST ART EXPERIENCES

Marvel at masterpieces by local heroes Rembrandt, Vermeer and Van Gogh (as well as thousands of other works) at the ❶ **Rijksmuseum** (p90; pictured far left).

Roam around Rotterdam's impressive urban art, including the ❷ **Moments Contained** (p187) sculpture on the train station square.

Take an unusual tour of a museum's storage facility at the ❸ **Museum Boijmans van Beuningen** (p193), a limited-time offer during renovations.

Ogle Dutch and Flemish masters at Den Haag's ❹ **Mauritshuis** (p209), including Vermeer's *Girl with a Pearl Earring*.

Go down the rabbit hole in a stately former palace showcasing Escher's logic-defying art in Den Haag's ❺ **Escher in Het Paleis** (p205).

FROM LEFT: ERIK SMITS/RIJKSMUSEUM, CHRISTIAN MUELLER/SHUTTERSTOCK

15

OH-SO-FINE DESIGN

Throughout history, the Dutch have carved out a reputation as innovators, devising ingenious solutions to practical problems and vastly improving the quality of life. In fields as diverse as engineering, architecture, furnishings, appliances, homewares, fashion and technology – even water management – Dutch designs display signature style and wit, while keeping communities connected. Landscaping and horticulture are longstanding traditions, while sustainable structures shape a new horizon. Discover Dutch design across urban skylines and natural environs alike.

FROM LEFT: DMITRY RUKHLENKO/SHUTTERSTOCK, AARONCHENPS2/SHUTTERSTOCK, MENNO VAN DER HAVEN/SHUTTERSTOCK

Architectural Marvels

Rotterdam is a powerhouse open-air art gallery of some of Europe's most imaginative (and often wacky) modern architecture. The best part? It's still under construction.

Treasuring Topography

Dutch landscaping and horticulture are credited with manicuring terrain, while also leaving ancient areas to evolve naturally while remaining accessible via cycling and hiking trails.

Sustainable Innovation

Ingenious water management and agricultural infrastructure has long protected vulnerable, low-lying lands. A new era of green architecture aims to reach ambitious climate goals.

BEST ARCHITECTURE & DESIGN EXPERIENCES

Discover the floating auction village Broek op Langedijk, once an innovative 19th-century marketplace where farmers sold produce off rowboats, at ❶ **Museum BroekerVeiling** (p133).

Go on a guided architecture walking or cycling tour and attend workshops and free exhibitions during ❷ **Rotterdam Architecture Month** (p205).

Cultivate knowledge of green innovation at Amsterdam's ❸ **Hortus Botanicus** (p112), aiming to become the Netherlands' first climate-neutral public greenhouse.

Gaze at gigantic Amazonian water lilies and rare flora galore in the tropical greenhouse 'wilderness' of Leiden's ❹ **Hortus Botanicus** (p214).

Roam the ❺ **Philips Museum** (p294) in Eindhoven, housing illuminating artefacts from the electronics pioneer and a prestigious factory-housed architecture and design institute.

FROM LEFT: V_E/SHUTTERSTOCK, COLORMAKER/SHUTTERSTOCK, JOCAA/SHUTTERSTOCK

CANAL CRUISING

Canals ribbon the Netherlands' low-lying land, from magnificent cities such as Haarlem and Leiden, to lesser-known gems like Enkhuizen and Hoorn. Webs of waterways are historic lifelines, providing transport and pure pleasure. Strolling along canal banks and picturesque bridges is nice, but the more intimate, memorable experience is getting out on the water. Cruising experiences are eclectic and bountiful – board a vintage boat for a scenic cruise or become the captain of your own raucous party boat.

Out-Venicing Venice

Counting more canals than Venice (approximately 165 collectively stretching more than 100km), it's easy to see why Amsterdam's waterways are UNESCO-recognised.

Double the Fun

Utrecht's canals aren't as illustrious as Amsterdam's, but they are unique in their own right, thanks to being set across two levels.

Smooth Sustainability

Zero-emissions vessels, from e-boats to pedal boats and kayaks, provide an opportunity to drift all day without putting out carbon.

BEST CANAL-CRUISING EXPERIENCES

Skim Amsterdam's canals and hear immigration stories aboard ❶ **Rederij Lampedusa** (p115), a former refugee boat.

Clean polluted waterways on a do-good 'plastic-fishing' trip offered by ❷ **Canal Motorboats** (p71), Amsterdam's oldest boat operator.

Follow canals and channels dug by peat harvesters and farmers of yore into ❸ **Weerribben-Wieden National Park** (p273), near the canal-laced rural idyll of Giethoorn.

Indulge in the lush sceneries that inspired Hieronymus Bosch's paintings on a scenic cruise along semi-underground canals in ❹ **Den Bosch** (p282).

Cycle around a Dutch postcard brought to life at ❺ **Kinderdijk** (p197). Historic windmills nestle between meandering canals and picturesque greenery.

REGIONS & CITIES

Find the places that tick all your boxes.

Haarlem & North Holland

WINDMILLS, TULIPS, CHEESE AND MUSTARD

Haarlem, a commuter haven, evokes the Middle Ages and the Netherlands' 'Golden Age' with as much charming beauty as neighbouring Amsterdam (and with fewer crowds). Further out, the region flaunts small, cute places like cheese hot spot Edam, beaches and windswept dunes. Kitesurf, hike, sail and cycle around, spotting bountiful bird life and seal colonies. p122

Friesland (Fryslân)

PROUD LAND OF LAKES

Indulge in your water nymph fantasy on the Netherlands' northern coasts. Nomadic types feel right at home sharing empty beaches and endless waves with abundant sea and bird life. Float your boat out to islands, foray onto the mudflats and cycle back to reality with historic fishing towns. p218

Northeastern Netherlands

A DYNAMIC CITY, QUIET PARKS AND DEEP HISTORY

Take a journey through time across the northeast. Between farmland and forest lies fascinating history, including *hunebedden* (old burial sites) and a preserved fortress town. The regional centre, Groningen, has echoes of the 'Golden Age' and ancient times, yet a lively student population keeps an upbeat, urban pulse. p238

Northeastern Netherlands p238

Friesland (Fryslân) p218

Haarlem & North Holland p122

Central Netherlands p258

AMSTERDAM p46

Amsterdam

TRADITIONAL CHARM MEETS VISIONARY INNOVATION

Amsterdam is on every traveller's bucket list with good reason. It boasts more canals than Venice, cobblestone streets offering kaleidoscopic discovery, gabled canal houses, flower power and sprawling world-class museums immortalising artists from Rembrandt to Van Gogh. Though 17th-century glamour paints a timeworn landscape, rest assured that the capital is truly a contemporary powerhouse. p46

Rotterdam & South Holland

QUIRKY AND QUAINT DUTCH LIVING

An eclectic ensemble of small cities packs cool surprises around every corner. Rotterdam, Europe's largest port, is an open-air gallery of wacky architecture and street art. Delve into the weird and wonderful scientific history in Leiden, the 'City of Discovery', and vibrant cultures beyond Den Haag's world-peace governance. p170

Utrecht Province

OLDER AND WISER THAN AMSTERDAM

Utrecht vaunts an Amsterdam vibe without the crowds. Cool murmurs go 'underground' thanks to the city's unique two-storey canals. Explore cavernous bars and restaurants hidden in medieval warehouses, plus the city's deep subterranean archaeology. Across the province, fortifications and towns surrounding castles deliver high contrast. p150

Central Netherlands

NATURAL AND CULTURAL SPLENDOUR

Going off-path is this region's primo pleasure. Discover unchanged Hanseatic trade buildings in town alley time-warps, and follow canals and channels dug over the centuries by peat harvesters and farmers. WWII monuments and museums recalling fierce battle horrors are counterpoints to the idyllic rural life, yet offer poignant historical resonance. p258

Southeastern Netherlands

'BURGUNDIAN' JOIE DE VIVRE

Maastricht brings out the art buff and history nerd in any traveller, with sights from treasure-packed museums to underground tunnels and forts spanning Roman times and wars. Stop for caffeine at the city's vibrant cafes, though strong yet exquisite monastic brews present a formidable challenge in not getting too tipsy. p278

Utrecht Province p150

Rotterdam & South Holland p170

Southeastern Netherlands p278

NGCHIYUI/SHUTTERSTOCK

Binnenhof (p202), Den Haag

ITINERARIES

Splendid Cities Circuit

Allow: 1 week   **Distance:** 150km

Amsterdam may be a famous city break, but after discovering other pint-sized urban places, you'll probably find a different favourite. Cute 'second cities' offer equally enticing landmarks and authentic glimpses into everyday Dutch life. Desert the capital's crowds and catch a laid-back vibe across historic towns and windmill-speckled scenery.

①
AMSTERDAM ⏱ 2 DAYS

Spend three days in the capital **Amsterdam** (p46) to take in a couple of world-class museums, do some shopping and hop aboard a canal cruise. Make sure to spend time strolling aimlessly around Amsterdam's neighbourhoods, too. The perfect itinerary covers Jordaan, De Pijp, the Jewish Cultural Quarter and trendy Noord.

🔄 *Detour: Visit Lisse's Keukenhof Gardens (p216) and take in the season's tulip fields (mid-March to mid-May).*

🔄 *Detour: Cycle to Haarlem (p126) and hit the beach. For many, the 20km designated bike path connecting the two is a one-hour daily commute.*

②
UTRECHT ⏱ 2 DAYS

Scoot over to the cosmopolitan university city of **Utrecht** (p154). Arguably, it's even better for canals than the capital. Discover medieval architecture and subterranean Roman archaeology. Roam along the Oudegracht canal and wander into wharf cellars hiding atmospheric restaurants, bars and other secrets.

🔄 *Detour: Amersfoort (p166), a historic city off most travellers' radars, delights with its alluring fine-dining scene. Cycling the 20km here from Utrecht is a fabulous idea. Between mid-April and mid-September, you can jump aboard the riverboat Eemlijn, stopping in Amersfoort and then getting off at either Spakenburg or Huizen and cycling on.*

FROM LEFT: TAIGA/SHUTTERSTOCK, MISTERVLAD/SHUTTERSTOCK

Markermeer
IJmuiden
Zaandam
Zuid-Kennemerland National Park
START
Haarlem
1 AMSTERDAM
Almere
NORTH SEA
1hr
1½hr
Hoofddorp
Amstelveen
30min
Bussum
Noordwijk aan Zee
Lisse
Hilversum
Katwijk aan Zee
Leiden
Amersfoort
Alphen aan den Rijn
15min or 1hr
Den Haag
3
2
Utrecht
Zeist
Utrechtse Heuvelrug National Park
Zoetermeer
Nieuwegein
45min
Gouda
Delft
30min
4
Rotterdam
30min or 1hr
END
Kinderdijk
Tiel
Spijkenisse
Gorinchem
Dordrecht
0 20 km
0 10 miles

3

DEN HAAG 1 DAY

There's more than meets the eye in the Netherlands' seat of government and monarchy. The 'International City of Peace and Justice', **Den Haag** (p199), is also home to the Peace Palace (p202; pictured top left) and excellent cultural attractions such as the renowned art gallery Mauritshuis and modern performance complex Amare. Most importantly, Den Haag is made for spending time outdoors. Grab drinks on the Grote Markt square, seek out plentiful green parks and gardens such as the urban nature reserve Koekamp and stroll along Scheveningen beach.

4

ROTTERDAM 2 DAYS

There probably isn't enough time to discover the endless weird and wonderful murals, sculptures and art installations canvassing the streets of **Rotterdam** (p176) – locals don't even know them all – but two days will do just fine. Also packed with marvellous modern architecture, it's arguably the Netherlands' more surprising 'Dam.

Detour:** Windmill-heavy, countryside sweetheart* ***Kinderdijk *(p197) is a 30-minute waterbus or a 16km cycling journey away. Hiring a bicycle at Kinderdijk is easy, but you can also bring one on the waterbus from Rotterdam for free.*

FROM LEFT: KIEV.VICTOR/SHUTTERSTOCK, SEAN PAVONE/SHUTTERSTOCK

Gouda (p196)

ITINERARIES

Beyond the Capital

Allow: 4 days   **Distance:** 80km

Already annoyed by Amsterdam's crowds? Good, because the most quintessentially Dutch sights lie on a pleasant-paced journey around the south. Skip across eclectic culture- and history-packed centres strung together with charming smaller cities. Now those are double-Dutch jumps to remember! Afterwards, continue along the coast; Belgium and Germany run along the border.

❶ LISSE ⏱ 1 DAY

Revel in the vibrant colours of the Keukenhof Gardens (pictured), the world's largest floral show, in **Lisse** (p216). The Netherlands' ultimate petal paradise opens only in springtime. Off-season, Lisse stays sleepy – in fact, a little too so. Skip it and spend a day in more attractions-packed Den Haag or Rotterdam instead. Alternatively, shorten to a half-day in season if Keukenhof's crowds become too much.

🚣 *Detour: From Lisse, laid-back **Haarlem's** (p126) beaches and greenery are perfect antidotes to Keukenhof mania. It's an easy, breezy 20km bike ride. Taking a train won't save you any time; it's about the same duration.*

❷ LEIDEN ⏱ 1 DAY

Now we're talking surprises! Lisse is also an easy 15km bicycle ride or a 30-minute tram ride from underrated **Leiden** (p214), the 'City of Discovery'. Unexpected gems abound around its historic canals, and the city is more than just Rembrandt's birthplace. Leiden's historical botanical garden is the oldest in Western Europe; check out the distinguished tulip tree presiding over the front garden. Its mighty blooms are an evocative reminder of how the first tulips were successfully grown here by Carolus Clusius at the beginning of the 17th century.

FROM LEFT: STUDIO BARCELONA/SHUTTERSTOCK, BORIS STROUJKO/SHUTTERSTOCK

Map legend:

N

| 0 | 20 km |
| 0 | 10 miles |

NORTH SEA

Overveen
Zandvoort
Haarlem
AMSTERDAM

Hoofddorp
Amstelveen
Aalsmeer

START **1** Lisse
Noordwijk aan Zee

30min

Katwijk aan Zee

2 Leiden

Scheveningen

15min

Den Haag

Alphen aan den Rijn

Woerden

Zoetermeer

Monster

Oudewater

4 Gouda
END

Delft **3**

Hoek van Holland

45min

Schiedam
Rotterdam

Vlaardingen

3
DELFT ⏱ 1 DAY

The iconic blue and white porcelain you see everywhere across the Netherlands finds its origins in **Delft** (p211), a quick train ride from Leiden. From the city-centre Markt square (pictured), explore picturesque 17th-century streets and quaint boutique displays of Delftware pottery. If you hire a bicycle, you can explore more of the cityscapes that inspired native son Johannes Vermeer (though none of his works are on display here). Cute, independent lodgings – slightly cheaper than neighbouring Den Haag – and excellent cafes also make for lovely overnights.

4
GOUDA ⏱ 1 DAY

Grand finale **Gouda** (p196; pictured top left) serves up authentically Dutch cheesy goodness across a historic market and museums dedicated to its dairy origins. At the cheese market on Thursday mornings (April to August), delicious Dutch delicacies go well beyond dairy, including *stroopwafels* filled before your eyes (the famous caramel-wafer dessert originated in Gouda), traditional cookies and cakes, and seafood vendors selling *kibbeling* (fried fish bites). Train connections from Rotterdam are fast and frequent, making for an easy day trip. Gouda is also reachable via a direct sprinter (one hour) from Amsterdam.

FROM LEFT: WERNER LEROOY/SHUTTERSTOCK, WJAREK/SHUTTERSTOCK

Nature's Splendour

Allow: 11 days   **Distance:** 250km

Few travellers venture into the north and central inland, but they're missing out. The Netherlands' rural heart is where traditions are kept alive and prehistoric relics dot the landscape. Hire an electric vehicle and freely spin around remote islands and farmland. Groningen and Leeuwarden, with culture-rich historic centres, are wonderful bases to explore from.

Leeuwarden (Ljouwert; p222)

① GRONINGEN ⏱1 DAY

Get your bearings in **Groningen** (p242), the north's most charming hub. Around the historic city centre, striking architecture and impressive art collections are at hand. The youthful energy across student cafes and bars is infectious. Take quaint countryside stops en route to the lakeside tranquillity of Noorderplantsoen park. Ramble on deeper into the Dutch heartland.

② DRENTHE ⏱3 DAYS

If there's an off-the-radar part of the Netherlands, **Drenthe** (p252) is it. Without sea access or a major city, this region endures as Van Gogh described it in 1883: 'Here is peace'. Serene, remote nature is offered in spades. Discover canvas-worthy rural landscapes across a growing collection of national parks, and marvel at the mystery of megalithic *hunebedden* (burial chambers).

③ LEEUWARDEN (LJOUWERT) ⏱1 DAY

An unexpected combination of style and grit across graffitied alleyways and cafe-lined canals, Friesland's capital of **Leeuwarden** (Ljouwert; p222) is well worth a stop. It offers a superb trinity of museums and inventive cultural projects stemming from its 2018 crown as European Capital of Culture. Bars and cafes throbbing with fun-loving Liwwadders (as the locals are officially known) promise true northern hospitality.

WOLF-PHOTOGRAPHY/SHUTTERSTOCK

4
FRISIAN LAKES ⏱ 3 DAYS

The **Frisian Lakes** (p232) are idyllic Dutch countryside epitomised. Seek solitude across 20 serene bodies of water that form a meandering network of quaint canals, historic villages and gorgeous landscapes. Indulge in unpretentious seafood restaurants between active days of paddleboarding and kitesurfing.

🚢 *Detour:* Take a ferry to the **Wadden Islands** (p230) for quiet white-sand beaches and mudflats.

5
ZWOLLE ⏱ 3 DAYS

Zag eastwards to Overijssel, the Central Netherlands' most charmingly rural neck of the woods, to discover remote forests and medieval historic villages. On the province's eastern side, bordering Germany, the land is refreshingly hilly compared to elsewhere in the Netherlands, while 'flat and soggy' mostly sums up the landlocked, former western coastline. Anchor yourself in a picture-postcard Hanseatic town like **Zwolle** (p275).

6
GIETHOORN ⏱ 3 DAYS

Meander south through pastoral farmland to the wetland of **Giethoorn** (p271). Here in this Venetian-style canal village, waterways and boats famously outnumber paved roads and cars. Paddle about peacefully and discover Giethoorn's bucolic beauty around every bend. The lush, green landscape abounds with hydrangea and orchid shrubs, thatched-roof cottages, and button-sized bridges for perfect fairy-tale adventures.

TAIGA/SHUTTERSTOCK

ITINERARIES

Tour de Nederland

Allow: 10 days   **Distance:** 150km

The ultimate rewarding journey through the Netherlands is by *fiets* (bicycle). Pedalling Amsterdam's canals is cool, but the country's cycling network offers endless freedom as it glides by dyke- and windmill-covered countryside. This itinerary covers the main destinations in about 20km to 60km rides (about one to 3½ hours each).

① AMSTERDAM ⏱ 3 DAYS

Pick up your trusty two-wheeled steed in **Amsterdam** (p46), and get to know each other over three days of exploring renowned museums and landmarks. Get the hang of cobblestone streets in historic districts from Jordaan to De Pijp, and take your wheels on the free ferry to Noord, where they're especially handy for the distances. Park for a canal cruise and cafe stops.

② HAARLEM ⏱ 1 DAY

Just 20km north, **Haarlem** (p122) is a pleasant ride – so much so that many people who live here cycle daily to Amsterdam. Discover commuter life in this upscale, family-friendly city. Picturesque canals lace around 'Golden Age' townhouses, and the city centre has atmospheric terrace restaurants and many boutiques.

🚲 *Detour:* Cycle to **Zuid-Kennemerland National Park** (p131) for lakes, wildlife and beach-bar-lined white sands.

③ DEN HAAG ⏱ 2 DAYS

Take your pick of scenic routes through picturesque towns, past canals and dunes en route to the seat of the Dutch government, **Den Haag** (p199). Venture into towns like Leiden and Delft or stroll along Scheveningen Beach to discover wide, windswept dunes, WWII bunkers, and beach bars and restaurants.

FROM LEFT: TAIGA/SHUTTERSTOCK, TRABANTOS/SHUTTERSTOCK, Z. JACOBS/SHUTTERSTOCK

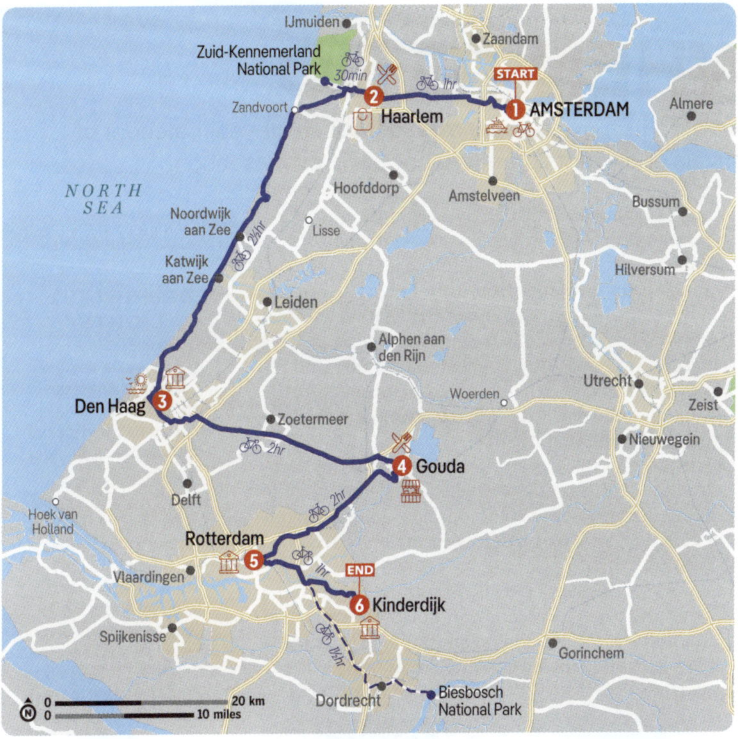
IJmuiden
Zaandam
Zuid-Kennemerland National Park
30min
1hr
START
1 AMSTERDAM
2 Haarlem
Zandvoort
Almere
NORTH SEA
Hoofddorp
Amstelveen
Bussum
Noordwijk aan Zee
2¼hr
Lisse
Katwijk aan Zee
Hilversum
Leiden
Alphen aan den Rijn
Utrecht
Woerden
Zeist
3 Den Haag
Zoetermeer
2hr
Nieuwegein
4 Gouda
Delft
2hr
Hoek van Holland
Rotterdam
5
1hr
END
Vlaardingen
6 Kinderdijk
Spijkenisse
1½hr
Gorinchem
0 20 km
0 10 miles
Dordrecht
Biesbosch National Park

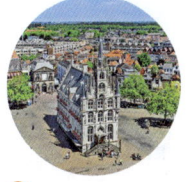

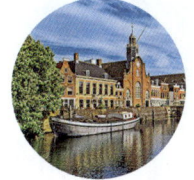

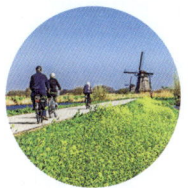

4

GOUDA ⏱ ½ DAY

Den Haag to **Gouda** (p196) takes you through 70km of lush Dutch countryside. It's one of the most classic day trips on two wheels. Park and wander around the compact city centre, discovering the historic cheese market and related attractions. Gorge on Gouda and *stroopwafels*, which originated here.

5

ROTTERDAM ⏱ 3 DAYS

Pastoral paths take you to **Rotterdam** (p176). Beyond infectious maritime vibes, Rotterdam is a venerable open-air gallery of funky modern architecture. It has fantastic art museums, too. Trendy nightlife and dining, from jazz cafes and rave warehouses to sustainable restaurants and craft brewpubs, keep a cool pace.

***Detour:** Reach **Biesbosch National Park** (p198) after a 28km ride through Dordrecht.*

6

KINDERDIJK ⏱ ½ DAY

Cycle over cute countryside bridges and past windswept dykes to iconic, 18th-century windmills. The 19 giants at **Kinderdijk** (p197) are loud and creaky, but some still work and can be entered. Sore legs by now? Return to Rotterdam on the speed waterbus (30 minutes). From there, take the train to Amsterdam (one hour) or directly from Kinderdijk (two hours).

FROM LEFT: STEVE PHOTOGRAPHY/SHUTTERSTOCK, PANI GARMYDER/SHUTTERSTOCK, LEOKS/SHUTTERSTOCK

WHEN TO GO

Tulip blooms may draw the masses, but an all-year calendar of festivals and events promises hoopla in every season.

Any time is prime to visit the Netherlands, and here's a controversial take: it probably isn't even when tulips are in bloom.

Summer's peak tourist season draws gigantic crowds around the country, and in compact city centres, you feel the squeeze. That's especially true in Amsterdam, where long museum queues, fully booked restaurants and attractions requiring months-ahead reservations put the kibosh on spontaneity. City officials even launched an 'anti-tourism' campaign in 2023.

The truth is that there is no poor time to visit the Netherlands. Low and shoulder seasons offer considerable perks, such as cheaper accommodation, longer lingering on gallery floors, and meeting locals more freely in their natural habitat.

The country's eclectic, calendar-spanning programme of festivals and events, especially in Rotterdam and Amsterdam, delivers lively vibes year-round. With speedy train rides effortlessly connecting towns and cities, there's no excuse not to be a *sociale vlinder* (social butterfly).

⊙ I LIVE HERE

DELIGHTFUL LIGHTS

Li Chao is a UX designer from Los Angeles who's been working in Amsterdam's fast-paced tech scene for a decade.

In December and January, it's fun to see the Amsterdam Light Festival (*amsterdamlightfestival. com*) aboard a boat with a group of friends. Different artists create light sculptures along the canals, and some are interactive. You can walk or bike the route, but the best way to see it is on the water.

FROM LEFT: IVO ANTONIE DE ROOIJ/SHUTTERSTOCK, KIEV.VICTOR/SHUTTERSTOCK

ENDLESS DAYS OF ENTERTAINMENT

The Netherlands' motley crew of multiday to monthlong festivals makes it easy to catch a performance or a party. The Holland Festival (May), Rotterdam Architecture Month (May) and Amsterdam Pride (July and August) are highlights.

Amsterdam Pride (p330)

Weather Through the Year

JANUARY	FEBRUARY	MARCH	APRIL	 MAY	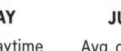 JUNE
Avg. daytime max: **6°C**	Avg. daytime max: **7°C**	Avg. daytime max: **10°C**	Avg. daytime max: **13°C**	Avg. daytime max: **17°C**	Avg. daytime max: **19°C**
Days of rainfall: **17**	Days of rainfall: **13**	Days of rainfall: **14**	Days of rainfall: **13**	Days of rainfall: **13**	Days of rainfall: **12**

WINTER WONDERLAND

Colder months promise heartwarming cheer during Carnaval in February, charming Christmas markets in December and *gezelligheid* (conviviality) at skating rinks and *bruin cafés* (traditional pubs). Many Amsterdam museums and attractions open on public holidays (Christmas, New Year's Day), offering special holiday fun.

World-Famous Festivals

Carnaval (p297) In Maastricht, this annual event boasts big parades, raucous drinking and traditions like hoisting the 'Cabbage Woman'. **February or March**

Holland Festival (p83) Draws in big-name theatre, dance and opera as part of the Netherlands' biggest performing-arts extravaganza in Amsterdam. **June**

North Sea Jazz Festival (p189) Rotterdam hosts the world's largest event for the musical genre, when about 1000 musicians swing into the city. Take your pick of jazz concerts from soloists to experimental. In the weeks prior, the North Sea Round Town fringe festival puts on jazz acts in public spaces and concert halls. **July**

Amsterdam Dance Event (p85) One of the world's largest electronic-music celebrations sees 2200 DJs, producers and more than 300,000 clubbers attending 450 citywide events for five sweaty nights. **October**

⊘ **I LIVE HERE**

MAGIC GATHERINGS

Viona Terleth is a Dutch culture strategist and leadership company founder from Amsterdam. linkedin.com/in/vionaterleth

I love going to festivals, and especially attending smaller ones for techno music. The Netherlands is known for throwing big celebrations, but with the smaller ones, you really have a chance to connect with people. My favourite festival is Gardens of Babylon *(thegardensofbabylon).com)* in Amsterdam. Four times a year, about 3000 attendees dress up in the most magical way for art, music and spiritual workshops.

Cultural Celebrations

National Tulip Day (p87) Dazzling displays of 200,000 tulips cover Amsterdam's Museumplein to kick off the Dutch tulip season. Admire a captivating mix of vibrant colours and aromas, and collect a tulip for free to take with you. **January**

King's Day (p101) Dutch festival season truly kicks off on 27 April with Koningsdag, the biggest countrywide street party in Europe. Pack your brightest orange getup – in Amsterdam, hundreds of thousands show up in the royalty's colour. **April**

Oerol Festival (p231) The Frisian Island of Terschelling turns into a stage, where you can enjoy theatre performances among dunes, beaches turned into artworks and live music played in remote locations. **June**

Holland Festival Oude Muziek (p153) Head to Utrecht for this weeklong showcase of European Middle Ages, Renaissance and baroque music. **August**

TULIPMANIA

Tulip frenzy takes flower in mid-January with National Tulip Day, when the capital's Dam square fills with about 200,000 tulips. Flowers can be taken home at the end of the day. Keukenhof Gardens' flowering-bulb show, the world's largest, happens from mid-March to mid-May.

JULY	**AUGUST**	**SEPTEMBER**	**OCTOBER**	**NOVEMBER**	**DECEMBER**
Avg. daytime max: **21°C**	Avg. daytime max: **21°C**	Avg. daytime max: **18°C**	Avg. daytime max: **14°C**	Avg. daytime max: **10°C**	Avg. daytime max: **7°C**
Days of rainfall: **13**	Days of rainfall: **14**	Days of rainfall: **13**	Days of rainfall: **15**	Days of rainfall: **17**	Days of rainfall: **17**

FROM LEFT: SINA ETTMER PHOTOGRAPHY/SHUTTERSTOCK, PHOTO 12/ALAMY

Delft (p211)

GET PREPARED FOR THE NETHERLANDS

Useful things to load in your bag, your ears and your brain.

Clothes

Layers It doesn't matter what time of year you go, you need a good range of easily changeable clothes. Wind and rain are all-too-familiar features of mild, yet temperamental, weather.

Backpack The Dutch love sleek yet functional design, so a stylish Scandinavian-type backpack helps you blend in anywhere. Inside, keep a couple of layers and maybe a swimsuit. (Bathing spots are easy to happen upon.)

Hand fan Heatwaves are increasing. As hotel rooms and establishments typically don't have air-con, bring your own breeze.

Smart casual wear Fancy dining stays relaxed: think a nice shirt and jeans. Bring sneakers rather than flip-flops, which scream 'tourist' and are bad for cycling.

Manners

Directness, openness and pragmatism inform Dutch manners. Formality-free, straightforward delivery is culturally standard. It's not to be stern, but rather ensure that communication stays clear and efficient.

Small talk with strangers can be cringy and awkward, but deep down, the Dutch are highly social and fun-loving, especially after a few pints when 'Dutch courage' sets in.

Punctuality is highly regarded; tardiness is considered impolite.

Cycling-friendly gear Stay cool and dry with lightweight nylon wares of the breathable variety. The right jacket, cycling trousers and shoes are musts.

📖 READ

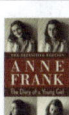

The Diary of a Young Girl (Anne Frank; 1947) The Netherlands' most iconic tome: 30 million copies in 70 languages sold.

Max Havelaar (Multatuli; 1860) Novel written under a pseudonym on Dutch colonial exploitation; a policy-changing masterpiece.

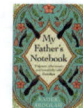

My Father's Notebook (Kader Abdolah; 2000) A fictional Iranian's Dutch immigration story, exploring identity, culture and family.

The Dinner (Herman Koch; 2009) Psychological thriller revolving around a dinner in Amsterdam that exposes family secrets.

Words

Hallo (hah-loh) Standard 'hello'.

Joe (yo) Slang for 'hello', 'goodbye' and getting attention

Groetjes (khroot-yes) 'Greetings'

Tot ziens (tot zeens) Formal 'goodbye'

Dag (dakh) 'Goodbye' for everyday interactions

Tjuus (choos) 'Goodbye' but a little cute

Excuseer mij (eks-kew-zeyr mey) 'Excuse me'

Dank je wel (dahnk yuh vell) 'Thank you', often shortened to 'dank'

Goedemorgen (hood-mor-khun) 'Good morning' (formal)

Goedenavond (hood-un-ah-vohnd) 'Good evening' (formal)

Ja (yah) 'Yes'

Nee (nay) 'No'

Alstublieft/Alsjeblieft (al-stew-bleeft/a-shuh-bleeft) **Please** (polite/informal)

Hoe gaat het met u/jou? (hoo khaat huht met ew/yaw) 'How are you?' (polite/informal)

Goed, en met u/jou? (khoot en met ew/yaw) 'Fine, and you?' (polite/informal)

Sorry Said the same as in English

Proost (prohst) 'Cheers' (toasting)

Eet ze (ate zay) 'Enjoy your meal'

Lekker (leh-kur) Useful term for 'delicious', 'cool' or 'awesome' for food, fashion and places

Top (top) Slang for anything excellent

Vet (feht) Slang for 'cool'

Gezellig (heh-zell-ikh) Describes a cosy, warm and enjoyable atmosphere

Chillen (chill-en) A 'Dunglish' (Dutch-English) term for hanging out

Strand (strahnd) 'Beach'

Fiets (feets) 'Bicycle'

▶ WATCH

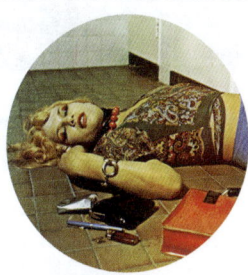

Turkish Delight (Paul Verhoeven; 1973; pictured) Erotic romantic drama from legendary auteur.

Vincent: The Life and Death of Vincent van Gogh (Paul Cox; 1987) Engrossing documentary-style drama exploring the artist's final years through written letters.

Soldier of Orange (Paul Verhoeven; 1977) Romantic war thriller depicting a Dutch student's time as a WWII resistance fighter.

Character (Mike van Diem; 1997) Dutch-Belgian mystery and psycho-drama set in the 1920s.

Capo di Famiglia (Annemarie Libbers; 2017) *Godfather*-esque crime thriller about a Dutch-Italian family harbouring dark secrets.

🎧 LISTEN

A Heart Full of Music (Denise Jannah; 1990) This album with powerful vocals helped establish the Suriname-born chanteuse as the country's queen of jazz.

Dekmantel 10 Years – The Collection (various artists; 2017) The electronic music festival's anniversary series offers tasters of its signature sounds.

Horizon (Jeangu Macrooy; 2021) The Surinamese-Dutch soul-pop crooner competed in the 2021 Eurovision Song Contest with a track from this album.

It's a Good Day (Shishani Vranckx; 2015) The Namibian-Dutch singer-songwriter's eclectic style represents a new generation of Dutch music.

LEFT: KAJAHIIS/SHUTTERSTOCK. BOTTOM RIGHT: MILOS RUZICKA/SHUTTERSTOCK.

Poffertjes (mini pancakes)

THE FOOD SCENE

The Netherlands is Europe's diverse dining hot spot. Multicultural cuisines and warm hospitality promise a *lekker* (delicious) time.

The Dutch ethos of keeping curious but unfussy informs a food scene that offers fabulous variety, from cuisine types to price points. Service is outstanding everywhere, from the most upscale eateries to traditional pubs, and *gezelligheid* (a state of cosiness, similar to Swedish *hygge*) is gloriously valued over putting on airs.

Modern cuisine embraces farm ingredients and artisan producers, and pays homage to Dutch cooking traditions. Despite these meat-centric traditions, thoughtful vegan and vegetarian options deliver satisfaction.

Beyond dinnertime indulgence, snacking in a *bruin café* (traditional pub) is a must. These centuries-old, tobacco-stained brown cafes, beloved by young and old, serve *borrelhapjes* (deep-fried snacks) with beer. Order a bunch to enjoy in what the Dutch call a 'brown buffet'.

Overall, the Netherlands has the most diverse, multicultural foodscape you'll find anywhere, but it's important to remember this stems from a complicated history encompassing high immigration, merchant trade and colonialism. Imperialism in Caribbean, Asian and African countries (some now sovereign, others not) shapes a culinary scene of homeland and fusions.

Dutch Classics

Traditional cuisine is highly influenced by the Netherlands' geography and history. Classic dishes, starring diet staples like dairy, meat and fish, greatly reflect overseas trade, as well as successful fishing and farming industries.

Successful exporting has increasingly prized quantity over quality, but to call the national cuisine bland is a misrepresenta-

---

Best Dutch Dishes

BROODJE	BITTERBALLEN	HARING	PATATJE
'Little bread' sandwich that's a staple for cycling journeys; a buttered roll with meat, cheese or other fillings.	The most beloved *borrelhapje*: deep-fried, ragu-filled balls with dipping mustard.	Raw, preserved herring with onions, pickles and bread, typically sold from stands.	Fries in a cone-shaped paper wrapping topped with ketchup and/or mayo.

tion. The colonial spice trade, though a contentious time period, counts flavourful, fascinating dishes, which are today truly Dutch favourites. Street snacks are often served with Indonesian-style peanut satay sauce, including *patatje oorlog* ('war fries') – a bouquet of fries topped with a lighter version of mayonnaise, satay sauce and diced raw onions – and *frikandel* (minced-meat sausage).

Cold winters have influenced filling, hearty creations, such as *boerenkool met worst* (mashed potatoes topped with kale and smoked sausage), *erwtensoep* (split pea soup with bacon or smoked sausage and thick rye bread), *stamppot* (mashed potatoes crowned with a veggie-sausage medley), as well as pub-staple *borrelhapjes*.

Meanwhile, industrialisation has seen Dutch sweets becoming beloved worldwide, including *poffertjes* (mini pancakes), *hagelslag* (sprinkles on buttered toast) and *stroopwafel* (caramel-syrup-filled wafers). Of course, there's also the country's favourite confection, *zoute drop* (salty liquorice) – beloved by the Dutch and their Nordic neighbours, but not so much by everyone else.

Where to Eat

Bruin cafés are traditional drinking dens where *borrelhapjes* are served, which might include croquettes and *kaassoufflé* (breaded and fried pastry filled with cheese). *Eetcafés* are traditional pub-cafes that serve meals and *borrelhapjes*.

A *koffiehuis* is an espresso bar or cafe (distinguishable from a coffeeshop, which sells cannabis), often selling all things *gebak-*

ken (baked), including pastries, sandwiches and cakes.

Boerenmarkten (farmers markets) sell fresh produce and also have stands such as a *kaaswinkel* (cheeseshop), a *bakkerij* (bakery), a *slagerij* (butcher), a *vijshandel* (fishmonger), and sometimes a *wijnhandel* (wine shop) or *ijsmaker* (ice-cream maker), too.

IMAGO/ALAMY

FESTIVALS FOR FEASTING

Amsterdam Coffee Festival (pictured) Celebration of local coffee culture, from tastings to barista competitions, in April.

Amsterdam Wine Festival In September, sip and savour among a 20,000-strong crowd of winemakers, sommeliers and vino buffs.

Preuvenemint (p297) Maastricht becomes the 'largest open-air restaurant in the world' for the Netherlands' biggest food festival in August.

Keti Koti (p104) Delicious food lies at the heart of nationwide celebrations on 1 July, marking the abolition of slavery in Suriname.

Ontzet (p205) This annual fest on 3 October in Leiden commemorates the end of Spanish starvation in 1574 with the same traditional feast over centuries: *hutspot* (stew of boiled and mashed potatoes, carrots and onions), herring, white bread and gallons of beer.

Rollende Keukens Sample Dutch and global cuisine across more than 100 'rolling kitchens' (street food trucks).

Kaassoufflé (fried pastry filled with cheese)

PANNENKOEKEN	POFFERTJES	RIJSTTAFEL	BAMI GORENG	KROKET
Large, thin pancakes with sweet (syrup, fruit) or savoury (cheese, mushrooms) toppings.	Puffy mini-pancakes generously layered with butter and powdered sugar.	'Rice table': a grand feast of prepared dishes like curries; a Dutch-Indonesian highlight.	A Dutch-Indonesian noodle (not rice) stir-fry that's beloved in Dutch culture.	A deep-fried meat ragu fast-food snack; sometimes eaten in a bun *(broodje kroket).*

Specialities

Best Borrelhapjes (Bar Snacks)

Bitterballen The most classic bar snack; a carnivore's treat. Try them in *bruin cafés* or find upscale versions at gourmet restaurants, such as the bone-marrow *bitterballen* at Clos in Amsterdam.

Kaasblokjes Deep-fried cubes of Gouda and Edam on toothpicks; served with dipping mustard like *bitterballen*.

Gefrituurde uienringen Dutch take on fried onion rings.

Mini saté Marinated skewers, often chicken or pork, served with peanut sauce.

Food Markets

Gouda Kaasstad Traditional wedges and kitschy costumes at Gouda's historic cheese market.

Foodhallen (p97) Amsterdam's epicentre of multicultural dining across 20-some food stands.

Markthal (p191) Rotterdam's striking market hall boasts fresh produce stands and modern eateries.

Postcolonial Cuisine

Indonesian Try a traditional *rijsttafel*, a large spread of small

Bitterballen

savoury and spicy dishes with rice as the centrepiece.

Surinamese A fusion of African, East Indian, Javanese and Dutch influences. In Amsterdam's multicultural Oost area, take your pick of authentic Surinamese street food at the Dappermarkt (p104).

Caribbean Soul food from Aruba, Bonaire and Curaçao blends Dutch, African and Indigenous influences. Dishes include *keshi yena* (steamed or baked cheese stuffed with spiced meat) and *stoba* (beef stew).

Chinese Discover Chinese-influenced dishes often at Indonesian restaurants. Head to Chinatown in Amsterdam (p46) and Den Haag (p199).

INNA TARAN/SHUTTERSTOCK

MEALS OF A LIFETIME

Witloof In Maastricht, this internationally renowned restaurant boasts Belgian classics, an atmospheric beer cellar and surreal dining-room decor.

De Kas In a 1926-built greenhouse on a former country estate, dine on sustainable, modern Dutch fare. All produce is grown in the gardens right outside.

Pannenkoekenhuis Upstairs Amsterdam's most exclusive address might be at this unsuspectingly famous pancake restaurant with only four tables.

Zala's Fairly priced, gourmet multicourse dinners in Utrecht; stay over afterwards in its elegant B&B.

François Geurds Rotterdam's best-known chef promises wowing menus from his restaurant and adjoining food lab.

Simonis aan de Haven Seaside canteen and Den Haag harbour institution with a truly eclectic seafood menu.

THE YEAR IN FOOD

SPRING

Fresh farm produce starts to hit market stands. Don't miss the most beloved regional harvests: strawberries and asparagus. Standout dishes include asparagus in Hollandaise sauce (obviously), *aspergesoep* (asparagus soup) and *aardbeientaart* (strawberry tart).

SUMMER

Splurge on a fine-dining tasting menu. Chefs go crazy with abundant seasonal produce, and many restaurants pluck from their own gardens. Passion and creativity promise surprising, experiential gastronomic affairs.

AUTUMN

Venture out to grand estates and charming orchards (close to the cities) to pick apples and pears. Sweet treats like *pannenkoeken* and *poffertjes* are dolloped with fresh *appelmoes* (applesauce), and *perentaart* (pear cake) hits eatery menus.

WINTER

Cosy up with hearty dinners or *borrelhapjes* in candlelit *bruin cafés*. At Christmas markets, indulge in *oliebollen* (deep-fried Dutch beignets) and *stamppot*. Dip *pepernoten* (mini spiced cookies) into hot chocolate.

OLENA RUDO/SHUTTERSTOCK, SUSANNA8976/SHUTTERSTOCK, RUUD MORIJN PHOTOGRAPHER/SHUTTERSTOCK, POLEIJPHOTO/SHUTTERSTOCK

Cyclists, Kinderdijk (p197)

TRIP PLANNER

CYCLING NATION

The Netherlands is the ultimate country to explore by *fiets* (bicycle). From pedalling along Amsterdam's canals to rolling past tulip fields and dykes, two-wheeled adventures offer a rewarding taste of the freedom that Dutch folks simply live for. Low-lying landscapes and excellent cycling infrastructure, including parking garages and paved paths, promise smooth sojourns.

Cycle Like the Dutch

ROUTES

The Netherlands' mostly flat landscape, without many hills or steep inclines, and excellent webs of long and short cycling routes make the country a joy to ride through. Thousands of routes across cities – and between them – fabulously connect coasts and borders, with most neighbouring cities only a one- to two-hour journey from each other.

CYCLING 'MOTORWAY'

Standing for *landelijke fietsroutes* (long-distance routes, also called 'national bike routes'), LF routes are the Netherlands' epic journeys on two wheels. The network of routes criss-crosses the country and, like motorways, is designed to get you from one locale to another. Go your own way, whatever that may be, via the Holland Cycling website's route planner *(nederlandfietsland.nl)*.

BICYCLE HIRE

Bike shops are everywhere – every town and larger train stations have at least one. Costs range from about €10 to €15 per day. Often, shops take a copy of your passport and require a cash or credit card deposit (usually €25 to €100). Helmets are not commonly used in the Netherlands and are not included. They typically cost €5 per day. Before riding into the sunset, check for a working lock, bell, back-pedal coaster brakes and hand brakes. Document any existing damage with your phone for a smooth return.

ACCELERATED FREEDOM

Get around quicker and easier
● Thanks to plentiful, well-paved routes and flat terrain, cycling is convenient (and budget-friendly).

Understand the culture
● No activity better exemplifies the Dutch hallmarks of 'true freedom' and egalitarianism. Bikes became popular here because, unlike elsewhere in Europe, they've always been an accessible, non-luxury item.

Ride between cities
● National routes span approximately 35,000km. Travelling between neighbouring urban centres in South Holland and beyond boasts gorgeous countryside.

Discover modern innovation
● Seek out stretches that take comfortable two-wheeling to a high gear, including solar-panelled paths and a night-illuminated 'smart highway'.

Kick it into high gear
● The Dutch are famously skilled cyclers (training starts as young as age two) for whom speeding up to 25km/h is no sweat. Stay to the right to be passed.

Seek out covered and underground parking
● Garages are inexpensive and essential in rainy times.

Consider winter cycling
● Many cities keep cycling paths clear of snow, and heated bike lanes prevent ice.

Get familiar with Dutch-only traffic features
● Cyclist-only roundabouts *(fietsrotondes),* skyways, as well as traffic lights *(verkeerslichten)* and lanes *(fietsstrook)* designated for cyclists comprise key cycling infrastructure. Navigating such road features, as well as the fast-paced, crowded nature of Dutch cycling routes, might take some getting used to.

MARC VENEMA/SHUTTERSTOCK

BEST CYCLING DAY TRIPS

Amsterdam to Waterland Loop (37km)
One of the most picturesque rides, with greenery galore and village life.

Amsterdam to Haarlem (50km to 70km return)
Follow Dutch commuters to a cute suburb-like town and hit the beach.

Den Haag to Gouda (70km to 80km return)
Day trip through classic Dutch countryside ending in a deliciously cheesy payoff.

Rotterdam to Kinderdijk (25km one way)
Cycle to UNESCO-listed heritage windmills and take a speedy ferry back.

Rotterdam to Biesbosch National Park (60km return)
Go from a buzzy harbour city to a beautiful nature park. Explore vast marshlands and spot beavers.

The Dutch railway operator NS hires out 'OV-fiets' bikes for much cheaper than shops (€4.65 per day for three days, €9.65 per day afterwards, to a seven-day maximum). There are more than 300 hire stations nationwide, most at train stations. OV-fiets must be returned to the same station, or there's a €10 fee.

TRAIN TRAVEL

Take your bicycle onto trains at certain times (and depending on space). Bike tickets (€7.95 per day) are valid Netherlands-wide regardless of distance, but only outside designated peak periods (9am to 4pm and 6.30pm to 6.30am Monday to Friday). On weekends, throughout July and August and on public holidays (except for King's Day), bikes are allowed on trains at any time. Tickets can be purchased from machines or service desks.

Cyclists near Groningen (p249)

SECURITY

Bike theft is common. Hardened chain-link or T-hoop locks are the most secure. Don't ever leave your bike unlocked.

MAINTENANCE

Beyond repair shops, free repair stations are often found in public spaces, such as outside of train stations.

PARKING

Parking facilities *(fietsenstallingen)* are abundant, well-covered or underground, and often have video or guarded surveillance. Some, like the one at Amsterdam's Centraal Station, are among the world's largest. Be sure to note your location (or digitally pin it). Public parking allowances range anywhere from hours to weeks.

RULES OF THE ROAD

Watch for cars Cyclists have the right of way, except when vehicles enter from the right (although not all motorists respect this).

Watch for pedestrians Tourists often zig-zag into lanes.

Use the right-hand lane Look for white lines and marks.

Make sure to signal Put out your hand.

Use lights at night (by law) Front and rear clip-on lights also allowed.

Ring the bell when passing It's polite.

'Offroading' Experiences

TOURS & TRIPS

Endless companies offer bike tours of cities and countryside, including multiday trips.

Nature campsites abound along bike paths, often adjoined to local farms. They're generally smaller, simpler and cheaper than regular campgrounds and free of cars and caravans. Accommodation with bike storage and e-charging points is common.

ARTS & CULTURE

Don't forget to park and discover cycling as a cultural activity. Vibrant street art and sculptures offer a fantastic visual ride, from abstract to historic. Look for tunnels and bridges sporting murals. Many repair shops double as cute cafes showcasing local life. Check out a cycling festival incorporating culture and sport with live music, food stands and velophiles.

BICYCLE GRAVEYARDS

Discover a so-called 'bicycle graveyard', like the Fietsdepot (Bicycle Depository) in Amsterdam, where stolen and removed bikes are reclaimed by owners or otherwise donated and recycled.

WINTER CYCLING

Cycling across snow and ice is not for the faint of heart; the Dutch do so expertly. Warm layers are essential, and hiring special gear is advised.

UNUSUAL ATTRACTIONS

The Netherlands is full of surprising, uncommon activities related to its national obsession. In Utrecht, discover the library's 'cycling desks' allowing patrons to exercise and charge their devices. In Eindhoven, an extraordinary floating roundabout suspends cyclists in the air.

LF ICON ROUTES

In 2022, the LF network unveiled 'Icon Routes', each offering a themed journey. Infrastructure upgrades include the addition of info displays to landmarks along the way. Find maps, tours and more digital resources on the LF app *(nederlandfietsland.nl)*.

LF Maas Route (477km)
Marathon route from Maastricht to the Hook of Holland.

LF Zuiderzee Route (434 km)
Discover North Sea villages, harbours and reclaimed polders starting and ending in Amsterdam.

LF Waterline Route (405 km)
Follows ancient Dutch defences such as dykes and fortresses between Edam and Bergen op Zoom.

LF Coastal Route (626km)
Cruising the southern coast and islands.

R. DE BRUIJN_PHOTOGRAPHY/SHUTTERSTOCK

Dwingelderveld National Park (p253)

THE **OUTDOORS**

The Netherlands' lowlands bring together wetlands, lakes and verdant countryside. With nary an elevation in sight, the features of this landscape become even more impressive.

The Netherlands turns any couch potato into an active nature buff. Don't let the flat terrain fool you; outdoor recreational opportunities are endless and regionally diverse. The Dutch way is simply appreciating nature as the key to a fulfilling, enjoyable life. Lush terrain promises thrilling and relaxing outdoor escapes. Endless cycling routes connect land and water, putting seclusion within pedal's reach, though travelling by bike is only the start to airy, green Dutch discoveries. Across the country, float and ramble to your heart's delight.

Cycling

The Netherlands, perhaps the world's most bicycle-friendly place, promises pedal-powered trips of a lifetime. The landscape, flat as a *pannenkoek* (pancake), is easy riding. Thousands of kilometres of cycling lanes and paths link virtually the entire country.

Trading cities for the countryside, where you can really ride like the wind, is an unforgettable experience. The Netherlands' *landelijke fietsroutes* (LF) routes, essentially cycling highways, offer enchanting scenery: cow-filled farmland, creaky windmills and tulip blooms in springtime.

Even if you're not a big cycling person, consider this type of trip – it's less exerting than you might think. Standard touring bikes suit the Netherlands' flat terrain just fine. E-bike hire and taking wheels onto long-distance trains and buses are also allowed.

Boating & Paddling

Strolling around canals and bridges is nice, but it doesn't compare with the experience of being out on the water. An afternoon

Alfresco Adventures

ICE SKATING
Strap on some skates and join locals on the ice in **Elfstedenhal** (p226) in Leeuwarden.

MUDFLAT WALKING
Experience the filthy fun that is *wadlopen* (p228) from the mainland to the Wadden Islands.

CLIMBING
In Groningen, scale **Bjoeks** (p248), one of the world's highest towers and, if you're wily, camp up top.

FAMILY ADVENTURES

Build sandcastles and enjoy ice cream on **Scheveningen Beach** (p203).

Picnic and explore gardens in Amsterdam's excellent green lungs, such as **Vondelpark** (p86) and **Oosterpark** (p106).

Zip line between towering ancient trees in the lush forests of **Amsterdamse Bos** (p102).

Explore dunes and dunk into North Sea swells at **Bloemendaal aan Zee** (p131).

Encounter seals, sharks and all sorts of other native coastal animals at Texel's **Ecomare** (p137) nature centre.

Learn to windsurf off the artificial sands of Amsterdam's **IJBurg** (p111).

Skip and cycle around tulip fields at the famous **Keukenhof Gardens** (p216).

Enjoy bird-watching, swimming and eating *broodjes* (sandwiches) at the **Zuid-Kennemerland National Park** (p131) near Haarlem.

skimming along rivers, lakes or inland seas is the epitome of fun and relaxation. Myriad Dutch canals and waterways offer endless twists and turns for unexpected discovery. The opportunity to play captain comes in all shapes and sizes, from canoes and small sailboats to motorboats. Opt for an emissions-free electric boat; they're easy to hire most everywhere these days.

For the most definitive boating experience, head to Friesland (p219). From inland lakes to island coasts, empty sandy stretches and low, verdant farmland provide big, open views of rolling skies.

Much less known but equally impressive are the dinghy drifts in the Netherlands' underrated central regions. Finding your 'sea legs' on canals is gloriously rewarded. Giethoorn (p271), for example, is a Venetian-style village cut with watery trails.

Canal cruises in Amsterdam (p46) and Utrecht (p150) are much more mainstream experiences, but still savour-worthy. Unconventional boating tours are good for more than just panoramic seclusion. Amsterdam's Plastic Whale *(plasticwhale.com)* runs 'plastic fishing' trips to clean polluted waterways. On the Rederij Lampedusa (p115), listen to immigrant tales aboard a former refugee boat.

Walking & Hiking

Wandering around the Netherlands' dashing countryside comes with a stark realisation: no brushstrokes could ever do such landscapes justice. See for yourself what the masters have tried to immortalise: dense forests, colourful heathlands and tulip fields, not in museum paintings but in real life. Wonderfully low-lying Dutch terrain promises non-challenging walks and endless horizons. About 10% of the country is untamed protected land. Dwingelderveld National Park (p253), Europe's largest wet heathland, offers more than 60km of hiking paths amid bogs, meadows and forest.

ACTION AREAS

For the best outdoor locations, see p42

FOKKE BAARSSEN/SHUTTERSTOCK

Hindeloopen (p233), Friesland

CYCLING	**HIKING**	**PADDLING**	**WATERSPORTS**
Glide through Den Haag's **urban forest** (p199) and along a beach leading to discoveries of dunes and WWII bunkers.	Choose your perfect treasure hunt of prehistoric relics and ancient forests such as **Dwingelderveld** (p253) in Drenthe.	Swan along the waters in **Amsterdamse Bos** (p102), but do so sustainably by canoe.	Take your pick of wet 'n' wild thrills from kitesurfing to waterskiing on **Bloemendaal aan Zee** (p131) in North Holland.

ACTION AREAS

Where to find the Netherlands' best outdoor activities.

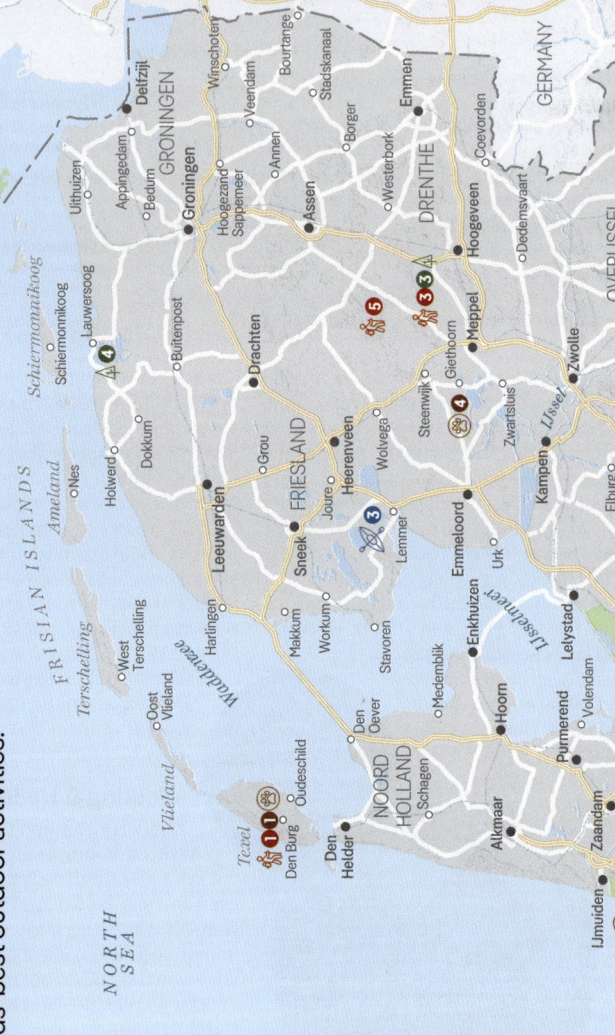

Walking/Hiking

1. Duinen van Texel National Park (p135)
2. Utrechtse Heuvelrug National Park (p165)
3. Dwingelderveld National Park (p253)
4. Hoge Veluwe National Park (p267)
5. Drents-Friese Wold National Park (p256)

Boating

1. Den Bosch (p282)
2. Utrecht (p150)
3. Frisian Lakes (p232)
4. Haarlem (p126)
5. Amsterdam (p46)

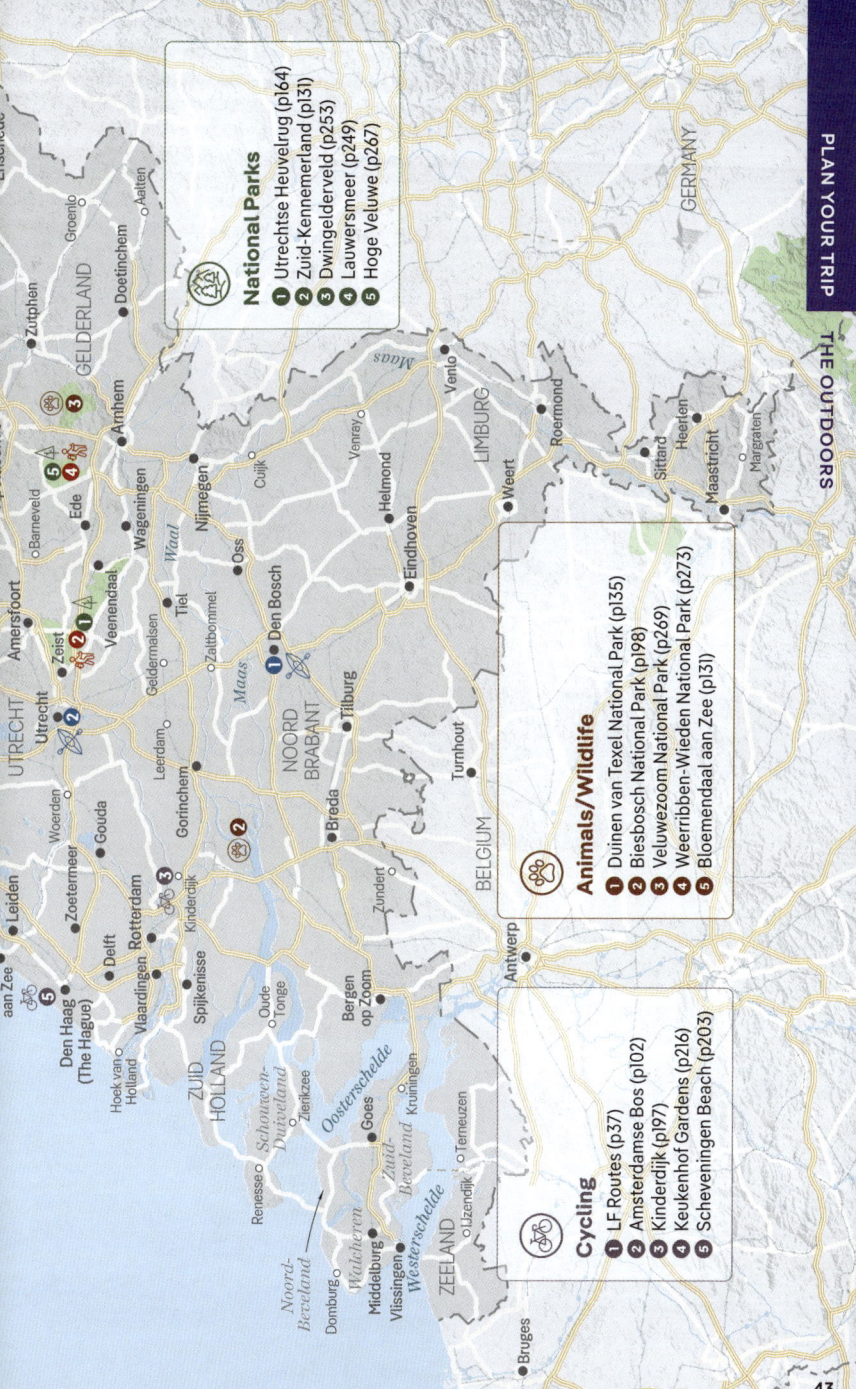

National Parks

1. Utrechtse Heuvelrug (p164)
2. Zuid-Kennemerland (p131)
3. Dwingelderveld (p253)
4. Lauwersmeer (p249)
5. Hoge Veluwe (p267)

Animals/Wildlife

1. Duinen van Texel National Park (p135)
2. Biesbosch National Park (p198)
3. Veluwezoom National Park (p269)
4. Weerribben–Wieden National Park (p273)
5. Bloemendaal aan Zee (p131)

Cycling

1. LF Routes (p37)
2. Amsterdamse Bos (p102)
3. Kinderdijk (p197)
4. Keukenhof Gardens (p216)
5. Scheveningen Beach (p203)

THE GUIDE

Friesland
(Fryslân)
p218

Northeastern
Netherlands
p238

Haarlem &
North Holland
p122

AMSTERDAM
p46

Central
Netherlands
p258

Utrecht
Province
p150

Rotterdam &
South Holland
p170

Southeastern
Netherlands
p278

Chapters in this section are organised by hubs and their surrounding areas. We see the hub as your base in the destination, where you'll find unique experiences, local insights, insider tips and expert recommendations. It's also your gateway to the surrounding area, where you'll see what and how much you can do from there.

Giethoorn (p271)

FOKKE BAARSSEN/SHUTTERSTOCK

For places to stay in Amsterdam, see p120

KERTU/SHUTTERSTOCK

Above: Cyclists crossing a canal; Right: Vondelpark (p86)

THE MAIN AREAS

**MEDIEVAL CENTRE &
RED LIGHT DISTRICT**
Amsterdam's historic
heart. **p52**

**WESTERN CANAL RING,
JORDAAN & THE WEST**
Charming waterways
and shopping. **p63**

SOUTHERN CANAL RING
Grand canal houses,
entertainment and
nightlife. **p78**

**VONDELPARK, OUD-
WEST & OUD-ZUID**
Monumental museums
and parks. **p86**

Curated by
Catherine Le Nevez

Amsterdam

TRADITIONAL CHARM MEETS VISIONARY INNOVATION

The Netherlands' multifaceted capital combines extraordinarily rich, influential history with the cosy, free-spirited atmosphere of a global village and inspired ambitions for its sustainable future.

Amsterdam celebrated its 750th birthday in 2025, but evidence of human activity goes back much further. Excavations during the 2005–12 tunnelling of the Noord/Zuidlijn (metro line 52) unearthed artefacts from the Amstel's depths (now home to the main thoroughfares of Damrak and Rokin) that show humans have lived here (at least transiently) since about 2600 BCE.

Water has been Amsterdam's lifeblood since its inception. Lying at or below sea level, its swamps, lakes and rivers were repeatedly reshaped by storms and floods. This fluid landscape presented challenges but also defining opportunities.

It was around the 13th century that the city's story began in earnest, with the construction of dams retaining the IJ river between the Zuiderzee and Haarlem. In 1275, inhabitants were granted toll-free status, and Amsterdam gained direct ocean access via the Zuiderzee (now the IJsselmeer) and then free access to the Baltic to become a global player.

The pivotal 1600s saw major advances in engineering (especially its World Heritage–listed canal ring), art (Rembrandt was among the artists who lived and painted here) and trade (Amsterdam was the site

WOLF-PHOTOGRAPHY/SHUTTERSTOCK

of the world's first stock exchange when the Dutch East India Company traded its own shares). In recent years, the city has confronted the era's dark colonial history; in 2023, King Willem-Alexander formally apologised for the Netherlands' involvement in slavery at Oosterpark's National Slavery Monument.

Today, the vibrant capital, with a population of 934,374, is home to 174 nationalities, making it one of the world's most multicultural cities. Its long history of counterculture and creativity spills into traditional, contemporary and futuristic art spaces; fantastic entertainment venues; and diverse drinking, dining and shopping opportunities.

Amsterdam's charms aren't lost on visitors. The 22.9 million overnight stays in 2024 (alongside 15.1 million day trips) represent an increase of 472.5% since 2000. In response, it ramped up efforts to address overtourism, deter nuisance behaviour, and reduce pollution and bottleneck crowds to rebalance the city for residents and visitors. Aiming for a fully circular, climate-proof city by 2050, Amsterdam is already leading the way, topping the Arcadis Sustainable Cities Index as the most sustainable city in the world.

DE PIJP & ZUID
Buzzing markets, lively dining and expansive greenery. **p98**

OOSTERPARK & EAST OF THE AMSTEL
World cultures and green spaces. **p104**

NIEUWMARKT, PLANTAGE & THE EASTERN ISLANDS
Gardens, museums and architecture. **p108**

AMSTERDAM NOORD
Evolving ex-industrial creative district. **p116**

47

AMSTERDAM
THE GUIDE

Find Your Way

Charming, compact and famously flat, Amsterdam's canal-laced historic centre is easily walkable, while the surrounding neighbourhoods are perfect for cycling. The city also has a superb public transport network of trams, buses and metros, as well as free five-minute passenger and bicycle ferries across the IJ river to Amsterdam Noord.

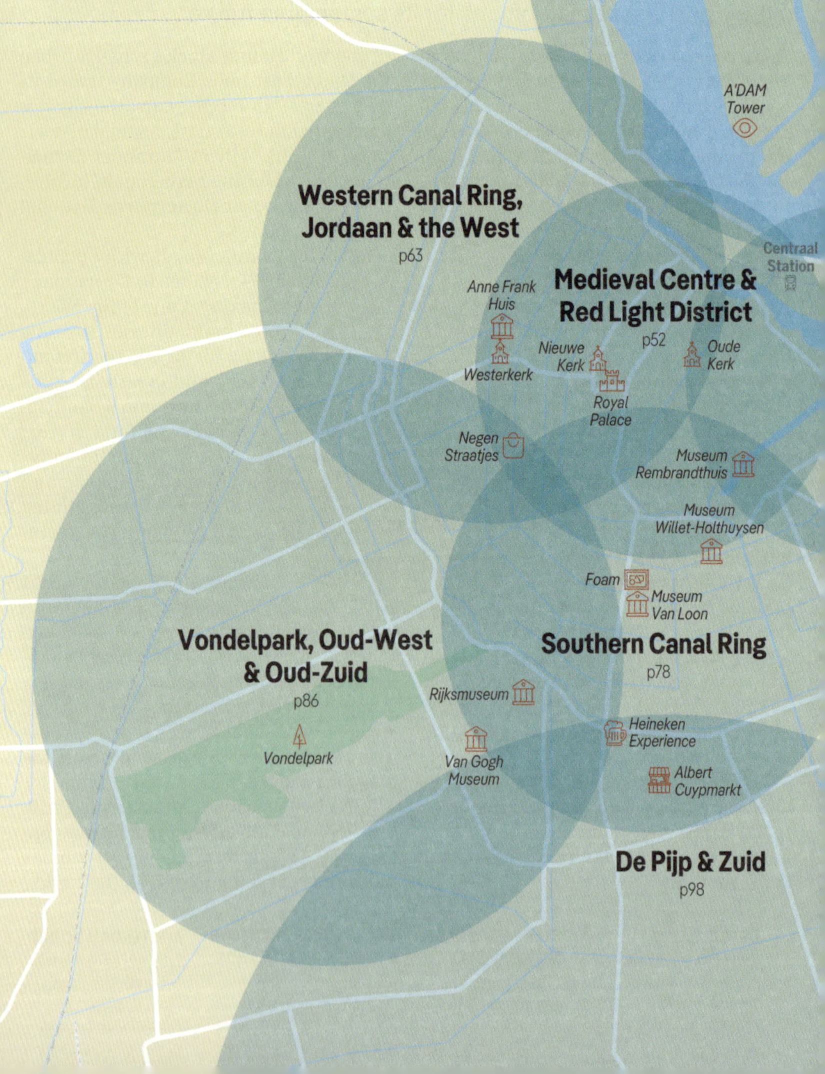

NDSM  Straat

A'DAM
Tower

Centraal
Station

Western Canal Ring,
Jordaan & the West
p63

Medieval Centre &
Red Light District
p52

Anne Frank
Huis

Nieuwe
Kerk

Oude
Kerk

Westerkerk

Royal
Palace

Negen
Straatjes

Museum
Rembrandthuis

Museum
Willet-Holthuysen

Foam

Museum
Van Loon

Vondelpark, Oud-West
& Oud-Zuid
p86

Southern Canal Ring
p78

Rijksmuseum

Vondelpark

Van Gogh
Museum

Heineken
Experience

Albert
Cuypmarkt

De Pijp & Zuid
p98

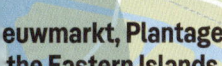
Amsterdam Noord
p116

Nieuwmarkt, Plantage and the Eastern Islands
p108

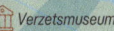
Verzetsmuseum

Hollandsche Schouwburg

🏛 *Wereldmuseum Amsterdam*

Oosterpark 🌳

Oosterpark & East of the Amstel
p104

Het IJ

FROM THE AIRPORT

Frequent trains from Schiphol International Airport's train station make the 15-minute trip to Amsterdam Centraal Station. Amsterdam Airport Express buses are a handy 30-minute trip to Museumplein and Leidseplein. An Amsterdam Travel Ticket includes travel to and from Schiphol Airport.

WALK

Busy streets, narrow lanes and canals make the centre easiest to explore on foot, and allow you to discover the gabled buildings, cosy cafes and tiny shops that make Amsterdam so special. Beware of walking in bike lanes and always look both ways before crossing them.

BICYCLE

Amsterdam has more bicycles than residents. Cycling is the most popular way to get around, and 42% of all journeys are on *fietsen* (bikes). Amsterdam has extensive bike lanes and plentiful parking. Bike hire outlets are everywhere, or use pay-per-minute hire apps like Donkey Republic *(donkey.bike)*.

PUBLIC TRANSPORT

Most public transport is on distinctive blue and white trams. Many of the 15 lines converge at Centraal Station. Buses fill the gaps, and all buses will be electric by 2030. Of Amsterdam's five metro lines, M52 conveniently runs from Noord via the centre to Zuid.

Plan Your Days

Amsterdam's condensed size means you can pack a lot into even a short visit. Book in advance to visit sights and bring comfortable shoes to explore the city's standout attractions and hidden surprises.

OIZA00/SHUTTERSTOCK

Co-kathedrale Basiliek van de Heilige Nicolaas (p53)

Day 1

Morning

● Begin by viewing the masterpieces at one of the three big museums at Museumplein: the mighty **Rijksmuseum** (p90), the intimate **Van Gogh Museum** (p94), or modern and contemporary art at the **Stedelijk Museum** (p92).

Afternoon

● Explore the secret courtyard and gardens at the **Begijnhof** (p56) in the Medieval Centre. Stroll to the Dam, where the **Royal Palace** (p57) and **Nieuwe Kerk** (p53) provide a dose of Dutch history. In the Red Light District, the **Oude Kerk** (p60) has historical and art exhibitions.

Evening

● Sip *jenever* (traditional Dutch gin) standing like a local at **Wynand Fockink** (p58) and settle in for cocktails made from heritage recipes at **Dutch Courage** (p58).

You'll Also Want to...

Dive deeper into Amsterdam and escape the crowds by getting further off the beaten track, with unique experiences found all over the city.

EXPLORE A 'CULTURAL VILLAGE'

Visit the 19th-century buildings of a disused gasworks that now house drinking, dining and entertainment venues, as well as sights like Amsterdam in Motion's scale model of the city, at **Westergas** (p76).

SEE THE WORLD'S LARGEST STREET ART MUSEUM

Check out extraordinary street art and graffiti at **Straat** (p118) in a vast warehouse at NDSM's disused shipyards in Amsterdam Noord.

SIP JENEVER IN A WOODLAND DISTILLERY

Head to fairy-tale-like **Distilleerderij 't Nieuwe Diep** (p107), in Oost's wooded Flevopark, an enchanting place to try its *jenever* and liqueurs.

Day 2

Morning
● After brunch in De Pijp at a local hangout like **Bakers & Roasters** (p102), browse Amsterdam's largest street market, the **Albert Cuypmarkt** (p100). Afterwards, get shaken up, heated up and 'bottled' like a beer at the **Heineken Experience** (p98).

Afternoon
● Cross into the Southern Canal Ring to check out the opulent canal-house lifestyle at **Museum Van Loon** (p78) and edgy photo exhibitions at **Foam** (p83).

Evening
● After dark, party at hyperactive, neon-lit **Leidseplein** (p84), surrounded by good-time clubs and *bruin cafés* (traditional pubs), or nearby **Rembrandtplein** (p84). **Paradiso** (p85) and **Melkweg** (p85) host the coolest agendas. Catch atmospheric gigs at **Jazz Café Alto** (p83).

Day 3

Morning
● Take a spin around Amsterdam's beloved **Vondelpark** (p86). It's easy to explore on a morning jaunt – and all the better zipping by the ponds, gardens and sculptures by bike.

Afternoon
● Immerse yourself in the speciality shops of **Negen Straatjes** (p63). At the nearby **Anne Frank Huis** (p67), the claustrophobic rooms give an all-too-real feel for Anne's life in hiding, as does seeing her diary.

Evening
● Set sail with operators like **Pure Boats** (p71) to see the waterways illuminated at night. Spend the evening in the Jordaan, enjoying a glass on a canal-side terrace at **'t Smalle** (p70) or heaps of other *gezellig* (cosy) haunts.

CATCH A MEMORABLE CONCERT	RIDE A VINTAGE TRAM TO AMSTERDAM'S FOREST	LEARN ABOUT DUTCH SEAFARING HISTORY	UNDERSTAND WORLD CULTURES
Take in a performance at the glass and steel landmark of the **Muziekgebouw aan 't IJ** (p112) concert hall or its jazz stage, the Bimhuis, which also hosts free Tuesday jam sessions.	Board one of the wonderful old vintage trams run by 'mobile museum' **Electrische Museumtramlijn Amsterdam** (p97) to the sprawling recreational area of Amsterdamse Bos.	Clamber aboard a replica galleon at maritime museum **Het Scheepvaartmuseum** (p110), which powerfully reinterprets historic voyages in a 17th-century Admiralty of Amsterdam storehouse.	View eye-opening exhibitions unflinchingly addressing the Netherlands' colonial history amid the old-world elegance of the **Wereldmuseum Amsterdam** (p104), which celebrates world cultures.

Medieval Centre & Red Light District

AMSTERDAM'S HISTORIC HEART

GETTING AROUND

Small, narrow streets mean this neighbourhood is most easily covered on foot. Rideshare vehicles aren't permitted throughout the centre; there's a designated pick-up point at Muntplein on the neighbourhood's southern edge.

Many of the city's tram lines go through the neighbourhood en route to Centraal Station. The metro travels from Centraal to Amsterdam's outer neighbourhoods, and to Amsterdam Noord and Station Zuid via Rokin in the Medieval Centre.

Free ferries to Amsterdam Noord depart from the piers behind Centraal Station.

Amsterdam's oldest quarter is remarkably preserved. The Amstel's original rivermouth, Damrak, stretches south to the Royal Palace on the Dam, the site of the herring-fishing settlement Aemstelredamme ('the dam built across the Amstel') that gave the city its name. Its extension, Rokin, continues south to Muntplein.

Side streets brim with 17th-century *jenever* (Dutch gin) tasting rooms, cosy *bruin cafés* (traditional pubs), boutiques and atmospheric restaurants. To the west is the shopping strip Kalverstraat. East, in the area known as De Wallen, are the narrow alleyways of the Red Light District. A clean-up agenda has so far curbed bar and club opening hours, banned on-street cannabis smoking and barred guided tours (and proposed relocating brothel windows), though it can still be a walk on the wild side and rowdy at night. De Wallen is also home to Amsterdam's oldest surviving building, the 1306-built Oude Kerk, and the oldest canal, the 1385-dug Oudezijds Voorburgwal.

See the City's Foundations

The Dam in Amsterdam

Dam is the very spot where Amsterdam was founded in the 13th century, before it was granted toll-free status in 1275. It's still a national gathering spot, and if there's a major speech or demonstration, it takes place here. The fallen of WWII are honoured at the **Nationaal Monument** on 4 May.

The square was historically split into two sections: Vissersdam, a fish market where department store **De Bijenkorf** (*debijenkorf.nl*) now stands (head to its rooftop cafe for fabulous views), and Vijgendam, probably named for the figs and other exotic fruits unloaded from ships. Various markets and events have taken place here through the ages, including executions – you can still see holes on the front of the Royal Palace (p57) where the wooden gallows were affixed

MIROSLAV POSAVEC/SHUTTERSTOCK

Nationaal Monument

Catch Exhibitions at the 'New Church'

Medieval showcase

Consecrated in 1409, the late-Gothic **Nieuwe Kerk** *(nieu wekerk.nl; adult/child from €7.50/6.25),* only 'new' in relation to the Oude Kerk (p60) – the city's Old Church, built a century earlier – is the site of royal investitures and weddings. Check the agenda for exhibitions and concerts. The annual photojournalism and documentary exhibition World Press Photo takes place here from mid-April to mid-September.

Visit a City Landmark

Cupola-topped co-cathedral

From the turreted 1889 Centraal Station (p61) and Damrak's canal-boat docks, the magnificent cupola and neo-Renaissance towers of the **Co-kathedrale Basiliek van de Heilige Nicolaas** *(Co-cathedral Basilica of St Nicholas; nicolaas-parochie .nl/nicolaas; entry by donation)* dominate the skyline.

Named for the patron saint of seafarers (and the city) and completed in 1887, it was the first church to be built after Catholic worship became legal again in the 19th century. Its high altar and crown of Emperor Maximilian I are highlights of the interior. The church was elevated to a basilica minor in 2012 and elevated again by Pope Francis to a co-cathedral in 2025.

Sightseeing isn't permitted during services or on Sundays.

☑ **TOP TIP**

The city's history museum, the Amsterdam Museum, is closed until 2028 while its historic building, Amsterdam's former civic orphanage for almost 400 years, undergoes renovations. Check *amsterdammuseum. nl* for updates and to find out where museum programmes are running until it reopens.

MEDIEVAL CENTRE & RED LIGHT DISTRICT

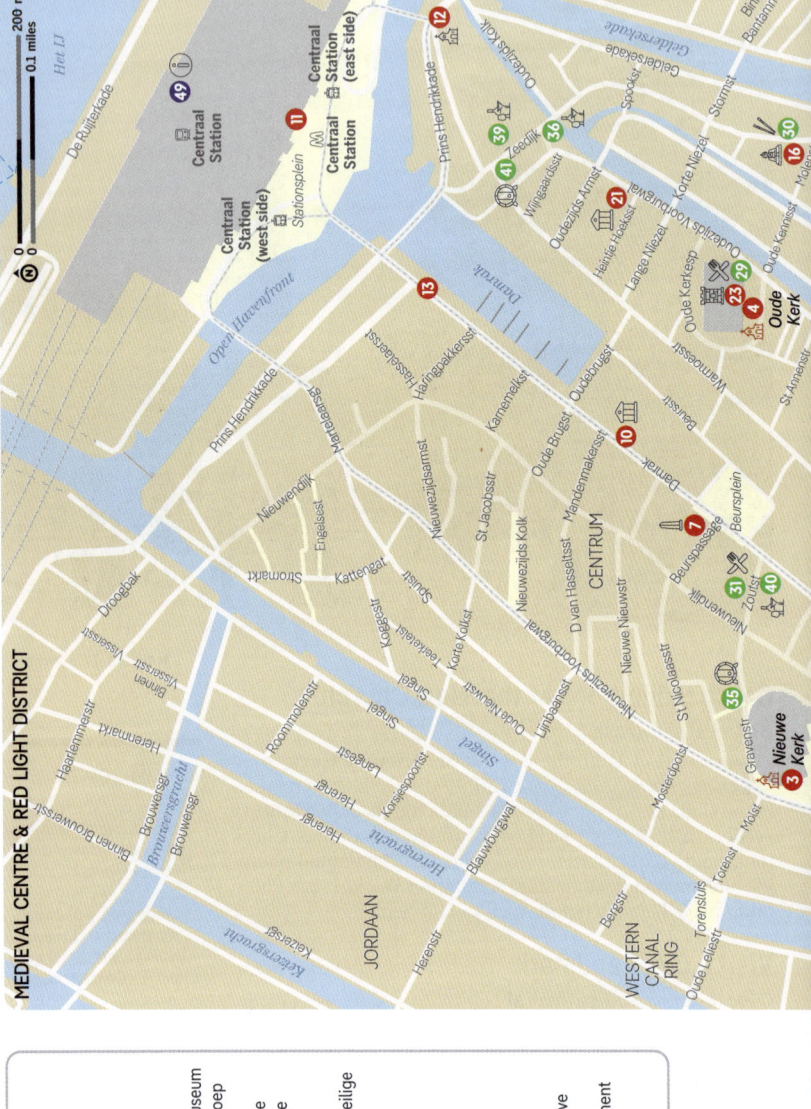

★ HIGHLIGHTS

1 Begijnhof
2 Dam
3 Nieuwe Kerk
4 Oude Kerk
5 Royal Palace

● SIGHTS

6 Allard Pierson Museum
7 Amsterdam Oersoep
8 Begijnhof Kapel
9 Below the Surface
10 Beurs van Berlage
11 Centraal Station
12 Co-kathedrale
Basiliek van de Heilige
Nicolaas
13 Damrak
14 De Papegaai
15 Engelse Kerk
16 He Hua Temple
17 Het Muizenhuis
18 Houten Huis
19 Kalverpassage
20 Kalverstraat
21 Museum Ons' Lieve
Heer op Solder
22 Nationaal Monument
23 Oudekerkstoren
24 Spui

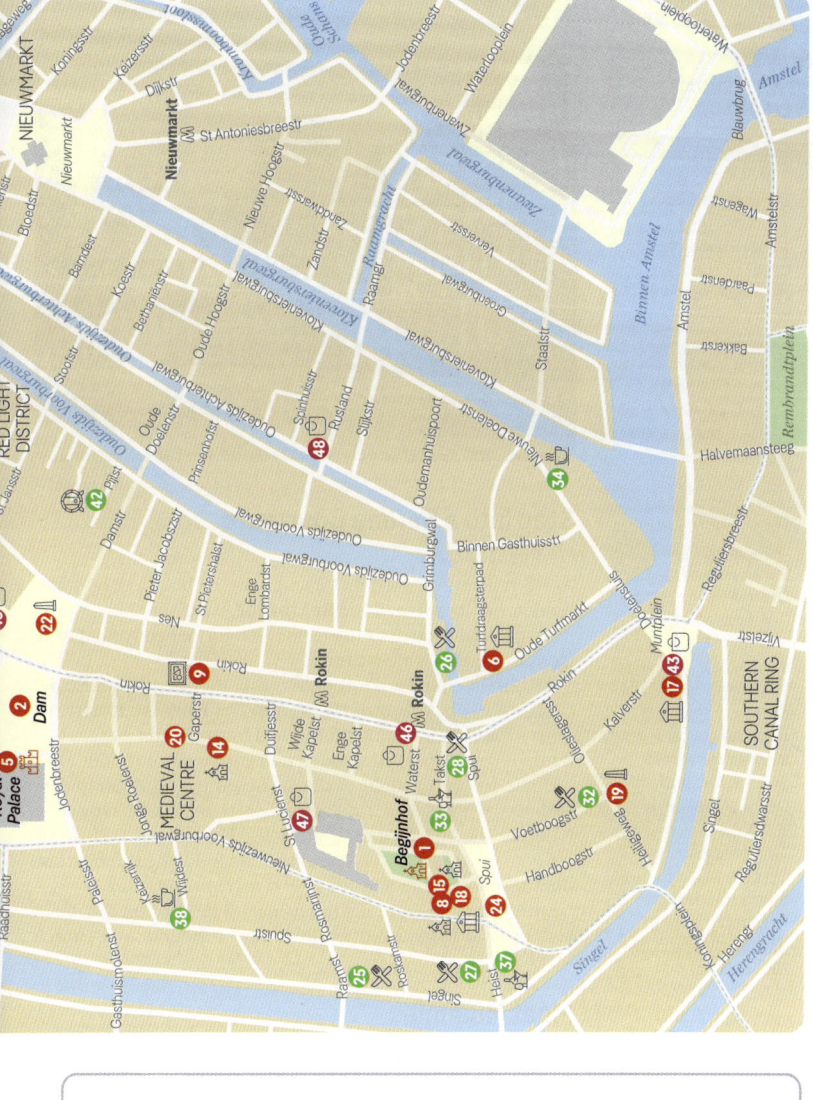

● **EATING**
25 Broodje Bert
26 De Laatste Kruimel
27 Dutch Delicacy
28 Gartine
29 Koffieschenkerij
30 Nam Kee
31 Rob Wigboldus
   Vishandel
32 Vleminckx

● **DRINKING & NIGHT-
LIFE**
33 Café de Dokter
34 Café de Jaren
35 De Drie Fleschjes
36 Dutch Courage
37 Hoppe
38 Hummingbird
39 In 't Aepjen
40 Oporto
41 Proeflokaal de
   Ooievaar
42 Wynand Fockink

● **SHOPPING**
43 Andries de Jong BV
44 By Popular Demand
45 De Bijenkorf
46 PGC Hajenius
47 Posthumus
48 WonderWood

● **INFORMATION**
49 I amsterdam Store

I AMSTERDAM CITY CARD

If you plan on doing a lot of sightseeing and using public transport, the **I amsterdam City Card** *(iamsterdam. com)* includes GVB trams, metros, buses and ferries (but not transport to/from Schiphol Airport), 24 hours' bike hire and a canal cruise, along with admission to more than 70 museums and attractions (notable exceptions include the Anne Frank Huis and Van Gogh Museum. Durations range from one day (€90) to five days (€135).

You can buy a digital card on the website or a physical card at the **I amsterdam Store** at Amsterdam Centraal Station, which also sells Amsterdam-themed gifts like tulip-shaped bottle stoppers and Playmobil figurines from Rembrandt's *The Night Watch*.

ZEBRA0209/SHUTTERSTOCK

Begijnhof

Step into a Serene Courtyard

Medieval enclave

Amid central Amsterdam's cacophony is the pin-drop-quiet hidden *hof* (courtyard) of **Begijnhof**, with tiny houses and postage-stamp gardens in an enclosed former convent dating from the early 14th century.

Within the courtyard is the charming 1671 **Begijnhof Kapel** *(begijnhofkapelamsterdam.nl)* and the **Engelse Kerk** *(erc. amsterdam)*, built around 1392. The **Houten Huis**, the Netherlands' oldest preserved wooden house, dates from about 1465.

Home to the Catholic order of Beguines – unmarried or widowed women who lived religiously without monastic vows – before the last died in 1971, today 105 women still reside here, so visitors must be respectful (no food, drink, smoking, photography of the houses, or excessive noise).

Enter via Gedempte Begijnensloot. (The door on the north side of Spui is reserved for Begijnhof residents and church services.)

Meet Mummies

Archaeological treasures

Run by the University of Amsterdam and named for its first professor of archaeology, Allard Pierson (1831–96), the **Allard**

EATING IN THE MEDIEVAL CENTRE: BEST DUTCH SNACKS

Vleminckx: Hailed as Amsterdam's best *friterie,* this 1887-opened kiosk offers crispy fries in traditional cones, plus more than 20 sauces. *11am-7pm or later* €

Broodje Bert: Canal-side sandwich shop named after its lamb meatball twist on the classic Dutch *broodje* (sandwich). *9am-5.30pm Tue-Sun* €

Dutch Delicacy: Savour Dutch cheeses on a board or vacuum-packed to take away, as well as Gouda sandwiches and *appeltaart* (apple pie). *9am-7pm* €

Rob Wigboldus Vishandel: Hole-in-the-wall fish shop serving excellent sandwiches with herring, Dutch prawns and fried whitefish. *8am-5pm* €

Royal Palace

The Royal Palace (Koninklijk Paleis) began life as a city hall and was completed in 1665. Its architect, Jacob van Campen, spared no expense to display Amsterdam's wealth in a way that rivalled the grandest European buildings of the day. The result is opulence on a big scale. Visitors can explore the building when no events are scheduled.

History of the Building

In 1808, Napoleon's brother, Louis Bonaparte, the newly installed king of the Dutch Republic, moved in, transforming it into a lavish regal abode. After the French were overthrown in 1813–14, it remained a royal palace, though never a permanent royal residence, and today it functions as the monarch's official reception palace.

Visiting the Palace

A self-guided tour with a free audio guide explaining everything in vivid detail takes about an hour. You also receive a copy of the booklet 'Traces of Slavery', shedding light on the building, which was partly financed from trade involving the exploitation and trafficking of people.

Palace Highlights

Most rooms are spread over the 1st floor, which is awash in chandeliers (51 in total), along with damasks, gilded clocks and spectacular paintings by artists including Ferdinand Bol and Jacob de Wit. In the great *burgerzaal* (citizens' hall), maps inlaid in the floor show the eastern and western hemispheres, with a 1654 celestial map in the middle.

Louis Bonaparte left behind about 1000 pieces of Empire-style furniture and decorative artworks, one of the world's largest collections from the period.

TOP TIPS

● Check the website's calendar for closures and book tickets with a designated timeslot in advance online to ensure entry.

● Don't miss seeing the exterior at night, when the palace is dramatically floodlit.

PRACTICALITIES

● 10am–5pm ● adult/child €13.50/free

● paleisamsterdam.nl

DUTCHMEN PHOTOGRAPHY/SHUTTERSTOCK

AMSTERDAM'S CHINATOWN

Amsterdam's small, lively Chinatown centres on Zeedijk, the sea dyke to protect Amsterdam from the IJ. It's the site of New Year celebrations (there's a lion dance on 2 January as well as Chinese New Year later in January or February). The Chinese community first settled here around 1911, with city authorities collaborating with residents to breathe new life into the area from the mid-1980s.

Built in 2000, **He Hua Temple** *(ibps.nl; entry by donation),* Europe's largest Chinese Imperial–style Buddhist temple, is a shrine to Kuan Yin, the bodhisattva (Buddhist goddess) of mercy. Its classical roof carvings are visible at Zeedijk 106–118; entry is via the side gates.

Chinese grocery stores and restaurants congregate here, such as **Nam Kee** *(namkee.nl),* established in 1981.

Pierson Museum *(allardpierson.nl; adult/child €15.50/3.50)* contains a rich collection of Mediterranean and Near Eastern archaeology. You'll find actual mummies (humans and animals), vases from ancient Greece and Mesopotamia, a cool wagon from the royal tombs at Salamis (Cyprus), and galleries full of other items providing insight into daily life in ancient times.

With an extensive range of maps, atlases and nautical charts, its cartography collection is one of the world's largest. Like other Dutch institutions, since 2023 it has reviewed its collection to tell stories from lesser-heard perspectives, such as looking at maps and archives on Suriname up to its independence in 1975. This Surinamica Collection is now among its core archives.

Go Below the Surface

Unearthing the past

With a valid metro ticket, descending to Rokin metro station opens up a window on Amsterdam's long history.

During the construction of Amsterdam's Noord/Zuidlijn (north–south metro line), which opened in 2018, more than 134,000 archaeological finds were unearthed from beneath the streets and waterways. Now 9500 of them, dating as far back as 2400 BCE, are displayed in glass cases between Rokin metro station's escalators at the exhibition **Below the Surface** *(belowthesurface.amsterdam).* Transport, craft and industry, buildings and interiors feature at the southern entrance. Objects at the northern entrance span science, communications, weapons, armour, recreation, personal items and clothing.

Collection highlights include coins (from as early as 1371), ice-skating blades from the Middle Ages, 15th-century padlocks, 17th-century pottery, an 18th-century piggy bank, 19th-century pocket watches and military uniform buttons, a 1922 car radiator cap, and brick-like 1980s mobile phones.

Knock Back a Glass of Gin

Jenever tasting houses

The Medieval Centre has some fabulously atmospheric places to try the local firewater, *jenever,* along with liqueurs.

De Drie Fleschjes *(dedriefleschjes.nl)* is a 1650 jewel with a wall of master-shipbuilder-made barrels. Another 17th-century treasure, **Wynand Fockink** *(wynand-fockink.nl)* is an intimate tasting house (no seating) dating from 1679, with a house-speciality liqueur called Boswandeling ('secret of the forest'). Not much bigger than a vat of *jenever,* magnificent little **Proeflokaal de Ooievaar** *(proeflokaaldeooievaar.nl)* is a timber-lined tasting house that was deliberately built tilted in 1782.

New-generation, heritage-specialist cocktail bar **Dutch Courage** *(dutchcouragecocktails.com)* has 150 different types of *jenever* and old Dutch liqueurs.

Oudezijds Voorburgwal canal, Red Light District

Stay Updated on the Red Light District

Amsterdam's changing image

In Amsterdam's medieval area of De Wallen, the **Red Light District** dates from the 1300s, when women carrying red lanterns greeted sailors near the port. Its sex-worker windows, strip clubs, fetish shops, 'smart shops' (selling natural hallucinogens), coffeeshops (cannabis-smoking cafes) and copious bars, especially on and around the Oudezijds Voorburgwal and Oudezijds Achterburgwal, have made it a magnet for hedonistic (and simply curious) visitors.

A clean-up agenda set out in 2007 has accelerated post-pandemic. Having reduced the number of brothel windows, the city is endeavouring to shift sex work out of the area altogether. A decision on whether to relocate the district's brothels by building a purpose-built, multistorey 'erotic centre' on Europaboulevard in Zuid (widely opposed by both residents and sex workers) will be made by the end of 2026.

To date, guided tours past sex-worker windows have been outlawed, as has smoking cannabis in central Amsterdam's streets (banning tourists from coffeeshops remains under discussion), with earlier closing times for bars and clubs (1am midweek and 2am on weekends, with no admittance after 1am). Meanwhile, city authorities have run 'anti-nuisance tourism' campaigns, including a targeted 'stay away' campaign to actively discourage rowdy partiers.

UNUSUAL SHOPS

Andries de Jong BV: Serving seafarers since 1787 with bells, bottled boats and other maritime gifts. *(andriesdejong.nl)*

By Popular Demand: Nifty gift-y wares and (mostly) easy to transport: windmill or bicycle lapel pins and rock 'n' roll–inspired Delftware. *(bpd.nu)*

Posthumus: Established in 1865 in a preserved-timber shop. Sells everything stamp-related – lacquer and rubber stamps, wax and ink – in Dutch-themed designs. *(posthumuswinkel.nl)*

PGC Hajenius: The Dutch royal family frequents this tobacco emporium, where Cuban cigars are sold in gilded and marbled interiors. *(hajenius.com)*

WonderWood: As much a museum as a vintage furniture and decorations shop; look up to see the 1565-built timber ceiling. *(wonderwood.nl)*

DRINKING IN THE MEDIEVAL CENTRE: BEAUTIFUL BROWN CAFES

Hoppe: Take in interiors and exteriors listed as historical monuments at Hoppe, filling glasses since 1670. *9am-1am Sun-Thu, to 2am Fri & Sat*

In 't Aepjen: In a 15th-century building, this former inn was once frequented by sailors bartering *aapjes* (monkeys) for lodging. *2pm-1am or later*

Café de Dokter: Eyeball chandeliers, a birdcage and smooth jazz in a seventh-generation family-run bar. *4pm-1am Wed-Sat*

Oporto: Cool decor untouched in decades: woodwork zodiac signs and iron-framed parchment lighting. Play darts, down a glass. *11am-late*

TOP EXPERIENCE

Oude Kerk

Built to honour Amsterdam's patron saint, St Nicholas, Oude Kerk dates from 1306, making it the city's oldest surviving building. Originally Catholic and now Protestant, the Gothic-style structure holds the city's oldest church bell (1450), a stunning Vater-Müller organ, 15th-century choir stalls with graphic wooden carvings, and Europe's largest medieval wooden vaulted ceiling.

ANTON_IVANOV/SHUTTERSTOCK

TOP TIPS

● Buy tickets online or at the entrance.

● Midweek mornings are quietest. Church services take place outside visiting hours on Sundays.

● The attached **Koffieschenkerij** serves lovely cakes, tarts and apple pie and has a sunny garden blooming with tulips in spring.

PRACTICALITIES

● 10am-6pm Mon-Sat, 1-5.30pm Sun ● adult/child €13.50/7, incl Oudekerkstoren €21/14.50
● oudekerk.nl

Church History

Originally, this site was home to a graveyard built on a mound next to the Amstel river and a wooden chapel constructed around 1213. A stone church replaced it in 1306, and it was consecrated in 1309 as the Catholic St Nicolaaskerk. It became known as the Oude Kerk (Old Church) once the Nieuwe Kerk opened in 1409. After Amsterdam's Catholic city council was deposed in 1578, the ransacked Oude Kerk became Protestant.

Graves

Many famous Amsterdammers are buried under the floor's worn tombstones, including Rembrandt's wife, Saskia van Uylenburgh (2 August 1612 to 14 June 1642). Each year on 9 March at 8.39am, a beam of light touches her grave. In all, some 60,000 citizens lie beneath the church.

Concerts & a Tower Climb

Contemporary art exhibitions are a highlight. During concerts, you can hear the magnificent Vater-Müller organ (first built in 1726 and rebuilt in 1742), the 1965 transept organ, the Italian organ and the cabinet organ.

Oudekerkstoren, the church's tower, rises 67m and is reached by 155 steps. Guided tours run from mid-May to October hourly from 1pm on Wednesdays, Fridays and Saturdays, and from 1.30pm on Sundays.

Seek Out Clandestine Churches
Hidden houses of worship

On the Oudezijds Voorburgwal, what might look like a typical Amsterdam canal house outside contains an entire church. In the mid-1600s, when the Calvinist rulers outlawed public Catholic worship, local merchant Jan Hartman built a covert church inside his home for his son to study to be a priest.

Unexpectedly elaborate, **Museum Ons' Lieve Heer op Solder** *(Our Dear Lord in the Attic; opsolder.nl; adult/child €16.95/7.50)* has a marble-columned altar, a painting by Jacob de Wit, a grand organ and a capacity for 150 worshippers. The building, with its maze of staircases, nooks, oak furniture and porcelain-tiled kitchen, provides a snapshot of 17th-century canal-house life.

An unexpected oasis in the sea of consumerism on busy shopping street **Kalverstraat**, the curious Petrus en Pauluskerk, aka **De Papegaai** *(nicolaas-parochie.nl/papegaai; entry by donation),* is a Catholic church from the 17th century that was a clandestine house of worship, hidden in the garden behind a bird trader's house. Note the *papegaai* (parrot) over the door.

Find Unexpected Art
Under-the-radar exhibition spaces

Cuyperspassage, a tunnel cutting through the middle of **Centraal Station**, is a shortcut covered in porcelain art. Some 80,000 Delft Blue tiles, handcrafted by Dutch artist Irma Boom, tell the story of Amsterdam's maritime past.

Off high-street chain-store-lined Kalverstraat, shopping centre **Kalverpassage** *(kalverpassage.nl)* unassumingly doubles as a gallery with various statues and installations by international artists. Scan QR codes beneath each artwork for an art audio tour.

Chandeliers crafted from bicycle parts, stained-glass lamps, a shimmering fish fountain dispensing 'tolerance elixir' (water), and ship-wheel-and-anchor floor tiles enveloping 19th-century De Beurspassage illustrate how water formed life in the city in the work **Amsterdam Oersoep** (Amsterdam Primordial Soup, as the city's canal water is known) by artists Arno Coenen, Iris Roskam and Hans van Bentem.

Steps away, architect and ardent socialist HP Berlage's 1903 **Beurs van Berlage** *(beursvanberlage.com),* Amsterdam's financial exchange, venerates labour in tile murals showing

NAVIGATING THE CITY

Amsterdam's concentric canals and similarly named streets make it all too easy to get lost. Some pointers: a *gracht* (canal), such as Egelantiersgracht, is distinct from a *straat* (street) such as Egelantiersstraat. A *dwarsstraat* (cross street) that intersects a *straat* is often preceded by *eerste, tweede, derde* and *vierde* (first, second, third and fourth; marked 1e, 2e, 3e and 4e on maps).

For example, Eerste Egelantiersdwarsstraat is the first cross street of Egelantiersstraat (ie the nearest cross street to the city centre). Streets preceded by *lange* (long) and *korte* (short) simply mean the longer or shorter street. Be aware, too, that seemingly continuous streets regularly change names along their length.

EATING & DRINKING IN THE MEDIEVAL CENTRE: CHARMING CAFES

De Laatste Kruimel: Despite being busy, the homey 'Last Crumb' has a canal-side terrace and serves pies, quiches, cakes and coffee. *8am-5pm or later* €€

Gartine: Alley-tucked charm with mismatched antique tableware and organic egg breakfasts. Come for high tea. *9.30am-4pm Wed-Sun* €

Café de Jaren: Watch the Amstel go by from the waterside terraces of this bright, spacious grand cafe. *10am-10pm Sun-Wed, to 11pm Thu-Sat*

Hummingbird: Speciality coffee and art are the draws of this simple yet stylish coffee bar with changing guest roasters and fair-trade beans. *8.30am-5pm*

AN ARCHITECTURAL HEAVE-HO

When you leave **Proeflokaal de Ooievaar** (p58), it's not that *jenever* making you woozy. The historic building is indeed leaning. Known as *op vlucht bouwen* (built on the fly), the design allowed goods to be hoisted into upper floors without risking facade damage.

Of course, Amsterdam's slumping landscape isn't solely by design. Many canal buildings lean because of age and shifting foundations. How to tell the difference? *Op vlucht bouwen* houses are perfectly tipped forward and might still have a hoisting beam or hook at the gable top. Windows and door frames appear parallel to the ground rather than warped in ageing constructions.

GINA RODGERS/ALAMY

Cuyperspassage, Centraal Station (p61)

the proletariat of the past, present and future. Catch art exhibitions on its former trading floor.

Marvel at a 'Mouse Mansion'

Enchanting world in miniature

Het Muizenhuis *(Mouse Mansion; themousemansion.com; free)* is the brainchild of artist and author Karina Schaapman, who crafted a 100-room home for adorable felt mice Sam, Julia and friends and then produced a series of children's books (22 to date) on their adventures. You can see the original mansion and sets for later books (even a mouse roller coaster) at this two-floor 'mini museum' and buy toys, books and materials to build your own mouse mansion.

Western Canal Ring, Jordaan & the West

CHARMING WATERWAYS, ENTICING SHOPPING AND NEW DEVELOPMENTS

Some of the city's loveliest canalscapes and grand, gabled canal houses are just west of the Medieval Centre in the Western Canal Ring, like scenes straight out of 17th-century paintings. By the Westerkerk, the Anne Frank Huis, where the young diarist hid with her family in WWII, is the area's main draw. Don't miss strolling these UNESCO-listed waterways, and shopping in the 'nine little streets' of Negen Straatjes and the Haarlemmerbuurt.

Across the Prinsengracht, the Jordaan's tiny streets, *bruin cafés* and markets recall its heritage, before its gentrification, as a former *volksbuurt* (workers' quarter) and are wonderful to wander, as are the lesser-explored peaceful Western Islands.

Northwest of the Jordaan, the West is one of Amsterdam's most up-and-coming areas, especially around the regenerated former gasworks, now the 'cultural village' of Westergas, adjoining leafy Westerpark, with new developments continuing to spring up around the one-time industrial lumber ports of Houthaven.

Browse the Negen Straatjes

Charming speciality shops

In a city filled with shopping opportunities, the **Negen Straatjes** *(de9straatjes.nl)* represent an especially dense concentration.

Between Raadhuisstraat and Leidsegracht, each of these 'nine little streets' is just a block long. The streets (from west to east, and north to south: Reestraat, Hartenstraat, Gasthuismolensteeg, Berenstraat, Wolvenstraat, Oude Spiegelstraat, Runstraat, Huidenstraat and Wijde Heisteeg) and four canals (west to east: Prinsengracht, Keizersgracht, Herengracht and Singel) form a tight grid packed with some 250 shops.

continues on p66

GETTING AROUND

mmediately west of the Medieval Centre, the narrow streets of the Western Canal Ring and, west again, the southern Jordaan are most easily explored on foot. Cycling is ideal in the spread-out northern Jordaan and West. Free ferries, including Ferry F7 from Pontsteiger to NDSM-werf, accept bikes.

The Western Canal Ring and southern Jordaan can be reached by tram (lines 2, 12 and 17) from Centraal Station. Trams travelling along the Jordaan's western edge (5, 7 and 13) don't go to Centraal. Buses are handy for northern Jordaan and the West.

WESTERN CANAL RING, JORDAAN & THE WEST

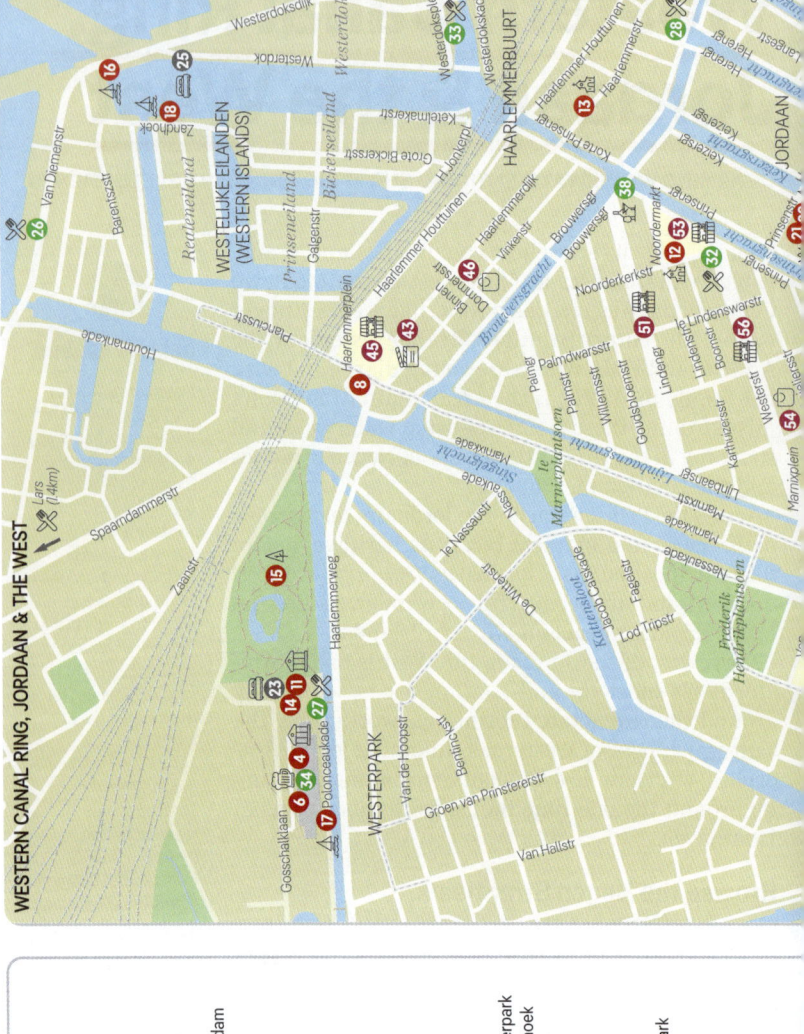

● **HIGHLIGHTS**
1   Anne Frank Huis
2   Negen Straatjes
3   Westerkerk

● **SIGHTS**
4   Amsterdam in Motion
5   Amsterdam Tulip Museum
6   Fabrique des Lumières
7   Grachtenmuseum Amsterdam
8   Haarlemmerpoort
9   Houseboat Museum
10 Huis Marseille
11 Museum Villa
12 Noorderkerk
13 Posthoornkerk
14 Westergas
15 Westerpark
    see 3 Westertoren

● **ACTIVITIES**
16 Canal Motorboats –
    Westerdoksdijk
17 Canal Motorboats – Westerpark
18 Canal Motorboats – Zandhoek
19 Kayak in Amsterdam
20 Pure Boats
21 Those Dam Boat Guys

● **SLEEPING**
22 BackStage Hotel
23 Conscious Hotel Westerpark
24 Dylan
25 Houseboat Ms Luctor

● **EATING**
26 BAK
27 De Bakkerswinkel
28 De Belhamel

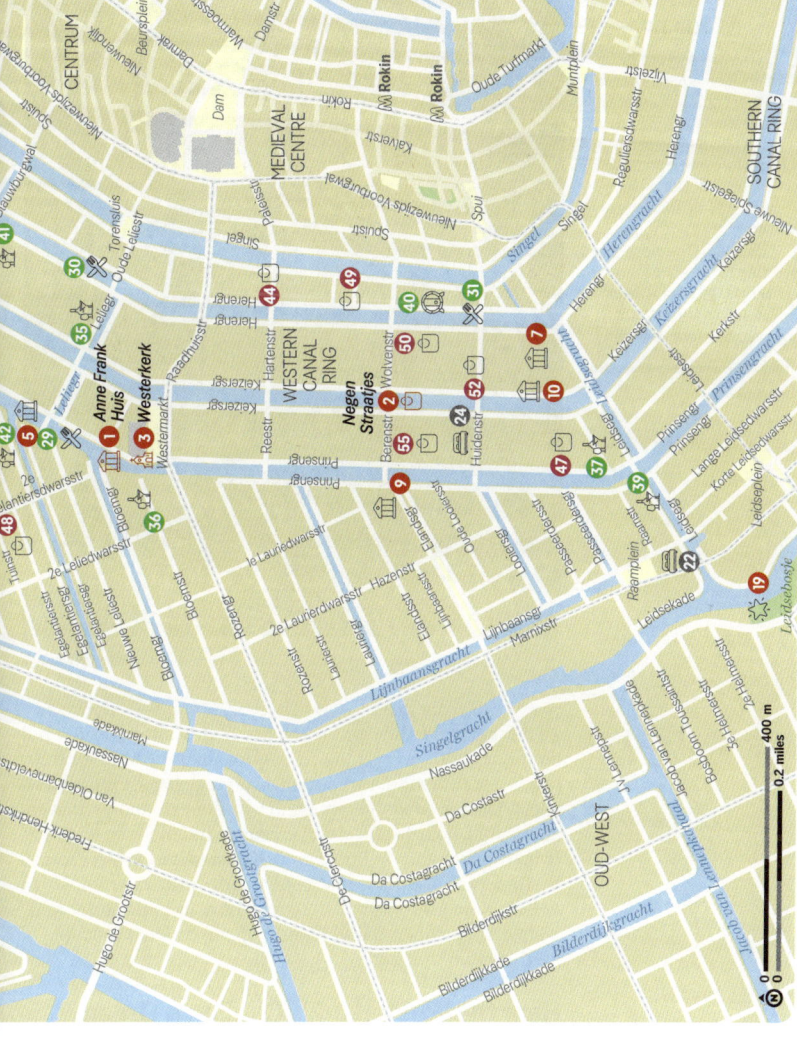

29 Eetcafé Roem
30 Miss G's Brunch Boat
31 Singel 404
32 Winkel 43
33 Wolf Atelier

● **DRINKING & NIGHTLIFE**
34 Brouwerij Troost Westergas
35 Café Brandon
36 Café Chris
37 Café het Molenpad
38 Café Papeneiland
39 Café Pieper
40 Proeflokaal A van Wees
41 't Arendsnest
42 't Smalle

● **ENTERTAINMENT**
43 Movies

● **SHOPPING**
44 Antonia
45 Boerenmarkt Haarlemmerplein
46 De Mof
47 Frozen Fountain
48 Het Oud-Hollandsch
     Snoepwinkeltje
49 Keesiedive
50 Laura Dols
51 Lindengracht Markt
52 Marie-Stella-Maris
53 Noordermarkt
54 POLSPOTTEN
55 Rain Couture
56 Westerstraat Markt

RESUL MUSLU/SHUTTERSTOCK

☑ **TOP TIP**

The massive urban renovation project Oranje Loper ('orange carpet'), stretching 2.8km from the Raadhuisstraat to Mercatorplein, is underway until 2029. During the works, some tram stops are closed and routes diverted. (The closest stop to the Anne Frank Huis is the Dam.) Check transport updates at *gvb.nl/en/oranje-loper*.

Westerkerk

continued from p63

The shops are tiny, and many are highly specialised. Find boutiques with everything from pure silk fabrics to buttons, beads, ceramic tiles, rare watches, vintage bags, vintage jewellery, leather goods, ceramics, art, antiques, candles, flowers and plants, board games, vinyl records and niche specialities, from flippers and diving gear at **Keesiedive** *(keesiedive.nl)* to slippers and slip-ons like clogs at **Antonia** *(depantoffelwinkel.nl)*. Numerous fashion designers have flagship stores here.

Most shops open daily. Plan to spend at least a couple of hours wandering here.

Hear the Westerkerk's Carillon & Organ

A beacon across the city

The **Westerkerk** *(Western Church; westerkerk.nl; entry by donation)* and its bell tower, the **Westertoren** (Western Tower), are beloved by Amsterdammers. Built in Dutch Renaissance style to designs by city architect Hendrick de Keyser, the Netherlands' first Protestant church was consecrated in 1631. After Rembrandt died bankrupt in 1669 at nearby Rozengracht, he was buried here in an unidentified pauper's grave.

The 50-bell carillon rings out across the neighbourhood. Recitals typically take place from noon to 1pm on Tuesdays. Hear the organs during free lunchtime concerts from 1pm to 1.30pm on Wednesdays.

TOP EXPERIENCE

Anne Frank Huis

In the shadow of the Westertoren, the Anne Frank Huis is a heartbreaking and profoundly significant sight. It's where young Jewish girl Anne kept a diary while she and her family lived in hiding from the Nazis in a secret annexe of her father's business premises for more than two years until they were betrayed and deported. Visiting will stay with you forever.

Diary of a Young Girl

Anne Frank was born in Frankfurt, Germany, in 1929. Together with her older sister, Margot, and parents, Otto and Edith, the family fled when Hitler came to power in 1933, settling in Amsterdam, where Otto Frank founded companies selling foodstuffs in offices and warehouses on Amsterdam's Prinsengracht.

It took Hitler's forces a mere five days to occupy the Netherlands, Belgium and much of France in 1940. Anne's diary

DON'T MISS

Anne's red plaid diary

Secret annexe

Anne's bedroom

WWII newsreels

Peter van Pels' room

Former offices

PRACTICALITIES

● annefrank.org ● adult/child €16/7, with introductory programme €23/14 ● 9am-10pm

POWERFUL DETAILS

It's often the smallest details that are the most moving of all, for instance the film magazines Victor Kugler bought for Anne, displayed in his office; Anne's treasured children's tea set that she left with her next-door neighbour Toosje Kupers before going into hiding; and, in Anne's parents' bedroom, the markings charting their daughters' heights – Anne grew more than 13cm while living in the secret annexe.

describes how restrictions were gradually imposed on Dutch Jews, from being forbidden to ride streetcars to being forced to hand over their bicycles and not being allowed to visit Christian friends. Many Jews went into hiding. Otto and his colleague Hermann van Pels prepared a hidden 'secret annexe' of Otto's business in spring 1942.

In June 1942, Anne received her red plaid-covered diary for her 13th birthday. The following month, when 16-year-old Margot was summoned to Nazi Germany, the family took shelter in the hideout. Soon joining them were Hermann van Pels; his wife, Auguste; and their son, Peter (called the Van Daans in Anne's diary); and then dentist Fritz Pfeffer (called Mr Dussel in the diary). The household of eight lived with blacked-out windows in total daytime silence to avoid detection, and Anne's diary was the outlet for her fears and future ambitions. They were tragically cut short when the Gestapo arrived in August 1944 after the hiders were mysteriously betrayed. All eight were deported. Anne died in the Bergen-Belsen concentration camp in March 1945, just weeks before its liberation, aged only 15. Her diary was found in the deserted annexe, and published in 1947 by her father, Otto, the sole survivor. Millions of copies, translated in more than 70 languages, have since been sold worldwide.

Visiting the Anne Frank Huis

Accessed from Westermarkt, the Anne Frank Huis is contained within a modern, box-like shell that retains the building's original industrial character. Its museum shows multilingual news reels of WWII footage narrated using excerpts from Anne's diary. Temporary exhibitions also take place here.

You can see the former offices of Victor Kugler, Otto Frank's business partner, and office workers Miep Gies, Bep Voskuijl and Johannes Kleiman, who provided food, clothing, school supplies and other goods – often bought on the black market or with ration cards – for the hiders.

Above the office kitchen in the *achterhuis* (rear house), beyond the bookcase that ingeniously swings open on hinges, entering the annexe's stark former living quarters is to step back into 1942. At Otto's request, the annexe remains unfurnished, but Anne's pictures of Hollywood stars and Dutch royals remain where she glued them on the walls of her small bedroom, which she shared with Pfeffer. When the museum opened in 1960, Otto had models made of the house that preserved the cramped, concealed layout.

After visiting the annexe, view more poignant exhibits, including Anne's original red-checked diary, alone in a glass case.

The museum shop stocks copies of Anne's diary and historical books. Also here is a **cafe** for quiet contemplation.

IVO ANTONIE DE ROOIJ/SHUTTERSTOCK

Anne Frank Huis exterior

NIEUW AMSTERDAM TO NEW YORK

Enlisted by the Dutch East India Company (VOC), English captain Henry Hudson changed course to explore the North American river now named for him. The Dutch established a fort on the island of Manhattan, which grew into the settlement of Nieuw Amsterdam. In 1626, an agent of the recently established Dutch West India Company (GWC) purchased the island from Native Americans for 60 guilders (then equivalent to US$24).

In 1653, the Dutch colonists built a fortified wall (now Manhattan's Wall St), but in 1664, British warships invaded, and the GWC's local governor, Peter Stuyvesant, director-general of the colony of New Netherland, surrendered. The British swiftly renamed it New York.

Marvel at the Making of the Canal Ring

Secrets of the Grachtengordel

A 17th-century canal house on the Herengracht is a fitting place to discover the extraordinary engineering behind Amsterdam's Grachtengordel ('city canal belt', comprising the Western Canal Ring and Southern Canal Ring). At the **Grachtenmuseum Amsterdam** *(grachten.museum; adult/child €17.50/9.50),* audio-guided tours in small groups of up to 12 people depart every 10 minutes to avoid overcrowding and take in its permanent exhibition. Its high-tech holograms, videos, cartoons, and scale models of the city and canal houses demonstrate how the canals and tilting houses lining them were constructed and the problem-solving that went into the city's expansion.

There are thought-provoking temporary exhibitions, such as on the animals of Amsterdam's canals. The history of the symmetrical Dutch baroque house designed by Philips Vingboons is conveyed in glorious period rooms.

Visiting typically takes around 1½ to two hours in all. Afterwards, you'll look at the surrounding canals in a whole different light.

Catch Photography Exhibitions

Influential image museum

A pair of 17th-century canal houses is the showcase for photography that captures the zeitgeist at **Huis Marseille** *(huismarseille.nl; adult/child €12.50/free).* Its original building (Keizersgracht 401) was built around 1665 for French merchant Isaac Focquier (look for the map impression of Marseille's port on the facade's gable stone). Stuccowork and Jacob de Wit's ceiling painting were added in the following century. Exhibition spaces and a depot fill the adjoining Keizersgracht 399.

The museum doesn't have a permanent display; instead, it mounts several major exhibitions each year and closes for a week between each one.

Hang Out in the Haarlemmerbuurt

Food, film and sustainable fashion

Between Centraal Station and Westerpark, the hive of activity in the **Haarlemmerbuurt** *(haarlemmerbuurtamsterdam.nl)* is a legacy of the Brouwersgracht's former shipyards, breweries and warehouses. The neighbourhood's spine stretches along Haarlemmerstraat past the neogothic **Posthoornkerk**,

DRINKING IN THE WESTERN CANAL RING: BEST BROWN CAFES

't Arendsnest: Gorgeous *bruin café* with glowing copper *jenever* boilers, serving only Dutch beers, gins, ciders, whiskies and liqueurs. *noon–midnight or later*

Café Brandon: Rare corner canal house from 1826, adorned with pictures of Dutch royals and Ajax football players. *3pm–1am Mon–Thu, noon–3am Fri & Sat, to 1am Sun*

Café het Molenpad: Quietly romantic, with low lamps and candlelight illuminating its small tables beneath pressed-tin ceilings. *noon–1am Sun–Thu, to 2am Fri & Sat*

Proeflokaal A van Wees: Pours its Jordaan-distilled house brands: 17-plus *jenevers* and more than 60 liqueurs. *11am–11pm Sun–Thu, to 1am Fri & Sat* built in 1863 by Pierre Cuypers. Beyond the Prinsengracht, the street's western extension, the Haarlemmerdijk, continues to the neoclassical **Haarlemmerpoort** gate on the large square Haarlemmerplein. On Wednesdays, farmers market stalls set up here for its **Boerenmarkt**.

Today, this 1km-long thoroughfare is a buzzing commercial strip, lined with independent boutiques stocking fashion (vintage and new), cosmetics, books, music and homewares, with an increasingly sustainable focus, as well as food and drink specialists. Also here is Amsterdam's oldest cinema, 1912 art deco gem **The Movies** *(themovies.nl),* showing indie and mainstream films, including films with English subtitles.

Learn about the National Flower
The story of the tulip

Allow about 30 minutes or so at the charming Jordaan canal house containing the diminutive **Amsterdam Tulip Museum** *(amsterdamtulipmuseum.com; adult/child €7/4),* which offers an overview of the history of the country's favourite bloom. Through exhibits, timelines and two short films (in English), you'll learn how Ottoman merchants encountered the flowers in the Himalayan steppes and began commercial production in Türkiye, how fortunes were made and lost during 'tulipmania' in the 17th century, and how bulbs were used as food during WWII. You'll also discover present-day growing and harvesting techniques. There's a great collection of tulip art and artefacts, such as vases designed to accommodate separate stems.

Even if you're not visiting the museum, you can stop by its gift shop overflowing with high-quality floral souvenirs (many artist commissions), including jewellery, bags, books, homewares (tea towels, aprons and tableware), and antique and reproduction Delft tiles. It also stocks premium bulbs in season (spring-flowering varieties in autumn and summer-flowering bulbs in spring/early summer).

Treasure Hunt at the Jordaan's Markets
To market, to market

With the 1623-built Calvinist **Noorderkerk** *(noorderkerk. nl),* home to classical concerts *(noorderkerkconcerten.nl)* and immersive projections of 'Van Gogh & Rembrandt in Amsterdam' *(vangoghinamsterdam.com; adult/child €17/13)* as its
continues on page 74

BEST CANAL EXPLORATIONS

Pure Boats: Boutique operator with beautiful small boats. Options include 1½-hour daytime 'highlights' trips with apple pie or evening trips with cheese platters. *(pureboats.com)*

Those Dam Boat Guys: Laid-back trips lasting 90 minutes come with entertaining, irreverent commentary. BYO refreshments. *(thosedamboat guys.com)*

Miss G's Brunch Boat: Combines 90-minute weekend cruises with brunches, beats and Bloody Marys. *(missgs.nl)*

Canal Motorboats: Amsterdam's oldest operator offers boat hire from **Westerdoksdijk, Zandhoek** and **Westerpark,** including 'plastic fishing' equipment to clean up the canals. *(canalmotorboats. com)*

Kayak in Amsterdam: Guided one-hour 'Around Jordaan' tours pass landmarks like the Westerkerk. *(kayakinamster dam.com)*

 ## EATING IN WESTERN AMSTERDAM: BEST RESTAURANTS

De Belhamel: At the head of the Herengracht with canal-side tables, a split-level art nouveau interior and French-influenced plates. *9.30am-10pm* €€€

Wolf Atelier: Showcase for experimental chef Michael Wolf's tasting menus, with magical views at night. *6-10pm Tue-Fri, from noon Sat* €€€

BAK: Overlooking the IJ in a historic warehouse, crafting sustainable Dutch seafood, vegetables and wild game. *6-10pm Wed-Fri, 12.30-3pm & 6-10pm Sat & Sun* €€€

Lars: Michelin-starred address at Houthaven using produce from its rooftop garden in three-to eight-course menus. *6-10pm Tue & Wed, from noon Thu-Sat* €€€

Cycle Houthaven & the Western Islands

Spin through architectural advances and uncover layers of history on this 5km cycling tour. Starting at the 1920s-developed Spaarndammerbuurt, you visit the 1876-dug harbour, Houthaven (aka Houthavens for its four lumber ports), transformed from 2010 into Amsterdam's first climate-neutral neighbourhood. You then wind through a once-busy early-17th-century harbour that's now the tranquil Western Islands, passing historic bridges, wharves, warehouses and an ingenious 'bubble barrier', finishing at a waterside cafe.

❶ Museum Het Schip

The remarkable 1921-completed housing project **Het Schip** is a flagship of Amsterdam School architecture. Designed for railway employees, its triangular block has a rocket-shaped tower linking the complex's wings.

The Cycle: Cycle north along Oostzaanstraat to Spaarndammerdijk and cross over the top of the Spaarndammertunnel into Houthaven.

❷ Theater Amsterdam

With a 3800-sq-metre glass facade facing the IJ, the main hall of this **theatre**, built in 2014, can accommodate huge sets for large-scale theatre and music productions.

The Cycle: Ride northeast along Haparandadam, passing barges converted into houseboats and a vintage 1927 ex-vehicle and passenger ferry that now contains bar-restaurant Ferry.

❸ REM

Rising 22m at the end of the peninsula, red-metal rig **REM** (pictured) was a pirate radio and TV broadcasting station in the North Sea. In 2011, the rig was towed here and now houses a restaurant with 360-degree views from its three platforms, including the former helipad rooftop terrace.

The Cycle: Take the pedestrian and cycle bridge across the islands Wiborgeiland and Stettineiland to Revaleiland to the IJ.

4 Het Eikenhout

Out the front of apartment-hotel The July – Boat & Co, designed in a contemporary interpretation of the Amsterdam School style, stop to cool off at urban beach **Het Eikenhout**.

The Cycle: Ride southeast along Gevlebrug to Oude Houthaven and then east along Van Diemenstraat.

5 Muurschildering Willem Barentsz

Covering four building facades, a series of Delft Blue murals by Klaartje Bruyn (2008) depict the 16th-century expeditions of Dutch seafarer and scientist **Willem Barentsz**.

The Cycle: Navigate south to Realengracht and then west to the Drieharingenbrug.

6 Drieharingenbrug

Linking the Western Islands of Realenei-land and Prinseneiland, the double wooden

drawbridge **Drieharingenbrug** ('Three Herrings Bridge') is named for the gable stone on the 18th-century house on its northern side.

The Cycle: Head southeast to Prinseneiland and north to Han Lammersbrug, crossing the Westerdok canal. On your right, look for the diagonal line of bubbles. Installed in 2019, the Great Bubble Barrier lifts plastic waste to the surface, where it flows to a collection point without hindering the passage of fish or watercraft.

7 Hoogendam

Hoogendam has a vast timber-floored interior with a copper-green bar. But its biggest draw is the south-facing dockside terrace, which stays sunny throughout the afternoon – perfect for a frothy Dutch beer, Amsterdam-roasted coffee or house-made lemonade.

GABLE STONES OF THE JORDAAN

Before street numbers were introduced in the 19th century, *gevelstenen* (gable stones) identified homes and businesses. Like stained-glass church windows, these stone tablets above doors on buildings' facades used illustrations (many with religious symbolism and imagery) and text.

Some 850 exist today, with plenty in the historic Jordaan's streets that tell stories of the people who lived and plied their trades here, like the horseshoe gable stone of the former blacksmith at Lindengracht 73, copper barrels used to make potash at the former soap maker at Tuinstraat 46 and goose-feather quill of the former scribe at Egelantiersstraat 52. Look up as you stroll.

PICTURE PARTNERS/SHUTTERSTOCK

Noordermarkt

continued from page 71

backdrop, the **Noordermarkt** *(noordermarkt-amsterdam.nl)* has been a marketplace since the early 17th century.

Saturdays see the Noordermarkt host a general market in front of the church, with everything from antiques and bric-a-brac to artisan crafts, ceramics, prints, posters, vintage fashion, bags, hats and jewellery, as well as a **farmers market** *(boerenmarkt)* with organic produce.

On Mondays, a general market takes over the Noordermarkt. Along the adjacent Westerstraat (once the Anjeliersgracht, meaning Carnation Canal, dug in 1650 and backfilled in 1861 to create a thoroughfare), the **Westerstraat Markt** (aka the Westermarkt) sells bolts of colourful fabrics.

Around the corner from the Noordermarkt, Saturday's lively **Lindengracht Markt** has been a neighbourhood tradition since 1894. Join locals browsing more than 230 stalls selling fresh fruit, vegetables, seafood, fabulous cheeses, breads and Dutch delicacies like caramel-filled *stroopwafels,* colourful cut flowers, clothing and homewares.

Discover Boat Life in the Jordaan

All about houseboats

The 23m-long *Hendrika Maria,* a former cargo ship from 1914, is now the **Houseboat Museum** *(houseboatmuseum. nl; adult/child €9.50/5).* It offers a good sense of how *gezellig* (cosy) life can be on the water. Restored in 2008, there's some fantastic vintage decor from 1967 to 1997 when it was a residence. An audio guide lets you navigate its surprisingly spacious 80-sq-metre interior; the actual displays are minimal, but you can watch a presentation on houseboats (some pretty and some ghastly) and inspect the sleeping, living, cooking and dining quarters with all the mod cons.

WANDER THE HISTORIC WESTERN CANAL RING

Discover 17th-century bridges, buildings and waterways on this walk through the charming Western Canal Ring.

START	END	LENGTH
Singel	Felix Meritis	2.8km; 2½ hours

The ❶ **Singel** was originally a moat that defended Amsterdam's outer limits. The canal's 1648-built ❷ **Torensluis** (named for the tower that stood here until 1829) is Amsterdam's oldest bridge in its original state. On its northern side, the ❸ **Multatuli Statue** commemorates Dutch literary giant Eduard Douwes Dekker, pen name Multatuli, and the nearby ❹ **Multatuli Museum** chronicles his life and work, with furniture and artefacts from his time in Indonesia.

Head north along the ❺ **Herengracht**, which intersects with the pretty ❻ **Brouwersgracht**. At the Herenmarkt is the 17th-century ❼ **West-Indisch Huis**, where the Dutch West India Company's governors authorised the creation of Nieuw Amsterdam (now New York City).

Turning south, cross onto ❽ **Keizersgracht** (Emperor's Canal), where the red-shuttered ❾ **Greenland Warehouses** used to store whale oil that powered lamps and stoves pre-electricity. Continue south to the 1622 Dutch Renaissance ❿ **Huis Met de Hoofden** ('House with the Heads'), with carvings of Apollo, Ceres, Mercury, Minerva, Bacchus and Diana. Designed by architect Hendrick de Keyser and his son Pieter, it now houses the Embassy of the Free Mind philosophical museum and library.

At Leliegracht, turn west and then south onto ⓫ **Prinsengracht**, home to the ⓬ **Anne Frank Huis** (p67) and ⓭ **Westerkerk** (p66). Back on Keizersgracht is theatre ⓮ **Felix Meritis**; its facade was a model for Concertgebouw (p93).

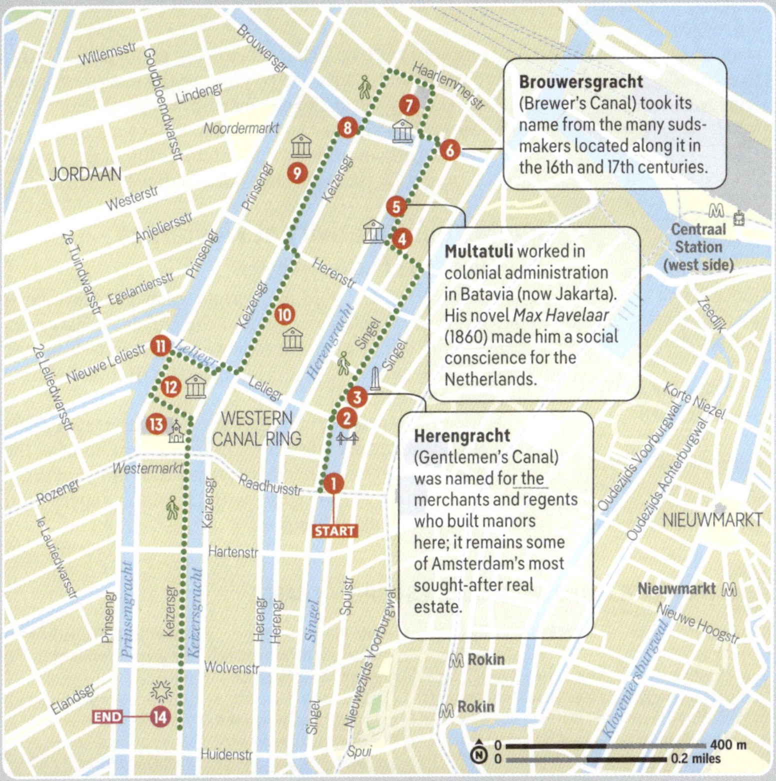

Brouwersgracht

(Brewer's Canal) took its name from the many suds-makers located along it in the 16th and 17th centuries.

Multatuli

worked in colonial administration in Batavia (now Jakarta). His novel *Max Havelaar* (1860) made him a social conscience for the Netherlands.

Herengracht

(Gentlemen's Canal) was named for the merchants and regents who built manors here; it remains some of Amsterdam's most sought-after real estate.

START

END ⓮

0   400 m
0   0.2 miles

BEST SHOPS

De Mof: Durable workwear and casual-wear since 1885. *(demof kleding.nl)*

Rain Couture: Multi-seasonal wet-weather trench coats, jackets and parkas. *(rain-couture.nl)*

Laura Dols: Everything from 1920s beaded dresses to '40s hand-stitched leather gloves and shawls. *(lauradols.nl)*

Marie-Stella-Maris: Ethical plant-based skincare products and home fragrances. *(marie-stella-maris.com)*

Het Oud-Hollandsch Snoepwinkeltje: Jar after apothecary jar of Dutch penny sweets, including *zoute drop* (salty liquorice). *(snoepwinkeltje.com)*

Frozen Fountain: Dutch design platform showcasing striking interiors and homewares. *(frozenfountain.com)*

POLSPOTTEN: Brand store of the 1986-founded Dutch design pioneer. *(polspotten.com)*

Amsterdam's 2500 or so houseboats are connected to utilities, including water, electricity, gas and the sewage system, thanks to the city's Project Schoonschip (Project Clean Ship), which saw every houseboat connected to the sewage system by 2017, dramatically improving the water quality of the canals. Museum tickets are cheaper before noon (online bookings only).

Ignite Your Creativity at Westergas

Gasworks turned 'cultural village'

Just northwest of the Jordaan, former gasworks have been repurposed in recent years as 'cultural village' **Westergas** *(westergas.nl)* with a growing collection of art museums and venues, as well as diverse places for drinking, dining, clubbing and entertainment, and a slew of festivals.

Westergas' 19th-century buildings now contain creative spaces like the grand former engineer's residence, now housing the artist-designed, 2025-opened **Museum Villa** *(museumvilla. com; adult/child from €17.50/9),* with changing experiential contemporary art exhibitions.

 DRINKING IN THE JORDAAN: BEST BROWN CAFES

't Smalle: Dock your boat at this 1786 former *jenever* distillery with its convivial terrace. *2pm-midnight Mon-Thu, to 1am Fri & Sat, 2-10pm Sun*

Café Papeneiland: With Delft Blue tiles and a central stove, this *bruin café* is a 1642 gem. *10am-1am Mon-Thu, to 3am Fri & Sat, noon-1am Sun*

Café Pieper: Antique beer mugs hang from the bar with an 1875 working Belgian beer pump at this stained-glass-windowed 1665 treasure. *noon-1am or later*

Café Chris: Allegedly the Jordaan's oldest *bruin café*, dating from 1624: workers building the Westertoren collected their pay here. *noon-midnight or later*

CLAUDIO ARMANDI/SHUTTERSTOCK

TULIPMANIA

The Dutch tulip craze of 1636–37 ranks alongside history's greatest economic booms and busts. After successfully growing and cross-breeding tulips in the Netherlands' cool, damp climate, exotic frilly, flame-streaked specimens attracted the attention of wealthy merchants, and tulip growers arose to service demand.

A speculative frenzy ensued: bidding often took place in taverns, and people paid top florin (even more than an Amsterdam canal house) for the finest bulbs, many changing hands time and again before they sprouted. When traders failed to fetch expected prices in February 1637, the market abruptly collapsed. Within weeks, many people lost everything. Enthusiasm for tulips endured – the Netherlands remains the world leader of tulip cultivation.

Westerpark

The former purification hall, where sulphur was extracted, is home to the 2022-opened immersive digital art gallery **Fabrique des Lumières** *(fabrique-lumieres.com; adult/child €18/14)*. Also in the purification hall is the 2025 arrival **Amsterdam in Motion** *(amsterdaminmotion.nl; adult/child €18/free)*. Curated by the under-renovation Amsterdam Museum, it incorporates a 15-minute journey through the city's past via projection mapping on a 200-sq-metre city model of 30,500 buildings at 1:1300 scale, and upper-floor interactive installations showcasing Amsterdam's present and future.

On-site brewery **Brouwerij Troost Westergas** *(brouwer ijtroost.nl; brewery tours per person €10)* has big silver tanks cooking up saison, blond ale and smoked porter varieties, distils its own *jenever* and other gins, and makes sodas. Brewery tours last 45 minutes and take place on Saturdays.

Linked to Westergas by a long wading pool and tree-shaded paths, expansive **Westerpark** is a favourite local hangout on sunny days.

EATING IN WESTERN AMSTERDAM: BEST CAFE DINING

De Bakkerswinkel: Situated at Westergas, with mezzanine seating, sofas and a sunny terrace. Great-value cafe dishes. *9am-5pm* €

Eetcafé Roem: Sandwiches, toasties and giant sweet or savoury Dutch pancakes looking down the Leliegracht from the Prinsengracht. *9am-9pm* €

Winkel 43: Popular from breakfast to evening drinks, and for Amsterdam's most coveted *appeltaart*. *8am-1am Mon-Fri, 7am-2am Sat, 9am-1am Sun* €€

Singel 404: Tucked-away canal-side spot (look for the red awning) for all-day breakfast, lunch and honey-mint lemonade at its handful of tables inside or out. *9am-6pm* €€

Southern Canal Ring

GRAND CANAL HOUSES, ENTERTAINMENT AND NIGHTLIFE

GETTING AROUND

Walking is the perfect way to take in this neighbourhood's magnificent architecture and interesting boutiques.

This area is well served by trams. For the Leidseplein area, take tram 1, 2, 5, 7, 12, 17 or 19. To reach Rembrandtplein, take tram 4, which travels down Utrechtsestraat, or tram 14. Tram 24 runs along the neighbourhood's southeastern edge, turning south to De Pip.

Metro line 52 between Amsterdam Noord and Zuid stops at Vijzelgracht.

A crescent stretching from the Leidsegracht to the Amstel, Amsterdam's Southern Canal Ring is a magnet for visitors day and night. The neighbourhood has some of the city's most beautiful stretches of waterways, including the grand properties gracing the Golden Bend, little changed since the 17th century when the city's splendid canal ring was expanded south and the wealthy merchant owners successfully lobbied city planners for deep gardens and double-width gables.

There are wonderful museums (not least the extravagant canal houses of the Museum Van Loon and the Museum Willet-Holthuysen); dining options galore, with some of the most exciting places popping up along Utrechtsestraat; and countless opportunities for shopping, from bulbs and flower-themed souvenirs at the waterside Bloemenmarkt to the antiques, bric-a-brac and art in the Spiegelkwartier. After dark, the action gravitates to the bars, clubs and entertainment venues surrounding the large squares of Leidseplein and Rembrandtplein.

Visit a Grand Canal House

Architectural splendour

Dating from 1672 and set in a beautiful canal house, the **Museum Van Loon** *(museumvanloon.nl; adult/child €16/9)* was first home to acclaimed painter Ferdinand Bol. By the late 1800s, the Van Loons, a prominent patrician family, had moved in and have lived here ever since; they still occupy the building's upper floors. It's filled with opulent furniture and family portraits, but the main exhibit is the house itself. It's full of set-piece interior decoration, with intricate wedding-cake stucco on the ceilings. Temporary art exhibitions and concerts take place throughout the rooms.

Downstairs is the old-fashioned basement kitchen. Original blueprints were used to restore the wine cellar, pantry and storage room.

Museum Van Loon

This is the only such mansion where you can still see a rear coach house, which once housed up to eight horse-drawn carriages. It's outside, at the end of the pristine formal courtyard garden. Its small cafe is a lovely place for a coffee and *appelschnitt* (apple strudel).

Imagine the 19th-Century High Life

Canal house elegance

Built in 1687 as a home for Amsterdam mayor Jacob Hop and redesigned in 1739, the **Museum Willet-Holthuysen** *(amsterdammuseum.nl/tentoonstelling/huis-willet-holthuysen/9511; adult/child €15/free)* offers insight into the 19th-century lives of the merchant class's super-rich. It's named for Louisa Willet-Holthuysen, who lived a lavish, bohemian life here with her husband Abraham from 1861. Their rich selection of furniture and art includes notable paintings by Jacob de Wit. The preserved kitchen and scullery provide a glimpse of the work required to keep the house running.

Louisa Willet-Holthuysen bequeathed the property to the city in 1895, and it's now managed by the Amsterdam Museum. Every six months, a leading artist or collector is offered the opportunity to exhibit throughout the property's fabulous rooms.

Its garden is a highlight of June's **Open Tuinen Dagen** *(Open Garden Days; opentuinendagen.nl).*

continues on page 82

☑ **TOP TIP**

Opened in 1955, the Netherlands' largest music shop **Concerto** *(concerto.nl)* is a rare audiophile's paradise. Along with new and secondhand vinyl and CDs spanning rock to classical and jazz, and an impressive selection of electronic music genres, it also has an awesome roster of free live gigs and DJ sessions in-store.

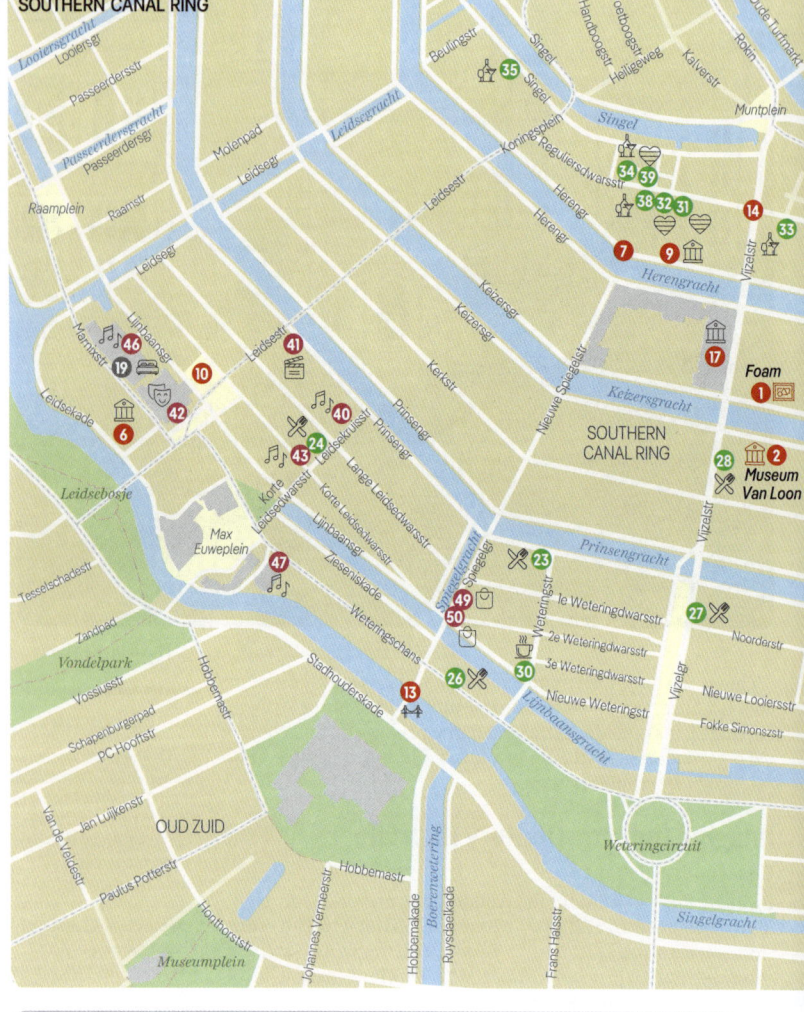

SOUTHERN CANAL RING

★ HIGHLIGHTS
1 Foam
2 Museum Van Loon
3 Museum Willet-Holthuysen

● SIGHTS
4 Amstelsluizen
5 Blauwbrug
6 Clayton Hotel Amsterdam American
7 Golden Bend
8 H'ART
9 Kattenkabinet
10 Leidseplein
11 Magere Brug
12 Museum van de Geest
13 Museumbrug
14 Reguliersdwarsstraat
15 Reguliersgracht
16 Rembrandtplein
17 Stadsarchief

● SLEEPING
18 ClinkCoco
19 Hotel La Boheme
20 Hotel V Frederiksplein
21 Seven Bridges

● EATING
22 Bakhuys Amsterdam
23 Buffet van Odette
24 De Blauwe Hollander
25 Dignita Hoftuin
26 Levant
27 Patisserie Holtkamp
28 Petit by Sam
29 Zoldering

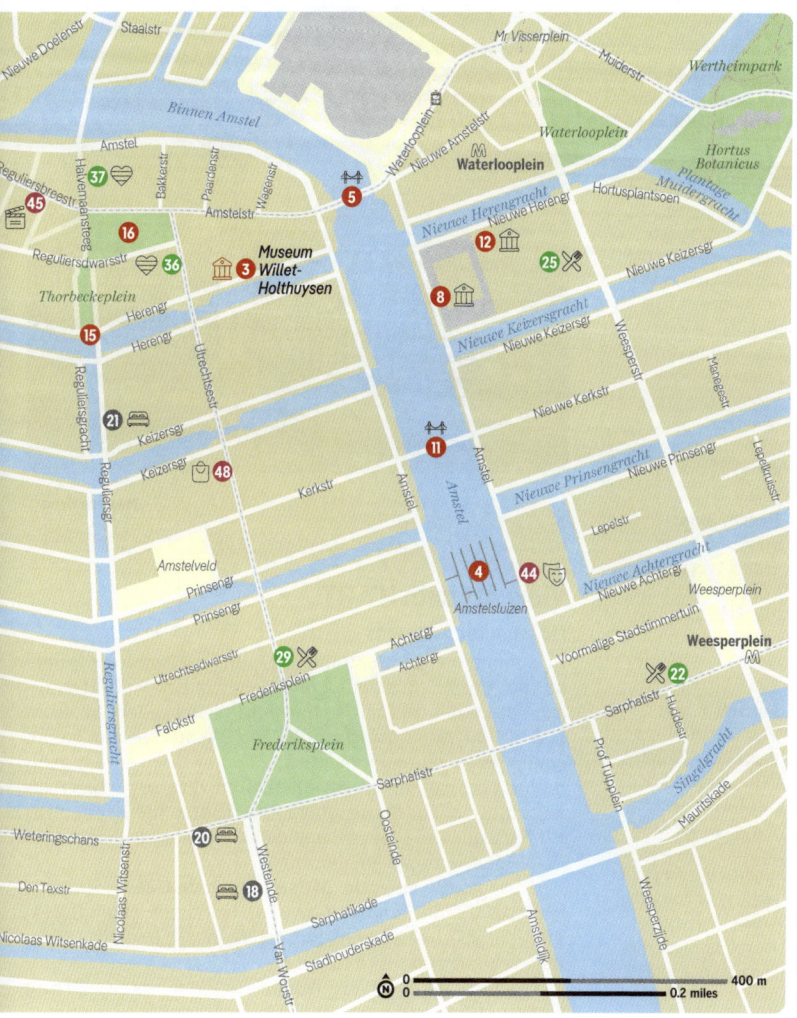

● **DRINKING & NIGHTLIFE**
30 Back to Black
31 B'Femme
32 Blend XL
33 Door 74
34 Duke of Tokyo
35 Flying Dutchmen Cocktails
36 Lellebel
37 Montmartre

38 Secret Garden
39 Taboo Bar

● **ENTERTAINMENT**
40 Bourbon Street Jazz & Blues Club
41 De Uitkijk
42 Internationaal Theater Amsterdam
43 Jazz Café Alto

44 Koninklijk Theater Carré
45 Koninklijk Theater Tuschinski
46 Melkweg
47 Paradiso

● **SHOPPING**
48 Concerto
49 Hoogkamp Antiquariaat
50 Spiegelkwartier

BEST BRIDGES

Blauwbrug: The beautiful 1884 Blue Bridge features tall, ornate street lamps topped by the imperial crown of Amsterdam.

Reguliersgracht: Lean over the bridge facing the Herengracht to see seven humpbacked arches leading down the canal straight ahead.

Magere Brug: With a hand-operated central section (raised to let boats through), the Skinny Bridge is especially pretty at night, when it glows with 1200 tiny lights.

Amstelsluizen: Dating from 1674, these locks allow the canals to be flushed with fresh water. The sluices on the city's west side are left open as the stagnant water is pumped out to sea.

Museumbrug: Idyllic canalscapes with blooms on railings and grandiose architecture.

MILOS RUZICKA/SHUTTERSTOCK

Magere Brug

continued from page 79

View Art with H'ART

Museum for museums

In a monumental 1683 building with its 102m-long facade on the Amstel – a satellite of St Petersburg's State Hermitage Museum until the Ukraine War – independent museum **H'ART** *(hartmuseum.nl; adult/child €38.50/free)* now has an emphasis on contemporary art and offers three or four exhibitions per year and programming from diverse perspectives and cultures. The Smithsonian American Art Museum, British Museum and Centre Pompidou are among an impressive roster of upcoming collaborations.

In a separate wing, the **Museum van de Geest** *(Museum of the Mind; museumvandegeest.nl)* has single, changing exhibitions spotlighting 'outsider art' produced by artists while in psychiatric institutions.

H'ART's front courtyard is home to the museum's **Grand Café** in summer. It moves to the indoor upper level in winter.

In the leafy garden is the glass-walled cafe **Dignita Hoftuin** *(eatwelldogood.nl)*.

 EATING IN THE SOUTHERN CANAL RING: BEST BAKERIES & CAFES

Bakhuys Amsterdam: Watch as bakers knead sourdough and work the wood-fired oven. Toast, sweet pastries, pizzas and sandwiches. *7am-5pm €*

Patisserie Holtkamp: Chocolate truffles are most beloved. Also fluffy Bavarian cream-topped cakes, *koekjes* (cookies) and tarts. *8.30am-6pm Mon-Fri, to 5pm Sat €*

Petit by Sam: Little patisserie using natural ingredients (date puree, honey and almond flour). Vegan, dairy- and gluten-free pick-me-ups. *9am-5pm €*

Back to Black: Ultra-cool neighbourhood cafe with teal walls and cakes, pies and powerballs baked in-house. Also roasts its own beans. *9am-6pm*

Explore the Municipal Archives

City memory bank

A distinctive striped former bank dating from 1923 now houses more than 50km of shelving storage at the **Stadsarchief** *(City Archives; amsterdam.nl/stadsarchief; free)*. Amsterdam archival gems, such as the 1942 police report on the theft of Anne Frank's bike and a letter from Charles Darwin to Artis Zoo in 1868, can be viewed in the enormous tiled basement vault. Upstairs, a gallery space mounts temporary exhibits, some of which charge a fee to see.

Admire Feline Art

Museum on the Golden Bend

Wealthy financier Bob Meijer founded an entire museum in memory of his late red tomcat, John Pierpont Morgan III. The **Kattenkabinet** *(Cat Cabinet; adult/child €12.50/7.50)* collection includes artworks by Tsuguharu Foujita, Théophile Steinlen and Amsterdam's chief sculptor, Hildo Krop. You may get the chance to admire the cats that live in the building along with the art collection.

A visit here allows you to explore one of the famously double-wide, anything-but-humble canal-side homes on the **Golden Bend** (Gouden Bocht); this is the only one open to the public.

Take in Photography at Foam

Renowned photo museum

A visit to **Foam** *(foam.org; adult/child €16/11.75)* is always an eye-opening experience. It's one of the world's leading museums for international photographic exhibitions, and the diverse programming spans fashion retrospectives and travel photographers' image storytelling. From the outside, Foam (short for 'Fotografiemuseum') looks like a grand canal house, but these three buildings linked by staircases and passageways are the backdrop for spacious galleries, with an emphasis on experimental installations.

The **Foam Editions** gallery, featuring established and emerging photographers, supports the museum's educational projects. Some of Foam's rotating exhibitions require an additional charge.

BEST ENTERTAINMENT VENUES

Koninklijk Theater Tuschinski: Fantastical 1921-completed art deco cinema. *(pathe.nl)*

De Uitkijk: Arthouse cinema in a 17th-century warehouse. *(uitkijk.nl)*

Koninklijk Theater Carré: Historic Amstel theatre. *(carre.nl)*

Internationaal Theater Amsterdam: Plays, operettas and festivals, such as late May/early June's Holland Festival, the Netherlands' biggest arts fest *(hollandfestival.nl)*. *(ita.nl)*

Jazz Café Alto: Staging jams and performances since 1953, with live gigs nightly; no reservations. *(jazzcafe-alto.nl)*

Bourbon Street Jazz & Blues Club: Intimate venue with open jam sessions and performances including jazz, blues and soul. *(bourbonstreet.nl)*

EATING IN SOUTHERN CANAL RING: BEST RESTAURANTS

Buffet van Odette: Chef-restauranteur Odette serves decadent mains at her enchanting canal-side restaurant. *noon-3pm & 5.30-11pm Wed-Sat* €€

De Blauwe Hollander: It's all comfort food at this red-lamp-lit place with staples like *stamppot* (mash with pork sausage). *noon-10.30pm* €€

Zoldering: Michelin-starred bistro serving refined French-Dutch cuisine with seasonal and foraged ingredients. *5.30-10pm Mon-Fri, from 4pm Sat* €€€

Levant: Elegant Turkish eatery serving meze and grilled meats by candlelight. Reserve a spot on the back terrace right against the water. *5-11.30pm* €€€

GABLES GALORE

Some of the most significant architectural features of canal houses are their gables, or roof-level facades. The gable hid the roof from public view and helped to identify the house until the French occupiers introduced house numbers in 1795. Gables later became a reflection of aesthetics rather than functionality.

There are four main types: simple spout gables, with a diagonal outline and semicircular windows or shutters (used mainly for warehouses from the 1580s to the early 1700s); step gables, a late-Gothic design favoured by Dutch Renaissance architects; neck gables, a durable design introduced in the 1640s; and bell gables, which appeared in the 1660s and was popularised in the 18th century.

Hit Leidseplein & Rembrandtplein
Nightlife zones

Historic architecture, bars, pubs, clubs, theatres and live-music venues – **Leidseplein** has a bit of everything. The square and its surrounding streets are always busy, especially since several tram lines converge here. After dark, Leidseplein is a major nightlife hub that gets thronged by a mainstream crowd of party lovers (more tourists than locals).

Nearby **Rembrandtplein** was first called Reguliersplein and then Botermarkt for the butter markets that took place here until the mid-19th century. It gained its current name in 1876, when Louis Royer's 1852 cast-iron statue of the painter, the Rembrandt Monument, was moved from the edge of the square to the centre. It's a major nightlife hub, ringed by cafes, pubs and clubs.

Compile a Cabinet of Curiosities
Art and antiques quarter

The perfect Delft vase or 16th-century wall map will most assuredly be hiding among the antique stores, bric-a-brac shops and commercial art galleries in the **Spiegelkwartier** *(spiegelkwartier.nl)*.

In the early 20th century, dealers set up shop around Nieuwe Spiegelstraat, with surrounding stately canal houses ensuring a steady flow of collectors. **Hoogkamp Antiquariaat** *(Prints & Maps Hoogkamp; fineartprints.nl)* has wonderful prints of Amsterdam.

Party on Reguliersdwarsstraat
Amsterdam's main LGBTIQ+ street

The Southern Canal Ring has a longstanding, lively queer scene. Romp through some of its best nightlife on its major gay street, **Reguliersdwarsstraat** *(reguliers.net)*. The pedestrian strip is lined by gay bars and nightclubs, cocktail joints and restaurants enjoyed by a diverse (gender, age and otherwise) crowd. Warm, summer evenings see everyone – partygoers to drag queens – melt outside into one big street party.

Gay nightlife institutions here range from the twinkling disco-ball-lit dance floor at **Blend XL** *(barblend.nl)* to the lesbian cafe **B'Femme** *(instagram.com/bfemme__)* and laid-back, chatty vibes at **Taboo Bar** *(instagram.com/taboo.amsterdam)*.

 DRINKING IN THE SOUTHERN CANAL RING: BEST COCKTAIL BARS

| Door 74: Innovative cocktails in a classy, dark Prohibition era–inspired atmosphere. Themed cocktail lists change regularly. *8pm-3am Sun-Thu, to 4am Fri & Sat* | Duke of Tokyo: Trendy karaoke bar with a serious focus on Japanese-inspired cocktails, spiked with sake, plum liqueur and rum. *5pm-1am Sun-Thu, to 2am Fri & Sat* | Flying Dutchmen Cocktails: Amsterdam's best cocktail bar. Monthly changing mixology and the Netherlands' largest backbar with more than 800 spirits. *5pm-4am* | Secret Garden: Rainforest decor and an equatorial-inspired cocktail list packing mezcal and pisco punch. *6pm-1am daily, plus 12.30-3pm Fri-Sun* |

JASON WELLS/SHUTTERSTOCK

Reguliersdwarsstraat

AMSTERDAM DANCE EVENT

Thanks to its historic, large-scale theatres and nightlife, the Southern Canal Ring plays a big role in Amsterdam Dance Event *(ADE; amsterdam-dance-event.nl)*, one of Europe's biggest electronic music festivals. For five days in late October, more than 500,000 participants – DJs, labels, clubbers and everyone in between – come to dance to their favourite DJs and genres in massive club nights. During the day, ADE gets a bit serious with a conference-like atmosphere and talks on sound production, trends and getting along in the industry.

The church-turned-nightclub **Paradiso** is one of the venues most associated with unforgettable ADE nights – tickets to events here sell out quickly. You'll also find big events in the former factory **Melkweg**.

Nearby, off Rembrandtplein, popular venues include **Lellebel** *(lellebel.nl)*, specialising in drag queen fabulousness, and **Montmartre** *(cafemontmartre.nl)*, known for its Dutch music sing-alongs, karaoke, drag, and '80s and '90s hits.

Dance at Legendary Venues

Nightlife icons

In a former dairy factory squatted in and repurposed by a theatre collective in 1970, the nonprofit **Melkweg** *(Milky Way; melkweg.nl)* is one of the Netherlands' most important concert venues, hosting up to 1500 people for DJ club nights and live bands – everything from reggae and punk to heavy metal and mellow singer-songwriters. Its free, weekly 'Techno Tuesday' is a decade-long institution seeing hundreds of people stomp to high-BPM beats. Check for cutting-edge cinema, theatre and multimedia offerings, too.

In 1968, a beautiful 19th-century church was turned into the 'Cosmic Relaxation Center Paradiso'. Today, at the **Paradiso** *(paradiso.nl)*, a smaller hall hosts emerging artists, but there's something special about the main hall, where it seems the stained-glass windows might shatter under the force of synthesiser beats.

Vondelpark, Oud-West & Oud-Zuid

MONUMENTAL MUSEUMS AND SPRAWLING PARKS

GETTING AROUND

Cycling is ideal for getting around this neighbourhood, and it's especially handy for the more spread-out streets of Oud-West and for exploring within the Vondelpark.

Trams are also handy. Tram 1 traverses Overtoom, and tram 3 serves Concertgebouw. Trams 2, 3, 5 and 12 stop at Museumplein. Tram 5 continues to Amsterdam Zuid, which is linked by metro 52 to Centraal Station, and trains to Centraal Station and the airport.

Connexxion's Amsterdam Airport Express (bus 397; Niteliner N97) directly connects the airport with Museumplein, which can be convenient if you're staying in this area.

At this neighbourhood's heart, Vondelpark has rambling English-style gardens within strolling distance from the mega-museums of elegant Oud-Zuid and vibrant street life in and beyond Oud-West. Ranging over 47 hectares, the Vondelpark's lawns, roses, sculptures, fountains, ponds and winding paths are only moments from frenetic Leidseplein, and they are a favourite escape for Amsterdammers and visitors on sunny days.

Footsteps southeast, the vast, grassy square Museumplein is ringed by Amsterdam's biggest-hitting museums: the Netherlands' monumental national museum, the Rijksmuseum; the Van Gogh Museum, with the world's largest collection of the artist's works; and the Stedelijk Museum, with modern and contemporary art and installations.

On the Vondelpark's northern side, cafes, restaurants, shops and bars line Overtoom and surrounding streets, which blend into the up-and-coming Oud West. Converted tram sheds here now house cultural and food hub De Hallen. Luxury boutiques and eateries grace the leafy streets to the Vondelpark's south.

Laze in the Vondelpark
Urban idyll

Originally opened in 1865 as a private park only for the wealthy, the **Vondelpark** is home to English-style gardens that were laid out on marshland, and they were expanded between 1875 and 1877 to the current size. In 1867, a statue of poet and playwright **Joost van den Vondel** (1587–1679) was created by sculptor Louis Royer. Locals began referring to the park as Vondelspark (Vondel's Park), and it was formally renamed. The **rose garden** was added in 1936. Bought by the city council in 1953, the park finally opened to the public.

During the 1960s and '70s, Amsterdam became the *magisch centrum* (magic centre) of Europe. A housing shortage saw

Vondelpark

squatting (illegal since 2010) become widespread, and Dutch authorities turned the park into a temporary open-air dormitory. Although the sleeping bags are long gone today, an indie spirit persists.

Sculptures dotted throughout the park include Picasso's 6m-high abstract work *Figure découpée l'Oiseau* (The Bird; 1965), commonly known as **The Fish**, which he donated for the park's centenary on the condition it remains here.

Refreshments inside the park gates include the blue and white, flying-saucer-shaped **Proeflokaal 't Blauwe Theehuis** *(brouwerijhetij.nl)*, a **Brouwerij 't IJ** (p112) taproom; garden cafe **De Vondeltuin** *(devondeltuin.nl)*; and Hansel-and-Gretel-like chalet **Groot Melkhuis** *(grootmelkhuis.nl)*.

The **Openluchttheater** *(Open-Air Theatre; openluchttheater.nl)* hosts free performances (world music, dance, plays and more) from Friday evenings to Sunday afternoons from May to September.

Het Documentaire Paviljoen, in the colonnaded Italian Renaissance–style Vondelparkpaviljoen, is the home base of November's citywide **International Documentary Film Festival Amsterdam** *(IDFA; idfa.nl)*.

On neighbouring Overtoom, **This Is Soul** *(thisissoul.com; day/overnight skate hire from €10/5)* rents in-line skates. Amsterdam's 20km **Friday Night Skate** *(fridaynightskate.com)* sets off from the park.

☑ **TOP TIP**

Museumplein hosts Amsterdam's biggest celebrations, including Nationale Tulpendag (National Tulip Day; the third Saturday in January), when it's carpeted with 200,000 tulips; Bevrijdingsdag (Liberation Day; 5 May); Keti Koti (1 July, the anniversary of 1863 abolition of slavery in Suriname and the Netherlands Antilles), plus Christmas markets and New Year's Eve fireworks.

WOLF-PHOTOGRAPHY/SHUTTERSTOCK

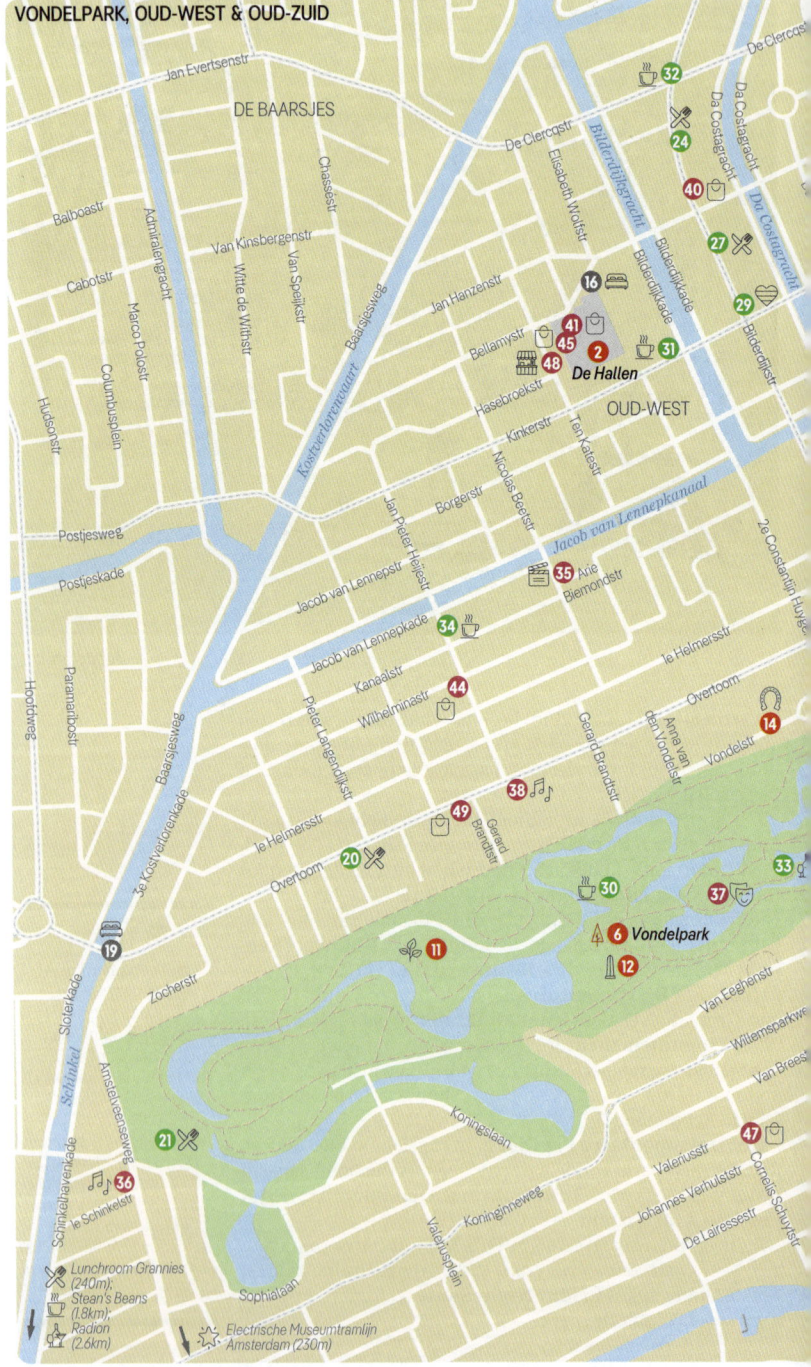

VONDELPARK, OUD-WEST & OUD-ZUID

DE BAARSJES

OUD-WEST

De Hallen

Jacob van Lennepkanaal

Arie Biemondstr

Vondelpark

Lunchroom Grannies (240m);
Stean's Beans (1.8km);
Radion (2.6km)

Electrische Museumtramlijn Amsterdam (230m)

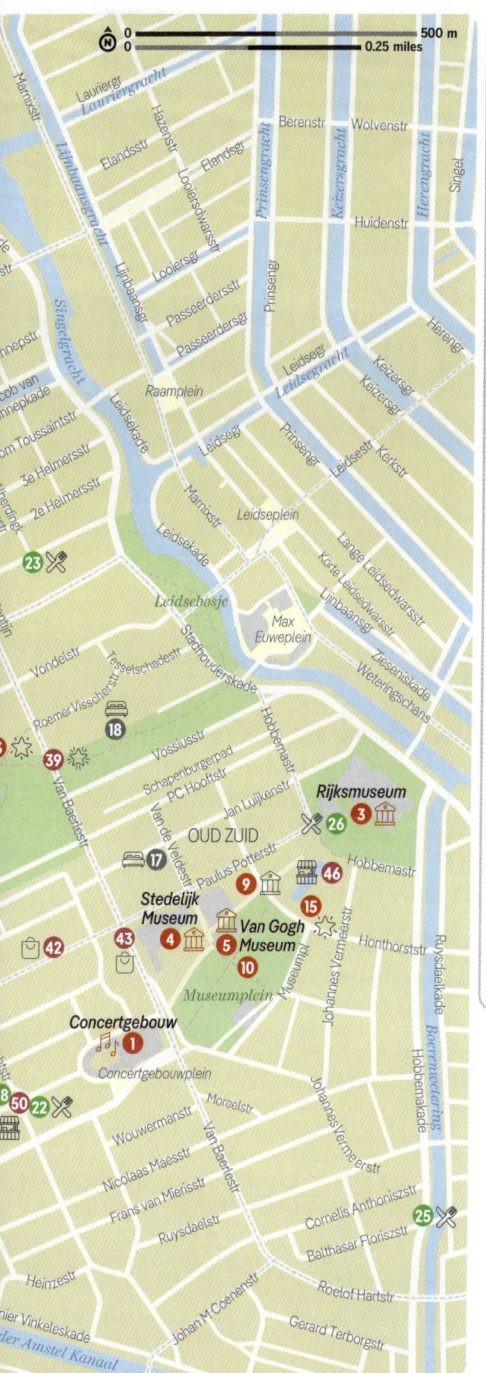

⭐ HIGHLIGHTS
1 Concertgebouw
2 De Hallen
3 Rijksmuseum
4 Stedelijk Museum
5 Van Gogh Museum
6 Vondelpark

🔴 SIGHTS
7 Het Documentaire Paviljoen
8 Joost van den Vondel Statue
see 14 Levend Paarden Museum
9 Moco Museum
10 Museumplein
11 Rose Garden
12 The Fish

🔴 ACTIVITIES
13 Friday Night Skate
14 Hollandsche Manege
15 Skatepark Museumplein

⚫ SLEEPING
16 Hotel De Hallen
17 Hotel Fita
18 Stayokay Amsterdam Vondelpark
19 SWEETS Hotel Overtoomsesluis

🟢 EATING
20 Alchemist Garden
21 De Vondeltuin
see 2 Foodhallen
22 Friet Boutique
23 Hap Hmm
24 Meatless District
25 Old Soul
26 Rijks
27 Soil
28 Visque Winkel

🟢 DRINKING & NIGHTLIFE
29 De Trut
30 Groot Melkhuis
31 LOT61
32 Monks Coffee Roasters
33 Proeflokaal 't Blauwe Theehuis
34 Trakteren

🔴 ENTERTAINMENT
see 2 Filmhallen
35 Lab 111
36 OCCII
37 Openlucht-theater
38 OT301
39 Vondelbunker

🔴 SHOPPING
see 2 Art, Design & Vintage Market
40 Cane & Grain
41 Denim City
42 Donsje
43 Floris van Bommel
44 J&B Craft Drinks
see 2 Maker Market
45 Maker Store
46 Museum Market
47 Nixx
48 Ten Katemarkt
49 This is Soul
50 Zuidermarkt

ERIK SMITS/RIJKSMUSEUM

TOP EXPERIENCE

Rijksmuseum

Resembling a castle with its towers rising above its grand red-brick facade, the Rijksmuseum is one of the world's most magnificent museums, and a fitting showcase for the Netherlands' rich collection of art. Masterpieces by the nation's greatest artistic talent, such as Rembrandt, Vermeer and Van Gogh, are displayed alongside some 8000 other treasures across 1.5km of gallery space.

DON'T MISS

Rembrandt's *The Night Watch*

Vermeer's *Milkmaid*

Jan Asselijn's *The Threatened Swan*

Delftware pottery

Dollhouses

Rijks Michelin-starred restaurant

History of the Museum

Today's Rijksmuseum (pronounced 'rikes') was more than two centuries in the making. The first museum conceived to hold national and royal collections opened in Den Haag's Huis Ten Bosch in 1800. (Jan Asselijn's *The Threatened Swan,* c 1650, was its first acquisition.) During French rule, the collections moved to the new capital, opening on the top floor of Amsterdam's Royal Palace in 1809, where they were joined by paintings including Rembrandt's *The Night Watch*.

Following King Willem I's ascension to the throne, the collections shifted locations until architect Pierre Cuypers was

PRACTICALITIES

● rijksmuseum.nl ● adult/child €25/free, guided tour €7.50
● 9am–5pm

chosen to design a purpose-built permanent home for the national museum. Construction of the building, incorporating neogothic and Renaissance styles, began in 1876, and it opened in 1885.

Floor 0 Highlights

Covering the years 1100 to 1600, the ground floor's Special Collections span magic lanterns, armoury, ship models and Dutch status symbols from previous eras, such as musical instruments and silver miniatures. Early gems include Charles V's cutlery and works by Albrecht Dürer.

The serene Asian Pavilion, a separate sandstone and glass structure, holds first-rate artworks from China, Indonesia, Japan, India, Thailand and Vietnam.

Floor 1 Highlights

Highlights on the 1st floor, spanning 1700 to 1900, include the Rijksmuseum's largest painting, Jan Willem Pieneman's *The Battle of Waterloo* (1824), Van Gogh's famous 1887 *Self-portrait*, and a gilded, recreated 18th-century canal-house room.

Floor 2 Highlights

On the 2nd floor, the Gallery of Honour, with masterpieces spanning 1600 to 1700, is the best place to begin your visit. Among the masters here are Frans Hals; *The Merry Drinker* (1628–30) shows his broad, fluid brushstrokes. Beautiful works by Johannes (Jan) Vermeer featuring intimate, almost photographic-like domestic details include *The Milkmaid* (1660; also called *The Kitchen Maid*) and *Woman Reading a Letter* (1663). Jan Steen depicted chaotic households to convey moral teachings, as in *The Merry Family* (1668).

Works by Rembrandt include his self-portrait as the Apostle Paul, and a couple's intimate caress in *The Jewish Bride* (1665). The Rijksmuseum's star is Rembrandt's colossal *The Night Watch* (1642). The extensive research and conservation project Operation Night Watch has provided visitors the unique opportunity to witness it undergoing studies and repairs surrounded by a glass chamber. No completion date for the multiyear project is set, but it remains in full public view.

Splendid 17th-century treasures are displayed in rooms on either side of the Gallery of Honour. On one side is delicate blue and white Delftware pottery from the late 1600s. The other features extraordinary dollhouses. Merchant's wife Petronella Oortman employed carpenters, glassblowers and silversmiths to make items using the same materials as for full-scale versions.

Floor 3 Highlights

The museum's top floor encompasses 1900 to 2000. Works include paintings by Karel Appel, Constant Nieuwenhuys and fellow CoBrA members of the post-WWII movement, and Dutch design furniture.

REFRESHMENTS AT THE RIJKSMUSEUM

When you need a break, the Rijksmuseum has options for dining and drinking at all price points. The museum has two espresso bars (plus another in the garden pavilion in summer); a cafe in the atrium (with breakfasts, pastries, soups, salads and sandwiches); and a Michelin-starred restaurant, **Rijks**, which can be accessed without a museum ticket.

TOP TIPS

● Buy tickets and reserve a timeslot in advance, even if you already have a ticket or museum pass.

● Download the museum's excellent free app. It features self-guided tours, or create your own personalised route (BYO headphones). You can also hire a device (€5) at the multimedia tours desk.

● Mornings before noon and weekday afternoons from 3pm are usually the quietest.

● While you can see the highlights in a couple of hours, the collection is huge, so allow much longer.

● It's free to stroll the museum's gardens amid the roses, hedges, fountains and a greenhouse.

BEST EX-SQUATS

Vondelbunker: A 1947 fallout shelter contains this underground venue hosting music, film, poetry and more. *(vondelbunker.nl)*

Radion: Former dental centre with 24-hour clubbing and cultural events. *(radion.amsterdam)*

Lab 111: Once a university science laboratory, now a cinema screening cult films. *(lab111.nl)*

OCCII: Legalised squat in former stables and tram sheds with an alternative scene from folk to punk. *(occii.org)*

OT301: Street-art-covered ex-squat in the former Netherlands Film Academy, hosting bands, DJs, theatre and workshops. *(ot301.nl)*

De Trut: Once-squatted printing-machine factory that's a decades-strong volunteer-run LGBTIQ+ club famed for its Sunday parties. *(trutfonds.nl)*

WOLF-PHOTOGRAPHY/SHUTTERSTOCK

Skatepark, Museumplein

Striking masterpieces

The fabulous **Stedelijk Museum** *(stedelijk.nl; adult/child €22.50/free)* is an impressive, light, bright, modern art museum, displaying artworks from its 90,000-strong collection that dates from 1870 onwards.

Of the Stedelijk's vast repository, some 500 works are displayed in the permanent collection presentation at any one time. While it rotates, you're likely to see works by Monet, Picasso, Kandinsky, Matisse, Chagall, Warhol, Rothko, De Kooning and more. It's housed in a gabled, red-brick, Dutch Renaissance–style masterpiece designed by Amsterdam city architect AM (Adriaan Willem) Weissman in 1895. Temporary installations of the latest in contemporary art show in its 2012-opened wing that's known as 'the Bathtub' (for reasons that are immediately apparent).

The entrance incorporates the **Don Quixote Sculpture Hall**, showcasing works by sculptors such as Henry Moore, Anne Imhof and Damien Hirst. There's free access (no ticket required) when the museum's open, and after-hours views of the illuminated sculptures.

 EATING IN VONDELPARK, OUD-WEST & OUD-ZUID: CLASSIC DUTCH

Visque Winkel: Fishmonger with ready-to-eat *kibbeling* (pieces of fried fish), sandwiches, smoked eel and herring. *noon-6pm Mon, 8am-6pm Tue-Sat* €

Friet Boutique: Deep-fried goodness: crispy fries (with sauces), *frikandellen* (sausages) and *bitterballen* (meat croquettes). *noon-10pm* €

Lunchroom Grannies: Dutch gems, such as *chocoladebroodje* (chocolate sprinkles on bread) and *zuurvlees* (vinegar-stewed beef). *9am-5pm Wed-Sun* €

Hap Hmm: Comfort food since 1935, from grandmother's recipe meatballs to chicken casserole, schnitzel and pancakes. *5-9.15pm Mon-Fri* €€

Go Moco
More modern and contemporary art

Overlooking Museumplein's northwestern corner from Honthorststraat, the beautiful 1904 Villa Alsberg has been converted into the **Moco Museum** *(mocomuseum.com; adult/ child from €17.95/15.95),* short for 'Modern Contemporary', an independent museum founded by couple Lionel and Kim Logchies, private collectors and curators, who opened it in 2016. Its collection includes modern, contemporary, digital, immersive and street art by artists such as Andy Warhol, Keith Haring, Damien Hirst, Jeff Koons and Banksy. Sculptures displayed in the garden include a giant red gummy bear by artist WhIsBe and an outsized rocking horse by Dutch designer Marcel Wanders. Temporary exhibitions run in parallel throughout the year.

Skate at Museumplein
Scenic blading, boarding and biking

More than just a park for relaxing and attending celebrations and major events, Museumplein is also home to a state-of-the-art **skatepark** for skateboarders, BMXers and in-line skaters. It's open 24 hours, with lighting until 10pm. Ice skating has taken place here since 1864, and the ice rink *(ijsbaanmuseumplein.nl)* is set to reopen in 2027.

Appreciate the Concertgebouw's Exceptional Acoustics
Celebrated concert hall

One of Museumplein's trio of late-19th-century architectural beauties, along with the Stedelijk and Rijksmuseum (the architect of the under-construction Rijksmuseum, Pierre Cuypers, helped purchase the land), Amsterdam's magnificent concert hall the **Concertgebouw** *(concertgebouw.nl)* was built for its 1888 debut by AL (Adolf Leonard; 'Dolf') van Gendt, who engineered its near-perfect acoustics. Former Royal Concertgebouw Orchestra conductor Bernard Haitink remarked that the world-famous hall was the orchestra's best instrument.

The Concertgebouw was designated a protected monument in 1972 and renovated between 1985 and 1988 to prevent the building from sinking. The home of the Netherlands Philharmonic and the Netherlands Chamber Orchestra, it presents
continued on page 96

BEST MARKETS

Museum Market:
Art, crafts, design and food stalls on Museumplein on the third Sunday of the month. *(museummarket.nl)*

Ten Katemarkt:
Fresh produce, nuts, cheeses, flowers and other staples fill this 1912-established street market from Monday to Saturday. *(tenkatemarkt.nl)*

Zuidermarkt:
Co-op–run market selling mostly organic fruit, vegetables, mushrooms, olives, breads, cheeses and wines every Saturday. *(zuidermrkt.nl)*

Maker Market:
Browse sustainable, handcrafted designs and meet the artisans on Saturdays and Sundays. *(dehal len-amsterdam.nl)*

Art, Design & Vintage Market:
Glassware, ceramics, painting and jewellery are among the preloved treasures at this market on the second Sunday of the month. *(facebook .com/anafternoon withthecollector samsterdam)*

 DRINKING IN VONDELPARK, OUD-WEST & OUD-ZUID: BEST COFFEE

Monks Coffee Roasters: Sources and roasts outstanding coffee, with a phenomenal house blend; brilliant for brunch. *8am-4pm*

LOT61: See (and smell) beans being roasted in the open cellar. Coffees are double shots unless you say otherwise. *8am-6pm Mon-Fri, from 9am Sat & Sun*

Trakteren: Preparation methods of single-origin beans include Aeropress, V60 pour-over, Chemex, syphon and cold press. *8am-5pm Mon-Fri, from 9am Sat*

Stean's Beans: Only a glass window separates the roastery from the cafe at this fabulous Hoofddorppleinbuurt space. *10.30am-4pm Mon, from 9am Tue-Fri*

ULUS/SHUTTERSTOCK

TOP EXPERIENCE

Van Gogh Museum

Opened on Museumplein in 1973 to house the collection of Vincent van Gogh's younger brother Theo, his benefactor and confidant, the Van Gogh Museum manages to feel personal and intimate, while containing the world's largest collection of the complex artist's work. It's home to some 200 paintings and 500 drawings by Vincent and his contemporaries, including Gauguin and Monet.

DON'T MISS

The Potato Eaters

The Yellow House

Wheatfield with Crows

Sunflowers

Congregation Leaving the Reformed Church at Nuenen

Self portraits

Museum Backstory & Layout

Vincent van Gogh died in 1890, aged 37, having sold only a single painting in his lifetime, and leaving his prolific collection to his brother, Theo, who died the following year. Theo's widow, Johanna van Gogh-Bonger, then left it on her death in 1925 to her son, Vincent Willem van Gogh, who loaned it to the Stedelijk Museum (p92) until the Dutch government commissioned this dedicated museum.

De Stijl architect Gerrit Rietveld designed the 1973 building. Architect Kisho Kurokawa's glass exhibition wing (nicknamed

PRACTICALITIES

● vangoghmuseum.nl ● adult/child €24/free, audio guide €3.75/2
● 9am-6pm (to 9pm most Fri) May-Sep, shorter hours Oct-Apr

'the Mussel') was completed in 1999, and in 2015, an extension providing an additional 800 sq metres of space incorporated the striking entrance hall.

Spread over four levels, from the ground-level Floor 0 to Floor 3, the museum's chronological layout allows you to see Van Gogh's work evolve from his early depictions of sombre countryfolk in the Netherlands to his vivid, swirling landscapes in southern France. The individual paintings often move around depending on the current exhibition theme.

Collection Highlights

Van Gogh's earliest works are from his time in the Dutch countryside and studying at Antwerp's Royal Academy of Fine Arts. Peasant life is celebrated in many of his early works, such as *The Potato Eaters* (1885).

After his father became pastor of the Dutch Reformed Church in Nuenen in 1882, Van Gogh stayed at the vicarage and painted *Congregation Leaving the Reformed Church at Nuenen* in early 1884, which he modified in late 1885, painting out a peasant with a spade in the foreground and adding mourning clothes to the congregation, after his father's death earlier that year. The painting, along with *View of the Sea at Scheveningen* (1882), was stolen in 2002 and recovered in 2016.

In 1886, Van Gogh moved to Paris, where his brother Theo was working as an art dealer. Unable to pay for models, Vincent started painting multiple self-portraits to improve his portraiture techniques. He met some of the Impressionists, and his palette began to brighten.

Van Gogh headed south to Provence in 1888 to paint its colourful landscapes and intense Mediterranean light. *Sunflowers* (1889) dates from this period, as does *The Yellow House* (1888), a rendering of the property Van Gogh rented in Arles. *The Bedroom* (1888) depicts Van Gogh's sleeping quarters at the house. Painter Paul Gauguin came to stay, but their artistic differences led to fierce arguments. It was here, in 1888, during a bout of psychosis, that Van Gogh sliced off part of his ear.

Van Gogh had himself committed to an asylum in St-Rémy in 1889, where he continued to paint with a wild, expressive fervour. The countryside's olive and cypress trees feature in his works, as do its irises. In 1890, he returned north to Auvers-sur-Oise to be closer to Theo. The ominous *Wheatfield with Crows* (1890) was among his last works before his suicide on 29 July 1890.

Other Artists

The museum also contains works by Vincent's peers, including Gauguin, Monet and Toulouse-Lautrec. There are also paintings by Van Gogh's precursors, as well as by later artists Van Gogh influenced.

VAN GOGH'S LETTERS

What makes the museum so special is the intimate connection you experience with the artist. In addition to his paintings and drawings, it holds more than 800 handwritten letters, mainly between Vincent and his brother, as well as artists such as Gauguin and Émile Bernard. You can hear recordings at multiple listening stations. The museum has categorised all of Van Gogh's letters online at vangoghletters.org.

TOP TIPS

● Buy tickets and reserve a timeslot in advance, even if you already have a ticket or museum pass. (The I amsterdam City Card isn't valid here.)

● Plan around two hours to visit (longer if you're a serious fan).

● Before 11am, after 3pm and Friday evenings are the quietest.

● Check dates for 'Vincent on Friday' evening events (€11) with live performances and DJs.

● Ask at the information desk about treasure hunts and other activities for kids.

● Along with ground-floor cafes, Bistro Vincent has cuisine inspired by Van Gogh's paintings.

BEST SHOPPING

Maker Store: Showcases 80-plus Amsterdam artisans. *(themakerstore.nl)*

Donsje: Adorable handmade kids' clothing with nature themes. *(donsje.com)*

Floris van Bommel: Ninth-generation-run shoemaker established in 1718. *(florisvanbommel. com)*

Denim City: Stocks startup labels' latest collections, recycles denim into original pieces and does repairs. *(denimcity. org)*

J&B Craft Drinks: Huge range of international craft beers, ciders and sodas, available cold from the fridge. *(jbcraftdrinks.com)*

Nixx: Has a superb range of Dutch cheeses, roasts nuts in store, and sells dried fruit and natural wines. *(nixx-noten-kaas-amsterdam.nl)*

Cane & Grain: Specialises in *jenevers* and Caribbean rums. *(caneandgrain.nl)*

TOURALBY AKBARI/SHUTTERSTOCK

De Hallen

continued from p93

a wide-ranging programme. In addition to the 1974-capacity **Grote Zaal** (main hall) and 437-seat **Kleine Zaal** (recital hall), the 150-capacity **Koor Zaal** (choir hall) is often used as a jazz club.

From September to June, free half-hour concerts take place at 12.30pm on Wednesdays (arrive early), with substantially discounted concerts from 11am to noon on Sundays.

Be Whisked Back in Time at the Hollandsche Manege

Neoclassical riding school

Bordering the Vondelpark's northern side, the grandiose indoor **Hollandsche Manege** *(Dutch Riding School;*

 EATING IN VONDELPARK, OUD-WEST & OUD-ZUID: BEST VEGAN

Alchemist Garden: This bright, high-ceilinged cafe features dishes like almond-cheese and courgette quiche. *9am-9pm Mon-Sat, from noon Sun* €

Soil: Fermentation, curing and smoking are used in mushroom *bitterballen*, tempeh burgers and other innovations. *noon-10pm* €€

Meatless District: Industrial-style space with classy dishes like braised artichoke with lemon aioli, Korean fried cauliflower and watermelon sashimi. *5.30-10pm Wed-Mon* €€

Old Soul: Daily changing Surinamese vegan dishes such as yams and fried plantains and stuffed bitter melon and jackfruit stew. *5-10pm Wed-Sun* €€

dehollandschemanege.nl; 30-minute riding/side-saddle lesson €49/55) was inspired by Vienna's famous Spanish Riding School.

Built in 1882 by architect AL van Gendt (who also designed the stations along the Amsterdam–Den Helder line), the neoclassical building retains its charming horsehead facade and is a national monument. Its **Levend Paarden Museum** *(Living Horse Museum; museum adult/child €12.50/8.50; closed Mon)* details the building's history alongside the 'world of the horse' through equine art and displays including historic riding equipment.

A highlight is watching a balletic carousel display with women riding side-saddle, which has a UNESCO Intangible Cultural Heritage designation. It's also possible for visitors to book ahead for one-off 30-minute or hour-long standard private riding lessons at its arena.

Ride Aboard a Historic Tram

A museum on the move

Not a museum in a static sense, the **Electrische Museumtramlijn Amsterdam** *(museumtramlijn.org; Heritage Line adult/child return €7.50/5, City Tour adult/child €10/5)* allows you to travel on historic trams from the Netherlands, Austria and Poland collected between the 1950s and '70s – the earliest date from the 1890s. On Sundays from April to October, the Heritage Line (line 30) departs from red-brick Haarlemmermeer Station near the Vondelpark to Amstelveen via **Amsterdamse Bos** (p102). A return trip takes about 1¼ hours; you can hop off at scheduled stops en route.

Head to De Hallen

Food and cultural hub

Cavernous red-brick sheds now house **De Hallen** *(dehallen-amsterdam.nl),* with sustainable Dutch design and fashion boutiques; an antiques shop; a bike seller and repairer; a hairdressing academy-salon; a library; galleries; **Filmhallen** *(filmhallen.nl),* a nine-screen cinema; and a **hotel** (p120).

At De Hallen's heart, its skylit food hall, **Foodhallen** *(foodhallen.nl),* is an airy, open-plan communal dining area surrounded by 21 stands cooking everything from Mumbai street food to Dutch-speciality meatballs. 'Beats & Bites' on Fridays and Saturdays, with DJs, and 'Bands & Bites' when live musicians play on the first Thursday of the month, add to the party atmosphere. There's also a reading cafe with cultural events and an all-day bar-restaurant.

Regular events include markets, sustainability workshops and pop-up exhibitions.

Directly outside De Hallen is the street market **Ten Katemarkt** (p93).

WHY I LOVE THE VONDELPARK

Catherine Le Nevez, Lonely Planet writer

What's really special about this neighbourhood is that while it's home to Amsterdam's biggest and busiest sights around Museumplein and one of my favourite green escapes, the Vondelpark, heading only a few footsteps away in any direction, you're immersed in local life.

The whole neighbourhood is filled with small localities like the international restaurants along Amstelveenseweg; buzzing shops, cafes and bars on and around Jan Pieter Heijestraat; vegan restaurants and Amsterdam's best coffee around Bilderdijkstraat; elegant boutiques and cafes around Cornelis Schuytstraat; ritzy window shopping along PC Hooftstraat; and up-and-coming areas like the post-industrial spaces and happening addresses in Hoofddorppleinbuurt.

De Pijp & Zuid

BUZZING MARKETS, LIVELY DINING AND EXPANSIVE GREENERY

GETTING AROUND

The Noord/Zuidlijn (north–south metro line; M52) from Amsterdam Noord via Centraal, the Medieval Centre and Southern Canal Ring, has stations at De Pijp, Europaplein and its southern terminus, **Amsterdam Zuid**, which is becoming a major transport hub, with international rail services.

Tram 24 rolls north–south from Centraal Station along Ferdinand Bolstraat. Tram 4 travels from Centraal via Rembrandtplein to De Pijp. Tram 3 traverses De Pijp between the Vondelpark and Oost. Tram 12 from Centraal via Leidseplein cuts through De Pijp and neighbouring Rivierenbuurt.

Some further-flung areas are served by Connexxion *(connexxion.nl)* buses.

☑ **TOP TIP**

Discover De Pijp's global food scene is on an insiders' tour with **Hungry Birds** *(hungrybirds.nl)*.

Vibrant De Pijp has a distinct community spirit and character forged throughout its history. An island linked to surrounding districts by 16 bridges, De Pijp's straight, narrow streets reflect the stems of old clay pipes, hence its name, 'the Pipe'.

The city expanded here in the 19th century, when tenement blocks were rapidly constructed to relieve pressure on the densely populated Jordaan and provide cheap housing for workers. In the 1960s and '70s, when many residents relocated for more space, the government refurbished the properties for immigrants. Artists, creatives, university students and entrepreneurs all flocked here, and gentrification took off, but it retains a village atmosphere. It's the gateway to a host of lesser-visited and under-the-radar sights across Amsterdam Zuid (Amsterdam South), including peaceful residential areas, Amsterdam School architectural icons such as the 1928 Olympisch Stadion, glitzy new developments and glorious parks, as well as the sprawling forest of Amsterdamse Bos.

Visit the Heineken Experience
Interactive brewery tour

Since it began brewing in Amsterdam in 1864, Heineken has become a global juggernaut: upwards of 25 million serves of its pilsner are drunk daily worldwide. Production at its old De Pijp brewery ceased in 1988, but it's been repurposed as the whizz-bang, multisensory **Heineken Experience** *(heinekenexperience.com; tours from €24.95).*

On high-spirited 90-minute self-guided tours, you experience the brewing process from the inside out as you're immersed in the production process via 360-degree multimedia wizardry. Tours include two tastings. Various upgrade options are available, including canal cruises on Heineken-bedecked boats.

Browse the Albert Cuypmarkt
The Netherlands' biggest and best-known street market

A hive of activity, the **Albert Cuypmarkt** *(albertcuyp-markt. amsterdam)* has been the heart and soul of De Pijp since

DE PIJP

Amstel

Weesperzijde

Amsteldijk

Van Woustr

Rijnstr

200 m
0.1 miles

DE PIJP

Pieter Lodewijk Takstr

Burgemeester Tellegenstr

Henrick de Keijserstr

Karel du Jardinstr

2e Van der Helststr

Van der Helstplein

Lutmastr

Cornelis Troostplein

Ferdinand Bolstr

Frans Halsstr

Dusartstr

Ruysdaelkade

Boerenwetering

Hobbemakade

Heineken Experience

Albert Cuypmarkt

Sarphatipark

Amstelkanaal

Jozef Israëlskade

⭐ **HIGHLIGHTS**	**13** Kaasbar
1 Albert Cuypmarkt	**14** Little Collins
2 Heineken Experience	**15** Miri Mary
	16 Sol El Luna
🔴 **SIGHTS**	**see 8** Yamazato
3 Museum De Dageraad	
4 Sarphatipark	🟢 **DRINKING & NIGHTLIFE**
	17 Bar Mokum
🔴 **ACTIVITIES**	**18** Barça
5 Boaty	**19** Brouwerij Troost
6 SUP Tropisch	**20** Café Sarphaat
⚫ **SLEEPING**	🔴 **ENTERTAINMENT**
7 Bicycle Hotel Amsterdam	**21** Cinetol
8 Hotel Okura Amsterdam	**22** Rialto
9 Sir Albert Hotel	🔴 **SHOPPING**
	23 Bier Baum
🟢 **EATING**	**24** De Kleine Parade
10 Bakers & Roasters	**25** Elcie
see 8 Ciel Bleu	**26** Love Stories Archive
11 GlouGlou	**27** Maats
12 Juno	**28** Mercer

PLAN ZUID

At the turn of the 20th century, HP (Hendrik Petrus) Berlage was tasked with urbanising Amsterdam's then-undeveloped south. In line with the city's 1901 housing legislation to improve workers' housing supply, affordability and standards, and avoid slums, Berlage's 1915 Plan Zuid (South Plan) of wide streets, greenery-filled courtyards and decorative bridges was brought to life by architects from the expressionist Amsterdam School, including the Netherlands' first practising female architect, Margaret Staal-Kropholler.

Boosted by Amsterdam's 1928 Olympic Games, the Amsterdam School's design philosophy spanned housing blocks with sculptural brick facades and rocket-shaped towers to streetlights, bridges, rubbish bins and electricity substations.

1905. Named for landscape painter Aelbert Cuyp (1620–91), this unmissable street market stretches for 700m along Albert Cuypstraat between Ferdinand Bolstraat to its west and Van Woustraat to its east. From 9.30am to 5pm on Monday to Saturday, some 260 stalls sell everything from fresh produce, ready-to-eat treats and bouquets of flowers to fabrics, clothing, cosmetics and much more.

Picnic in Sarphatipark
Urban oasis

De Pijp's favourite hangout on sunny days is the **Sarphatipark**. Created in 1885, this English-style park takes in 4.5 hectares of ponds, meadows and wooded fringes.

Its gently sloping lawns are idyllic for picnics. Pick up provisions at the Albert Cuypmarkt and chilled craft brews at **Bier Baum**.

Catch Emerging Musicians & Films
Music and screen

With a capacity of just 150, **Cinetol** *(cinetol.nl)* is an intimate place to catch established and emerging local acts across all genres. About 250 concerts take place each year, and it also hosts exhibitions, screenings and album launches.

Opened in 1921, art deco cinema **Rialto** *(rialtofilm.nl)* shows eclectic arthouse fare from around the world (often in English or with English subtitles).

Study Up on the Amsterdam School
Architectural dawn

Designed by two of the Amsterdam School's founding members, Piet Kramer and Michel de Klerk, social housing complex De Dageraad (meaning 'the dawn') was a game-changer when it was completed in 1922. The architects devised buildings that were not only functional but also artistic, as evident in the wave-like brick facades' rounded edges, flowing balconies, integrated sculptures and wrought-ironwork.

Plans of De Pijp, floor plans, stained glass, sculptures and photos are displayed at its **Museum De Dageraad** *(hetschip. nl; museum adult/child €16.50/5, architectural walks €13.50).* Museum tickets include a tour of the complex. (The 3.30pm tour is in English.)

DRINKING IN DE PIJP & ZUID: BEST BARS

Bar Mokum: Ode to Mokum, mixing local spirits into cocktails. The decor recreates the streetscapes. *5pm-1am or later Mon-Sat*

Brouwerij Troost: Watch beer being brewed in stainless-steel vats at the original location of this organic craft brewery. *4pm-1am Mon-Fri, noon-2am Sat, to 11pm Sun*

Café Sarphaat: Perennial local favourite opposite Sarphatipark with a lovely old bar and outdoor terrace that's heated in chilly weather. *9am-1am or later*

Barça: On bar-filled Marie Heinekenplein, with a 'Barcelona in Amsterdam' theme, Spanish wines and sparkling cava. *noon-midnight or later*

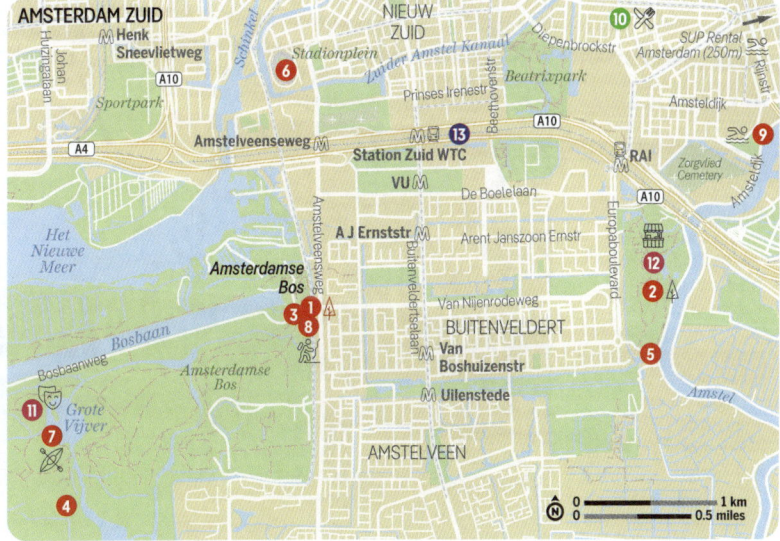

Cruise the Waterways

DIY boating and paddling

See the waterways under your own steam with **Boaty** *(boaty. nl; 3hr hire from €89)*. Its Amstelkanaal floating jetty is an ideal launching pad before approaching busy city-centre canals. Electric boats carry up to six people, and hire includes a map outlining suggested routes. No boat licence is needed.

For SUP hire *(from about €13 per hr),* try **SUP Tropisch** *(suptropisch.nl),* **SUP Rental Amsterdam** *(amsterdamboo thuur.nl)* or **SUP SUP CLUB** *(supsupclub.com).*

Admire Amsterdam's Old Olympic Stadium

Sporting glory

Built for the 1928 Olympic Games, the elegant **Olympisch Stadion Amsterdam** *(olympischstadion.nl; tours from €12.50)* is a triumph of Amsterdam School architecture, designed by Jan Wils. It has a soaring tower from which the Olympic flame burned for the first time during the competition. Arrange guided one-hour tours (minimum of five people) in advance.

As well as track and field events, concerts and events also take place here. On King's Day, it hosts the massive music festival **Kingsland** *(kingslandfestival.nl).*

Explore the Amstelpark

Expansive green space

Rose and rhododendron gardens, a glasshouse and an orangery grace the **Amstelpark** *(amstelpark.info),* created for the 1972 flower show Floriade. At its southern edge, near the 1636 polder-drainage windmill **De Riekermolen**, is a statue

⭐ **HIGHLIGHTS**
1 Amsterdamse Bos

🔴 **SIGHTS**
2 Amstelpark
3 De Boswinkel
4 De Ridammerhoeve
5 De Riekermolen
6 Olympisch Stadion Amsterdam

🟠 **ACTIVITIES**
7 Kanoverhuur Amsterdamse Bos
8 Klimpark Fun Forest
9 SUP SUP CLUB

🟢 **EATING**
10 Vinnies

🔴 **ENTERTAINMENT**
11 Bostheater

🔴 **SHOPPING**
see 10 De Winkel van Nijntje
12 Pure Markt

🔵 **TRANSPORT**
13 Amsterdam Zuid
see 1 De Boshalte

MOKUM MOTIFS

Amsterdam's Jewish inhabitants gave Amsterdam its nickname, Mokum – the Yiddish word for 'town' or 'safe haven' (from the Hebrew *makom*, meaning 'place'). Amsterdam natives are known as Mokummers.

The city's motto, *Heldhaftig, Vastberaden, Barmhartig* (Valiant, Steadfast, Compassionate), is emblazoned on the coat of arms, whose escutcheon (heraldic shield) is the basis of Amsterdam's flag: two horizontal red stripes and a central black stripe with three diagonal white St Andrew's crosses.

Appearing on municipal buildings and merchandising everywhere, this symbol 'XXX' likely originated in 1505 when Amsterdam was a fishing town; St Andrew is the patron saint of fishers.

FOKKE BAARSSEN/SHUTTERSTOCK

of Rembrandt sketching it. Look out for artisan food, drink and design-filled **Pure Markt** *(puremarkt.nl)* and numerous food festivals.

Kids love its playgrounds, city farm, yew-hedge maze, mini golf *(minigolfamstelpark.nl; from €9)*, and the delightful miniature **Amstel Trein** *(Amstel Train; amsteltrein.nl; €3.50)*, as well as rides for tots such as bumper boats at the **Speeltuin Amstelpark** *(speeltuin-amstelpark.nl; 1/10 tokens €1.30/12)*; check individual seasonal opening times online.

Climb into the Treetops

Activity-filled forest

On the city's southwestern edge, **Amsterdamse Bos** *(Amsterdam Forest; amsterdamsebos.nl; free)* offers an accessible escape to the countryside. Planted from 1934 to provide employment during the Great Depression, it sprawls over 1000 hectares of polder (drained land) now alive with woodland,

 EATING IN DE PIJP & ZUID: BEST FOR BRUNCH

Bakers & Roasters: Brazilian-Kiwi favourite for banana nut bread French toast, Navajo eggs, smoked salmon stacks and caipirinhas. *8.30am-3pm or later* €€

Little Collins: Creative dishes include oat milk panna cotta with rhubarb or poached eggs with smoked labneh and dukkah. Walk-ins only. *9am-4pm* €€

Vinnies: Fabulous all-day brunches spanning blueberry spelt pancakes, coconut granola, spicy shakshuka and mimosas. *7.30am-5pm Mon-Fri, from 9am Sat & Sun* €€

Miri Mary: Weekend brunches with an Indian twist, like butter chicken eggs Benedict and masala omelettes. *5.30-10pm Mon-Thu, 10.30am-3pm & 5.30-10pm Fri-Sun* €€

Amsterdamse Bos

meadows, lakes and waterways.

De Boswinkel visitors centre sells tickets for 90-minute boat cruises (€10; Wed & Sat May-Sep). Hire bikes from adjacent **De Boshalte** *(deboshalte.com; bicycle hire per hr/day from €6/10; closed Tue)* to explore 50km of cycling trails.

The **Klimpark Fun Forest** *(funforest.nl; adult/child from €32/23)* has 10 ropes courses and zip lining through the trees. Water activities include canoeing, with hire from **Kanoverhuur Amsterdamse Bos** *(kanoverhuur-adam.nl).* There's also a working organic goat farm, **De Ridammerhoeve** *(geitenboerderij.nl);* an open-air theatre, the **Bostheater** *(bostheater.nl);* and markets and festivals galore.

Amsterdamse Bos is served by Connexxion buses (lines 178, 257 and 357) and, on Sundays from April to October, vintage trams run by the **Electrische Museumtramlijn Amsterdam** (p97).

BEST SHOPS

Elcie: Elsbeth Schiphorst makes dresses, jackets and more from leftover fabrics at her studio. *(elcie.nl)*

Mercer: Sustainable streetwear and vegan sneakers made from pineapple leather, grapes, cacti or plastic ocean waste. *(themercerbrand.com)*

Maats: Cycling clothing and accessories; also organises countryside bike rides. *(maats.cc)*

De Winkel van Nijntje: Dedicated Miffy (Dutch: Nijntje) emporium. *(dewinkel vannijntje.nl)*

De Kleine Parade: Kids' and babies' clothing, shoes, accessories and toys, and a children's hair salon. *(dekleineparade.com)*

Love Stories Archive: Samples, stock sales, and discounted lingerie and swimwear. *(loves toriesintimates.com)*

EATING IN DE PIJP & ZUID: BEST TAPAS-STYLE DINING

Kaasbar: Classy space with a conveyor belt of 20-plus cloche-covered Dutch cheeses to pair with by-the-glass wines. *5-11pm Mon-Thu, 1pm-1am Fri-Sun* €€

GlouGlou: Convivial wine bar with all-organic, additive-free wines and cheese, charcuterie and escargot platters. *3pm-midnight Mon-Fri, from 2pm Sat & Sun* €€

Juno: Grilled dishes complement more than 40 natural wines in the dark-timber interior or under the fairy-light-strung trees. *5pm-midnight Tue-Fri, from 1pm Sat & Sun* €€

Sol El Luna: Tapas and cocktail bar with sharing dishes like Padrón peppers, grilled octopus and jamón ibérico (cured leg of pork). *5-11pm Tue-Fri, from noon Sat & Sun* €€

Oosterpark & East of the Amstel

WORLD CULTURES AND GREEN SPACES

GETTING AROUND

From Centraal Station, tram 14 skirts Oosterpark's northern edge. Trams 1 and 3 run past Oosterpark on their east–west routes across the city. Tram 19 runs north–south through the neighbourhood's centre.

Metro lines 51, 53 and 54 run south from Centraal Station along the neighbourhood's western border.

This spread-out area and its sprawling parks are especially suited to exploring by bike. A 2km cycling loop goes around Oosterpark, and Park Frankendael has a 5km loop.

Oost (East) is one of Amsterdam's most culturally diverse neighbourhoods. It grew up in the 19th century, a heritage recalled in its grand architecture, wide boulevards and beautiful English-style Oosterpark, where, in 2023, King Willem-Alexander formally apologised for the Netherlands' involvement in slavery. The Keti Koti ('broken chains') commemoration takes place here on 1 July every year.

Adjoining Oosterpark, the splendid neo-Renaissance Wereldmuseum Amsterdam (World Museum Amsterdam) changed its name in 2023 from the Tropenmuseum (Royal Tropics Museum) – a symbolic break with more than 150 years of tradition – and has since undertaken a sweeping decolonising mission.

East of the multicultural Dappermarkt, bustling with shoppers from Monday to Saturday, Javastraat leads to neighbourhood square Javaplein. Lush expanses and wetlands further east date from when this area was a country retreat. Today's Oost is one of Amsterdam's most rapidly gentrifying areas. Scout out trendy restaurants and bars, including rooftop bars with stupendous views.

Understand World Cultures

Human connections at the Wereldmuseum Amsterdam

The Dutch slave trade, understanding cultural appropriation and returning stolen artefacts to Indonesia – at the **Wereldmuseum Amsterdam** *(amsterdam.wereldmuseum.nl; adult/ child €18/7.50),* themes around race, ethnicity and identity are explored from multiple perspectives. Such exhibits are part of the ethnographic museum's greater vision to examine and undo the colonial practices of its past.

The Wereldmuseum's origins go back to 1871, when it was initially established as the Koloniaal Museum (Colonial Museum). Like many 19th-century European museums, the museum's collections grew out of colonial expansion and scientific

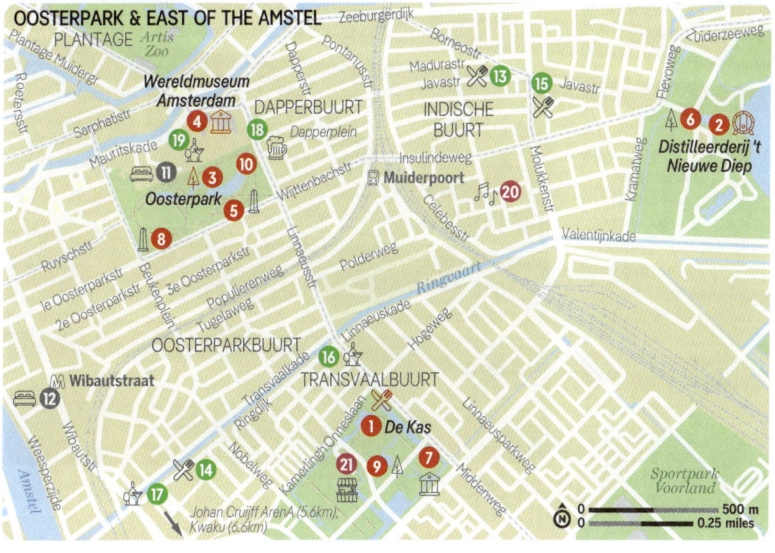

HIGHLIGHTS
1 De Kas
2 Distilleerderij 't Nieuwe Diep
3 Oosterpark
4 Wereldmuseum Amsterdam

SIGHTS
5 De Schreeuw
6 Flevopark
7 Huize Frankendael
8 National Slavery Monument

9 Park Frankendael
10 Spreeksteen

SLEEPING
11 Generator Amsterdam
12 Volkshotel

EATING
13 La Douzaine
see 7 Merkelbach
14 Vergulden Eenhoorn
15 Wilde Zwijnen

DRINKING & NIGHTLIFE
16 Cafe Mojo
17 Dakterras GAPP
18 De Biertuin
19 Fitz's on the Roof

ENTERTAINMENT
20 NedPhO-Koepel

SHOPPING
21 Pure Markt

research. After the Dutch colonial empire ended, the institution became the Royal Tropics Museum in 1950, shifting its focus to regions from Africa to the Middle East and beyond.

Contrasting the atrium's stunning, old-world elegance with brightly lit, modern displays, the 2018-installed permanent exhibition 'Things That Matter' explores universal cultural themes such as language, belief, climate and activism, homing in on questions such as 'When is culture yours?'.

Spanning 1200 sq metres, the exhibition 'Our Colonial Inheritance' is a profound, comprehensive inspection of Dutch colonial history. Most movingly, the Digital Names Monument is inscribed with the names of nearly 200,000 people who were enslaved during the colonial period in Suriname, Curaçao and Indonesia.

Excellent temporary exhibitions (included in admission) dive deeper into topics such as restitution and martial arts around the world.

☑ TOP TIPS

Free public rehearsals and concerts by the Netherlands Philharmonic and Netherlands Chamber Orchestra take place beneath the dome of the **NedPhO-Koepel** (orkest. nl) in the Byzantine-inspired church Gerardus Majellakerk, designed by Jan Stuyt in 1925, with a 12-sided conical tower.

DREW MCARTHUR/SHUTTERSTOCK

MULTICULTURAL FESTIVAL

On summer weekends, typically from mid-July to early August, the massive food-and-football fair **Kwaku** (*kwakufestival. nl*) is a prime reason to head to Amsterdam's southeast.

What started in 1975 as a small football tournament is now the Netherlands' largest multicultural festival, welcoming 300,000 participants every year. Come to feast on spicy Surinamese cuisine and cocktails, enjoy live performances from Afro-Caribbean singers and bands, and participate in dance workshops.

Kwaku takes place in Nelson Mandelapark, renamed in 2014 from Bijlmerpark, shortly after the South African leader's passing. (Mandela visited Amsterdam, once a vocal hub for anti-apartheid activism, multiple times throughout his life.)

Oosterpark

Unwind in the Oosterpark

Picturesque place

The **Oosterpark**'s lush greenery, with wild parakeets in the trees and herons stalking the large ponds, brings an almost tropical richness to this diverse neighbourhood, despite being laid out in English style. Designed by Leonard Antonij Springer, it was established in 1891 as a pleasure park and still retains an elegant, rambling feel. Tango sessions take place on alternate summer Sundays in the wrought-iron bandstand. Families will enjoy the playground (with a summer wading pool) on the park's north side.

On the south side, look for two monuments. The **National Slavery Monument** commemorates the abolition of slavery in the Dutch colonies in 1863, and **De Schreeuw** is a metal profile shouting into the sky, celebrating free speech and, specifically, the late filmmaker Theo van Gogh. Another (living) monument to Van Gogh is the **Spreeksteen**, a rock podium marking a speakers' corner.

 EATING IN OOSTERPARK & EAST OF THE AMSTEL: LOCAVORE DINING

Vergulden Eenhoorn: Seasonal dining in a restored 1702 farmhouse with leather sofas, an indoor fireplace and a summer terrace. *10am-11pm* €€

Wilde Zwijnen: Rustic-industrial space using regional, sustainable produce in daily three-to five-course menus. *6-10pm Mon, Tue & Thu-Sat, from noon Sun* €€

La Douzaine: Oysters and seafood with bubbles and wine at outdoor barrel tables on Javastraat. *3-9.30pm Wed & Thu, noon-10.30pm Fri & Sat, to 8pm Sun* €€

De Kas: Michelin-starred multicourse dining, growing most produce at its 1926 greenhouses and adjacent gardens. *noon-1.45pm & 6-9pm Mon-Sat* €€€

Trace Park Frankendael's History

The city's only surviving country estate

During the 17th century, Amsterdammers sought respite from the crowded city. Drained in 1629, the polder area of Watergraafsmeer made way for landscaped country estates, farmlands and pleasure gardens. It was annexed in 1921 and absorbed into Amsterdam-Oost. Wildlife around the reedy areas of **Park Frankendael** includes waterbirds, frogs and, on an old chimney, nesting storks.

Restored Louis XIV–style mansion **Huize Frankendael** (*Frankendael House; huizefrankendael.nl; free*) is Amsterdam's last remaining country estate. Within its coach house is the elegant restaurant **Merkelbach** (*restaurantmerkelbach. nl*). Huize Frankendael opens to the public on the last Sunday of every month, when the artisan **Pure Markt** (*puremarkt. nl*) also sets up. For Michelin-starred greenhouse dining, book into **De Kas** (p106).

Visit a Hidden Distillery

Flevopark fairy tale

Flevopark has a wilder, more rambling atmosphere than Amsterdam's central green spaces.

Appearing out of the woods like a *Hansel and Gretel* cottage, the quaint architecture and setting of an old pumping station, with a lakeside terrace next to an orchard, is enchanting. **Distilleerderij 't Nieuwe Diep** (*nwediep.nl*) makes about 100 small-batch *jenevers*, herbal bitters, liqueurs and fruit distillates from organic ingredients according to old Dutch recipes.

Tour AFC Ajax' Home Turf

Renowned football ground

The Netherlands' most famous football team, AFC Ajax, plays its home games at the 68,000-capacity **Johan Cruijff ArenA** (*johancruijffarena.nl; match tickets from €80, stadium tours adult/child €27.50/19.25*). Match tickets are sold on the stadium's website.

Highlights of self-guided stadium tours include emerging from the 'Players Tunnel' to the edge of the pitch and commemorative Delftware porcelain in the memorabilia-packed Ajax Gallery of Fame.

ORANGE FEVER

If you've attended a sporting event where the Dutch national team is playing, you're already familiar with *oranjegekte* (orange craze) or *oranjekoorts* (orange fever). The custom of wearing the traditional colour of the Dutch royal family, the House of Orange-Nassau, was originally limited to celebration days for the monarchy, such as King's Day (Koningsdag), but particularly since the 1974 FIFA World Cup, when tens of thousands of orange-clad football supporters cheered on every match, wearing outlandish orange getups – clothes, scarves, wigs, fake-fur top hats, face paint, feather boas, you name it – has become a cultural phenomenon.

 DRINKING IN OOSTERPARK: BEST ROOFTOPS & TERRACES

Dakterras GAPP: On Hotel Casa's rooftop terrace, sip creative cocktails within an aromatic herb garden. *noon-10pm Fri & Sat, 9am-5pm Sun*

De Biertuin: Covered terrace with heaters for chillier weather, plus a long beer list and pub grub. *3pm-1am Mon-Thu, to 2am Fri, noon-2am Sat, to 1am Sun*

Fitz's on the Roof: Umbrella-shaded, 4th-floor rooftop terrace overlooking Oosterpark. *5pm-midnight Sun-Thu, 4pm-1am Fri & Sat*

Cafe Mojo: Lovely open-fronted bar by the canal. Superb terrace perfect for summer drinks. *noon-midnight or later Mon-Sat, 11am-11pm Sun*

Nieuwmarkt, Plantage & the Eastern Islands

LEAFY GARDENS, FAMILY-FRIENDLY MUSEUMS, AND CONTEMPORARY ARCHITECTURE

GETTING AROUND

It's often quicker to walk in the western half of this area. In the more distant islands and docklands, however, a bicycle or public transport makes sense.

IJburg-bound tram 26 starts behind Centraal Station, following the IJ waterfront and intersecting with tram 7 at Rietlandpark. Tram 14 goes via Waterlooplein and Plantage. Buses 22 and 43 are useful in the Eastern Island areas.

Short hops on metro lines 51, 53 and 54 connect Centraal Station via Nieuwmarkt and Waterlooplein to Weesperplein, from where tram 7 heads to Azartplein via De Gooyer Windmill and Rietlandpark.

Sewn through with rich seams of history, Nieuwmarkt's heart is its 'new market'. The turreted, castle-like Waag was built as a city-wall gate in 1488. Rembrandt painted the area's picturesque canals; his home and studio during his most successful years is now the Museum Rembrandthuis. Centuries-old synagogues house insightful museums in Nieuwmarkt's old Jewish quarter, now called the Joods Cultureel Kwartier (Jewish Cultural Quarter), which also has significant memorials.

To the east, leafy Plantage evolved from marshland in the 17th century, and plots unsold during an economic crisis were developed into parks. Greenery also fills the Hortus Botanicus botanical gardens and Artis Zoo. Continuing east brings you to the Eastern Islands (Oostelijke Eilanden) and their docklands (Oostelijk Havengebied), where historic architecture such as the Het Scheepvaartmuseum meets contemporary showpieces. At this area's easternmost edge is the recently constructed IJburg neighbourhood on artificial islands in the IJmeer lake, offering numerous watersports.

See Where Rembrandt Lived & Painted

The artist's former home and studio

Step back into the 17th century at the **Museum Rembrandthuis** *(rembrandthuis.nl; adult/child €21.50/8),* the 1606 canal house that one of the Netherlands' greatest artistic geniuses, Rembrandt van Rijn, bought in 1639, helped by his wealthy wife, Saskia van Uylenburgh. The interiors are meticulously reconstructed based on a detailed inventory made in 1656 when bankruptcy forced Rembrandt to sell the home.

Prebook timeslot entry; at quiet times (typically midweek afternoons), walk-ins are usually possible. Highlights include a handful of Rembrandt's etchings, paintings by artists inspired by Rembrandt's work, Rembrandt's recreated cabinet of

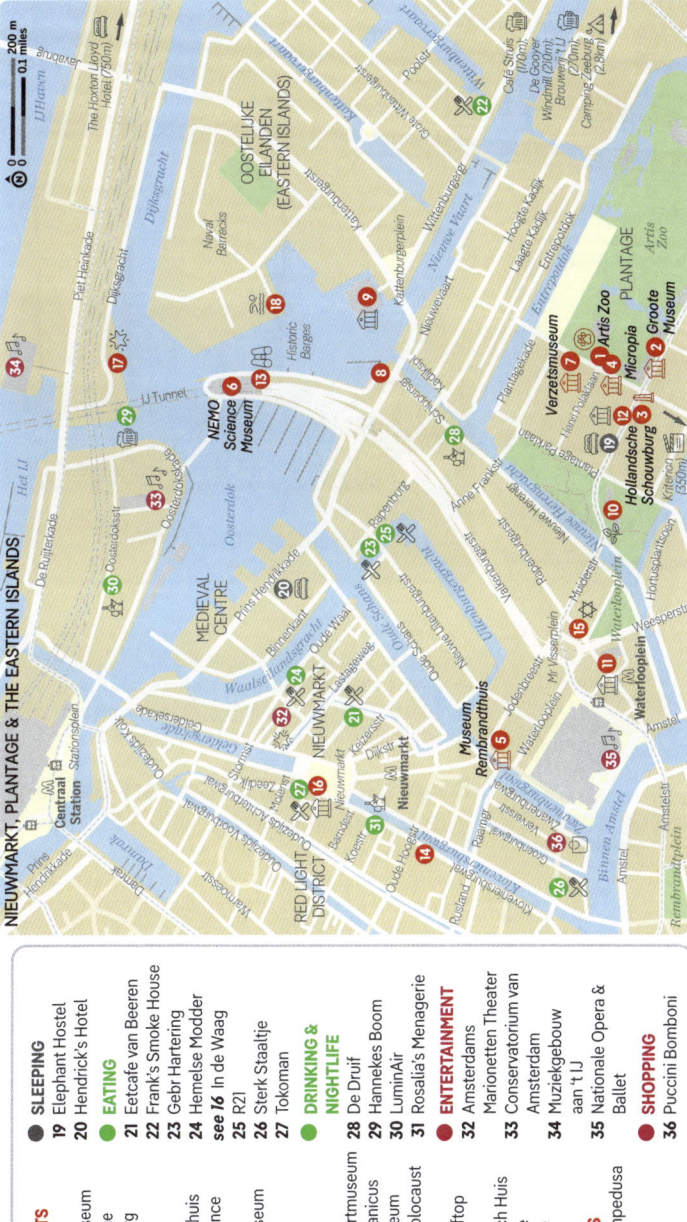

THE GUIDE

AMSTERDAM NIEUWMARKT, PLANTAGE & THE EASTERN ISLANDS

NIEUWMARKT, PLANTAGE & THE EASTERN ISLANDS

★ HIGHLIGHTS
1. Artis Zoo
2. Groote Museum
3. Hollandsche Schouwburg
4. Micropia
5. Museum Rembrandthuis
6. NEMO Science Museum
7. Verzetsmuseum

● SIGHTS
8. Arcam
9. Het Scheepvaartmuseum
10. Hortus Botanicus
11. Joods Museum
12. National Holocaust Museum
13. NEMO Rooftop Viewpoint
14. Oost-Indisch Huis
15. Portuguese Synagogue
16. Waag

● ACTIVITIES
17. Rederij Lampedusa
18. SUP to Go

● SLEEPING
19. Elephant Hostel
20. Hendrick's Hotel

● EATING
21. Eetcafe van Beeren
22. Frank's Smoke House
23. Gebr Hartering
24. Hemelse Modder *see 16* In de Waag
25. R21
26. Sterk Staaltje
27. Tokoman

● DRINKING & NIGHTLIFE
28. De Druif
29. Hannekes Boom
30. LuminAir
31. Rosalia's Menagerie

● ENTERTAINMENT
32. Amsterdams Marionetten Theater
33. Conservatorium van Amsterdam
34. Muziekgebouw aan 't IJ
35. Nationale Opera & Ballet

● SHOPPING
36. Puccini Bomboni

109

NIEUWMARKT EVOLUTION

The centrepiece of low-key, cafe-ringed Nieuwmarkt is the **Waag**, a multi-lobed brick mini castle, originally built in 1488 as a gate in the city walls. In 1601, those walls were demolished as the city expanded, and the Waag was turned into Amsterdam's main weigh house.

By the 17th century, it was home to various guilds, including that of the surgeons who, after intoning suitable prayers, would perform human dissections in front of a paying crowd. One such scene is famously captured in Rembrandt's *The Anatomy Lesson of Dr Nicolaes Tulp* (displayed in the Mauritshuis (p209) in Den Haag).

Today, most of the ground floor is the eponymous cafe-restaurant, **In de Waag** *(indewaag.nl)*. Out front, Nieuwmarkt hosts a variety of events, including a Saturday farmers market.

NICK N A/SHUTTERSTOCK

curios that he collected and sketched, and fascinating exhibits in his light-filled painting, etching and student studios. Live demonstrations of pigment making or etching are included on alternate days (10.30am to noon and 12.30pm to 3pm).

Board a Replica 17th-Century Galleon

National maritime museum

Exploring a full-scale replica of the 700-tonne galleon *Amsterdam* is the highlight of a visit to **Het Scheepvaartmuseum** *(National Maritime Museum; hetscheepvaartmuseum.com; adult/child €18.50/free)*. The original, one of the VOC's largest tall-mast ships, was wrecked by storms during its maiden voyage to East Asia. A 180-degree multi-screen projection takes you downriver on a virtual journey into the 18th-century port of Amsterdam.

Inside the main museum, the powerful 'Shadows on the Atlantic' exhibition examines colonial reverberations. Other rooms display historic ship figureheads, navigational instruments

EATING EAST OF NIEUWMARKT: COSY DINING

Eetcafe van Beeren: Trad-French restaurant meets Dutch brown cafe, wafting tempting aromas. Meal of the day €15. *5-9.30pm Mon-Fri, from 4pm Sat & Sun* €

Gebr Hartering: Founded by foodie brothers in a tiny shophouse. Menus barely hint at the five- or seven-course adventure ahead. *6-9pm* €€

Hemelse Modder: Neat, simple decor leaves little to distract you from the entrancing flavours created in the chef's inventive multicourse menus. *6-10pm* €€

R21: Refined yet completely unstuffy gastronomic dining across three connected antique buildings at a cosy canalside location. *6-10pm Tue-Sat* €€€

Het Scheepvaartmuseum

ON THE WATER

Amsterdam's rapidly developing outer suburb of IJburg, reached via tram 26, is an urban watersports getaway.

Surfcenter IJburg: At the wide, sandy artificial beach Strand IJburg, this container-housed shop hires out SUP boards, wingfoils and windsurfing gear. *(surfcenterijburg.nl)*

King of Boardsports: Has wingfoil lessons and equipment hire. *(kingofboardsports. com)*

Zeilschool IJburg: Rents small skiffs and motorboats by IJburg's marina. *(zeilschoolijburg.nl)*

Amsterdam Watersports: Offers numerous activities, including wakeboarding and flyboarding. *(amster damwatersports.com)*

SUP to Go: Has automated lockers with SUP boards; prebook online. *(supsupclub.com)*

and priceless naval charts. The imposing courtyard building is part of the attraction, a 1656 waterfront behemoth originally designed as a storehouse for the Admiralty of Amsterdam.

Perform Experiments at NEMO

Interactive science museum

State-of-the-art **NEMO Science Museum** *(nemosciencemuseum.nl; €21.50)* is truly interactive, with four floors of investigative mayhem that kids of all ages will enjoy. Experiment with lifting yourself via a pulley, making bubbles and designing your own wind turbine. Almost everything is labelled in English. You need several hours to see it all.

Italian architect Renzo Piano designed the impossible-to-miss green-copper building, and it's almost surrounded by water. The huge, sloping **rooftop** space, accessed via the museum or stairs in the southeastern corner, has some of the best views over Amsterdam.

 ## DRINKING IN NPEI: BEST BARS

Hannekes Boom: Waterside cafe built from recycled materials. Huge bench-tabled beer garden beneath colourful lights and winter fires inside. *11pm-late*

De Druif: In a 1566 building, 'The Grape' gained its first liquor licence in 1631. The wooden interior retains old gas chandeliers. *10am-1am or later*

Rosalia's Menagerie: Ring the doorbell to access this small, intimate but utterly exuberant drawing-room bar with its own bijou B&B. *6pm-1am*

LuminAir: On the triangular rooftop of the DoubleTree Inn, with light- and air-themed cocktails and 360-degree panoramas over Amsterdam. *noon-late*

ICONIC ENTERTAINMENT VENUES

Muziekgebouw aan 't IJ: Striking glass and steel concert venue, with two halls and an intimate jazz stage, Bimhuis. (muziekgebouw.nl)

Nationale Opera & Ballet: Home to the Netherlands Opera and the National Ballet, with a 1600-seat auditorium. (operaballet.nl)

Conservatorium van Amsterdam: The Netherlands' largest and most prestigious music academy, CvA hosts frequent student concerts. (conservatoriumva namsterdam.nl)

Amsterdams Marionetten Theater: Endearing puppet theatre that seems to exist in another era, presenting fairy tales and Mozart operas. (marionetten theater.nl)

Kriterion: Historic 1945 student Resistance-founded arthouse cinema; many English-language or subtitled screenings. (kriterion.nl)

Meet Animals at Artis

Historic zoo

Founded in 1838, **Artis Zoo** (artis.nl; adult/child €30.50/26.50) is one of Europe's oldest zoos and has gone to enormous efforts to update and enlarge its enclosures to ensure that its critters remain healthy and happy. Its 14 leafy hectares are home to more than 750 species, from lions, jaguars, elephants and giraffes to sea lions, golden-cheeked gibbons, iguanas, flamingos and cassowaries. There's a reptile house, butterfly pavilion, several aviaries and an aquarium. You can journey through the solar system and Milky Way at the 324-seat planetarium (included in zoo admission).

Combination tickets include entry to the neighbouring **Micropia** (artis.nl/en/artis-micropia; adult/child €17.50/free), which focuses on life-forms too small to see with the naked eye, and the **Groote Museum** (grootemuseum.nl; adult/child €17.50/free), probing such questions as 'What is the meaning of life?'

Take a Botany Lesson at the Hortus Botanicus

Tropical history

A botanical garden since 1638, the Plantage's 1.2-hectare **Hortus Botanicus** (dehortus.nl; adult/child €13.50/7) bloomed as Dutch trading ships brought in tropical seeds and plants. From here, coffee, pineapple, cinnamon and palm-oil plants were distributed throughout the world. Its medicinal gardens provided the Netherlands' doctors with remedies.

The gardens' 4000-plus species occupy wonderful structures, including a 1911 palm house, butterfly house and three-climate glasshouse renewed as the world's first fully sustainable, climate-neutral greenhouse. The 1875 orangery shelters a lovely cafe.

Sip Beer Beneath a Windmill

Iconic artisan brewery

Built in 1725 but moved here in 1814, **De Gooyer** is Amsterdam's largest windmill, complete with creaking sails and pretty nighttime lighting. It's now a private house, but the attached former bathhouse contains one of Amsterdam's leading microbreweries, **Brouwerij 't IJ** (brouwerijhetij.nl). It offers a dozen excellent draught beers to savour on the plane-tree-shaded terrace. Once the main tasting room closes, head to adjacent co-owned **Café Struis**.

Honour the Fate of a Community

Moving memorials

From the road, the **Hollandsche Schouwburg** (jck.nl; free) appears as it once was, an architecturally splendid 1892 theatre. However, behind the facade, the building is mostly a hollow shell: a powerful monument to the WWII deportations that

COLORMAKER/SHUTTERSTOCK

Hortus Bontanicus

virtually wiped out the Jewish community. A moving 12-minute audiovisual tells the story of how, from 20 July 1942, the playhouse became a holding place from which about 46,000 Jews were eventually sent to prison and death camps. After liberation, by the time the city could decide how to use the building, its rear section was in ruins. Ironically, the stark state of semi-collapse now serves to underline the sense of tragedy.

Across the road, the **National Holocaust Museum** *(adult/ child €20/8)* is housed in a former school from which some Jewish children were spirited away to safety when passing trams masked the view of the guards.

Learn about the Dutch Resistance

Extraordinary stories

What would you have done if you lived in Amsterdam during WWII, a city suddenly occupied by Nazis hell bent on reorganising society to their ideology? It's a question you can't help but ask yourself at the sobering yet inspiring **Verzetsmuseum** *(Dutch Resistance Museum; verzetsmuseum.org; adult/ child €16/8.50).* Allow at least a couple of hours to learn the background and then discover how people did react, whether by taking up arms or more subtly by helping those in hiding, forging documents or contributing to underground newspapers, radios and general strikes. Nuanced personal stories illuminate people's complex predicaments rather than simply condemning those who failed to choose heroism.

☑ **TOP TIPS**

Scenic picnic spots abound in this area. Stock up on house-smoked delicacies at deli-restaurant **Frank's Smoke House**; beautifully crafted sandwiches such as smoked beef, pesto and parmesan focaccia at gourmet deli **Sterk Staaltje**; or sensational fiery Surinamese sandwiches at **Tokoman**. Finish with a delicious choc-ball from Amsterdam institution **Puccini Bomboni**.

CONTEMPORARY ARCHITECTURE WALK AROUND THE EASTERN ISLANDS

Walk along the waterside to see how Amsterdam's Eastern Islands have transformed from decrepit docklands into inner-city suburbs.

START	END	LENGTH
Pacman Building	Azartplein tram stop	2.2km; 1 hr

Start at the **1 Pacman Building**, behind the RJH Fortuynplein stop on bus route 43 from Centraal Station. Dominating an area of otherwise low-rise housing, the building is a city planner's 'meteorite', ie disproportionately large construction. It contains **2 Borneo Architectuur Centrum**, an architectural practice whose free exhibition room fascinatingly details the area's five decades of development.

Notice the seagull-shaped streetlamps as you cross the red-metal, stepped footbridge, nicknamed **3 Pythonbrug** for its reptilian undulations. Beyond the **4 Zeeburg Passenger Ferry Jetty** is a **5 viewpoint** at the corner of Ertskade that simultaneously surveys Venetiëhof, a giant circular housing block by architect Jo Coenen, and, looking west, **6 The Wader**

(Steltloper), a tower block perched on distinctively in-pointing pillar 'legs'.

As greenery starts to hide flanking houseboats, you'll spy a giant, angled grey building widely known as **7 The Whale** (De Walvis). Cross the nearby causeway, pass a hippie garden area, and walk through the **8 Piraeus Building**, considered a classic of 1990s Dutch architecture with its quirky fold-out windows.

Across KNSM-laan, look inside daytime cafe **9 Kompaszaal**. Its interiors are little changed since 1956, when it was the waiting room for international passenger ships. Stretching west, the long **10 Loods 6** building contains galleries, a ceramics-makers' space and more. Return to central Amsterdam from **11 Azartplein** (tram 7).

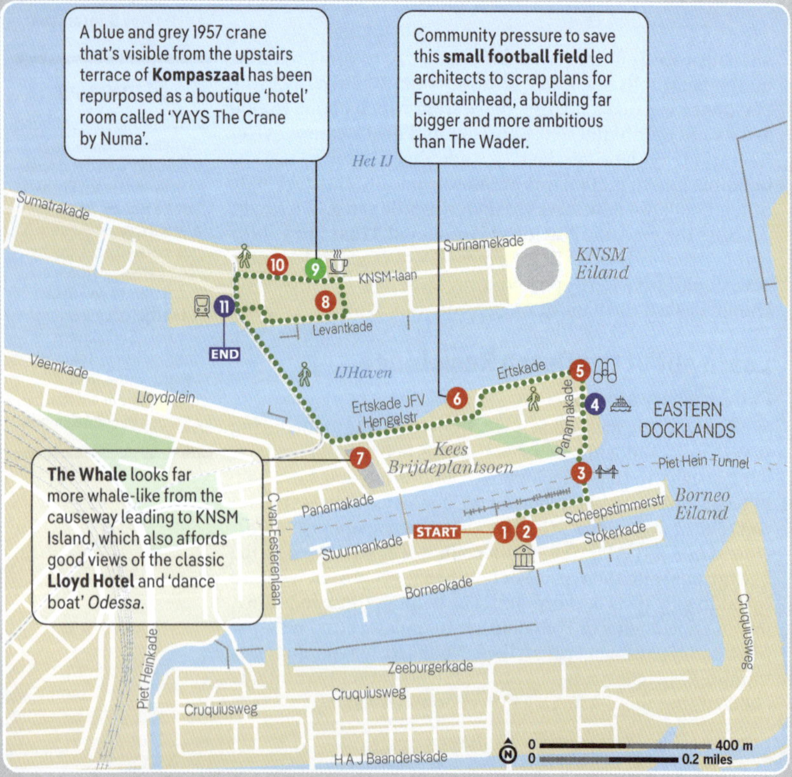

A blue and grey 1957 crane that's visible from the upstairs terrace of **Kompaszaal** has been repurposed as a boutique 'hotel' room called 'YAYS The Crane by Numa'.

Community pressure to save this **small football field** led architects to scrap plans for Fountainhead, a building far bigger and more ambitious than The Wader.

The Whale looks far more whale-like from the causeway leading to KNSM Island, which also affords good views of the classic **Lloyd Hotel** and 'dance boat' *Odessa*.

An important side exhibit covers the WWII situation in the Dutch colonies, particularly the crushed early hopes among Indonesian independence activists.

The 'Junior' section, which follows four Dutch children, is a highlight of the whole museum for adults as much as youngsters.

Visit Salvaged Synagogues
Rescued treasures

Also known as Esnoga, Amsterdam's **Portuguese Synagogue** (*jck.nl; adult/child €22/7*) was the largest in Europe when completed in 1675. Still active, it retains many of its 17th-century features, including sand-dusted floors. Without electric light, candles are still lit in the vast chandeliers for services after dark, and during evening concerts (usually held on one Thursday a month).

Tickets include entrance to the nearby **Joods Museum** (Jewish Museum), which illustrates key religious and cultural customs of Judaism and tells the history of Amsterdam's Jewish community.

Contemplate the VOC's Legacy
'Decolonial Dialogues'

Broach contentious history at the **Oost-Indisch Huis** (*uva. nl*), an imposing red and white edifice. Built between 1551 and 1643 and attributed in part to city architect Hendrick de Keyser, it was the headquarters of the 1602-founded Dutch East India Company (Vereenigde Oostindische Compagnie; VOC), trading spices, opium and more with Asia. It was here that the world's first share transactions were validated.

A video narrative now includes the voices of descendants of those exploited, calling for a fuller appreciation of the building's true historical implications, a common thread gaining traction more widely as Amsterdam grapples with its past.

Hear Refugees' Stories
Conscious cruising with Rederij Lampedusa

Cruises along Amsterdam's waterways with **Rederij Lampedusa** (*rederijlampedusa.nl; 90-min cruise €35*) are very special because your pilot/guide tells you not just about Amsterdam but also about their personal experiences as former asylum seekers from eye-opening, heartfelt perspectives. Trips depart beside the sustainability-arts centre Mediamatic.

Preview Amsterdam's Architectural Future
Exhibits and city tours

Generally abbreviated **Arcam** (*arcam.nl; adult/child €5/free*), the Amsterdam Architecture Foundation inhabits a small, curved metal and glass building by Dutch architect René van Zuuk. View exhibits on city planning and developments this century, and check for informative guided architectural tours, usually in English on Sundays.

JEWISH AMSTERDAM

Nieuwmarkt's Jewish quarter evolved from the 16th century, and by Napoleonic times, Amsterdam was Europe's largest Jewish centre. During French rule, guilds that prohibited Jews and remaining restrictions were abolished, and Amsterdam's Jewish community thrived in the 19th and early 20th centuries.

The Nazis' devastation of Amsterdam's Jewish community was near total. Of a prewar population of some 90,000 Jews (13% of the city's population), only 5500, scarcely one in 16 people, survived. Amsterdammers resisted: the city's motto, *Heldhaftig, Vastberaden, Barmhartig* (Valiant, Steadfast, Compassionate), presented by Queen Wilhelmina in 1947, commemorates citizens' protests against the WWII persecution of Jewish people.

Amsterdam Noord

EVOLVING EX-INDUSTRIAL CREATIVE DISTRICT

GETTING AROUND

Free 24-hour passenger ferries link Noord to the rest of the city every 10 to 15 minutes. Key routes are NDSM to/from Centraal Station and Pontsteiger (Houthaven), and Buiksloterweg to/from Centraal. Between Buiksloterweg and NDSM, it's often quicker to return and change ferries at Centraal than wait for buses.

The north–south metro line 52 links Amsterdam Zuid in the south via Centraal Station with Noorderpark and Noord stations, though both are a hike from the key waterfront areas, making ferries more convenient.

A bike is near essential for exploring spread-out Noord. Bringing bicycles on the ferry is free.

The fun of Noord starts right on the ferry. The free, five-minute cruise across the IJ from central Amsterdam is a sightseeing experience in its own right. Previously neglected, this area has been reinvented as one of the city's most happening neighbourhoods.

Around Buiksloterweg are the striking EYE Filmmuseum and the ex-Royal Dutch Shell oil company offices, transformed into the multi-attraction and entertainment hub A'DAM Tower. Heading some 3km northwest brings you to the vast NDSM shipbuilding yards. Art studios and galleries now occupy its huge hangars and warehouses.

Numerous cafes, bars, breweries and other creative enterprises, often built from recycled materials like shipping containers, have waterside terraces, though changing winds are seeing some obscure, alternative venues and once-treasured haunts edged out by shiny condominiums and commercial spaces. It's all minutes away from fields, horses and the odd windmill that are perfect for exploring by bike.

Head Up A'DAM Tower

Attraction-packed high-rise

The 22-storey **A'DAM Tower** *(adamtoren.nl; viewing platform adult/child €18.50/12.50)* was built in 1971 and used as the Royal Dutch Shell oil company offices. It's now a multivenue extravaganza, with a 360-degree viewing platform on its 100m-high rooftop, complete with interactive binoculars and super-size cushions for lounging in fine weather.

A six-person **giant swing** – Europe's highest – kicks out over the edge *(€7.50 per person)*. You can also add on an 'Amsterdam VR Ride' *(€7.50),* taking you on a wild simulated roller-coaster ride through the historic city.

On the 20th floor, bar/nightclub **Madam Amsterdam** *(madamamsterdam.nl)* has stunning, floor-to-ceiling windows and

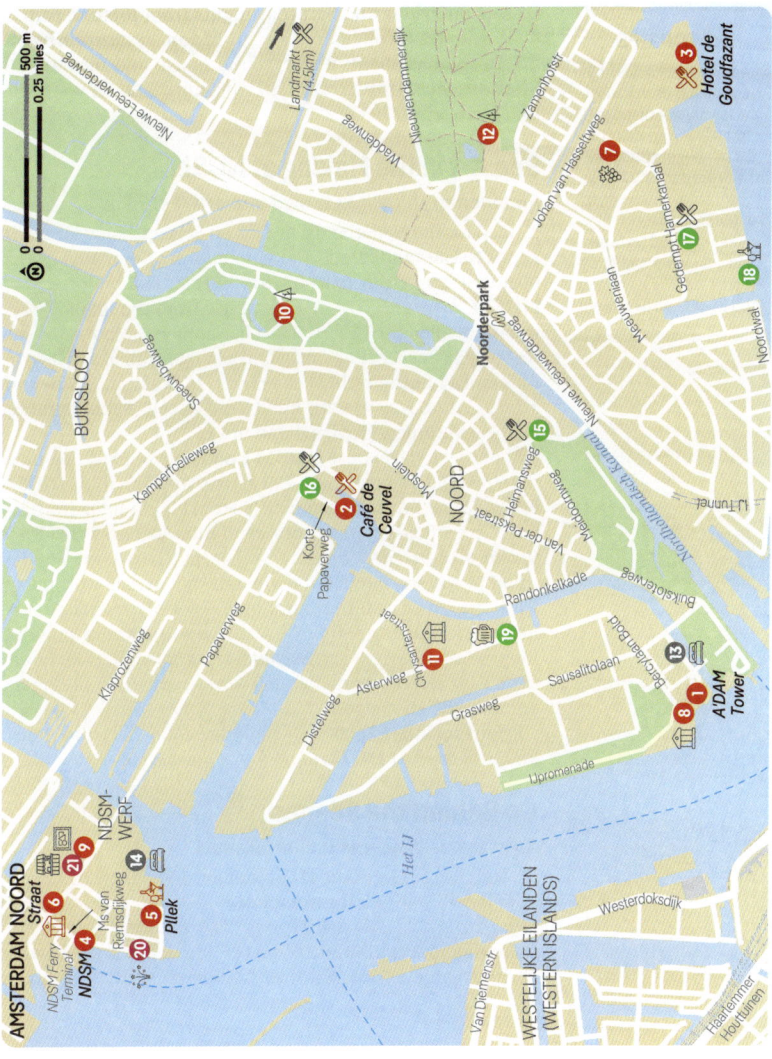

HIGHLIGHTS
1 A'DAM Tower
2 Café de Ceuvel
3 Hotel de Goudfazant
4 NDSM
5 Pllek
6 Straat

SIGHTS
7 Chateau Amsterdam
8 Eye Filmmuseum
9 NDSM Loods
10 Noorderpark
11 NXT Museum
12 WH Vliegenbos

SLEEPING
13 ClinkNOORD
14 Faralda
see 1 Sir Adam

EATING
15 Bunk
16 Cornerstore
17 Euro Pizza
see 1 Moon

**DRINKING &
NIGHTLIFE**
18 Lowlander
see 1 Madam Amsterdam
see 1 Shelter
19 Walhalla Taproom

ENTERTAINMENT
20 DGTL

SHOPPING
21 IJ Hallen

☑ **TOP TIPS**

Straddling both sides of the Noordhollandsch Kanaal, the lawns, woodland and formal rose gardens of the rambling, 41-hectare **Noorderpark** are home to regular events, such as outdoor art classes, film screenings and festivals, including September's Noorderpark Festival with food trucks and live music.

DJ sets on Friday and Saturday nights from 10pm to 5am. A floor below is revolving restaurant **Moon** *(restaurantmoon. nl)*. In the basement, underground house and techno club **Shelter** *(shelteramsterdam.nl)* runs until 7am on weekends thanks to a 24/7 licence.

See Art in the Making at NDSM

Abandoned shipyards turned into artist studios

Named for the Nederlandsche Dok en Scheepsbouw Maatschappij (Netherlands Dock and Shipbuilding Company), which operated here from 1946 to 1979, former shipbuilding yard **NDSM** *(ndsm.nl; free)* fell out of use from the 1980s, before squatters filled the void. Today it has numerous cool waterside restaurants, a street-art museum, a hangar full of artists' studios and a huge monthly flea market, **IJ Hallen** *(ijhallen.nl; adult/child €6/2.50)* with hundreds of stalls selling vintage clothes, antiques, vinyl, art and more.

At massive warehouse **NDSM Loods** *(ndsmloods.nl),* more than 80 studios have some 250 artists working in the NDSM *broedplaats* (breeding ground). Huge artworks hang from rafters. Up scaffolding-like stairs, exhibition space **NDSM Fuse** *(ndsm-fuse.eu; entry by donation)* opens Thursday to Sunday.

Follow the smell of fresh paint and spot artists working up fresh designs. Graffiti around here is legally regulated, and new works appear regularly. At the world's largest museum for graffiti and street art, **Straat** *(straatmuseum.com; adult/ child €19.50/free),* more than 150 works created on-site spread across 8000 sq metres.

Events include Easter weekend's three-day electronic music and arts festival **DGTL** *(dgtl-festival.com).*

Go Behind the Scenes

Amsterdam's eye-conic film museum

On the riverbanks of the IJ (pronounced 'eye'), the modernist angular white **Eye Filmmuseum** *(eyefilm.nl; film screenings adult/child €13.50/8, exhibitions €21/free)* peers over the city. Its permanent exhibition 'What is Film?' lets you see how the earliest cameras worked, insert yourself into a film using

 EATING IN NOORD: OUR PICKS

Café de Ceuvel: Off-grid spot built from recycled materials with an all-vegan menu. *noon-11pm or later Tue-Sun €€*

Cornerstore: Vinyl DJ booth, Asian-influenced plates and drinks from sake to agave. *6pm-1am Wed-Sat, 1.30-10pm Sun €€*

Hotel de Goud-fazant: Cavernous former garage with cars parked inside, where chefs cook up a French-influenced storm. *6pm-midnight Tue-Sun €€*

Euro Pizza: In a former garage, this cult favourite serves sourdough pizza paired with natural wines. *6-11pm Mon-Thu, from 1pm Fri & Sat, 1-10pm Sun €€*

green-screen technology and make your own animated movie. Virtual reality puts focus on the future, and all these eras come together in an installation called 'Film Catcher', where an AI-powered, image-based search allows you to call up films from a collection of more than 60,000 clips in mere seconds.

Eye's four state-of-the-art cinemas screen everything from blockbusters to experimental arthouse in Original Version; one has an organ for live sound effects.

Check Out the Nexus of Art & Tech

'New media art' museum

In a 1400-sq-metre warehouse space, **NXT Museum** *(nxt museum.com; adult/child from €19.50/13.50)* is a radical departure from traditional art forms. Artists, scientists, sound engineers, coders and designers collaborate to create immersive digital experiences of light, sound and movement using cutting-edge tech such as robotics, facial recognition, AI and VR. Large-scale, multisensory installations explore themes such as virtual worlds and digital identity through exhibits like evolving data sculptures.

Explore a Wildlife Haven

Forest trails

Planted from 1912, Noord's 20-hectare **WH Vliegenbos** *(vlie genbosamsterdam.nl; free)* is Amsterdam's oldest forest, with elm, ash, and black alder trees, and birdlife including woodpeckers, kingfishers, falcons and blackbirds. Walking and cycling trails weave through the greenery and past ponds and waterways.

Head to a Covered Market

Countryside dining

Farm-shop-style covered market **Landmarkt** *(landmarkt.nl)* is piled high with fresh fruit and vegetables, locally caught seafood delivered by boat, Dutch cheeses and artisan breads. There's a great cafe-restaurant and outdoor seating that feels immersed in the countryside.

GENTRIFICATION ON THE WHARF

Within just a few years, Noord has transformed dramatically from an industrial dockland into a speedily developing residential area. A persistent housing shortage and dispersing tourism from the city centre steer a municipal vision for taming a rebellious neighbourhood.

Alternative digs have raised speculative interest and resulted in many warehouses being razed to build new commercial and residential projects – and, of course, the creative businesses within them have been displaced. Slick, sanitised high-rises between Buiksloterweg and IJplein's ferry terminals heavily contrast graffitied corners. NDSM and other legacy institutions face increased pressure from developers, and many warehouse-situated businesses remain subject to construction timelines.

 DRINKING IN NOORD: OUR PICKS

Pllek: Come for afternoon beer on the waterfront and stay for live DJs and dance parties pumping until late. *9.30am-1am Sun-Thu, to 3am Fri & Sat*

Lowlander: Plant-filled former warehouse with a sun-soaked, south-facing terrace. Brews botanical beers and local, seasonal food. *11am-midnight Sun-Wed, to 1am Thu-Sat*

Walhalla Taproom: Relaxed microbrewery for unpretentious, delicious pours. *4pm-midnight Thu & Fri, from 2pm Sat, 2-9pm Sun*

Chateau Amsterdam: Grapes from around Europe become vino on site. Tour the solar-powered production facility. *5pm-midnight Wed-Fri, from 2pm Sat, 2-7pm Sun*

Places We Love to Stay

€ Budget €€ Midrange €€€ Top End

Medieval Centre & the Red Light District p52

St Christopher's at the Winston € Rock 'n' roll rooms, a busy nightclub with live bands nightly, a bar and restaurant, a beer garden and a smoking deck downstairs. En-suite dorms designed by artists (some are kinda 'out there').

Hotel The Exchange €€ Eye-popping rooms designed by students from the Amsterdam Fashion Institute. Rooms range from one- to five-star (with concept-driven designs). All have en-suite bathrooms.

Die Port van Cleve €€€ Opened in 1870 on the site of Heineken's first brewery, three monumental buildings give palatial vibes. Elegant design cues from blue and white Delftware.

Hotel de L'Europe €€€ Heineken family-owned, Amsterdam's 'other royal palace'. Classical elements (doorkeepers in top hats) and modern luxury rooms with canal views.

Western Canal Ring, Jordaan & the West p63

Houseboat Ms Luctor €€ An organic breakfast basket (included) is delivered daily at this solar-powered, mahogany-panelled 1913 houseboat, moored in a quiet waterway. Guests can borrow bicycles and a canoe for canal explorations. Minimum stay is three nights.

BackStage Hotel €€ Music-themed hotel loved by musicians, with a band-signature-covered piano and pool table in the bar, gig posters (many signed) lining the corridors, and retro-styled rooms with drum-kit lights, plus guitars, turntables and vinyl to loan.

Conscious Hotel Westerpark €€ Entirely wind-powered, Westergas' 89-room Conscious Hotel (there are three more near the Vondelpark) incorporates recycled materials, down to coat hangers made from radiator parts. Aquaponic walls grow the cafe's vegetables and herbs for all-organic breakfasts.

Dylan €€€ Exquisite Keizersgracht canal house set around a herringbone-paved, topiary-filled inner courtyard. Bespoke furniture like silver-leaf and mother-of-pearl drinks cabinets adorns its 40 rooms. Its two-Michelin-starred Restaurant Vinkeles also hosts private chef's tables aboard its boat.

Southern Canal Ring p78

ClinkCoco € Once a high-end brothel, this boutique hostel's doubles and dorms are light, bright and airy. There's a relaxing back garden, a well-equipped kitchen and a super-comfy lounge.

Hotel La Boheme €€ Small, sustainably focused hotel. Rooms are clean and simple, but the central location makes it a favourite. Book well in advance.

Hotel V Frederiksplein €€ Soothing, leafy views and designer digs over a lush square. Only a quick shimmy from the bars and restaurants of Utrechtsestraat.

Seven Bridges €€ Beautifully set on a lovely canal, aristocratic opulence is alive and well across these sumptuous rooms with oriental rugs, polished antiques and breakfast on fine china.

Clayton Hotel Amsterdam American €€€ Magnificent, historic art nouveau beast on Leidseplein. Today's hotel is an expansion of the original 1880s Viennese Renaissance–style building. Its grand Café American is dubbed 'Amsterdam's living room'.

Vondelpark, Oud-West & Oud-Zuid p86

Stayokay Amsterdam Vondelpark € Practically in the Vondelpark, this HI-affiliated 536-bed hostel offers private rooms and fresh dorms sleeping four to 10. Generous breakfasts in the plant-filled bar-restaurant cost extra.

Hotel Fita €€ One of the best-value digs near Museumplein (it books up fast!), family-owned Fita has 21 light-filled rooms in mint condition with modern bathrooms; fantastic free breakfasts of eggs, pancakes, cheeses and bread; and a lift.

Hotel De Hallen €€ Housed in a former tram depot, this designer hotel has 58 industrial-chic rooms and six loft-style apartments, and cool art and sculptures in its lobby, lounge areas, restaurant, bar and wraparound terrace. Breakfast costs extra.

SWEETS Hotel Overtoomsesluis €€ One of 28 historic bridge houses citywide converted into suites by a team of architects, designers and builders. There's a cosy bed nook, kitchenette and local life buzzing around you; expect a bit of noise.

De Pijp & Zuid p98

Bicycle Hotel Amsterdam €€ Green-minded hotel with six comfy, familiar rooms (the cheapest share bathrooms), fab organic vegetarian breakfasts and affordable bicycle hire for guests. No lift.

Sir Albert Hotel €€€ At the peaceful western end of market street Albert Cuypstraat, a 19th-century diamond factory houses 90 designer rooms.

Hotel Okura Amsterdam €€€ Rising 23 storeys with rare-for-Amsterdam panoramas, three Michelin stars (two at top-floor Ciel Bleu, one at ground-floor Japanese restaurant Yamazato), and a health club with an 18m pool.

Oosterpark & East of the Amstel p104

Generator Amsterdam € Outpost of a cool designer hostel chain. Occupies a century-old zoological university building with large windows overlooking lush Oosterpark. Great bars and restaurants nearby.

Vergulden Eenhoorn (p106) **€€** Restored 1702-built farmhouse with modern, stylish rooms. Excellent on-site restaurant. Hiring a bicycle makes the stay more enjoyable.

Volkshotel €€ Designer, eco-certified rooms and a rooftop hot tub. Coworking spaces and a full cultural programme (film screenings, DJs etc) at the restaurant-bar Canvas attract youthful, creative professionals.

Nieuwmarkt, Plantage & the Eastern Islands p108

Camping Zeeburg € Colourful waterside cabins (single, double and quad) and tent and van pitches, plus bike, kayak and SUP hire.

Elephant Hostel € Friendly hostel with a gloriously preserved common room and cafe in an 1884 mansion. Dorms have box bunks, air-con and decent lockers. Showers are small but well designed.

Hendrick's Hotel €€ One of several good options on Prins Hendrikkade, a 10-minute walk from Centraal Station, the 25 rooms come in 11 different categories with wide price variations, but all have air-con and a coffee-maker, and most are lift-accessible.

The Hoxton Lloyd Hotel €€€ The 1921 Lloyd Hotel is worth visiting even if you don't stay in one of the 136 rooms, restored to show off the hotel's stylishly retro sense of early art deco.

Amsterdam Noord p116

Bunk € Trendy budget rooms and 'pod' rooms in a converted, neogothic church.

ClinkNOORD € In a 1920s laboratory on the IJ riverbank, hostel dorms with designer edge. By Buiksloterweg's ferry terminal (a free, five-minute ride to Centraal Station 24/7).

Faralda €€€ Fantasy-world suites perched at varying heights on a crane atop NDSM-werf. Rooftop hot tub with astounding views.

Sir Adam €€€ Cool design hotel located in the A'DAM Tower.

KIEVVICTOR/SHUTTERSTOCK

Clayton Hotel Amsterdam American

Researched by
Abigail Blasi

Haarlem & North Holland

WINDMILLS, TULIPS, CHEESE AND MUSTARD

Head north of Amsterdam to discover the Holland seen on Delft tableware, a place of canal-laced towns, historic ports and waterside windmills above pea-green fields.

The lovely town of Haarlem is only 20km from Amsterdam (a 15-minute train ride), and many of its residents live a quiet life here, commuting to the country's capital for work. The heart of Haarlem centres on its great church, and the city has several fabulous museums. It's close to the rural expanse of Zuid-Kennemerland National Park, which boasts swimming lakes, wild deer, ponies, russet brown and horned Highland cattle, and a long beach-bar-lined white-sand beach. Spring brings lots of tulip fields to the land around Haarlem.

North of the city is Alkmaar, with its famous cheese market and superb 'floating auction' museum, and further still is the island of Texel, beloved by locals for wholesome beach and cycling holidays, with its sandy landscapes of dunes and strands.

One of the Netherlands' most-visited sites is just north of Amsterdam, at Zaanse Schans, where traditional houses and windmills were relocated to create a historic neighbourhood that is a kind of outdoor museum. To the east is Waterland, with cows grazing on tidy fields crisscrossed by waterways, beyond which are mast-filled ports such as Hoorn and Enkhuizen. A short bus trip from Amsterdam is the famous cheese town of Edam and the touristy port of Volendam, the place to get dressed up in clogs and Dutch traditional costume and have your photo taken.

NERPY/SHUTTERSTOCK

THE MAIN AREAS

HAARLEM
Handsome mini Amsterdam with beach and forest. **p126**

TEXEL
Largest Wadden Island, a rural escape. **p135**

ZAANSE SCHANS
Windmills, museums and historic houses. **p139**

For places to
stay in Haarlem
& North Holland,
see p149

FOKKE BAARSSEN/SHUTTERSTOCK

Left: Zaanse Schans (p139); Above: Eirland Lighthouse (p137), Texel

Find Your Way

It's generally easy to get around by public transport. Ferries link Den Helder and Texel. Another service makes the trip from Volendam to Marken. Every town has bicycle hire and, of course, cycle lanes aplenty.

Texel, p135

The largest and most easily accessible of the Wadden Sea Islands, this rural escape offers lots of local produce, sheep and wholesome outdoor pursuits.

Zaanse Schans, p139

A line of eight riverside windmills north of Amsterdam, with small museums, local craft demonstrations and historic houses from all over the Zaan region.

Haarlem, p126

The charm-packed historic capital of North Holland has fine architecture, museums and canals. Beaches and forests are an easy trip away.

TRAIN, BUS & FERRY

The national rail service links the main towns and cities with Amsterdam. Buses cover most other areas. It's a 20-minute car/passenger ferry crossing between Den Helder and Texel.

CAR & BICYCLE

A car or a bicycle is handy for exploring. Towns usually have some free parking, or you can pay for timed street parking via the Easypark app (*easypark.com*). Hire an e-bike on Texel.

BEARPOTOS/SHUTTERSTOCK

Teylers Museum (p129), Haarlem

Plan Your Time

You can see a lot in a few days in this area because distances are short and transport is easy. Many of these places could be visited on a day trip from Amsterdam.

A Two-Day Stay

● Go boating and wandering in Haarlem, exploring its superb **Teylers** (p129) and **Frans Hals** (p129) museums. Spend the afternoon in nearby **Zuid-Kennemerland National Park** (p131) or hit the **beach** (p131).

● Visit **Zaanse Schans** (p139), a heritage village with a waterway lined by eight windmills and small museums and gabled, green-painted townhouses.

With One Week

● Follow the two-day itinerary and then explore historic maritime **Hoorn** (p145) and **Enkhuizen** (p145). Don't miss the latter's fantastic open-air museum.

● Check out cheese-centric, surprisingly untouristy **Edam** (p142), eat herring in **Volendam** (p143) and take the ferry to **Marken** (p144), a lovely back-in-time place.

Seasonal Highlights

SPRING
Tulip season in March or early April is short but oh-so sweet. Lambing season is delightful on Texel.

SUMMER
The warmer months of May to September are the prime time to visit towns and villages. Alkmaar hosts the **TAPT** beer festival *(taptfestival.nl)* in June.

AUTUMN
It's a lovely time to explore the area's national parks, including Zuid-Kennemerland, and to see Zaanse Schans with a dash of autumn colour.

WINTER
Zuid-Kennemerland National Park is beautiful in winter. It's quiet, misty and a good time to spot birds. Haarlem has a Christmas market in early December.

Haarlem

MUSEUMS | HISTORY | ART

GETTING AROUND

Haarlem's 1908 art nouveau station is served by frequent trains linking Amsterdam and Rotterdam. Bus 300 runs between the bus station behind Haarlem's train station and Schiphol airport (40 minutes, every 15 minutes).

The best way to get around is by bike. You can cycle the 20km to Amsterdam along bike paths, but it's an urban rather than a scenic route.

☑ TOP TIP

The I amsterdam Card covers many sights in Haarlem, including the Teylers (p129) and Frans Hals (p129) museums, a Haarlem canal cruise, and public transport between the two cities.

Charm-packed Haarlem is only a 15-minute train ride from Amsterdam. The capital of North Holland has it all: flower-fronted gabled houses, canals, fine museums, restaurants, bars and a laidback feel. West of the city are coastal dunes, white-sand beaches and the wildlife-filled Nationaal Park Zuid-Kennemerland.

The name Haarlem derives from Haarloheim, roughly meaning 'forest homestead on a dune'. It dates from the 10th century, when the counts of Holland set up a toll post on the Spaarne River. It soon became the most important inland port after Amsterdam until the Spanish pillaged the city in 1572. In the 1600s, Haarlem became the focus of 'tulip mania' as the stately flower became the ultimate status symbol.

After Willem the Silent finally repelled the Spanish, Haarlem again boomed and in 1658 gave its name to the Dutch town of Harlem in what's now New York City.

Explore Haarlem's Historic Heart

Architectural highlights

The florid, crenellated 14th-century **Stadhuis** (Town Hall) dominates Grote Markt, fronted by a balcony. In the past, the high court announced its judgments from here. It opens to the public only on Open Monuments Day (the second weekend of September). Adjoining the town hall is the **Hoofdwacht**, or 'head watch', which dates from the 13th century and once served as the town jail.

The square also houses an 1856 bronze statue of local printer **Laurens Coster**, thought to be one of the inventors of movable type.

Off Grote Houtstraat, about a 10-minute walk southwest of Grote Markt, is the enchantingly pretty **Proveniershuis**, three residences around an inner courtyard. It started life as a *hofje* (almshouse) and for a time became the headquarters of St Joris Doelen (the Civic Guard of St George).

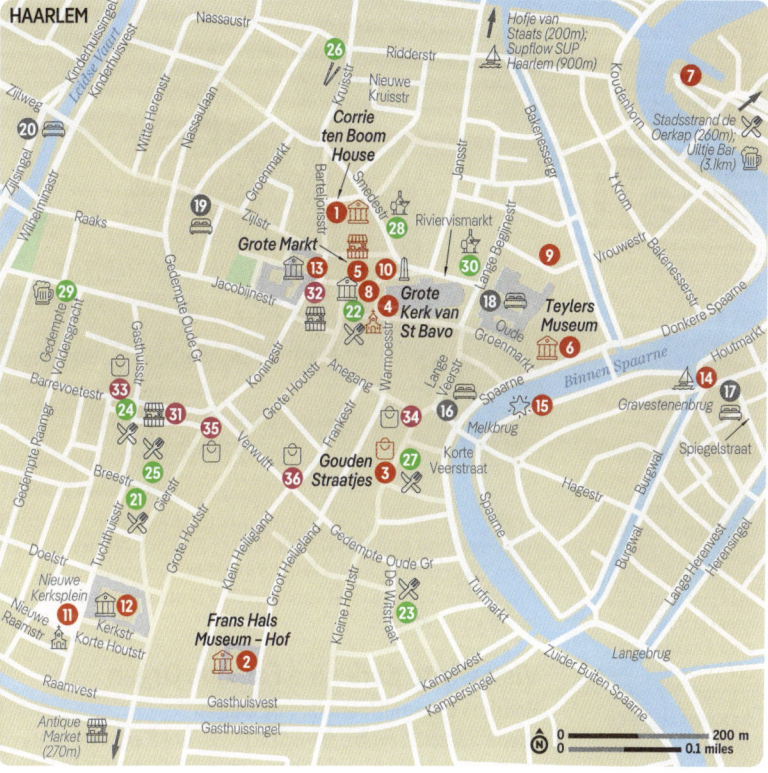

HAARLEM & NORTH HOLLAND HAARLEM

⭐ **HIGHLIGHTS**
1 Corrie ten Boom House
2 Frans Hals Museum – Hof
3 Gouden Straatjes
4 Grote Kerk van St Bavo
5 Grote Markt
6 Teylers Museum

🔴 **SIGHTS**
7 De Molen Adriaan
8 Frans Hals Museum – Hal
9 Hofje van Bakenes
10 Laurens Coster Statue
11 Nieuwe Kerk
12 Proveniershuis
13 Stadhuis

🔴 **ACTIVITIES**
14 Free Movement
15 Haarlem Canal Tours

⚫ **SLEEPING**
16 Brasss Hotel Suites
17 Hello I'm Local Boutique Hostel
18 Hotel ML
19 MAF Haarlem Boutique Hotel
20 Niu Dairy Haarlem

🟢 **EATING**
21 Brick
22 De Haerlemsche Vlaamse
23 DeDakkas
24 Mogador Cafe

25 Native
26 Ramen Brothers
see 18 Restaurant ML
27 Toast

🟢 **DRINKING & NIGHTLIFE**
28 Bar Wigbolt
29 Jopenkerk
30 Proeflokaal in den Uiver

🔴 **SHOPPING**
31 Botermarkt
32 Christmas Market
33 De KaasKampanje van Haarlem
34 Dille & Kamille
35 Drogisterij van der Pigge
36 Sûr Atelier

BEST SHOPS

Gouden Straatjes: Haarlem's 'Golden Streets' are full of independent boutiques selling clothing, vinyl and accessories.

Sûr Atelier: Slow fashion with lovely pared-down Scandi style stitched by migrants who have settled in the Netherlands. *(sur-atelier.nl)*

Drogisterij van der Pigge: Historic apothecary selling herbal remedies since 1849 that features a gaper (a traditional model head with an open mouth) outside. *(vanderpigge.nl)*

De KaasKampanje van Haarlem: Superb Dutch cheeses, charcuterie and olives, plus tastings and wine and beer pairing suggestions. *(kaaskampanje.nl)*

Dille & Kamille: Chain of homewares shops selling nicely designed, reasonably priced kitchen items. *(dille-kamille.com)*

WOLF PHOTOGRAPHY/SHUTTERSTOCK

Grote Kerk van St Bavo

Take a right along charming Korte Houtstraat and turn right again to find the 17th-century red-brick **Nieuwe Kerk** *(New Church; bavo.nl; closed Sun)*. The ornate tower by architect Lieven de Key is supported by a boxy design by artist Jacob van Campen.

Visit Grote Kerke & a Famous Organ

Haarlem's magnificent Gothic church

Dominating the centre of town is the **Grote Kerk van St Bavo** *(bavo.nl; adult/child €4/free; closed Sun),* with a towering 50m-high steeple. Dating from the 13th century, the building was rebuilt in the 1400s, retaining its Gothic look. Topped by a lantern tower, it was once the city's Catholic cathedral, but it was stripped of much of the interior decoration and turned into a Protestant place of worship during the Reformation. Look at the beautiful 16th-century choir screen, beyond which is the grave of painter Frans Hals. In the **Battery Chapel**, you can see a cannonball, preserved from the Spanish siege of 1573. On the other side, the **Dog-Whipper's Chapel** is devoted to the medieval role of keeping dogs in order in the church.

Several times weekly, you can listen to musicians play classical music on Grote Kerk's splendid, 30m-tall organ, constructed by organ builder Christian Müller with sculptor Jan van

---

EATING IN HAARLEM: OUR PICKS

Ramen Brothers: Authentic Japanese ramen served in a small, high-ceilinged interior with a few outdoor tables. *4.30-9pm, plus noon-3pm Sat & Sun* €€

Brick: An open kitchen, glass floor and spectacular bistro-style food. *5.30-10pm, plus noon-3pm Fri-Sun* €€

De Haerlemsche Vlaamse: The best fries in Haarlem, if not the Netherlands. *noon-6pm Mon-Sat, from 11am Sun* €

Toast: Lovely, relaxed place decorated with blonde wood, plants and oatmeal-coloured cushions. Serves delicious salads, eggs and cakes. *8am-5pm* €€

Logteren in 1738. Georg Friedrich Händel came here twice to play it, and it was also tinkled by a 10-year-old Wolfgang Amadeus Mozart.

Come Face to Face with the 17th Century
Frans Hals, Haarlem's adopted genius

Reason alone to visit Haarlem is the Hof branch of the superb **Frans Hals Museum** *(franshalsmuseum.nl; adult/child €17.50/free; closed Mon)*. Here you'll see firsthand what led painters such as Cézanne, Van Gogh and Courbet to revere his work.

Hals' work fizzes with life, the faces as vivid as the people you pass in the streets outside. You'll also see other great artists' work, from Pieter Brueghel to Sarah Lucas, and an 18th-century Dutch favourite: a monumental doll's house that's a miniature museum rather than a plaything.

The **Frans Hals Museum – Hal** is the contemporary-art branch, open only when there is an exhibition on. It occupies a 17th-century butcher and fish *hal* (hall) a short walk away.

WWII History at the Corrie ten Boom House
WWII hiding place

Like the Anne Frank House (p67) in Amsterdam, a visit to the **Corrie ten Boom Huis** *(corrietenboom.com; free; English tours 10am, noon & 2pm Tue-Sat)* takes you into viscerally painful WWII history, as you visit the secret compartments used to hide Jews and Dutch resistors from the Nazis. Corrie ten Boom and her family risked their lives to save those persecuted. In 1944, they were betrayed and sent to concentration camps, where three of them died. Visit via free guided hourlong tours; reserve at least five days ahead.

Visit Teyler's Extraordinary Museum
Home and treasure trove

If you like beautiful museums that feel like they themselves should be in a museum, you will love this place. With polished wood atriums and glass cases, **Teylers Museum** *(teylersmuseum.nl; adult/child €17.50/free; closed Mon)* was founded after wealthy cloth merchant and philanthropist Pieter Teyler died without an heir and specified in his will that he wanted his collections preserved for posterity.

BEST MARKETS

Grote Markt: Haarlem's 'Big Market' is on Mondays and Saturdays, with stalls selling fresh produce, cheese, preserves, spices, snacks, clothes (vintage and new) and antiques.

Botermarkt: On a small city square, the 'Butter Market' has vintage stalls on Mondays and Wednesdays, and it's piled high with food and produce on Fridays and Saturdays.

Antique Market: Every second Saturday from April to October brings out stalls along the Dreef selling vintage items and antiques.

Christmas Market: For a weekend in mid-December, the historic centre is filled with traditional Christmas stalls selling arts, crafts and *bischopswijn* (mulled wine).

 EATING IN HAARLEM: RELAXED EATS

DeDakkas: A fabulous cafe-restaurant in a greenhouse on top of a multistorey car park. *10am-10pm Sun, Tue & Wed, to 11pm Thu, 10am-midnight Fri & Sat €€*

Native: Artsy cafe in the Golden Streets area, serving brunch, soups and salads. *8am-5pm Mon-Fri, from 9am Sat & Sun €*

Mogador Cafe: Small place with excellent cakes, brownies and coffees. *8am-5pm Mon-Sat, from 9am Sun €*

Stadsstrand de Oerkap: Beach bar just outside the city centre, with street food and beers on tap. *10am-11pm Tue-Fri, from 11am Sat & Sun €€*

NIGEL J. HARRIS/SHUTTERSTOCK

HAARLEM'S HOFJES

Haarlem is particularly well known for its 21 *hofjes*, charitable almshouses centred on courtyard gardens. These almshouses were for women only, as elderly single men were housed in group homes, such as the building that houses the Frans Hals Museum (p129).

Haarlem has the oldest *hofjes* in the Netherlands, the 13th-century **Hofje van Bakenes**, just off the Bakenesser- gracht. **Hofje van Staats**, off Jansweg, is one of the prettiest and the largest, with 30 houses around a courtyard, founded by a yarn merchant for women over 50.

De Molen Adriaan

As part of your visit, you can visit the graceful townhouse where first Teyler and then the museum creators lived. The museum contains well-labelled fossils (including fascinating fake fossils with a great backstory), early inventions, and fac- similes of drawings by Michelangelo, Rembrandt and Piranesi.

Climb Haarlem's Windmill

Tours of De Molen Adriaan

The windmill that dominates a bend on the Spaarne River is **De Molen Adriaan** *(molenadriaan.nl; adult/child €7.50/3.50)*, built in the 18th century to help produce cement. During a 45-minute visit guided by volunteers, you get to climb its nar- row stairs to see a great view across Haarlem. The much-loved windmill burned down in 1932, and Haarlemmers collected money to rebuild it.

Boating in Haarlem

Views from the water

It's wonderful to see the city from the water. **Haarlem Canal Tours** *(haarlemcanaltours.com; adult/child €19/9.50)* offers a 75-minute tour in vintage open-top boats, with commentary by local guides. Hire a standup paddleboard or book a tour with **Supflow SUP Haarlem** *(supflow.nl; 1½hr per person €25)*. **Free Movement** *(freemovement.nl; 1hr kayak/SUP hire €25/17.50)* also offers SUP yoga.

DRINKING IN HAARLEM: OUR PICKS

Proeflokaal in Den Uiver: A proper old- school Dutch brown cafe. *4pm-midnight Sun-Wed, to 1am Thu-Sat*

Bar Wigbolt: This cosy bottle-backed place mixes up great cocktails. *6.30pm-2am Wed-Sun*

Jopenkerk: Independent brewery inside a 1910 church. *10am-11.30pm Sun-Thu, to 1am Fri & Sat*

Uiltje Bar: Local brewery's cute little 'owl bar' (*uiltje* means owl). *3-11pm Mon- Wed, to midnight Thu, to 2am Fri & Sat, to 9.30pm Sun*

Beyond
Haarlem

It's easy to reach white-sand beaches, lush forests, historic towns and seasonal tulip fields using Haarlem as a base.

Only 7km northwest of Haarlem are the dunes, lagoons, lakes and forest of Zuid-Kennemerland National Park and Bloemendaal aan Zee. About 9km south is Europe's largest playground, Linnaeushof. If you're here in March and early April, there are some huge tulip fields both to the south and the north of the city.

A little further, still just an hour by train north of Haarlem, Alkmaar has an excellent art museum and some fine architecture, and is famous for its cheese market. Make time to visit the nearby Museum BroekerVeiling, with a chance to take part in a floating auction. Find more tulip fields around here in spring.

Zuid-Kennemerland National Park

TIME FROM HAARLEM: 30MIN 🚲

Sights, cycling and swimming

Less than 5km west of Haarlem are the dunes, lakes, lagoons and Corsican firs of **Zuid-Kennemerland National Park** (*np-zuidkennemerland.nl*). It's a fantastic place to walk, cycle and swim.

A good starting point is **De Zandwaaier Visitor Centre** (*free; closed Mon*), which has bike hire, maps and a good cafe. Only a five-minute cycle from here is **Het Wed**, a lake ideal for swimming. Ten minutes further by bike is **Strand Oosterpas**, a lake that's hugely popular for a swim on sunny days.

At 50m tall, the **Kopje van Bloemendaal** is the highest dune in the country, just outside the eastern border of the park, with views of the sea and Amsterdam. Members of the Dutch Resistance are laid to rest at the cemetery, **Erebegraafplaats Bloemendaal** (*erebegraafplaatsbloemendaal.eu*).

To reach the park, take bus 81 from Haarlem train station, drive the N200 towards Bloemendaal aan Zee or cycle out of Haarlem along Brouwersvaart.

Fun at the white-sand beach

Around 7.5km west of central Haarlem is a long, gleaming beach, **Bloemendaal aan Zee**. On a hot day, it feels glorious, though the North Sea is distinctly less Caribbean than the soft white sands imply. It's backed by laid-back restaurants

Places

Zuid-Kennemerland National Park p131

Bennebroek p132

Alkmaar p132

GETTING AROUND

Haarlem has no bike-share programmes, but there is local bike hire. You can cycle, take the bus or drive to Zuid-Kennemerland National Park and the beaches at Bloemendaal aan Zee and Zandvoort. Parking is paid in central Haarlem, but there is some free parking in the streets outside the centre.

Haarlem is well connected by train and bus. As well as the 15-minute journey to Amsterdam, which has connections all over the Netherlands, it's 45 minutes north to Alkmaar.

FLORA & FAUNA IN ZUIDKENNEME-LAND

Zuid-Kennemerland National Park teems with wildlife, and it's a great destination for nature enthusiasts and bird-watchers. Among its most striking residents are the shy, shaggy Highland cattle, handsomely rust-coloured and horned, introduced in 2016. In the dune area of Kraansvlak, you might spot European bison. Spring carpets the sandy landscape with wildflowers, from desert orchids and rosettes of century weed to the delicate white blooms of Parnassus grass. Native red foxes, fallow deer and myriad bird species thrive throughout the park, and as evening falls, bats emerge from abandoned wartime bunkers to whirr through the twilight skies.

and cafes, with sunbeds and tasty food, especially the pirate-ship-centred **Woodstock 69** (p133) and **Rapa Nui** (p133). It starts to heat up on summer evenings with pop-up DJ events. Various outfits offer watersports such as kitesurfing. Take bus 81 here from Haarlem (every 15 minutes), or it's a half-hour bike ride.

Bennebroek

TIME FROM HAARLEM: 30MIN 🚲

Europe's largest playground

About 9km south of Haarlem is Europe's biggest playground, **Linnaeushof** *(linnaeushof.nl; €18)*. If you're travelling with kids, the colourful slides, tubes, climbing frames, water park, imaginative play areas, a lake with pedaloes, go-karts and mushroom-shaped playhouses make it a worthwhile trip for all-out entertainment. Separate areas with more challenging equipment are geared towards older children, and there's an indoor play area in case of bad weather. You can cycle or take bus 250 to get here.

Alkmaar

TIME FROM HAARLEM: 25MIN 🚌

Beer and cheese

Alkmaar is a handsome medieval town, most famous for the flourishing tourist spectacle of its **Kaasmarkt** (cheese market), held on Fridays between April and September. It's photo-op heaven, full of porters in colourful cheese-guild hats, pulling wedges piled on wooden sledges. Dealers in white smocks insert a hollow rod to extract a cheese sample, and sniff and crumble to check fat and moisture content.

The town centres on the pin-striped Gothic **Stadhuis**, Alkmaar's Town Hall, built between 1509 and 1520, with a Dutch Classicist wing added in 1694. A few hundred metres to the east is the **Waaggebouw** (Weigh House), a 14th-century chapel that two centuries later became the town's cheese weighing centre. The crenellated gable was added after the town withstood the 16th-century Spanish siege. It now contains the tourist office and **Hollands Kaasmuseum** *(kaasmuseum.nl; adult/child €6/2.50)*, a cheese museum.

Close by is the De Boom brewery, housing the **Nationaal Biermuseum** *(biermuseum.nl; tour €17.50; noon-5pm Thu-Sun),* a deep dive into the amber nectar, featuring beer-making equipment. Admission includes a drink in its sociable bar, and there's also the historic **De Boom** *(proeflokaaldeboom.nl)* downstairs, a lovely old pub on the canal.

INTO THE WOODS

For more forest and even more dunes, head to **Duinen van Texel National Park** (p135).

BEARFOTOS/SHUTTERSTOCK

Canal, Alkmaar

Alkmaar art

Art lovers should stop at the **Stedelijk Museum** *(stedelijk museumalkmaar.nl; adult/child €17/free, closed Mon)*, which includes artist Charley Toorop's fiercely realistic painting of the town cheese porters, as well as paintings by other members of the influential Bergen school, a modernist art movement that developed in the nearby village of Bergen, in the early 20th century. Like most Dutch museums, it has a great shop.

See floating farms and place an auction bid

The marshland area north of Alkmaar was once home to 15,000 tiny but productive farms, each on an island. Farmers tended their crops by rowboat. One of these farms, **Broek op Langedijk**, which oddly translates as 'trousers on the long dyke', has a historic floating auction village, now a museum.

The fascinating **Museum BroekerVeiling** *(broekerveiling. nl; adult/child €19.75/9.75; closed Mon)* is based around the

SIEGE OF ALKMAAR

This small town has a proud history. The townspeople used floodwater to beat back the invading Spanish in 1573. The Siege of Alkmaar took place during the Eighty Years' War, when Spanish forces attempted to capture the town.

Despite being outnumbered, Alkmaar's citizens mounted a fierce defence, using boiling tar and water, and eventually breaching dykes to flood the surrounding fields, forcing the Spanish to retreat. The victory at Alkmaar became a turning point in the war, and there's a costumed celebratory parade here every 8 October.

EATING & DRINKING IN ZUID-KENNEMERLAND: OUR PICKS

Het Duincafé: Indoor and outdoor seating and a playground at this cafe at the park's visitor centre. *8am-5.30pm* €	**Parnassia aan Zee**: Tuck into hamburgers, salads and fries while enjoying sea views from the terrace. *9am-9pm* €€	**Ron Gastrobar**: Upscale, creative Indonesian cuisine. *5-10.30pm Wed, from 11am Thu-Sun* €€	**Kraantje Lek**: Historic red-shuttered pub with a superb playground. *9am-5pm Mon & Tue, to 10pm Wed-Fri, 9am-midnight Sat & Sun* €€
Woodstock 69: Cool beach bar with pirate-style decor and wholesome food. *noon-10pm or later*	**Rapa Nui**: Tropical decor and Indonesian dishes at this beach bar. *10am-9pm Mon-Fri, to 10pm Sat & Sun* €€	**Ubuntu Beach**: Boho Zandvoort beach bar with Bali vibes. *9am-midnight*	**Hippie Fish**: Zandvoort cafe with lots of macrame and Buddha bowls. *9am-midnight* €€

ON THE WATER FROM ALKMAAR

Grachtenrondvaart Alkmaar: Runs 45-minute canal tours *(adult/child €6/4.50)* every hour, passing under some 22 bridges. Departs from the jetty on Mient. *(rondvaartalkmaar.nl)*

El Kombi SUP: Lessons, standup paddleboard hire *(per 1½hr €20)* or guided tours from its base close to the city centre. *(elkombi.nl)*

De Kraak: Offers self-drive boats *(per hr €15)*, as well as kayak and SUP hire. *(dekraak.nl)*

Alkmaar Cruises: Go further afield with this outfit, whose tours go as far as Zaanse Schans or Fort Marken. *(alkmaarcruises.nl)*

Pesie Rent a Bike: Hire a bike/e-bike/tandem/cargo bike *(per day €13/28/23/50). (pesierentabike.nl)*

OSSIP VAN DUIVENBODE/STEDELIJK MUSEUM AMSTERDAM

Stedelijk Museum (p133)

extraordinary 1877 auction house at the centre of a waterlogged area. The structure sits on 1900 piles and has canals running through it. Take a seat on the wooden benches in the auction room where buyers used to bid on produce as farmers paddled it through on boats. The museum gives you an opportunity to take part in an auction, which is great fun. Visitors can press a button to make a bid. The fastest bidder wins whichever vegetable is on sale, which you can take home to cook.

Tickets include a boat tour around the scenic floating fields, with about 200 surviving island plots that look like lozenges in the water. You can also hire an electric barge/canoe *(€27.50/7.50 per hr)* to explore the waterways yourself.

This peaceful village is clustered around its waterways, and lots of tulip fields bloom here in spring. You can cycle here from Alkmaar – the picturesque 9km bike path follows canals and passes through the tiny old village of Sint Pancras.

 EATING IN ALKMAAR: OUR PICKS

Abby's: Terrace bistro with a lovely greenery-filled outdoor seating area in the shade of a windmill. *11am-10pm Tue-Sun* €€

Cafe Restaurant De Buren: Canal-side restaurant with international dishes and lovely outdoor seating on the bridge. *10am-midnight* €€

De Vlaminck: Family run, with superb fries served with sauces from peanut to Zaanse mayonnaise. *11am-7pm Tue-Sat* €

Heeren van Sonoy: Eat sandwiches and light meals in a 16th-century nunnery amid carved wood furniture or outside in the cloister. *11am-midnight* €€

Texel

DUNES | SEALS | WATERSPORTS

The Wadden Islands speckle the UNESCO-listed Wad-denzee (Wadden Sea) above the Netherlands' northern coast. Texel (pronounced tes-sel) is the largest, closest and easiest to reach. It measures about 25km by 9km and is pancake-flat. Ringed by white-sand beaches, Texel is popular as a holiday destination for seal-spotting offshore, visiting the excellent Ecomare aquarium and Museum Kaap Skil (which displays artefacts rescued from shipwrecks), lounging on the beach, roaming around nature reserves and pedalling through forests. Sheep are everywhere. The local wool is highly prized, and there are numerous dairies producing cheese. During lambing season, people enjoy taking a *lammetjes wandeltrocht* (walk to look at the lambs).

Texel has more than 140km of well-signposted cycling routes. Swimming, sailing, kitesurfing, skydiving and horse riding are all popular pursuits. At the ferry terminal in Den Hoorn, Rijwielverhuur Veerhaven hires standard and electric bikes. The latter are worthwhile if you want to cover the whole island.

GETTING AROUND

Get to Texel on a 30-minute ferry from Den Helder. Bus 28, run by Texelhopper *(texelhopper.nl)*, operates throughout the year. Buy tickets in advance online, at Den Helder's train station, at Texel's tourist office or at large supermarkets. Alternatively, use an OV-chipkaart.

Texel is a great place to cycle, and you can cover a lot of ground with an e-bike.

Into the Dunes

Sand-scapes along Texel's west coast

Much of **Duinen van Texel National Park** *(npduinenvan texel.nl)* is a bird sanctuary and accessible only on foot. Book excellent two-hour ranger-led dune walks at **Ecomare** (p137).

South of Ecomare is the dark, leafy forest of **De Dennen**, between Den Hoorn and De Koog. Originally planted as a source of lumber, today it has an enchanting network of walking and cycling paths. In spring, snowdrops bloom, first planted here in the 1930s.

On the northwest coast, beautiful **De Slufter Nature Reserve** became a brackish wetland after land reclamation failed, while to the south, reclamation succeeded at the freshwater area of **De Muy**, renowned for its colony of spoonbills that are monitored with great zeal by local naturalists.

☑ **TOP TIP**

Texel is famous for its sheep cheese, fresh seafood and local beer from the Texel Brewery. It's worth carrying cash so you can buy produce using the honesty boxes.

TEXEL

NORTH
SEA

De Slufter

De Muy

De Cocksdorp

Klimpstraat

Hollandseweg

Hoofdweg

Postweg

Oosterenderweg

Hoofdweg

Slufterweg

Muyweg

Schorrenweg

De Koog

POLDER WAAL EN BURG

Oosterend

Ecomare

Duinen van Texel
National Park

Nieuwlanderweg

De Staart

De Waal

Hoofdweg

Oosterenderweg

Lancasterdijk

De
Dennen

Postweg

Rozendijk

Westerweg

Den Burg

Schilderweg

Oudeschild

Kaap Skil
Museum

Waddenzee

Bulb
Fields

Hemmerweg

Den Hoorn

Hoornderweg

N501

Portweg

Redoute

De Rade

Veerhaven

't Horntje

Hors

N

0 ——————————— 5 km
0 ——————————— 2.5 miles

★ **HIGHLIGHTS**
1 Duinen van Texel
  National Park
2 Ecomare
3 Kaap Skil Museum

● **SIGHTS**
4 De Dennen
5 De Kroon van Texel
6 De Muy
7 De Slufter
  Nature Reserve

8 De Zelfpluktuin
9 Eierland Lighthouse
10 Kaasboerderij
   Wezenspyk

● **ACTIVITIES**
see 23 De Eilander
11 Jan Plezier
12 Natuurmonumenten
13 Tessel Air
see 2 Texel 44
see 2 Texelstroom

14 TXGids

● **SLEEPING**
15 Bij Jef
16 Boutique Hotel Texel
17 Stayokay Texel

● **EATING**
18 De Winroos
19 Novalishoeve
see 2 't Pakhuus
see 2 Vispaleis Rokerij
   van der Star

● **DRINKING &
NIGHTLIFE**
20 Landgoed de
   Bonte Belevenis
21 Stokerij Texel
22 Texelse Bierbrouwerij

● **TRANSPORT**
23 Rederij de Vriendschap
24 Rijwielverhuur
   Veerhaven

Seal Spotting
Fascinating aquarium and nature centre
Ecomare *(ecomare.nl; adult/child €16/11)* was created as a refuge for sick seals. The huge aquariums are filled with fish from the Waddenzee and North Sea, including sharks. Playful *zeehonden* ('sea dogs', Dutch for seals) are the highlight.

Climb the Eierland Lighthouse
Superb windswept panoramas
Battered by storms and war, Texel's resilient mascot, 35m-high **Eierland Lighthouse** *(vuurtorentexel.nl; adult/child €6/free)*, on the northern coast, was built in 1864. Climb its 153 steps for sweeping views. Book tickets online.

See Treasure from Shipwrecks
Gloriously cluttered museum
Texel's marvellous **Kaap Skil Museum** *(Marine and Beach-combers Museum; kaapskil.nl; adult/child €12/8.50; closed Mon Nov-Mar)* has a mind-boggling array of treasure recovered from shipwrecks discovered around the island, including a 17th-century silver wedding dress. In the basement is a huge maritime model with about 160 exquisitely constructed sailing ships.

The Great Outdoors
Watersports, horse-drawn wagons and kitesurfing
Texel is a great place for outdoor pursuits. Ecomare, **Natuur-monumenten** *(natuurmonumenten.nl)* and **TXGids** *(txgids.nl)* offer fun mudflat walks.

Hire catamarans from **De Eilander** *(deeilander.nl; May-Oct)* near the Vlieland boat dock. The outfit also runs sailing courses. Take a cruise around the Waddenzee on a beautiful sailing ship, such as the **Texelstroom** *(texelstroom.nl)* or **Texel 44** *(tx44.nl)*. **Jan Plezier** *(janpleziertexel.nl)* has offered scenic horse-drawn wagon rides since 1928. Soar above the island on a scenic flight with **Tessel Air** *(boeking.tessel-air.nl)*.

Take a Boat to Vlieland
Trip across the Waddenzee
Rederij de Vriendschap *(waddenveer.nl; adult/child €42.50/32.50)* offers day trips (no bikes) to the neighbouring, car-free island of **Vlieland** from mid-May to September. The crossing takes an hour, and it's a fun way to see the smallest inhabited Wadden island and its desert.

BEST TEXEL TASTINGS

De Kroon van Texel: Vineyard tours run from May to September; tastings are year-round. *(wijngaarddekroon-vantexel.nl)*

Texelse Bierbrouwerij: Former dairy that's now a brewery with tours. *(texels.nl)*

De Zelfpluktuin: Pick your own fruit and vegetables. A cafe and a shop sell produce. *(zelfpluktuin.nl)*

Kaasboerderij Wezenspyk: Sample local cheeses at this small dairy between Den Hoorn and Den Burg. *(wezenspyk.nl)*

Landgoed de Bonte Belevenis: Beer and whisky tastings for the grownups and crafts for kids. *(landgoeddebonte belevenis.nl)*

Stokerij Texel: Artisanal gin and beer, with weekly tours. *(txtexel.nl)*

EATING ON TEXEL: OUR PICKS

Novalishoeve: This cafe supports people with disabilities. It has animals and a playground. *9.30am-4.30pm Mon-Sat* €

De Winroos: Forest- and dune-side garden cafe, with cakes and soups that use local organic produce. *10.30am-5pm Wed-Fri* €

Vispaleis Rokerij van der Star: Fishmonger with classic dishes, fish soup and *kibbeling* (pieces of fried fish). *8.30am-6pm Mon-Sat* €

't Pakhuus: Former warehouse serving fresh fish and Oosterschelde lobster with wow-factor seafood platters. *5.30-10pm Thu-Sun* €€€

Beyond
Texel

The naval port of Den Helder is the springboard for Texel, and it has an excellent museum, aquarium and 19th-century fort.

Places

Den Helder p138

GETTING AROUND

Den Helder station has good train connections to Amsterdam (1¼ hours). Bus 33 runs between the station and the ferry port for Texel, a distance of 2km, which you can also cycle or walk. Bus 37 takes about 10 minutes to the fort from the station and 35 minutes from the ferry port.

Den Helder, the Netherlands' principal naval base, might appear unremarkable at first glance, but for maritime history enthusiasts, it's a destination rich in naval heritage. Strategically located in the North Sea, Den Helder has served as a critical seafaring and defensive stronghold for centuries. It was significantly fortified during the Napoleonic era, and in 1814 it became the official home of the Royal Netherlands Navy. Its Marine Museum collection dates from this point.

Today, Den Helder remains the country's naval base and gateway to the Wadden Islands with regular ferries, but if you have time and an interest in maritime and military history, it's worth exploring the sights.

Den Helder

TIME FROM TEXEL: 20MIN

Explore the hands-on Marine Museum

You take the ferry to Texel from Den Helder, and the port is close to the armoury of the Royal Netherlands Navy, which now houses the magnificent **Marine Museum** *(marinemuseum.nl; adult/child €13/8; closed Mon Nov-Mar)*, with an impressive array of ships and models. Most exciting is the huge Tonijn submarine outside. You also have the opportunity to clamber into an extremely claustrophobic submarine berth and peer through working periscopes.

Roam around Fort Kijkduin

Built under Napoleon's orders in 1811 to accommodate 1400 soldiers, the hulking hilltop **Fort Kijkduin** *(fortkijkduin.nl; adult/child €11.50/9.50)*, 4km east of Den Helder, was originally called Fort Morland. It now houses a military museum incorporating an armoury and a fantastic subterranean aquarium with 14 tanks filled with every species of marine life from the Waddenzee and North Sea, one with a walk-through tunnel. It's a good one- to two-hour visit.

Zaanse Schans

WINDMILLS | LANDSCAPES | HISTORY

North of Amsterdam, herons stand sentinel over fields of rice-paddy green punctuated by houses and windmills. The Zaan region unfolds in flat, fertile fields sliced by canals and dotted with farmhouses, windmills, cows and woolly white sheep. It was, at the height of early industrial activity, home to about 1000 windmills.

At the heart of the region lies Zaanse Schans, one of the Netherlands' most popular heritage sites. Its beautifully preserved green-painted wooden houses and working windmills showcase historic crafts like oil pressing, spice grinding and paintmaking. Volunteers and artisans still demonstrate clog carving and cheese making, allowing insights into the Netherlands' industrial and rural past (with plenty of shops attached).

The village had 2.6 million visitors in 2024, and from 2026, visitors will be charged €17.50, which includes admission to several sights, in an effort to limit numbers. The area is much less busy outside the summer months.

GETTING AROUND

Zaanse Schans is 18km north of Amsterdam, and it's a lovely cycle ride. Starting from Amsterdam Centraal Station, take the IJ ferry. After this, the route heads northwest through Amsterdam Noord. You reach the small town of Zaandam first. It's a pretty (and flat) route. Bike hire is available in every town.

 ## EATING IN ZAANSE SCHANS: OUR PICKS

Het Zaanse Bakkertje: Across the bridge from the windmills, this excellent bakery is good for stocking up on picnic fare. *7am-3pm Wed-Sat* €

Het Zaanse Hoekje: Sunny, family-run restaurant with a Dutch take on brasserie food. *11am-10pm Thu-Sun* €€

't Groene Pandje: Cosy wooden house serving international fare and good Dutch pancakes. *9am-5pm Mon & Sat, to 6pm Tue-Fri, 10am-6pm Sun* €€

Brouwerij Hoop: Brewery with a restaurant serving burgers and similar grub. Less touristy than other local choices. *noon-11pm* €€

ZAANSE SCHANS

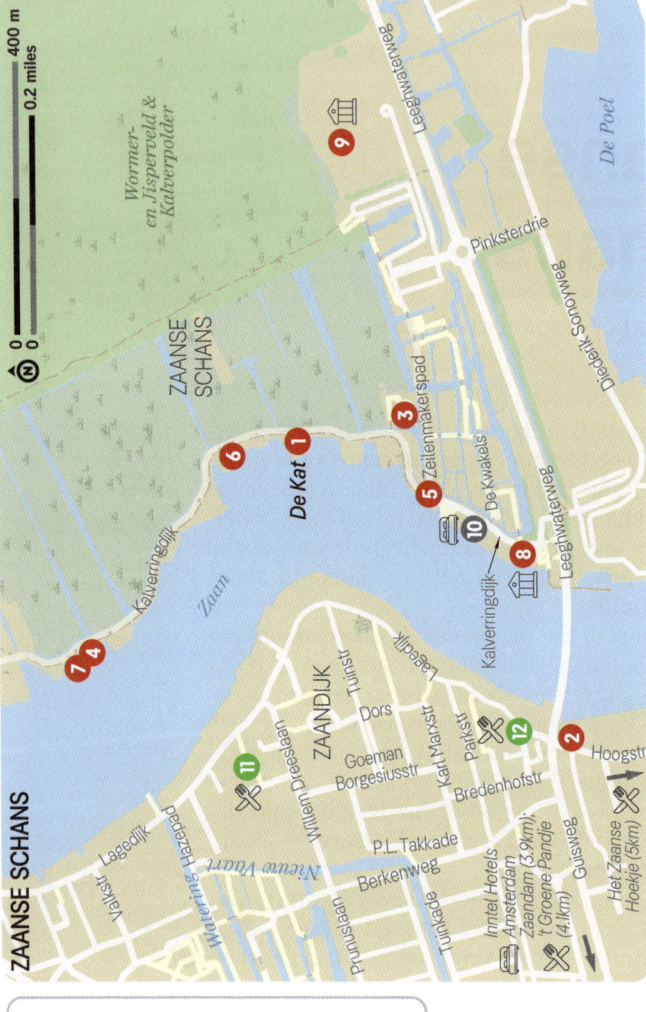

400 m
0.2 miles

Wormer-
en-Jisperveld &
Kalverpolder

ZAANSE
SCHANS

De Poel

Pinksterdrie

De Kat

Zeilenmakerspad

De Kwakels

Kalverringdijk

Zaan

Kalverringdijk

ZAANDIJK

Tuinstr

Lagedijk

Dors

Kat Marxstr

Parkstr

Goeman
Borgesiusstr

Bredenhofstr

Hoogstr

Valkstr

Lagedijk

Willem Dreeslaan

Wateringe Hazepad

Nieuw Vaart

P.L. Takkade

Berkenweg

Prunuslaan

Tuinkade

Guisweg

Inntel Hotels
Amsterdam
Zaandam (3.9km),
't Groene Pandje
(4.1km)

Het Zaanse
Hoekje (5km)

Leeghwaterweg

Diepedijk Sonoyweg

Leeghwaterweg

HIGHLIGHTS
1 De Kat

SIGHTS
2 Bleeke Dood
3 Catharina Hoeve Cheese Farm
4 De Bonte Hen
5 De Huisman
6 De Zoeker
7 Het Klaverblad
8 Museumwinkel Albert Heijn
9 Zaans Museum

SLEEPING
10 B&B Heerlijck Slaapen op de Zaanse
Schans

EATING
11 Brouwerij Hoop
12 Het Zaanse Bakkertje

Visit Zaanse Schans' Windmills

History in motion

Gloriously pretty and resembling a fantasy of Dutch early industrial life, Zaanse Schans' **windmills** *(dezaanseschans. nl; per windmill adult/child €7.50/3.75)* are mostly still functioning, with enthusiastic volunteers on hand to explain the processes as you explore and get up close with the vast and complex moving parts in their interiors.

These windmills had many different purposes: **De Huisman** was a former spice mill, which used to produce the famous mustard. It's worth buying some from the mill shop because it's spectacularly good. **De Kat** is the most-visited mill, and it still produces paint and pigment. You can climb this windmill for an excellent view.

De Zoeker and **De Bonte Hen** are both oil mills, with peanut and seed oils available in their shops. **Het Klaverblad** is a sawmill, open only by appointment. **Bleeke Dood** (the 'pale death') is a flour mill that's currently closed but viewable from the outside. It's the oldest windmill in the country.

Museums of Zaanse Schans

From clogs to cheese

As well as windmills, the Zaanse Schans area has various small museums with demonstrations of local traditional crafts. They are more like shops with museums attached, but still interesting.

A clog factory turns out wooden shoes as if grinding keys. It's worth visiting the **Zaans Museum** *(zaansmuseum.nl; adult/child €10/6)*, which tells the history of the area with some interactive exhibits and local artefacts, including a letter from Claude Monet to Camille Pisarro about Zaanse, which he visited and painted at the end of the 19th century.

Catharina Hoeve Cheese Farm *(henriwillig.com; free)* has vintage interiors constructed using antique beams and doors, and it hosts cheese-making demonstrations and tastings.

The First Albert Heijn Supermarket

Vintage shopkeeping

Albert Heijn supermarkets are a familiar sight all over the Netherlands – they're the biggest chain in the country. You can visit their first incarnation at **Museumwinkel Albert Heijn** *(albertheijnerfgoed.nl; free; closed Mon)*, a delightful green-fronted gabled building. Heijn started his business in Oostzaan in 1887 after buying the shop from his father, later expanding to a warehouse in Zaanse. The original building was moved from Oostzaan in 1966 together with authentic furnishings, such as the wooden counter, scales and a beautifully decorative coffee grinder. A lectern in the corner is where Heijn did his accounts.

CREATION OF ZAANSE SCHANS

The Zaan region was home to the world's largest timber port in the 16th and 17th centuries, dotted with hundreds of windmills. In the early 20th century, they began to be demolished, and Frans Mars, a painter and educator, founded an association to try to protect them.

Local mayor Joris in 't Veld suggested moving historic buildings to an area for their preservation. Architect Jaap Schipper found the location and created the layout. Mars suggested the name Zaanse Schans from 'Kalverschans', which reflects the fortified area where Zaan residents held off the Spanish in the 16th century during the Eighty Years' War.

☑ TOP TIP

The Zaanse Schans Card *(adult/child €29.50/20)* gives you access to the Zaans Museum, Weaver's House, Museum Zaanse Tijd, Heritage Chambres Kalverringdijk, Windmill Museum, two mills of your choice and a digital audio tour. The general admission ticket (from 2026, €17.50) includes entry to the museum and windmills.

Beyond
Zaanse Schans

The lush, pancake-flat province of Waterland
spreads to the east and along the coast to handsome historic towns.

Places

Edam p142
Volendam p143
Marken p144
Hoorn p145
Enkhuizen p145
Muiden p146
Naarden p147
Urk p148
Schokland p148
Lelystad p148

GETTING AROUND

Local towns are well connected by bus and train, with regular trains from Amsterdam to Zaandam, Hoorn and Enkhuizen. Ferries link Volendam and the former island of Marken, also accessible by road. A scenic way to reach Muiden is by boat from IJburg, which also stops at Fort Pampus.

Alternatively, Muiden is a pleasant 25-minute cycle along the Diemerzeedijk from Amsterdam, though the final stretch closes from November to April to protect migrating birds.

East of Zaanse Schans (northeast of Amsterdam) is Waterland, dotted with attractive small towns, such as Edam, Volendam and Marken.

Enkhuizen and Hoorn once thrived as busy fishing and trading ports on the Zuiderzee, a vast inlet of the North Sea. Repeated floods prompted the construction of the Afsluitdijk, a 32km-long dam built in 1932 that cut the inlet off from the sea. The reclamation created 640 sq metres of agricultural land. The new lakes, called Markermeer and IJsselmeer, turned gradually into freshwater.

South of the Markermeer lies Flevoland, the Netherlands' youngest province, created in 1986 from reclaimed land and incorporating the former island of Urk.

Edam

TIME FROM ZAANSE SCHANS: 1HR

Cheese, glorious cheese

The pretty flower-laden, cobblestone town of Edam, threaded through with canals, is synonymous with its eponymous, wax-covered rounds of cheese. In its 17th-century heyday, this former whaling port had 33 shipyards.

You can taste about 30 different cheeses at the wonderful and barely commercial **Gestam** *(gestam.com; free; closed Sat & Sun),* a warehouse for regional producers established in 1916. **Henry Willig's The Story of Edam Cheese** *(henriwillig. com; adult/child €8/4)* is a fun, interactive place to learn more than you could have imagined about the yellow gold.

See a floating floor in the Edams Museum

Don't miss the **Edams Museum** *(edamsmuseum.nl; adult/ child €8/3; closed Mon)* in a beautiful, historic canal-side townhouse that dates from 1540, crammed full of antiques. Most thrilling of all is the floating cellar, built to rise and fall with the river's swell to avoid flooding.

Across the canal in an annexe in the 1737 Town Hall, you'll find more exhibits, including the painting *Tall Girl,* depicting the 2.8m Trijntje Keever, who was born in 1616.

KIEV.VICTOR/SHUTTERSTOCK

Edams Museum

BEST TOURS IN VOLENDAM & EDAM

Fluisterbootjes: Boats seat up to seven people; no licence is required. Pay and pick up the key from the Edam tourist office or book online. *(fluisterboot-verhuur-edam.nl)*

Boat Tours: The Edam tourist office organises one-hour tours through the canals (called harbours) in a traditional, open-topped *praam* (cow boat).

Walking Tour: Leaves from the Edam tourist office every Saturday at 2pm.

Marken Express Ferry: Historic polished boat with a bar that makes the 30-minute trip from Volendam to Marken. *(markenexpress.nl)*

Rent & Event: Bike, motorcycle and e-bike hire; also offers two-hour guided bike tours around Volendam. *(rent-event.nl)*

Volendam

TIME FROM ZAANSE SCHANS: 1¼HRS 🚲

Go Dutch

The cute, touristy waterfront town of Volendam is one of the most popular places in the Netherlands to eat fresh *paling* (eel) and herring, and wander. Along the seafront are multiple small shops, such as **Foto de Boer** *(fotoinvolendamkostuum. nl),* where you can dress up and have your photo taken, perhaps holding an accordion or a wheel of cheese, in front of a Delft-tiled fireplace.

Volendam's History

Volendam means 'filled dam'. It was once the North Sea harbour for Edam, but then Edam constructed a direct canal to the Zuiderzee, so its old harbour was dammed and land reclaimed, and the town of Volendam became a base for fishers and sailors. It's a close-knit community with a strong musical tradition, the palingsound ('eel sound'). A surprising number of musicians hail from here, most famously the bands Cats and BZN.

EATING IN VOLENDAM & MARKEN: OUR PICKS

Vishandel Julianaweg: Volendam fishmongers: great for herring, smoked eel and *kibbeling*. *8.30am-6pm Mon-Sat* €

Eetcafé 't Havengat: Fresh fish, mussels and lobster dishes at this cosy wood-lined place on Volendam's seafront. *10am-2am* €€

Smit Bokkum: Smoking local eel, sea bass and mackerel since 1856, run by the sixth generation of a Volendam family. *10am-10pm Tue-Sun* €€

Taverne de Visscher: Good restaurants line Marken's harbour. Nautical-themed Fisherman's Tavern has great pancakes. *10am-10pm* €

THE 'GOLDEN AGE'?

Hoorn was a major trading port during the time of the Dutch East India Company, whose often exploitative trade overseas saw wealth pour into the country. In Hoorn's main square is a controversial statue of Jan Pieterszoon Coen, the governor general. He is notorious for ordering the massacre of the entire population of the Banda Archipelago when they refused to trade with him their precious cloves, nutmeg and mace, which grew only in this remote spot in what is now Indonesia.

JAYSI/SHUTTERSTOCK

Marken

History with a smoky twist

Five minutes' walk inland from the port is the charming little **Volendam Museum** *(volendamsmuseum.nl; adult/child €4/2)*. It has displays of traditional dress, a reconstruction of a cramped ship's sleeping quarters and the extraordinary Cigarbands House, where local eel sellers Nicolaas Molenaar and Jan Sombroek used 11 million cigar labels to create mosaics of famous world landmarks.

Marken

TIME FROM ZAANSE SCHANS: 30MIN 🚗

Island village

About 25km northeast of Amsterdam, Marken is an idyllic village of wood-slatted houses on an island. Until a bridge was built in 1957, it was accessible only by boat. It has a car-free centre, a quaint harbour with a few restaurants, a town museum and another devoted to clogs.

A row of six gloss-green eel-smoking houses in the Kerkbuurt area has been converted into the charmpacked **Marker Museum** *(markermuseum.nl; adult/child €4/2)*, which includes some startling waxwork figures and a recreated interior of a fisher's home.

The **Rederij Volendam Marken Express** *(markenexpress.nl; adult/child one-way €10/5, return €16/8)* ferry makes several trips a day between Volendam and Marken, which takes about 20 minutes.

MORE VINTAGE TRAINS

See more historic engines at the **Railway Museum** (p159) in Utrecht or ride the wheezing tram around the **Nederlands Openluchtmuseum** (p264) in Arnhem.

Hoorn

TIME FROM ZAANSE SCHANS: 30MIN

Strolling Hoorn's historic centre

Hoorn is named for the shape of its magnificent horn-shaped harbour. With its moorings, excellent restaurants and handsome buildings, the town attracts plenty of skippers and weekenders. It was once the capital of West Friesland and, thanks to the presence of the Dutch merchant fleet, a mighty trading city. As a member of the Republic of the Seven United Netherlands, it helped free the country from the Spanish, who occupied the town from 1569 to 1573. Those were Hoorn's glory days, and the architecture around its port reflects this time period. The defensive gate **Hoofdtoren** (1532) is topped by a tiny belfry. Check out the old warehouses on Bierkade, where lager was brought from Germany.

Set to reopen in 2027 after extensive refurbishment, the **Westfries Museum** *(westfriesmuseum.nl)* has a rich collection, including a 17th-century surgeon's room.

A vast former prison on Oostereiland houses the extremely entertaining **Museum van de Twintigste Eeuw** *(Museum of the 20th Century; museumhoorn.nl; adult/child €11/6)*, with lots of reconstructed sitting rooms and retro fashion.

All aboard the Stoomtram

It's great retro fun to take a trip on a vintage steam tram, which puffs from Hoorn's small **Museum Stoomtram** *(stoomtram.nl; adult/child €16.50/10; Apr–Sep, plus select dates Oct & Nov)*, housed in a train station, through lush flat green fields to Medemblik (22km, 1¼ hours), with volunteer staff dressed in historic uniforms.

From Medemblik, you can go on to take a boat to Enkhuizen, with its first stop at Zuiderzeemuseum.

Enkhuizen

TIME FROM ZAANSE SCHANS: 30MIN

Explore reconstructed historic houses

The attractive port of Enkhuizen, 20km northeast of Hoorn, has the wonderful **Zuiderzeemuseum** *(zuiderzeemuseum.nl; adult/child €21/14)*, with 130 relocated dwellings and workshops on the waterfront. The museum shows Zuiderzee life as it was from 1880 to 1932, after which life changed as the Zuiderzee was dammed.

You can explore the interiors of domestic houses and local shops and trades from the past, where every detail has been considered. Volunteers in costume bring the scenes to life.

BEST FAMILY EXPERIENCES IN NOORD-HOLLAND

Zuiderzeemuseum: Fantastic waterside open-air museum with activities from dinghy sailing to meeting costumed characters.

Zuid-Kennemerland National Park: Cycling, walking, swimming in lakes and fun at the beach, just outside Haarlem.

Zaanse Schans: An iconic row of windmills with small museums demonstrating local trades.

Volendam: Boat trips, a cute museum and dressing up in traditional costume to have your photo taken.

Ecomare: Texel seals and an aquarium at this eco centre.

Kaap Skil Museum: Fun museum on Texel with treasures from shipwrecks.

Naarden: Star-shaped fortress with cannon demonstrations.

 ### EATING IN HOORN: OUR PICKS

De Hoofdtoren: Superb restaurant inside Hoorn's historic Hoofdtoren, up a spiral staircase. *noon–midnight Tue–Sun* €€

Marque: Michelin-starred Mediterranean restaurant in a former cheese warehouse with courtyard tables. *noon–4.30pm & 6–10pm Wed–Sun* €€€

Havn: High-end spot with harbour views and playful seafood dishes from the creative kitchen of chef Robin Blaauw. *1pm–midnight Fri–Sun, from 6pm Wed & Thu* €€€

Eetcafé Skipperhuis: A historic brown cafe that's more about the harbourside setting than the simple pub food. *noon–10pm Mon–Thu, to 1am Fri & Sat, 10am–11pm Sun* €€

POP-UP PAMPUS

It's worth seeking out the **Summerlicht/ Winterlicht** pop-up dinners on Pampus Island (p146). It's a different way to see the fort. A boat transfer from Amsterdam is included, which leaves at 6pm, and you get to explore the illuminated fort as well as eat and drink before returning to Amsterdam by 11pm.

Start with an aperitif and a story about the island. In winter, there are fires outside, and dinner is served in the candlelit interior. It takes place on Friday and Saturday evenings and sells out quickly, so book ahead via the Fort Pampus website.

The displays join seamlessly: lime kilns from Akersloot stand a few metres from Zuidende and its row of Monnickendam houses, originally built outside the dykes. Don't miss the Urk quarter, raised to simulate the island town before the Noordoostpolder was drained. There's a superb collection of gapers (caricature heads with open mouths) in one gallery, which were traditionally hung outside shops. You can take dinghies out in the area near where the ferry docks. It's all tremendous fun; plan to spend the whole day here.

An indoor museum housed in the former home and warehouse of a Dutch shipping merchant includes a fine hall filled with historic boats.

The best way to approach is by boat, though you can also walk through the charming town from the train station. Drivers can park off the N302 and then take the ferry.

Muiden
TIME FROM ZAANSE SCHANS: 30MIN 🚗

Magnificent Muiderslot

Southeast of Amsterdam is the residential area of Het Gooi, full of villas with gardens, and lots of woodland, lakes and nature reserves. Because of its location, it is also the site of some of the country's most impressive, if defunct, fortifications. The oldest of these is **Muiderslot** (*muiderslot.nl; adult/child €15.50/9),* an exceptionally well-preserved medieval red-brick castle surrounded by a moat.

Muiderslot was built in 1280 by Count Floris V, son of Willem II. The count was a champion of the poor and a French sympathiser, two factors that inevitably spelt trouble. Floris was imprisoned in 1296 and murdered while trying to flee. The castle was destroyed shortly after and then rebuilt in the 14th century. Today, it's the Netherlands' most-visited castle.

In the 17th century, historian PC Hooft entertained some of the century's greatest writers, artists and scientists here, a group famously known as the Muiderkring (Muiden Circle), and this is the period reflected in the furnishings and gardens. The plum orchards are especially splendid.

A free audio tour leads visitors on three routes: start with the Knight's tour, followed by the Tower tour. Download the garden tour separately. The I amsterdam City Card allows free admission.

Visit a fortress island

Off the coast of Muiden lies **Fort Pampus** (*pampus.nl; adult/ child €18/14),* a derelict fort on an island. It's part of the Stelling van Amsterdam (Defence Line of Amsterdam), a ring of 42

EATING IN ENKHUIZEN: OUR PICKS

De Drie Haringhe: In an old Dutch East India Company warehouse, with a lovely garden and French-inspired cuisine. *6-9pm* €€€

Die Port van Cleve: Excellent Dutch restaurant with a characterful wood-beamed dining room and harbour views. *lunch from noon, dinner from 5pm* €€

De Mastenbar: Local favourite for its nautical-themed interior and tasty seafood. *noon-11pm Wed-Tue* €€

De Endracht in van Bleiswijk: Glorious grand cafe: a great place for a quick meal. *9am-11pm Sun-Wed, to midnight Thu-Sat* €

HANS ENGBERS/SHUTTERSTOCK

Pampus Island

fortresses stretching 135km. It's now a UNESCO World Heritage site and is great fun to explore. There's a free audio guide to download, or pick up a printed version.

You can take a direct 40-minute boat from the Amsterdam Ferry Service here from IJburg in Amsterdam, with 2½ hours to explore before the ferry returns. Another way to visit is to take the ferry to Muiden, visit Muiderslot, and then take a boat to Pampus. Regular ferries run from Muiden from April to October and take 25 minutes.

Naarden

TIME FROM ZAANSE SCHANS: 30MIN

Star-shaped fortress

A military work of art, the UNESCO-listed Naarden-Vesting Fortress contains the **Vestingmuseum** *(Fortress Museum; vestingmuseum.nl; adult/child €9/5; closed Mon),* which offers boat trips twice daily on weekends from April to October. These one-hour tours on 12-person vintage boats give an unparalleled view of the fortifications.

The fort was part of the 85km 'New Dutch' defence system and has the shape of a 12-pointed star with a double ring of moats. Built after the Spanish massacred the Naarden population in the 16th century, it was in use until the 1920s. Every third Sunday, Napoleonic-garbed gunners give demonstrations and fire cannons.

NAPOLEONIC WARS AT NAARDEN

The French occupied the Netherlands from 1795 to 1813 and used Naarden to control the surrounding region. After Napoleon's defeat at the Battle of Leipzig, the Dutch began to rebel, and with Russian and Prussian help, laid siege to Naarden in late 1813.

The French garrison refused to surrender because they would not believe that Napoleon had been captured, and they held out under harsh winter conditions for more than four months. It was only when a message got through to the fort's defenders from the French government that they finally evacuated the fortress and were given a retreat with honour.

✗ EATING & DRINKING IN MUIDEN & NAARDEN: OUR PICKS

Bob Bakt: Superb bakery in central Muiden serving excellent pastries and coffee. *8.30am-4pm Wed-Sat* €

Café Ome Ko: Napoleon came to this brown cafe in Muiden on horseback. *9am-midnight Sun & Mon, to 1am Tue-Thu, 9am-2am Fri & Sat*

Wijnbar Vijf: Waterside Muiden wine bar with French-influenced cuisine. *4pm-midnight Wed-Sat, from noon Sun* €

SEAson – Arsenaal: Michelin-starred spot in a 17th-century barracks in Naarden. *noon-2.30pm & 5.30-9.30pm Tue-Thu, noon-9.30pm Fri & Sat, 1-8pm Sun* €€€

NEW LAND FOR THE NETHERLANDS

Flevoland was built almost from scratch. The Netherlands' youngest province (inaugurated in 1968) is a masterpiece of Dutch hydroengineering, with more than 1400 sq km of land reclaimed between 1927 and 1932. When the Afsluitdijk (Barrier Dyke) was completed, it formed a dam between the IJsselmeer and the Waddenzee. Ringed dykes were erected so that water could be slowly pumped out to create land. The first residential rights were granted to workers who helped in reclamation and to farmers, especially those from Zeeland, who lost everything in the great flood of 1953.

If you're here in spring, the Noordoostpolder area is a superb place to see tulips.

Inside the fortress, quaint houses date from 1572, and the central **Grote Kerk** contains stunning 16th-century vault paintings of biblical scenes. You can climb the tower's 235 steps for a view of the leafy Gooi neighbourhood and the Vecht River.

Vestingvaart Naarden *(visitgooivecht.nl; adult/child €7/5)* offers one-hour cruises exploring Naarden-Vesting's moats and some of the reedy natural areas.

The fortress is 30 minutes by bus or bicycle from Muiden.

Urk

TIME FROM ZAANSE SCHANS: 1HR 🚗

Explore a former island

Urk was a proud island fishing community until 1939, when the surrounding Noordoostpolder was pumped dry to construct Flevoland. It might not be an island anymore, but Urk has a distinct character, with historic boats moored around the looking-glass waters of its harbour.

For sweeping views, climb the 295 steps of Urk's 18.5m-high lighthouse, **Vuurtoren van Urk** *(vuurtorenurk.nl; adult/child €3.50/2.50),* built in 1845. **Kerkje aan de Zee** *(free),* the village church, is partly constructed with masts of Dutch East India Company ships that brought back goods from the East Indies.

Museum het Oude Raadhuis *(museumopurk.nl; adult/child €7.50/4; closed Sun)* in Urk's former town hall is a charming small museum, including an authentic fisher's house interior, old photos and Urkian artefacts.

Schokland

TIME FROM ZAANSE SCHANS: 1HR 🚗

UNESCO-listed lost island

About 14km east of Urk is the fascinating **Schokland Museum** *(museumschokland.nl; adult/child €9.50/6; closed Mon Sep-Jun),* which affords glimpses into the adversities of the area's past. The former island of Schokland is now a UNESCO World Heritage site. A remote fishing and farming community lived on the hillocks that were gradually eroded by water and weather. Plucky locals hung on until their removal was ordered by Willem III in 1859. When the Noordoostpolder was reclaimed, Schokland became a dry island in the drained land. A gentle 9km walking route goes around the old island, starting at the museum.

Lelystad

TIME FROM ZAANSE SCHANS: 50MIN 🚗

Vessels in the air and sea

In Lelystad, Flevoland's capital, built on reclaimed land in 1967, **Batavialand** *(batavialand.nl; adult/child €14.95/6.95)* is a fun, hands-on museum with the opportunity to explore a replica of the 17th-century Dutch merchant frigate, the *Batavia.*

About 12km inland, at Lelystad's airport, the **Luchtvaart Themapark Aviodrome** *(aviodrome.nl; adult/child €19.95/16.95)* has 70 historic aircraft on display and is great fun. You can pretend to pilot a Boeing 747, try flight simulators and take a sightseeing flight.

Places We Love to Stay

€ Budget €€ Midrange €€€ Top End

Haarlem
p126

Hello I'm Local Boutique Hostel € Fabulous hotel-hostel with private rooms as well as dorms, a kitchen and a small restaurant. Mostly shared bathrooms.

Brasss Hotel Suites €€ Large, jazzily decorated suites, some of which have fish-themed feature walls and freestanding tubs; in the city centre.

Niu Dairy Haarlem €€ Snazzy yet good-value hotel, with rooms with cheery splashes of yellow. It's part of Holiday Inn.

MAF Haarlem Boutique Hotel €€ Deep blue or green walls, views, wood beams and chandeliers in this central gem.

Hotel ML €€ City-centre boutique hotel with period features and an attached bistro-restaurant.

Alkmaar
p132

Grand Hotel €€ Handsome rooms in a historic building in central Alkmaar. Some rooms have a Jacuzzi or sauna.

Hotel Stad en Land €€ Opposite the train station, with nicely neutral rooms decorated with sepia photographs of Alkmaar.

Luttik €€€ This gorgeous canal-side hotel features chairs suspended from the ceiling, sheepskins, freestanding bathtubs and views.

Texel
p135

Stayokay Texel € Well-run hostel surrounded by greenery with pleasant rooms, dorms, a restaurant and bar.

Boutique Hotel Texel €€ Scandi-style rooms, freestanding bathtubs, and big views over dunes and mudflats.

Bij Jef €€€ Former rectory turned boutique hotel with a charming view and a Michelin-starred restaurant.

Zaanse Schans
p139

Inntel Hotels Amsterdam Zaandam €€ This hotel has whimsical architecture – it looks like a sculptural structure combining traditional gabled houses.

B&B Heerlijck Slaapen op de Zaanse Schans €€ Amid the windmills, one of the rooms at this old-fashioned B&B has fantastic river views.

Volendam
p143

Art Hotel Spaander €€ Popular with artists in the 19th century, this hotel is a real grande dame, with wood-beamed rooms, views and a pool.

Posthoorn €€ This beautifully restored hotel, close to Volendam in the nearby handsome port of Monnickendam, dates from 1697 and has 12 romantic rooms blending antique furniture with contemporary comforts.

Hotel Old Dutch €€ Great views from this waterfront hotel, either over the Markermeer or the red roofs of Volendam, plus large rooms with panelled walls.

Marken
p144

Hof Van Marken €€ Marken's only hotel has a restaurant and seven cosy, pastel-hued rooms.

Edam
p142

L'Auberge Dam Hotel €€ Art- and antique-filled hotel in Edam's romantic centre.

De Fortuna €€ Cosy waterside hotel with a good restaurant and rooms with patchwork quilts and woodbeams.

Hoorn
p145

Bed & Breakfast Grote Noord € Hoorn's central square is just metres from this B&B, in a Dutch East India Company merchant's house dating from 1592.

Gevangis Hotel Hoorn €€ Hoorn's enormous former prison – still with bars on its windows – is now partly occupied by this hip hotel, with cells turned into boutique rooms. The harbour-view brasserie is filled with light.

Enkhuizen
p145

De Koepoort €€ Adjacent to the historic city gate of the same name, this hotel has 25 timber-trimmed rooms, some with balconies. Unwind in the leather armchairs in the lobby lounge.

Die Port van Cleve €€ A cosy small hotel with nice views over the canal. Decor is a bit dated, but it still has a lot of charm.

For places to stay in Utrecht Province, see p169

OLENA ZN/SHUTTERSTOCK

Above: Oudegracht canal (p155); Right: Railway Museum (p159)

Researched by
Mark Elliott

Utrecht Province

OLDER AND WISER THAN AMSTERDAM

The Netherlands' second-oldest city is a complete charmer with historic canals, a lively student vibe and a green periphery dotted with fascinating fortifications.

Petite but packing a punch, Utrecht Province boasts a fine selection of evocative castles and estate houses, plus a former ropemaking town that's now home to intriguing 'witch-weighing' scales. Utrechtse Heuvelrug, the Randstad's largest forest park, contains a wide variety of terrains and hides a bizarre grassy pyramid. Amersfoort is a dynamic city in its own right, with an adorable historic core, while being widely famed as the birthplace of abstract artist Piet Mondrian.

However, the main focus of the province is naturally on Utrecht city. With its pretty tree-lined canals, Utrecht is sometimes cited as a more liveable version of Amsterdam. Indeed, frequent, late-running train links mean that some travellers base themselves here to visit pricier Amsterdam as a series of day trips. But Utrecht is a cultural hub in its own right, packed with entertainment, great museums and throngs of young people – it's the Netherlands' top university city, with some 70,000 students in term time and a plethora of fun bars and cafes to match.

Historically, the city's Roman origins make Utrecht one of the country's three oldest towns. Its 'Waterline' location on what was then a major course of the Rhine was both a blessing and a curse as two fabulous out-of-town archaeology museums explain. Visually, the city's central axis is the soaring Domtoren (belfry), especially at night when cloaked in imaginatively creative illuminations.

HANS ENGBERS/SHUTTERSTOCK

Find Your Way

Utrecht Province is at the heart of the Netherlands, both historically and geographically. The city is well connected to most of the country with direct train services as far afield as Maastricht and Groningen.

TRAIN

Utrecht is just half an hour by rail from Amsterdam, and if you want to start your Dutch experience in this region, direct trains from Schiphol to both Utrecht and Amersfoort make it easy.

CAR & BICYCLE

In the bigger urban centres of Utrecht and Amersfoort, parking can be expensive (and a headache), but having wheels is handy for touring the castles. Consider hiring a bike instead of a car. Distances are manageable.

0	10 km
0	5 miles

FLEVOLAND

GELDERLAND

NOORD-HOLLAND

ZUID-HOLLAND

UTRECHT

Amersfoort

Hilversum

Loosdrecht

Loosdrechtse Plassen

Breukelen

A2
E35

Haarzuilens

Woerden

Oudewater

Utrecht
Domtoren

Nieuwegein

Bunnik

Zeist

Rietveld Schröderhuis

A12
E30

A27

A1

A28

A12

Doorn

Utrechtse Heuvelrug National Park

Wijk bij Duurstede

N225

Amerongen

Veenendaal

Rhenen

Nederrijn

Utrecht City, p154

The regional hub and undoubted star of the show is a charm-packed combination of canals, quirky independent shops, student-filled cafes and historical discoveries.

SINA ETTNER PHOTOGRAPHY/SHUTTERSTOCK

Amersfoort (p166)

Plan Your Time

However long you've planned for Utrecht, chances are that you'll want to stay longer. The city is addictive and also makes a great base from which to visit other Dutch destinations.

Only One Day

● Prebook an online slot for the **Rietveld Schröderhuis** (p159), perhaps picking a Friday when it opens late. That gives more of the daytime hours to join one of the city's excellent 'free' walking tours, visit the **DOMunder** (p154) Roman archaeological site and still have time to go for a splash or mini-cruise on the **canals** (p158).

Five Days or More

● Do all of the above over two or three days, adding the **Railway Museum** (p159) for train fans, **Castellum Hoge Woerd** (p163) for archaeology or **Fort bij Vechten** (p163) to learn about hydraulic military tactics. Drive or cycle to **Kasteel de Haar** (p164) and make an easy day trip by train to **Amersfoort** (p166), another city with a charm-filled central core.

Seasonal Highlights

SPRING	SUMMER	AUTUMN	WINTER
Dozens of bars turn into intimate mini theatres during the inventive **Café Theater Festival** *(cafetheaterfestival.nl)*, whose Utrecht iteration is in early March.	In late August, the **Holland Festival Oude Muziek** *(oudemuziek. nl)* features a week of music from the Middle Ages and baroque periods.	The 10-day **Netherlands Film Festival** *(filmfestival.nl)* presents the best of arthouse and independent Dutch movies in late September and early October.	In January, the **Sneeuwbal (Snowball) Winterfestival** *(sneeuwbalfestival. nl)* banishes new year blues with a techno-house festival in Transwijk Park.

Utrecht City

HIGHEST BELFRY | CRUISING CANALS | DE STIJL

☑ **TOP TIP**

Listen to great stories linked to the central sights on one of the entertaining 'Free' Walking Tours *(freewalkingtourutrecht. com)* at 1.30pm daily, plus some days at 10.30am. The tours aren't actually free; the guide relies on your tips, and there's a €2 booking fee if you reserve a slot online.

The Stormy Void

Roman remains and an invisible nave

Domtoren *(domtoren.nl)* is the city's iconic belfry tower and, at 112m, the Netherlands' tallest. Finally revealed after years of being hidden behind restorers' scaffolding, it forms a visual axis for the city seen from any direction, especially given cunning lighting effects that accentuate its features at night. Hour-long guided **belfry tours** *(adult/child €14.50/8.50)* climb steps to the highest accessible point (95m), stopping at 11m, 25m, 49m and 70m, after which the stairs get a little narrow.

Across the square is the **Domkerk** *(St Martin's Cathedral; domkerk.nl; entry by donation).* If you think its shape seems odd, that's because it's only half the original size. A once giant nave was destroyed by a freak summer hurricane in 1674. Catholics saw the disaster as God's retribution for the Reformation. Protestants saw it as a miracle that the belfry survived intact. The nave was never rebuilt, but if you look closely, you'll notice that the square (**Domplein**) is tiled in places with grey octagons. These tiles mark where the nave's soaring pillars once stood.

Beneath is a fascinating archaeological site that unlocks more than the former cathedral foundations. The site goes back to the Roman period, as you'll see if you visit **DOMunder** *(domunder.nl).* Tickets are sold online or through the nearby **tourist office**. The standard version *(adult/child €14.50/10)* reveals 2000 years of history with artefacts left lying where they were found. Use your lantern to unlock information as you go.

GETTING AROUND

The walkable small historic core (Binnenstad) is a 10-minute walk from Utrecht Centraal station via the Hoog Catharijne shopping mall. Some buses, such as bus 4 for Hoge Woerd, stop conveniently centrally at **Neude**. Others, including bus 41 for Wijk bij Duurstede via Vechter, depart from the station's west (Jaarbeursplein) side. Trams access park-and-

ride sites where you'd be wise to leave a car. Diesel cars are banned from the centre.

Het Zwarte Fietsenplan *(black-bikes. com)* hires out bicycles (one day/week from €17.99/71.96), or you could buy one for just €100 from **GH Velig Fietsen**. Subterranean bike-parking garages are free for stays under 24 hours.

OLENA ZN/SHUTTERSTOCK

Oudegracht

Another option explores the remains of **Paleis Lofen** *(pa leislofen.nl; adult/child €12.50/10),* a 12th-century residence of the Holy Roman Emperors, partly built by recycling Roman wall-stone for its floors. For a quick taster, you could spot some of that site's pillars by having a drink at **Walden** and asking to see their cellar bar (usually reserved for party groups). The **Domplein Highlights Tour** *(adult/child €25/12.50)* gives condensed versions of both DOMunder and Paleis Lofen tours, plus a climb up the first 25m of the belfry.

Double-Decker Canals

Kelders and canoes

The city's two most charming canals – buzzy **Oudegracht** and idyllically peaceful **Nieuwegracht** – cut right through the historic quarter. Both are unusual for their double-decker towpaths. Before Amsterdam was of any importance, Utrecht was a major river-trading hub, and merchants offloaded goods into *kelders* (storerooms) at water level.

Meanwhile, roadways were built above, creating the canals' special appearance. Cats were protected in Utrecht as a way to reduce rodents. Today, many of the Oudegracht *kelders* are used as cafes and restaurants, while some on Nieuwegracht are rented out as tourist accommodation, notably **Court Hotel** (p169).

continues on p158

A LITTLE HISTORY

Utrecht started life two millennia ago as Trajectum, a castrum (fort) on the Roman Empire's northern border. It guarded the Rhine, which flowed this way at that time. After Northumbrian monk-bishop St Willibrord founded a cathedral here around 695 CE, Utrecht grew into a major spiritual centre.

However, political and religious turmoil in the 16th century proved especially severe. Bishops lost their secular powers, and 1579's Union of Utrecht formed the core alliance of the Protestant anti-Spanish states that eventually led to the formation of the Netherlands.

Soon, Amsterdam was outshining Utrecht economically. Nonetheless, Utrecht's important university (founded in 1636) was developing fast, and today the city is the 'Cambridge of the Netherlands'.

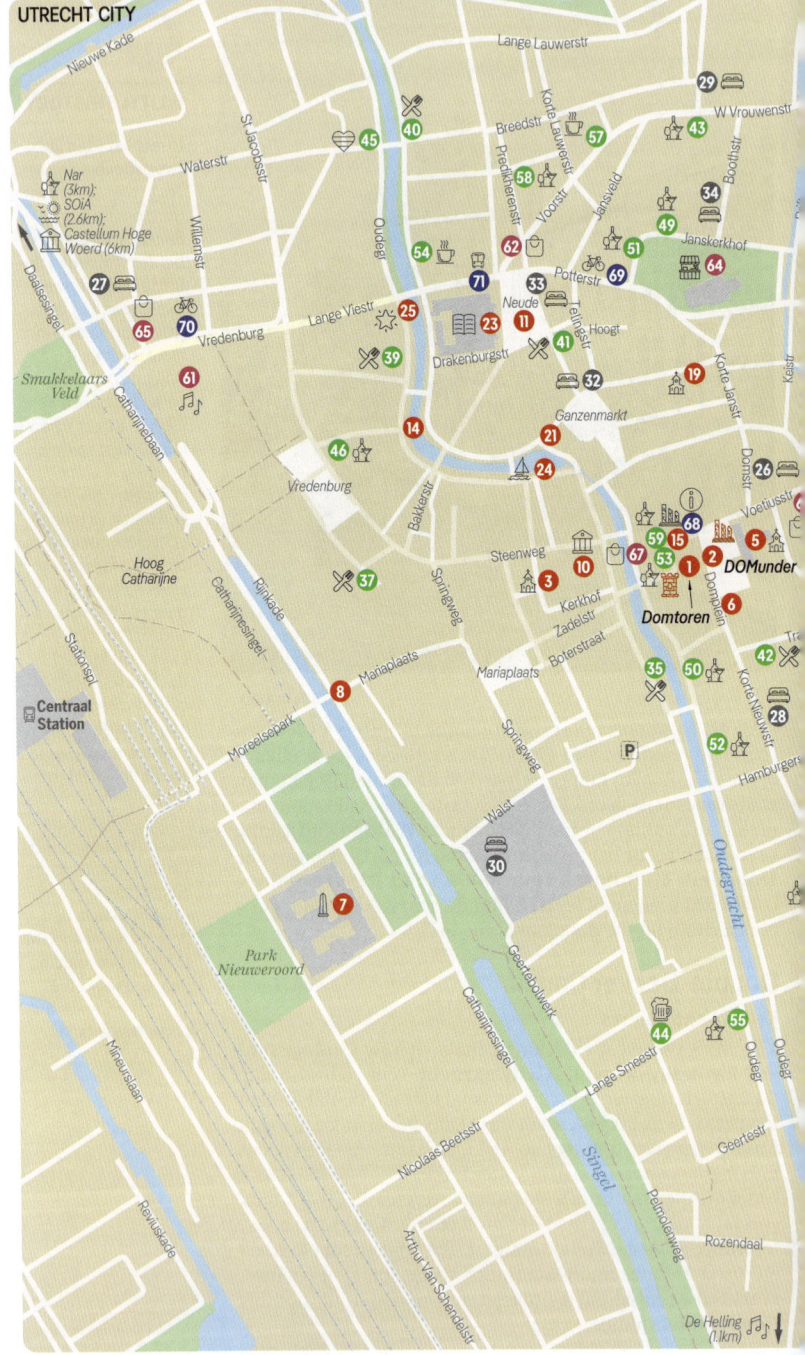

UTRECHT CITY

Lange Lauwerstr

Nieuwe Kade

Lange Lauwerstr

Korte Lauwerstr

Breedstr

W Vrouwenstr

29

43

St. Jacobsstr

Waterstr

45

40

57

Predikherenstr

58

Voorstr

34

Jansveld

49

Janskerkhof

Nar
(3km);
SOiA
(2.6km);
Castellum Hoge
Woerd (6km)

Oudegr

54

62

Pottersstr

51

69

64

27

65

70

Vredenburg

Lange Viestr

25

33

71

Neude

11

Telingstr

Hoogt

19

Korte Jansstr

Domstr

26

61

39

23

41

Drakenburgstr

Smakkelaars
Veld

Catharijnebaan

Bakkerstr

32

Ganzenmarkt

21

Voetiusstr

Vredenburg

46

14

24

Hoog
Catharijne

Catharijnesingel

Rijnkade

Steenweg

68

59 15

53

5

Domstr

Hoog
Catharijne

37

Springweg

10

67

1

2

DOMunder

3

Kerkhof
Zadelstr

Domtoren

6

Tra

Centraal
Station

Stationspl

Mariaplaats

8

Mariaplaats

Boterstraat

35

50

42

Moreelsepark

Springweg

Walstr

52

Korte Nieuwstr

28

Hamburger

P

Oudegracht

30

Park
Nieuweroord

7

Geertebolwerk

44

55

Oudegr

Mineurslaan

Lange Smeestr

Geertestr

Ravelijnkade

Nicolaas Beetsstr

Catharijnesingel

Singel

Pelmolenweg

Rozendaal

Arthur Van Schendelstr

De Helling
(1.1km)

156

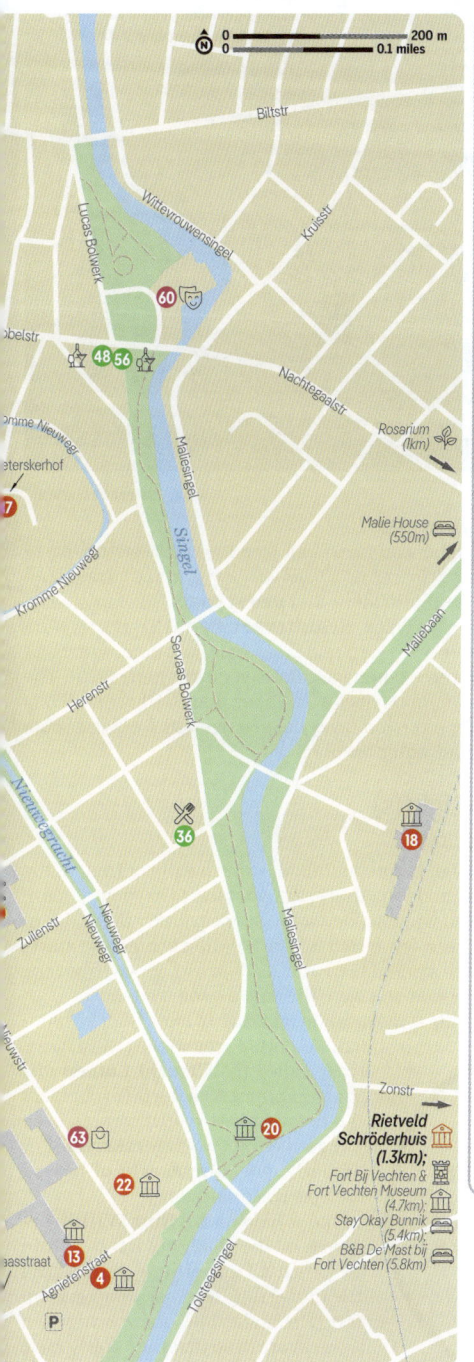

★ **HIGHLIGHTS**
1 Domtoren
2 DOMunder

● **SIGHTS**
3 Buurkerkhof
4 Centraal Museum
5 Domkerk
6 Domplein
7 Inkpot UFO
8 Mariaplaats
9 Museum Catharijneconvent
10 Museum Speelklok
11 Neude
12 Nieuwegracht
13 Nijntje Museum
14 Oudegracht
15 Paleis Lofen
16 Paushuize
17 Pieterskerkhof
18 Railway Museum
19 Sint Willibrordkerk
20 Sonnenborgh Museum & Observatory
21 't Tunneltje
22 UMU

● **ACTIVITIES**
23 Bibliotheek Neude
24 Pedal Boats
25 Schuttevaer Canal Tours

● **SLEEPING**
26 Anne&Max Boutique Hotel
27 Bunk Hotel Utrecht
28 Court Hotel
29 Eye Hotel
30 Grand Hotel Karel V
31 Hotel Beijers
32 Mother Goose Hotel
33 Stayokay Utrecht Centrum
34 Strowis Hostel

● **EATING**
35 Bistronome

des Arts
36 Heron
37 Olivier
38 Pand 33
39 Stadskasteel Oudaen
40 VandeStreek
41 Vegitalian
42 Zala's

● **DRINKING & NIGHTLIFE**
43 ACU
44 Café DeRat
45 Cafe Kalff
46 Club Poema
47 De Drie Dorstige Herten
48 De Kneus
49 Hofman
50 Jan de Winter
51 Jans Bar
52 Kafé België
53 Lebowski
54 't Koffieboontje
55 't Oude Pothuys
56 Villa Orloff
57 Village Coffee & Music
58 VinVin
59 Walden

● **ENTERTAINMENT**
60 Stadsschouwburg
61 TivoliVredenburg

● **SHOPPING**
62 Blackfish
63 Het Foto Atelier
64 Janskerkhof Bloemenmarkt
65 Kapsalon Cocopelo
66 Passemento
67 Rachmaninoff

● **INFORMATION**
68 Tourist Office

● **TRANSPORT**
69 GH Velig Fietsen
70 Het Zwarte Fietsenplan
71 Neude Bus Stops

LOCALS' SPOTS IN UTRECHT

Amanda Bond: cofounder of sustainability startup Bloom ESG, shares her Utrecht secrets.

Janskerkhof Bloemenmarkt:
In Amsterdam, the Flower Market doesn't focus on selling flowers. But Utrecht's really is a thing each Saturday. Go around 11am, and the bells will be playing

Rosarium:
Relaxing place for unwinding amid beautiful roses. Walk there through lovely Wilhelminapark.

SOiA:
For a chill-out afternoon that's family- and dog-friendly, head for SOiA (Strand Oog in Al) with waterside picnic spaces and a weekend cafe-restaurant on a little peninsula at the junction of two canals. Some people swim here, but you shouldn't. Huge ships pass by and won't see you!

TASFOTONL/SHUTTERSTOCK

Utrecht Lumen

continued from p155

To take to the water, you can hire 12-seater electric 'party boats' *(sloepdelen.nl* or *sloephurenutrecht.nl),* kayaks and canoes (several providers) and **pedal boats** *(stromma.com).* For a tour experience, **Schuttevaer Canal Tours** *(schutte vaer.com)* runs two loop routes several times daily with commentary in three languages. Both go down Oudegracht. The one-hour tour loops clockwise under Hoog Catharijne, while the 90-minute version takes the prettier anticlockwise route past parkland water bastions.

See the Light(s)

Magic after dark

After dark, but before midnight, stand awhile in front of the **Paushuize**, and something strange starts to happen. Some of the curtained windows develop a ghoulish flicker that gains in intensity over a few minutes. The building behind you starts behaving the same. Then, over its doorway, an owl appears. Chances are that you were the only person who saw it.

This is the most imaginative of more than 20 light-art installations dotted around the central area, collectively called the **Utrecht Lumen** *(dis cover-utrecht.com).* Seeking them out takes you into lovely, less-visited corners, such as the super-pretty **Pieterskerkhof** or similarly quiet **Buurkerkhof** behind the Speelgoedmuseum.

Find a halo above **Sint Willibror-dkerk** or the changing lights within the garish **'t Tunneltje**, a graffiti-laced little tunnel that descends from Ganzen-markt. The undersides of five bridges on Oudegracht are lit so that they slowly cycle through varying intensities of mellow blue.

MORE ROMANS REMAINS
Visit the sparklingly contemporary museum **Castellum Hoge Woerd** (p163), easily visited en route from Utrecht to Kasteel De Haar. There's another castellum site (Fectio) near **Fort bij Vechten** (p163).

The great Domtoren (p154) becomes a canvas for different lighting designs on different days. But can you find the **UFO**? Yes, a sizeable flying saucer hovers on the tower of the 1911 'Inkpot', the Netherlands' largest brick building. It's visible anytime from **Mariaplaats**, but things are more fun at night when it seems to fire its engines, albeit only occasionally.

De Stijl Classic

The unique Rietveld Schröder House

The chances are that if you walked past the residential building at Prins Hendriklaan 50, you wouldn't look twice. Yet this is the **Rietveld Schröderhuis** *(rietveldschroderhuis. nl; adult/child €19/3)*, a UNESCO World Heritage site. Look again, and it becomes clearer that this 1924 construction was years ahead of its time. Entering feels like you're walking into a 3D Piet Mondrian abstract.

Things get especially interesting when the walls start to move. To make for efficient use of space, celebrated Utrecht designer Gerrit Rietveld created a system that allows the room plan to be substantially adjusted. Guides demonstrate the mechanisms in action.

Prebooking online is essential because you must join a (small) group tour. It's worth arriving at least 20 minutes before your assigned entry time to see a contextualising video. The location is 2km out of the centre, accessible using bus 8 to the Hoogstraat stop.

See more of Rietveld's trademark furniture at Utrecht's **Centraal Museum** *(centraalmuseum.nl; adult/child €17.50/free)*.

Chug Around the Railway Museum

Not just for train spotters

Enter Utrecht's engrossing **Railway Museum** *(spoorwegmuseum.nl; €19.50)* via the gloriously restored 1874 Maliebaan Station, complete with art nouveau chandeliers. Move on to peruse countless historic locomotives, a vast collection of model trains and a range of rides and interactive science experiences for all ages. De Vuurproef is a Harry Potter meets Willy Wonka experience that starts as a history of railways and then morphs into an award-winning simulator ride.

One of the many other exhibits looks at the future of railways, including Dutch prototypes for hyperloop pods. The museum can be accessed by a pleasant amble across the canal ramparts from town. However, full-on railway enthusiasts love to arrive directly from Utrecht Centraal on a one-stop train service departing at 31 minutes past the hour.

Research Trip

Highlights of the University Museum

Utrecht University's museum, **UMU** *(umu.nl; adult/child €15.50/8)*, is a curious mixture of ultra-modern and super-traditional, all thrown together with a small botanical garden for unwinding in afterwards.

PROUDLY INDEPENDENT

'Buy Local – Keep Utrecht Weird' says a sign in many a shop window, underlining Utrecht's pride in its indie businesses.

Het Foto Atelier: A treasure trove for photographers; sells old cameras and fine B&W art prints. *(hetfotoatelier.nl)*

Passemento: Turret-topped building housing a remarkably niche shop specialising in coloured threads and ribbons. *(passemento.nl)*

Blackfish: Vintage and self-designed clothing store behind the preserved frontage of a historic pharmacy. *(blackfish.nl)*

Kapsalon Cocopelo: Hair salon with interior and signs little changed since the 1950s. *(kapsaloncocopelo.nl)*

Rachmaninoff: Furniture and furnishings in a whitewashed cellar chamber. *(rachmaninoffshop.nl)*

MORE GREAT MUSEUMS

Museum Speelklok:
A former church full of self-playing organs, musical boxes and assorted mechanised noise-makers from the 18th century onwards. *(museumspeelklok.nl)*

Museum Catharijneconvent:
Medieval religious art in a Gothic former convent complex. *(catharijneconvent.nl)*

Sonnenborgh Museum & Observatory:
A 19th-century observatory on the city ramparts. *(sonnenborgh.nl)*

Nijntje Museum:
Aimed at preschool-age children, this interactive museum is based on the cartoon characters created by local artist Dick Bruna (1927–2017), notably Nintje, known in English as Miffy. *(nijntjemuseum.nl)*

Start by picking up a mystery box to discover your 'research aims', giving purpose to your exploration of the startlingly varied series of exhibits. You can sit in a Philo-sofa to think about life or make a beeline for the gruesome highlight, a 19th-century collection of botanical specimens and skeletons designed as historical teaching aids. Spoiler alert: this includes humans with some utterly macabre deformities. Contrastingly beautiful are antique glass models of ephemeral creatures like jellyfish and slugs made as teaching aids. They would have lost their form if stored in formaldehyde.

Weekends in Utrecht
Let's party

On warm evenings, the restaurants on the twin-level canal sides are full to bursting around Bakkerbrug by about 6pm. Groups of friends fill the terraces of **Neude** and Stadhuisplein, which stay rammed until well after midnight. A gaggle of cafes in the northwest corner of Domplein are popular party starters, and from Thursday to Saturday, a DJ in the surprisingly cavernous interior of **Lebowski** invites folk to stay longer.

However, by midnight on Fridays and Saturdays, many have drifted to Janskerkhof, where **Jans Bar** (strictly 21+) and **Hofman** clear their interiors and become dance clubs, continuing until about 4am. Expect ID checks and queues.

Another small knot of bars on Drieharingstraat feeds the merry into **Club Poema**, a popular student nightclub. Some events require a student ID. The other area for 18+ crews is at the eastern end of Nobelstraat, with **De Kneus** a late-night party favourite. More sedate **Villa Orloff** next door has an appealing garden area for those who prefer to sit and chat.

Older locals gravitate instead some 3km west to artsy, Brooklynesque **Nar** in the Schepenbuurt wharf area. Despite looking a little edgy, it's a family favourite by day and then takes on a club vibe until 4am at weekends.

And then there's the very particular ACU.

Antiestablishment
Getting into the ACU...or not

It's a bar, but the intimate little **ACU** *(acu.nl)* doesn't necessarily want you to drink here. Run by volunteer activists, it's the meeting place of an anticapitalist community that describes itself as the 'rotten thorn' in the side of a gentrifying area.

 DRINKING IN UTRECHT: CLASSIC BROWN CAFES

De Drie Dorstige Herten: A 1687 *proeflokaal* (taproom) with beer and *baliekluiver* (local bitters) from a glass still. *3-10pm Wed-Sat, 2-7pm Sun*

Café DeRat: Cosy, board-floored cafe with whisky tastings and a selection of aged Belgian Lambics (sour, spontaneously fermented beers). *2pm-late*

Jan de Winter: Enticing brown cafe with a 1940s art deco feel and a cellar with canal-side seating. Half-litre beers from just €6. *2pm-late Wed-Sat*

Kafé België: A full-sized Madonna statue seems to be almost fainting with passion in welcoming beer lovers into paradise. *1pm-late*

WOLF PHOTOGRAPHY/SHUTTERSTOCK

Tivolivredenburg

Getting in might require connections, or at least some sensitivity. And certainly no meat or leather, as the ethos is vegan. Once you're in, however, expect fascinating conversations. The back bar, entirely invisible if you didn't know it was there, proudly offers the 'World's Worst Karaoke' and a roster of events that span folk-punk, shoegazing, queer nights and Caribbean fiestas.

In Concert

Many musical permutations

Architecturally, **Tivolivredenburg** *(tivolivredenburg.nl)* is a bold statement of 21st-century creativity. As a performance venue, its scope is bewildering, with two 2000-seater auditoria, four smaller halls and three foyer bar spaces allowing multiple concurrent shows.

Pick up the month's A5 printed calendar; you'll need a magnifying glass to read the details, which typically include dozens of free concerts. Even toddlers are catered for in this veritable palace of culture.

MORE GREAT PERFORMANCE VENUES

Stadsschouwburg: Large, architecturally protected 1941 theatre. *(stadsschouwburg-utrecht.nl)*

De Helling: Focuses on hip-hop, experimental and heavy bass musical styles for both concerts and club nights. One of several venues for Le Guess Who? *(leguesswho.com)* festival. *(dehelling.nl)*

Bibliotheek Neude: This magnificent 1924 Amsterdam School former post office is now the city library. The building's 400-capacity Great Hall doubles as a performance space. It's the spot for digital installations during the multi-venue Nederlands Film Festival *(filmfestival.nl)*. *(neude11.nl)*

't Oude Pothuys: Informal cafe-bar in a cellar-style chamber with jam sessions and band nights from 11pm on Tuesdays to Saturdays. *(pothuys.nl)*

DRINKING IN UTRECHT: OUR PICKS

VinVin: Cute street-corner wine bar with a wide choice of per-glass bottles displayed handily on the wall. Helpful staff. *4pm-midnight Tue-Sun*

Cafe Kalff: A focus of LGBTIQ+ social life for years, Kalff suggests you 'go where you are celebrated, not where you're tolerated'. *4pm-late Tue-Sun*

't Koffieboontje: Sociable and strictly laptop-free. The delicious aroma of the coffee beans hits you from the canal-side street outside. *9am-4.30pm*

Village Coffee & Music: A happy hipster bric-a-brac cafe with barista skills and eccentric vinyl soundtrack. *7.30am-6pm Mon-Fri, from 8.30am Sat & Sun*

🚶 WALKING UTRECHT'S HIGHLIGHTS

This unhurried stroll introduces you to the key sights of Utrecht's historic core.

START	END	LENGTH
Utrecht Centraal Station	Domplein	1.5km; 45 mins

From ❶ **Utrecht Centraal Station**, cut through ❷ **Hoog Catharijne Mall**, descending escalators and overlooking ❸ **Catharijnesingel**, a canal that was a highway until 2010.

Cross ❹ **Vredenburg**, home to three weekly markets and then follow cafe-lined Drieharingstraat to ❺ **Oudegracht** (p155), the classic double-decker canal. Expect lively scenes all the way down Vismarkt and then turn east on Servetstraat. Walk beneath the soaring ❻ **Domtoren** (p154) to discover the truncated ❼ **Domkerk** (p154). Immediately south, Utrecht University's ❽ **Academiegebouw** has an impressive 1892 facade but is actually centuries older. A doorway leads into a cloister called

❾ **Pandhof**. Exit into ❿ **Achter de Dom**, where a metal strip outlines what was once the eastern edge of the Roman fort within which Utrecht grew.

⓫ **Paushuize** (p158) is a splendid medieval palace designed for Utrecht-born Adrian VI, the only Dutch pope. Infamously humourless, he died before it was finished. ⓬ **Nieuwegracht** (p155), Utrecht's peaceful 'other' canal, heads south to Utrecht's compact museum district, but for a shorter walking route, take the passage through ⓭ **Catharijneconvent** (p160) and return up Lange Nieuwstraat towards ⓮ **Domplein** (p154) with the belfry towering ahead.

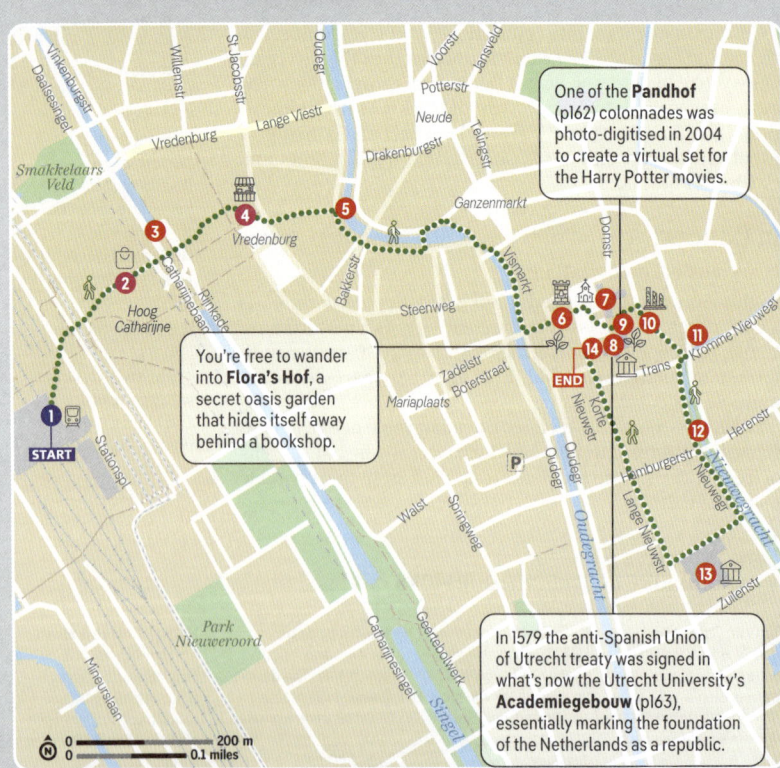

One of the **Pandhof** (p162) colonnades was photo-digitised in 2004 to create a virtual set for the Harry Potter movies.

You're free to wander into **Flora's Hof**, a secret oasis garden that hides itself away behind a bookshop.

In 1579 the anti-Spanish Union of Utrecht treaty was signed in what's now the Utrecht University's **Academiegebouw** (p163), essentially marking the foundation of the Netherlands as a republic.

0   200 m
0   0.1 miles

Creative Castellum

Roman remains reimagined at Hoge Woerd

Because it's out in one of Utrecht's furthest western suburbs, few visitors ever discover **Castellum Hoge Woerd** *(museum hogewoerd.nl; free)*. That's a pity because it's one of Europe's best archaeological museums, a family-friendly place with countless activities, a petting zoo and a garden designed to help preserve bees on top of its incredible centrepiece, a gigantic Roman barge that sank here in 192 CE.

Waterworks as Defence

Turn the taps at Fort bij Vechten

On the southern edge of Utrecht, **Fort bij Vechten** *(fortvechten.nl)* was one of the largest Waterline forts ever built. The moats and grassy ramparts are free to explore, as is the nearby marked outline of almost invisible Roman castellum **Fectio**, from which it was named.

A free info centre gives basic details, but it's well worth the entry fee to experience the **Fort Vechten Museum** *(adult/child €12/7)*. Press 2 on the 'phones' to activate your chip card in English. You'll need this to interact with the many fascinating attractions, including designing your own Waterline and a rather complicated four-minute game using taps, forts and troop assignments to see off the enemy. Snapshots of different eras show the development of Waterline technology and the importance of enough water (80cm), but not too much.

At the end, you get to 'fly' out across the Waterline in a VR plus simulator chair experience and to turn real taps while exploring a 1:1600 scale model of the whole system.

LIMES & WATERLINES

The Romans found that the going got tough when they reached the Rhine, so they decided to use the river as a de facto imperial border, a kind of water version of Hadrian's Wall.

Known as the Limes (limits), castellum sites were built at regular intervals to guard against Germanic incursions. From the 17th century, the general defensive idea was resurrected, adding cunning ideas using improved hydraulics to enable flooding of the surrounding fields at the time of an invasion.

The result was a 200km series of low-slung 'Waterline' fortresses, perfected in the 1860s with an extraordinary series of dykes. Along with the Limes sites, this Waterline in Germany and the Netherlands is now a collective UNESCO World Heritage site.

EATING IN UTRECHT: OUR PICKS

Vegitalian: Two very different rooms for small-plate vegetarian dishes designed to share. *8.30am-10pm* €

Olivier: Belgian beers and good-value pub fare in a characterful reworking of a large former church. *noon-late* €

Stadskasteel Oudaen: Restaurant, grand cafe and microbrewery in a 13th-century 'troubadour's castle'. *11am-late* €€

VandeStreek: Steak frites, vegan burgers and sharing plates with canal-side seating and many craft beers on tap. *3-11pm or later* €€

Bistronome des Arts: Wine bar with traditional French bistro food in an 1847 shophouse. *hours vary Wed-Sat* €€

Heron: Turns 100% locally sourced fare into seasonal and imaginative dinners. *6-8pm Tue-Sat* €€€

Zala's: Low-key yet gourmet multicourse surprise dinners at fair prices in a classy historic house setting. *6pm-1am Wed-Sun* €€

Pand 33: Unusually friendly spot for creative gastronomy. *6-10pm Tue-Sat Sep-Jun, special hours Jul & Aug* €€€

Beyond
Utrecht City

Utrecht's green hinterland and provincial towns sport castles, country houses and even witch-weighing scales.

Places

Kasteel de Haar p164
Amersfoort p166
Oudewater p167

GETTING AROUND

A car is handy for the castle loops, and there are appealing cycle paths, including the LF4 to Kasteel de Haar and the LF9 to Amersfoort. Alternatively, for Wijk bij Duurstede, take bus 41 from Utrecht or bus 56 from Amersfoort via Doorn. Amersfoort is as little as 26/35 minutes by regular train from Utrecht/Amsterdam. Oudewater is a stop on bus 107 between Utrecht (40 minutes) and Gouda (25 minutes).

The area around Utrecht combines a remarkable plethora of medieval and more recent castle-houses and fortresses, along with the archaeological echoes of the region's history at the Roman Empire's northern frontier.

Ideal for exploration by bicycle or on foot, the Utrechtse Heuvelrug is a 65km green arc of national park sweeping east of Utrecht city, with wildlife-rich forests, meadows and high dunes patchworked with areas of human habitation. Once predominantly heathland, its signature beech trees were mostly planted after 1804 when French revolutionary troops camped here and were set the task of building the Pyramide van Austerlitz to keep them out of trouble.

Amersfoort is an appealing historic city with Piet Mondrian connections.

Kasteel de Haar

TIME FROM UTRECHT: 45MIN

A Cuypers castle

West of Utrecht, **Kasteel de Haar** *(kasteeldehaar.nl; adult/child €20/12.50)* is everything you'd hope for in a 'medieval' fantasy castle, from the moat, drawbridge and spiky turrets to the panelled rooms filled with antiques. However, it's not medieval at all. The 13th-century original was almost entirely rebuilt over 20 years by Pierre Cuypers, the architect of Amsterdam's Rijksmuseum.

In its new 1912 guise, the castle's fame grew, and by the 1960s and '70s, it was home to lavish parties that attracted the global glitterati, including actors Gregory Peck, Joan Collins, Roger Moore and Brigitte Bardot.

EATING BEYOND UTRECHT CITY: OUR PICKS

Restaurant Laverie: Kasteel de Haar's cafe serves salads, sandwiches, snacks and drinks in a 1900 converted stable block. *10.30am-5pm* €

Liz Resto-Bar: Locally sourced salads and sandwiches, plus dinners blending international influences, all in Kasteel Amerongen's regal grounds. *11.30am-8pm* €€

De Engel: A cafe-pub in Wijk open since the 1670s serving brasserie fare, including croquettes, satay skewers and asparagus ravioli. *10am-9.30pm* €€

Restaurant Lutum: The organic gastronomy from chefs Roy Schipper and Rik Veen is a marvel of central Wijk. *6.30-8.30pm Wed-Fri, noon-2pm & 6.30-8.30pm Sat* €€€

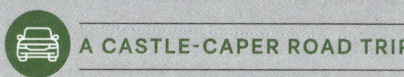

A CASTLE-CAPER ROAD TRIP

This relaxed day-trip driving itinerary takes you to contrasting castles and mansions with varied histories.

START	END	LENGTH
Utrecht	Utrecht	100km; 1 day

Soon after driving southeast out of **1 Utrecht**, you pass close to **2 Landhuis Oud Amelisweerd**, a well-preserved 1770 manor house and gardens repurposed as an art space. Nearby is the important Waterline site of **3 Fort Bij Vechten** (p163). Continue 18km to the interesting town of **4 Wijk bij Duurstede**. At the south edge of its compact historical core, its atmospherically shattered moated fortress **5 Kasteel Duurstede** is now an events venue that you can admire but not enter.

Continue east to Amerongen's moated chateau, **6 Kasteel Amerongen**, which has sumptuous salon interiors, restored original furnishings and regular garden concerts. After losing WWI in 1918, German Kaiser Wilhelm signed his abdication here and stayed on until 1920. He then moved to the less ostentatious **7 Huis Doorn**, about 10km northwest. He lived there until he died in 1941.

From Doorn, drive through the forested Utrechtse Heuvelrug National Park. Stop beside a small amusement park for the short woodland stroll to 'Europe's biggest pyramid', Napoleon's grassy **8 Pyramide van Austerlitz** (p167).

Fans of warplanes and military vehicles might add a visit to the **9 Nationaal Militair Museum** before returning to Utrecht.

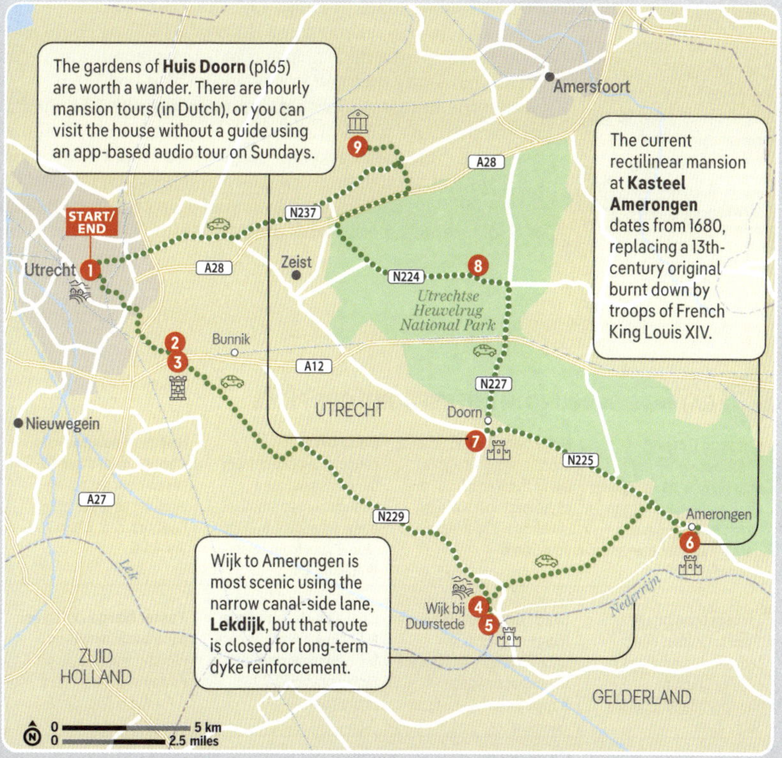

The gardens of **Huis Doorn** (p165) are worth a wander. There are hourly mansion tours (in Dutch), or you can visit the house without a guide using an app-based audio tour on Sundays.

The current rectilinear mansion at **Kasteel Amerongen** dates from 1680, replacing a 13th-century original burnt down by troops of French King Louis XIV.

Wijk to Amerongen is most scenic using the narrow canal-side lane, **Lekdijk**, but that route is closed for long-term dyke reinforcement.

Amersfoort

Utrecht

START/END

Zeist

Bunnik

Nieuwegein

Utrechtse Heuvelrug National Park

UTRECHT

Doorn

Amerongen

Wijk bij Duurstede

ZUID HOLLAND

GELDERLAND

Nederrijn

Lek

A28 · N237 · A28 · N224 · A12 · N227 · N225 · A27 · N229

0 — 5 km
0 — 2.5 miles

For a satisfying day trip by bike, add stops at **Slot Zuylen** (*slotzuylen.nl; adult/child €16/8*), another fine moated castle, and the brilliant archaeological museum, **Castellum Hoge Woerd** (p163).

THE MIRACLE OF AMERSFOORT

Amersfoort became wealthy enough to build its fabulous belfry thanks to the remarkable discovery of a Madonna statue, found under the ice of the frozen river by a maiden who'd been led to the exact spot by a dream. A flood of pilgrims quickly followed to venerate the icon, which reputedly bestowed miraculous cures upon many believers. Their generous donations paid for the belfry.

It's built on what is widely considered as the exact geographical centre of the Netherlands, an accolade marked by a little winking red light at the base of the tower.

Amersfoort

TIME FROM UTRECHT: 12–25MIN 🚆

Home of Mondrian

De Stijl artist Piet Mondrian (1872–1944; Mondriaan in Dutch) was born in the charming old centre of Amersfoort above a small canal-side school where his father was headmaster. He left aged eight, but **Mondriaanhuis** (*mondriaanhuis.nl; adult/child €13/8*) is now a well laid-out museum that traces his artistic evolution from realist landscapes through impressionism to the geometric rectangles of red, yellow and blue that became his hallmark after moving to Paris in 1911. One of his Parisian apartment-studios is also recreated, while upstairs there is a hands-on opportunity to make Mondrian-esque Lego designs and to play on the 'light organ'.

Bikes aboard: riding the Eemlijn

Most days between mid-April and mid-September, you can turn up at the Grote Koppel mooring in Amersfoort and jump aboard the top-heavy-looking two-storey **Fietsboot Eemlijn** (*eemlijn.nl*).

Departing at 10am, it chugs for about three hours downstream to either Spakenburg or Huizen. While you could just come for the views, the real idea is to bring a bicycle and cycle back. That's why they call it a *fietsboot* (bike-boat).

From the first stop, Soest (45 minutes, fare €3.50, plus €2 for the bike), it's a 5.5km ride back to Amersfoort, all along riverbank cycle paths. From Eemdijk (third stop, €10.50, plus €2), it's 17km, though between Baarn and Soest, you'll need to cut inland. You could return by train to Utrecht from Baarn or Soest, though both towns' railway stations are 2km from their respective jetties.

EATING & DRINKING IN AMERSFOORT: OUR PICKS

Corazon Coffee: Friendly central cafe with scrumptious cakes, sandwiches and vegan lunch plates, plus a game-filled toddler area. *10am-5pm* €

Het Zoete Zusje: Salads, croquettes and apple pie in the Kapelhuis, one of Amersfoort's oldest buildings. *10am-6pm Tue-Sun* €

Dolle Diva: Full sensory overload, from the colour-infused chandeliers to small-plate creativity. *5-11pm Mon & Tue, from noon Wed-Sun* €€

Het Bloemendaeltje: Choose from three to seven courses for an evening of fascinating flavours. *6-8.30pm Tue-Sat* €€€

Livingstone bij de Poort: Coffee, chai, lemonade and great pastries beside Kamperbinnenpoort. *9am-4pm*

Stadsbrowerij Drie Ringen: This 1626 microbrewery sits beside the canal near the Koppelpoort. *2-7.30pm Tue-Sun*

Crazy Louis Jazz Cafe & Eethuis: Antique cafe full of dark wood and faded brass. *10.30am-10pm Tue-Sat*

Zuster Margaux: Stylish wine bar in a historic cloister with music on Friday nights. *5-10pm Thu & Fri, from 3pm Sat & Sun*

WUT. MOPPIE/SHUTTERSTOCK

Amersfoort

No bike? Another option is to take one of the 45-minute tour-boat rides that putter around the **Amersfoort canals** *(amersfoort-rondvaarten.nl; adult/child €8.75/4.75).*

Oudewater

 TIME FROM UTRECHT: 40MIN

Fright or plump?

In the 16th century, about a million women all across Europe were put to death following suspicions of sorcery. Once accused of being a witch, the chances of any kind of reprieve were slim, but in some places, there was one hope. By a logic as absurd as the supposed crime itself, it was argued that, since a witch would need to fly on her broomstick to conduct her shenanigans, it stood to reason that 'real witches' could not be overweight. Indeed, her lack of a soul could explain her being lighter than expected for her apparent frame.

Incredibly, some comparatively merciful towns set up 'witch scales' to double-check. One such contraption has survived in the attractive former ropemaking town of Oudewater, where it forms the main exhibit of the little museum, **Heksenwaag** *(heksenwaag.nl; adult/child €8.25/4.25).* It occupies one of the historic houses on the canal, an area that's liveliest on Wednesdays (market day).

NAPOLEON'S GRASSY PYRAMID

In 1804, some 18,000 Napoleonic French troops were kept out of mischief by being set the make-work task of building a 36m artificial hill. Today, the huge **Pyramide van Austerlitz** *(pyramideva nausterlitz.nl; free)* is curiously hard to spot, hidden in 19th-century beechwoods.

These form part of the wildlife-rich **Utrechtse Heuvelrug** *(np-utrechtseh euvelrug.nl)*, the Netherlands' second-largest sweep of forest. A national park since 2003, the area also includes meadows and heathland with some unexpected patches of inland dunes, most notably around Soest near Amersfoort. There are ample opportunities for hiking and cycling, but you're never too far from civilisation.

MORE DE STIJL
De Stijl also influenced furniture and architecture, as you can see through the work of Gerrit Rietveld in **Utrecht** (p159).

STROLL HISTORIC AMERSFOORT

This short walk around Amersfoort is ideal for getting a taste of the city as a day trip from Utrecht or Amsterdam.

START	END	LENGTH
De Zonnewijzer	Mondriaanplein	4.2km; 2 hrs

Start on Stationplein (south exit) where the digital clock ❶ **De Zonnewijzer** tells two different times on a long, starkly bent lamppost, one standard and the other solar. Head southeast via treelined Spoorstraat and Vlasakkerweg and then northeast on Utrechtseweg. Prominently ahead rises Amersfoort's most defining architectural feature, ❷ **Onze Lieve Vrouwe Toren**, the 98m-tall belfry tower. Its church was destroyed in 1787 by a gunpowder blast. To climb the belfry's 346 steps, join a one-hour tour (12.30pm and 2pm). Get tickets from the ❸ **Tourist Office** on the photogenic square outside.

A pretty walk now follows a narrow canal past ❹ **Mondriaanhuis** (p166) and then around Muurhuizen. From the twin-turreted city gate ❺ **Kamperbinnenpoort**, Langestraat leads to ❻ **Sint Joriskerk**, Amersfoort's last surviving medieval church. Follow Havik along gorgeous canal sides to ❼ **Museum Flehite**, which explores city history. Along Spui, canal-spanning ❽ **Koppelpoort** is Amersfoort's icon and best-known historic gatehouse. Crossing under the railway bridge, Eemhuis cultural centre is contrastingly contemporary with a Dalek-style metallic skin. It contains ❾ **Kunsthal KAdE**, an excellent art gallery. Follow the railway along Piet Mondriaanlaan back to the station's north entrance, ❿ **Mondriaanplein**.

Like so much in the region, the 1425 **Koppelpoort** was rendered far more romantic thanks to an 1880s Gothic restoration by architect Pierre Cuypers.

A more direct route into town is less interesting but does pass an **electrical transformer hut**, enlivened with a Mondrian-esque paint job.

The small 1958 **Zonnehof** art space has little aesthetic charm, but it's a listed building, being a Gerrit Rietveld design.

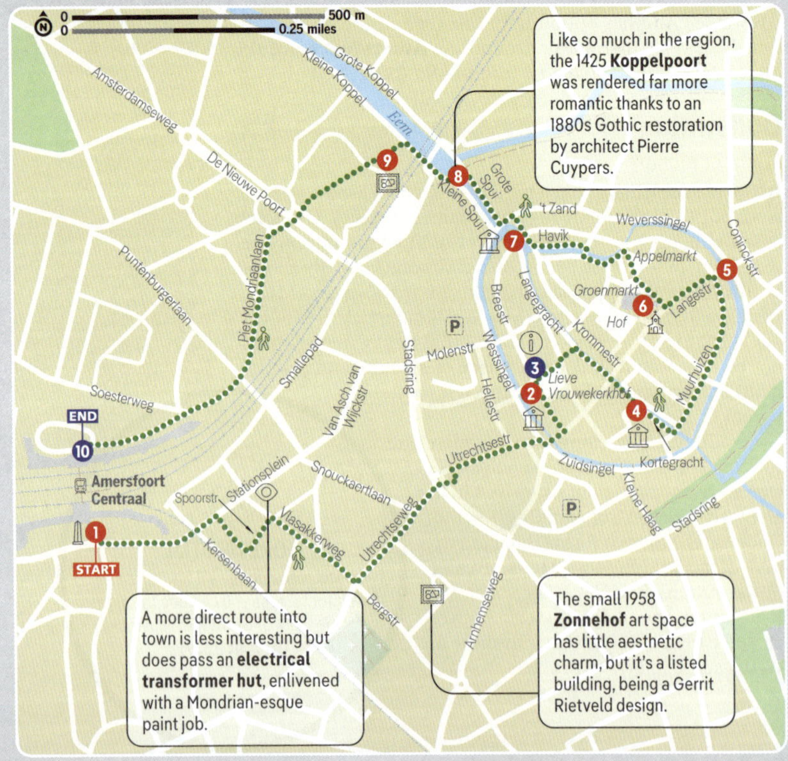

Places We Love to Stay

€ Budget €€ Midrange €€€ Top End

Utrecht City   p154

Bunk Hotel Utrecht €
Luxurious hostel with curtained pod-capsules, digital lockers and towels included. It's in a stylishly converted church that's part bar-cafe and part occasional music venue. Upstairs are often-missed balcony chill zones.

StayOkay Bunnik € Rural HI hostel just 5km from Utrecht in a 1830s mansion close to two huge Waterline fortresses.

Strowis Hostel € Promises 100% shark-free budget beds in a high-ceilinged 17th-century townhouse with garden, kitchen and bike hire.

Stayokay Utrecht Centrum €
Enthusiastically run bed factory with a superb location above a relaxed but stylish cafe. Game nights encourage phone-free interaction. Try to get a lower floor as the sensitive lift can malfunction.

Hotel Beijers €€ Beautifully appointed 17th-century mansion with period fittings tucked away in a quiet street just a stone's throw from the belfry.

Mother Goose Hotel €€
Highly personable staff add to the considerable appeal of this sensitively reworked 13th-century mansion. The nightlife square right outside can get noisy.

Eye Hotel €€ Beautifully conceived boutique hotel in what was, in 1858, the Netherlands' first eye clinic, hence all the ocular references.

Court Hotel €€ Stylishly modern, high-ceilinged rooms in midnight-blue with tongue-in-cheek 'see you in Court' photo art. Also has several canal-cellar rooms for a special Utrecht experience.

Malie House €€ Highly modernised interiors bring to life a large 19th-century property that's a little cheaper than the competition thanks to its location 1.5km east of the Domtoren in a sedate inner suburb.

B&B De Mast bij Fort Vechten €€ If you're travelling with your own wheels and a few friends, this peaceful three-bedroom farmstay can work out as an excellent option. Park the car for free and borrow bikes or take bus 41 to visit Utrecht.

Anne&Max Boutique Hotel €€€ Fashion-statement boutique hotel that's an unexpected addition to the Dutch coffee-house chain Anne&Max. Peaceful yet super central, suites have high ceilings, and one executive version has unparalleled views of the cathedral from its roof terrace.

Grand Hotel Karel V €€€
Five-star luxury in a converted historic hospital and former monastery that was visited by Holy Roman Emperor Charles (Karel) V in 1543.

Doorn, Wijk & Around   p165

Hotel 1851 €€ Eight unfussy rooms with coffee makers and kettles, plus a decent breakfast, three minutes' walk from the old core of Wijk bij Duurstede.

Kasteel Sterkenburg €€€
Indulgent B&B where most of the rooms are within a genuine castle-mansion, complete with a moat and period furnishings.

Parc Broekhuizen €€€
Lake-facing chateau-style mansion and associated coach house with rooms, suites and a Michelin-starred restaurant.

Amersfoort   p166

Amrâth Berghotel €€ Some 2km from the centre, this 80-room hotel has fairly functional business rooms that are reasonably priced in August and on Sunday nights.

Logement de Gaaper €€
Stay in the oldest surviving townhouse in Amersfoort, right on Hof, the biggest central square.

Leerhotel Het Klooster €€
Great value if slightly spartan rooms in a pseudo-medieval former monastery at the edge of Amersfoort. The staff are hospitality students.

Researched by
Barbara Woolsey

Rotterdam & South Holland

QUIRKY AND QUAINT DUTCH LIVING

This region is proudly a little offbeat. From naughty urban art to eccentric sights, the Netherlands' small southern cities offer a delightful combo of oddities and niceties.

Home to two of the Netherlands' major cities – Rotterdam and Den Haag – and many of its most traditionally pretty and historic towns, Zuid-Holland (South Holland) deserves kudos. Despite the region's popularity, its small urban centres keep true to their authentic flair and sincere hospitality.

Along with the provinces of Noord-Holland (North Holland) and Utrecht, South Holland is part of the Randstad, the Netherlands' economic heart, and half the Dutch population resides in this region. Traversing from coast to midland, South Holland offers vibrant landscapes and local life as you pedal past windmills (Kinderdijk), tulip-stuffed fields (Lisse), stately palaces (Den Haag) and sandy shores (Zeeland). As you cycle between canal-crossed cities (distances are short, usually only taking an hour or two), you get to know a multipack of memorable settings and landmarks.

Sightseeing can be charming and quaint, such as in 'Golden Age' darlings like Delft and Delfshaven (now part of Rotterdam), or Gouda's famously cheesy historic centre. Exploring unveils the unconventional and modern, too. Expect the unexpected out of Leiden landmarks shaped by famous intellectuals.

Meanwhile, Rotterdam, the second-largest Dutch city and home to Europe's largest port, moonlights as an open-air gallery. Crazily angled cube houses, pop-art protruding from office buildings and lots of naughty sculptures accentuate modern architecture and urban art. South Holland is anything but ordinary.

SINA ETTMER PHOTOGRAPHY/SHUTTERSTOCK

THE MAIN AREAS

ROTTERDAM
For geeks and art lovers alike. **p176**

DEN HAAG
Cultural sights, historical charm and world peace. **p199**

For places to stay in Rotterdam & South Holland, see p217

MIHAIULIA/SHUTTERSTOCK

Left: Den Haag (p199); Above: Erasmus Bridge (p192), Rotterdam

Find Your Way

South Holland is easy to navigate. City centres are smaller and closer together than they seem. Public transport is wonderfully efficient, though with a bike, you'll need it sparingly or not at all.

Den Haag, p199

Don't be fooled by the bureaucratic facade. Beyond its regal architecture and government institutions, the Netherlands' third-largest city offers astonishing cultural vibrancy, from museums to gastronomy.

Rotterdam, p176

The Netherlands' second-largest city (also Europe's biggest port) has proven itself the master of extreme urban makeovers thanks to world-class architecture and

WALKING

South Holland's cities, especially smaller centres like Lisse and Leiden, are a breeze for exploring on foot. Comfy sneakers are a must, though that's pretty much the Dutch dress code anyway. Still, a bicycle offers more freedom.

BICYCLE

Seeing South Holland's neatest old cities is best on two wheels. The longest regional distance between cities, Gouda to Lisse, is only 35km. Capture the scenery's full spectrum, from windmills to tulip spreads – plus, you never know what else will pop up en route.

PUBLIC TRANSPORT

Rotterdam and Den Haag, though seemingly bustling metropolises, are more compact than you think. You might never need to use metros, buses and trams if you're on foot or cycling, but the public transport systems are highly efficient and convenient.

Tilburg

Breda

NOORD BRABANT

Roosendaal

Bergen op Zoom

Sint Philipsland

Tholen

E312

Perkpolder

Zierikzee

Schouwen-Duiveland

Oosterschelde

Kruiningen

Goes

A58

Noord-Beveland

Zuid-Beveland

ZEELAND

Terneuzen

BELGIUM

Haamstede

N57

Veere

Walcheren

Middelburg

Vlissingen

Westerschelde

IJzendijke

Zeeuws-Vlaanderen

20 km

10 miles

Plan Your Time

Though among the smallest provinces (about 8% of the Netherlands' land area), Zuid-Holland packs in eclectic landscapes and attractions.

ALLARD ONE/SHUTTERSTOCK

Keukenhof Gardens (p216), Lisse

Short on Time

● Head to **De Rotterdam** (p195), a city-sized gallery of architecture, which, regardless of the season, has a *lekker* (awesome) programme of things to do.

● Beyond traipsing around taking in all the ubercool urban art, tour Europe's largest harbour port and visit the Depot exhibit by **Museum Boijmans van Beuningen** (p193), the **Maritiem Museum** (p184) and the architecturally striking food hall **Markthal** (p191).

● Get a taste for South Holland's eclectic, small-city-meets-traditional-countryside vibe in Rotterdam's 'Golden Age' remnant **Delfshaven** (p180), relaxing in beautiful *bruin cafés* (traditional Dutch pubs) such as **De Oude Sluis** (p189).

● Hop aboard a waterbus and sail to **Kinderdijk** (p197) to explore UNESCO-recognised windmills.

Seasonal Highlights

Booming tourism infrastructure – with lodgings and eateries at diverse price points – and a year-round events calendar make this region a seasonal all-rounder.

FEBRUARY

There's no better winter warmer than Den Haag's **Grauzone Festival** (p205). Duck into citywide venues for sweaty dancing to underground electronic music from disco to techno. Eye up annual themed exhibitions of avant-garde art.

MARCH

Keukenhof Gardens (p216), also known as the 'Gardens of Europe', sees seven million flower bulbs abloom. This attraction in Lisse is open only from mid-March to mid-May and welcomes more than a million annual visitors.

APRIL

Stay in a funky art installation or take artist-guided expeditions during Rotterdam's **Motel Mozaïque** (p205). The three-day festival for experimental and alternative culture spans live concerts and multidisciplinary art.

With a Few Days

● Make stops across the southern coast, starting with **Den Haag** (p199). The city's **Mauritshuis** (p209) unfurls a who's who of Dutch and Flemish masters, and the paintings *Girl with a Pearl Earring* and *The Goldfinch* are must-sees. Don't miss Escher's logic-defying graphic art in the grandiose **Paleis Noordeinde** (p208).

● Short train rides bring out the prismatic gamut of southern Dutch landscapes, from sandy beaches and the seasonal tulip fields at **Keukenhof Gardens** (p216) to attraction-filled **Leiden** (p214) and the diminutive, canal-woven streets of **Delft** (p211).

● Head into the heartland to get a smorgasbord of food and culture in **Gouda** (p196). A day admiring architecture, street art and museum exhibits in **Rotterdam** (p176) can be on the cards, too.

Two Weeks in South Holland

● Two weeks is more than enough for a leisurely spin, catching iconic Dutch sights. Hit the Netherlands' second- and third-largest cities, cutting-edge **Rotterdam** (p176) and governmental seat **Den Haag** (p199), plus an array of little cities and countryside between the two.

● From Rotterdam, savour the windmills of **Kinderdijk** (p197) and treats both savoury and sweet in **Gouda** (p196).

● From **Den Haag** (p199), spend a day among the old-world splendour of **Leiden** (p214) and a treasure chest of medieval and 'Golden Age' goodies in Vermeer's hometown, **Delft** (p211). Don't miss **Keukenhof Gardens** (p216), the world's largest bulb-flower garden. Leave the crowds behind for coastal dunes and invigorating, wide, windswept beaches in **Scheveningen** (p203).

JUNE
Rotterdam Architecture Month (p205) provides insider access, from guided tours of the city's coolest buildings to exhibitions hosted by local firms. Every year, the festival changes its main venue to a surprising pop-up location.

JULY
Rotterdam's don't-miss **North Sea Jazz Festival** (p205), the world's largest jazz extravaganza, attracts top-notch performers for 150-some concerts over three days. Even more performances take place in the weeks leading up to it.

AUGUST
Europe's biggest open-air cinema, **Pleinbioscoop** *(leinbi oscooprotterdam.nl),* hosts movie nights under the stars. **Duizel in Het Park** promises literary events, theatre and plenty of live music in **Vroesenpark** (p190).

OCTOBER
Leiden grinds to a halt for **Ontzet** (p205) commemorating the day the Spanish-caused starvation ended in 1574. Expect ceremonial servings of *hutspot* (stew), herring, white bread and beer-fuelled revelry.

175

Rotterdam

URBAN ART | MODERN ARCHITECTURE | MARITIME CULTURE

GETTING AROUND

Most of Rotterdam is easily walkable from Centraal Station. Otherwise, efficient tram, bus, and metro services and extensive bike paths keep the city well connected. Hail a watertaxi for an unconventionally cool sightseeing and transport experience. The digital **Rotterdam City Card** (*citycard. rotterdam.info; from €15/day*) offers unlimited rides on public transport (excluding watertaxis), as well as museum discounts.

☑ TOP TIP

A photo op on Rotterdam's harbour is essential, but do so mindfully. The decks of beautiful historic barges may seem inviting, but many are residents' doorsteps. Before you strike a pose, observe signs saying 'Private. No entry unless invited'. Respect the folks living on them by knocking and asking first.

The Netherlands' second metropolis and Europe's largest port makes for some of the continent's most fabulous (and surprisingly lesser-visited) cool hunting. Funky urban aesthetics, innovation and happening events are the local mantra, and the enthusiasm with which Rotterdammers do joie de vivre is mighty infectious. Despite rising word of mouth about local urban design and outdoor festivals, the city's vibe stays lovably personable and low-key.

Split by the Nieuwe Maas' vast shipping channel, waterways and tunnels are the stages for endless hustle and bustle. Visitors intermingle with city dwellers, zipping across sleek designer bridges, taking water taxis, and sauntering along picturesque inner-city canals and through a compact city centre. Prepare to be thoroughly impressed by an arts circuit spanning street art and sleek museums and galleries.

Who says Rotterdam is a second city? Overall, its authentic (less touristy) metropolitan charm gives Amsterdam a glorious run for its money.

Centrum

This neighbourhood is the heart of Rotterdam, a resplendent showcase of post-WWII architecture and heavy-hitting cultural institutions. As you walk around the city, you'll probably spend more time looking up than ahead, visually sidetracked by the profusion of interesting high-rise buildings. Many of these date from the 1940s and 1950s, but some are new – and extremely exciting – arrivals. Indoors, there are plenty of museums and galleries to visit, as well as an exciting lineup of restaurants, cafes, bars and clubs to investigate. Keep your eyes open for public art installations, too.

Centrum has loads to see and enjoy, so devise a plan of attack before hitting the streets. You need at least three days to do the neighbourhood justice – four days would be better. Most businesses and institutions don't open their doors until 10am, so treat yourself to some extra shut-eye before starting for the day.

MRFRED/SHUTTERSTOCK

Cube houses

SUPERDUTCH ARCHITECTURE

Rotterdam's cityscape is the calling card for the SuperDutch architecture movement that grew up here. Soaring to popularity in the 1990s and early 2000s, the Rotterdam skyline truly defines the SuperDutch concept's blending of purpose with playful aesthetic, such as mixed-use 'vertical cities' building up commercial and residential spaces.

The Rotterdam-based Office of Metropolitan Architecture, led by starchitect Rem Koolhaas, is largely credited with SuperDutch innovation, exemplified locally by buildings such as the **Kunsthal** (p184), **De Rotterdam** (p195) and **Timmerhuis**. Notable SuperDutch buildings by Dutch architecture firms abroad include the futuristic Mercedes-Benz Museum in Stuttgart, Germany, and the MVRDV architectural firm's so-called 'radical density' concepts in Tianjin, China, and Madrid, Spain.

Cubed houses galore

Perched high above the roads and intricately intertwined, Rotterdam's legendary row of cube houses, tilted at a 55-degree angle, never fail to captivate passersby departing from the city centre's **Blaak Station**.

In the 1970s, city planners faced the challenge of uniting residential blocks across Blaak St. Architect Piet Blom's ingenious solution was cubic homes. The resulting **Blaakse Bos** (Black Woods) development, inspired as an urban forest, comprises 38 vibrantly coloured residences and two 'super cubes' resting on hexagonal pylons.

All cubes are privately owned, spanning 100 sq metres across multiple floors connected by steep staircases. One apartment, the **Kijk-Kubus Museumwoning** *(Cube House Museum; kubuswoning.nl; adult/child €3.50/1.50),* has been transformed into a staged apartment you can visit.

The southernmost cube, **Stayokay Rotterdam** (p217), is a hostel, offering private rooms and dorms with awesome Old Harbour views and unique perspectives on the adjoining cubic troop and Rotterdam's skyline.

Rare, resilient skyscraper

Only 200m from the Overblaak Development, you'll find one of Rotterdam's sole survivors of the prewar period. Dating from 1897, Europe's first 'skyscraper' is the 10-storey, 45m-high **Witte Huis** *(inhetwittehuis.nl).* It's an art nouveau icon raised with load-bearing brick walls rather than a steel skeleton. An interior **cafe** *(closed Sun & Mon)* keeps with the gorgeous exterior style, elegantly flaunting multicoloured stained-glass windows, glass chandeliers and high ceilings. Head inside for a slick sundowner cocktail.

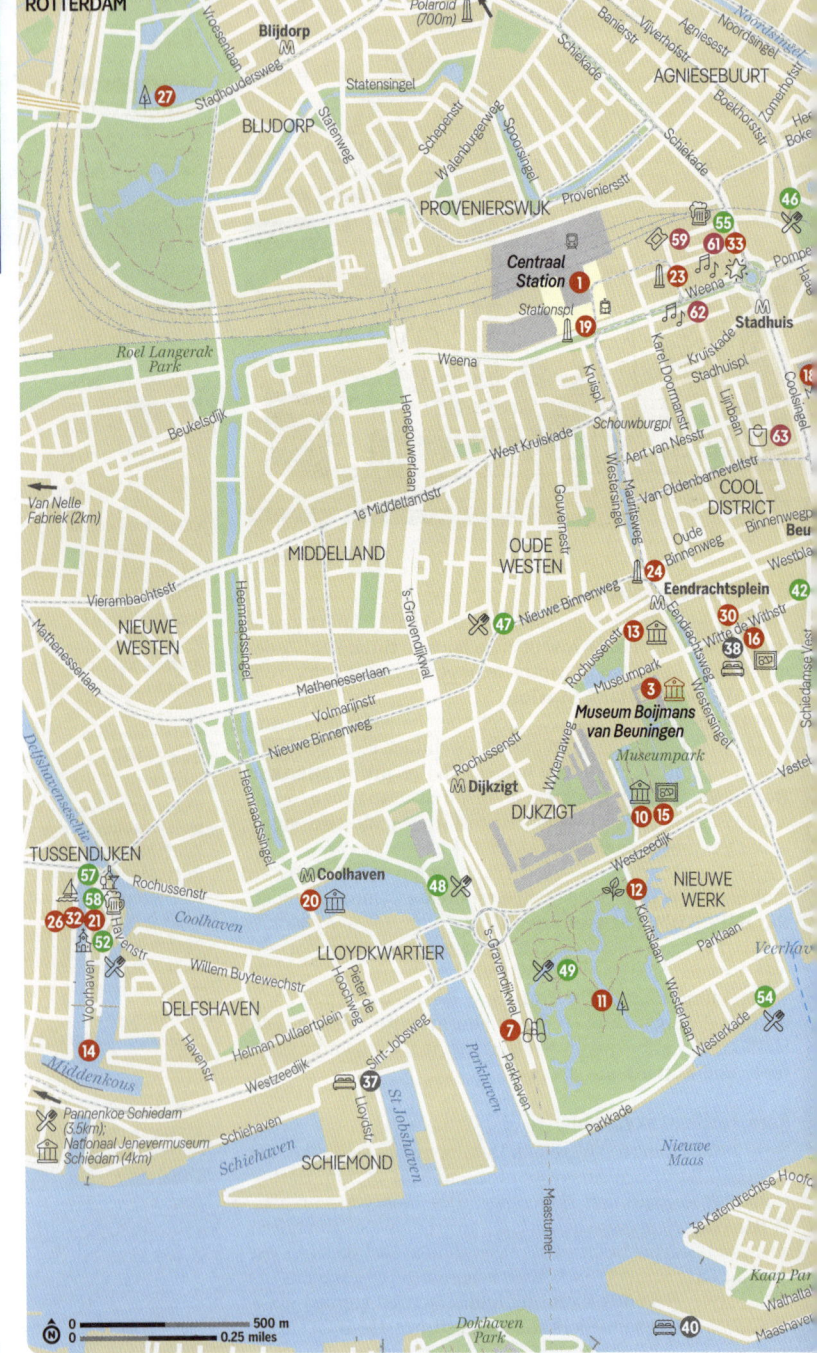

ROTTERDAM

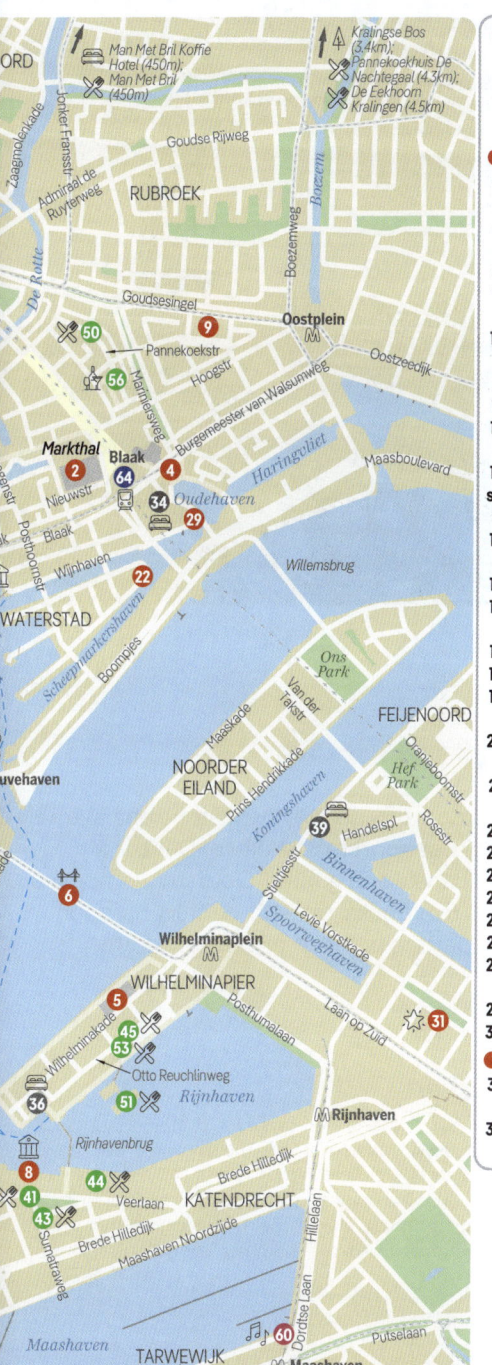

★ HIGHLIGHTS

1 Centraal Station
2 Markthal
3 Museum Boijmans van Beuningen

● SIGHTS

4 Blaakse Bos
5 De Rotterdam
6 Erasmusbrug
7 Euromast
8 Fenix
9 Het Industriegebouw
10 Het Natuurhistorisch Museum
11 Het Park
12 Historische Tuin Schoonoord
13 Huis Sonneveld
see 4 Kijk-Kubus Museumwoning
14 Korenmolen de Distilleerketel
15 Kunsthal
16 Kunstinstituut Melly
17 Maritiem Museum
18 McDonald's
19 Moments Contained
20 Museum Rotterdam
21 Oude of Pelgrimvaderskerk
22 Red Apple
23 Red BMW
24 Santa Claus
25 Timmerhuis
26 Tovertunnel
27 Vroesenpark
28 Wereldmuseum Rotterdam
29 Witte Huis
30 WORM

● ACTIVITIES

31 City Rotterdam Tours
32 iKapitein Boats & Bites
33 Urban Guides

● SLEEPING

34 CitizenM
35 Haven Hotel
36 Hotel New York
37 Hotel Stroom
38 King Kong Hostel
39 Pincoffs
40 SS Rotterdam
see 4 Stayokay Rotterdam

● EATING

41 CEO Baas van Het Vlees
42 De IJsmaker
43 De Matroos en Het Meisje
44 Fenix Food Factory
45 Foodhallen Rotterdam
46 François Geurds
47 Lilith
48 Old Scuola West
49 Parqiet
50 Pierre
51 Putaine
52 Restaurant Frits
53 Rolph's Deli
54 Zeezout

● DRINKING & NIGHTLIFE

55 Biergarten
56 Bokaal
57 De Oude Sluis
58 Stadsbrouwerij De Pelgrim

● ENTERTAINMENT

59 Cultuurpodium Perron
60 Maassilo
61 Operator Radio
62 Toffler

● SHOPPING

63 De Bijenkorf

● TRANSPORT

64 Blaak Station

DMITRY RUKHLENKO/SHUTTERSTOCK

TOP EXPERIENCE

Delfshaven

Just 3km southwest of Rotterdam city centre, the historic enclave of Delfshaven, once the official seaport for the city of Delft, is a spectacle of picture-perfect canals and gabled 'Golden Age' houses. Situated on the Nieuwe Maas riverbanks, the 14th-century harbour borough was a significant departure point for pilgrims to North America in 1620.

DON'T MISS

Harbour houses

Canal views

Tovertunnel

Pilgrim Fathers Church

De Oude Sluis

Historic Port

Once a two-sided area of working-class dwellings and wealthy harbour houses, Delfshaven was incorporated into Rotterdam as a poverty-stricken district after a 19th-century recession. One of the few neighbourhoods in Rotterdam to escape bombardment during WWII, this historic port area retains many traditional features, including a windmill, churches and *bruin cafés*.

New Port Order

These days, Delfshaven is a united front for new urban cool across art galleries, designer studios and eateries.

No aspect captures Delshaven's 'Golden Age 2.0' quite like **Tovertunnel** *(Magic Tunnel; free; daylight hours)*. One of the few *achterbuurt* (backstreet) alleys formerly connecting the rich and poor areas, the stretch on Schansstraat–Aelbrechtskolk was considered unsafe post-recession. In 1996, Rotterdam-based artist Willij Vanderlinden brought the passage from gloom to enchantment with colourful paintings and neon lights. The aesthetic, she says, is a symbolic combining of past and present and was also inspired by the desire to stop the dark alleyway from scaring children.

Pilgrim History

In 1608, 300-plus Calvinist Protestants split from the Anglican church and left persecution in England to settle in Leiden. Valuing a liberal atmosphere, influenced by the university and fellow Calvinist residents, they found solace here.

In 1618, when James I of England announced that he would assume control over them again, they set their sights across the Atlantic. The first group left Leiden in 1620 for Delfshaven, where they bought the *Speedwell* vessel.

Unfortunately, the leaky ship didn't live up to its name. After several attempts, the group gave up and, against their better judgment, sailed into Southampton, England. After repairs and a thwarted attempt to continue their journey, the group abandoned ship and joined the much more seaworthy *Mayflower* in Dartmouth and sailed, as it were, into history as pilgrims.

The Pilgrims prayed for the last time at the 15th-century **Oude of Pelgrimvaderskerk** (Pilgrim Fathers Church) before leaving for the 'New World' on 1 August 1620. Locals worship here on Sundays and also attend the regular cultural events, often musical evenings, hosted at other times.

Pilgrim Brewery

A short walk from Oude of Pelgrimvaderskerk, a 30-year-old *proeflokaal* (tasting room) speaks to modern times in Delfshaven's new Golden Age. The sight of bubbling wood and copper vats and the heady scent of hops greets you in the **Stadsbrouwerij De Pelgrim** *(City Brewery The Pilgrim; pelgrimbier.nl)*. The brewery is located in the atmospheric interiors of Delfshaven's former town hall. Take a voyage through its wonderful seasonal and standard beers in the bar, canal-side terrace or courtyard.

This brewery produces a wide variety of seasonal beers, but locals know they can rely on its best-known tipple, the Mayflower Tripel, to be available year-round. In winter, the historic taproom is a cosy spot, and in summer, the sunny canalside terrace beckons.

WONDERFUL WINDMILL

From the waterside, catch the **Korenmolen de Distilleerketel** windmill hard at work. The reconstructed 18th-century windmill is a testament to Delfshaven's industrial heritage, and it still grinds grain today. The interior is not open to the public, but the *bruin café* **De Oude Sluis** (p189) offers the perfect canal view.

TOP TIPS

● City life is slower in Delfshaven than elsewhere, particularly on weekdays. On weekends, visitors from Rotterdam descend.

● Have dinner at **Restaurant Frits** *(restaurantfrits.nl)* and then drinks at **De Oude Sluis** (p189) overlooking a windmill.

● The harbour is reached via a historical tram (or watertaxi) from Rotterdam's Centraal Station and makes for a lovely afternoon stop for strolling and canal-side dining. Tovertunnel is accessible only during the day.

● Rent a boat from **iKapitein** (p186) and explore Delfshaven's canals on the water. No boating licence is required; you'll get some guidance beforehand.

MORE CITY-CENTRE ARCHITECTURAL MARVELS

Huis Sonneveld: Outstanding example of Dutch Functionalism. A museum inside houses original 1930s decor. *(huissonneveld.nl)*

De Bijenkorf: The 1957-built 'Beehive' is one of Rotterdam's 'older' buildings. From the modern department store inside, you'd never know.

McDonald's: Rotterdam's chic 'Golden Arches' has a glass facade and a dramatic spiral staircase perfectly suited for Hamburglar getaways.

Het Industriege-bouw: National postwar monument embodying SuperDutch principles. Houses creative businesses, including powerhouse architecture firm MVRDV. *(hetindus triegebouw.nl)*

Red Apple: This crimson-hued, mixed-use tower, one of the city's tallest, is also publicly considered one of its most aesthetically controversial.

PICTOR PICTURES/SHUTTERSTOCK

Pop goes urban art

During the war, Rotterdam was destroyed and hastily recon-structed with uninspiring concrete buildings, which didn't impress its cheery, fun-loving residents. To inject creativity and beautify the city, a group of Dutch pop artists, Kunst en Vaarwerk, initiated art installations from 1979 to 1992 to in-geniously revamp existing buildings. Now, Rotterdam's urban design delightfully reflects locals' joie de vivre.

Most well-known is the gravity-defying art installation **Red BMW**. The vehicle protrudes from the glass facade of Weena 169 like a freeze-framed fender bender. It's one street away from Centraal Station (p187), but you have to look past the obscuring residential buildings.

A 20-minute walk north of Centraal on Gordelweg, a massive pinned **Polaroid** photo gussies up an ugly motorway viaduct. This intentionally skewed artwork features changing images of Rotterdam's harbour, from a ship's deck to a harbour cargo crane over the years.

Many more of these kooky art installations lurk around the city, including a hat on a lake, a tank transformed into an old-timey hat box (complete with a red buckle) and a metro line held up by a rolled newspaper (an otherwise lame con-crete column).

The website of Rotterdam's BKOR (Visual Arts & Public Space) foundation *(bkor.nl)* offers a zoomable map of the city's art installations, including these sculptures and more.

Buttplug or pine tree?

Rotterdam's most controversial art is the **Santa Claus** on Eendrachtsplein, and in this city, that's saying something. The 2001-commissioned bronze-cast sculpture by Ameri-can artist Paul McCarthy was meant for display on elegant

Red BMW art installation

Schouwburgplein, but it was eventually set here after locals expressed that it didn't resemble Santa holding a pine, but a dwarf with a sex toy.

The nickname 'Buttplug Gnome' has stuck, an inside joke for the city (though, at €280,000, an expensive one). Also on Eendrachtsplein, a hotel named Unplugged has no relation, supposedly.

Living cultures and a colonial past

The ethnographic **Wereldmuseum Rotterdam** (*rotterdam. wereldmuseum.nl; adult/child €18/8; closed Mon*) is as great as a cultural attraction can get.

Traipsing around the stately 19th-century Royal Yacht Club building, permanent and temporary exhibitions explore topics such as world culture, identity and immigration through engaging lenses, such as the customs of wedding dresses in different cultures or world peace through exhibits on ecocide, Islamophobia, female diaspora and Palestine. Educational moments are imbued with enjoyment, such as the interactive permanent children's exhibition, Superstreet, where little ones touch objects and explore world festivals and dance through multimedia displays.

Since 2023, the Wereldmuseum shares its name ('World Museum') with three other Dutch national museums (Leiden's former Museum Volkenkunde, Berg en Dal's Afrika Museum and the Tropenmuseum in Amsterdam). Each institution maintains its original collection and acts independently, but shares a greater vision of addressing colonialism's legacy in museums and ethnography. In 2024, Rotterdam's Wereldmuseum set a historic precedent through the restitution of colonial-era objects to Indonesia, the first time a Dutch city has done so. Pre-purchasing tickets online nets a small discount (*adult/child €16/6.50*).

ARCHITECTURAL MYSTERY BAG

Rotterdam is a vast open-air museum of 20th- and 21st-century architecture spanning ultramodern to retro. Important and eye-popping buildings are plopped around the city and are especially concentrated in its compact, easy-to-stroll centre. Rotterdam's municipality has long been a crusader for innovative, sustainable and exciting urban design. Even locals are hard-pressed to know their skyline's wide reach.

Today, Rotterdam's skyline is still a work in progress. Boundary-pushing blueprints currently under construction include the black marble-designed BaanTower and the MVDRV firm's 'The Sax' high-rise development, a new 'vertical city' with a sleek, silver silhouette inspired by the musical instrument.

ART HEIST

In the early hours of an October morning in 2012, thieves broke into the Kunsthal and stole seven paintings on loan from the Dutch Triton Foundation: two by Monet, and one each by Picasso, Gauguin, Matisse, Freud and de Haan (valued somewhere between €50 and €100 million).

Subsequent questions about inadequate security ensued. Using a rear emergency exit, the intruders were in and out in two minutes. A year later, authorities tracked down the paintings. Art lovers were horrified to hear they were taken to Romania and destroyed, with paint and canvas remnants located in the oven of one thief's mother. The burglary ring was convicted, as was the mother for hiding stolen property.

Always changing art exhibitions

A visit to **Kunsthal** *(kunsthal.nl; adult/child €14/free; closed Mon)* in Museumpark is always surprising, thanks to a cool rotation of temporary exhibitions showing the likes of big names from Andy Warhol to Roy Lichtenstein. That's only partially by choice – the Kunsthal was the victim of a major theft, and a touring program has taken place ever since. The museum's architecturally notable multifloored building always has at least three exhibitions to visit.

Galleries, cafes and boutiques

Winding along the Witte de Withstraat (which leads to Museumpark) unfurls a charming array of excellent cafes, independent shops and art galleries, prime for exploring. Along the strip, a diverse honeypot of establishments includes a soju bar, a design shop-gallery dedicated to the avant-garde CoBrA group and a strong candidate for Rotterdam's best ice cream shop, **De IJsmaker** *(deijsmaker.nl)*. Side streets reveal more arts venues, including the alternative nightlife and culture centre **WORM** *(worm.org)*.

Kunstinstituut Melly *(kunstinstituutmelly.nl; adult/child €10/5; closed Mon & Tue)* is worth a stop. The gallery gazes worldwide with experimental, political exhibitions. In 2017, a decolonial name change swapped a Dutch admiral's eponym for Melly, a new moniker inspired by Canadian artist Ken Lum's *Melly Shum Hates Her Job* (a 1989 local billboard that had a cult fanbase). The billboard now graces the gallery's facade.

Aboard seafaring history

The **Maritiem Museum** *(maritiemmuseum.nl; adult/child €17.50/12.50; closed Mon)* overlooking Leuvehaven offers a

TRABANTOS/SHUTTERSTOCK

Witte de Withstraat

EAT HERRING LIKE THE DUTCH

The Dutch have a traditional way of enjoying raw herring *(haring)* called *Hollandse Nieuwe* or *haringtje eten aan de staart* (eating herring by the tail). Grab the herring by the tail, tilt your head back and let the fish slide into your mouth all in one bite. The method comes from when street vendors once sold the fish whole. A firm tail grip ensured a bull's-eye of slippery, oily snack to mouth – no utensils or cleanup necessary. Serviettes weren't a thing back then, anyway.

The raw herring is freshly caught and lightly salted, and often served with finely chopped onions and sometimes pickles. Traditionally, the 'chaser' is a throat-searing shot of *jenever*. For a slightly less daring approach, order a *broodje haring* (herring in a bun), but don't expect to impress any locals.

touch of harbour history and strolling. Exhibits, from crane simulators to joystick-steered ships, entertain parental units, too. Moored out front, a functioning collection of historic vessels provides photo ops, and many can be boarded.

A watertaxi (p176) can take you right to the museum, but departing from here is a little less convenient as it's a popular embarkment stop. Phone ahead *(010-403 03 03)* to book your ride or visit the museum as an early stop on a day of Centrum exploring.

Adolescent fun for all ages

The exhibits at **Het Natuurhistorisch Museum** *(Natural History Museum; hetnatuurhistorisch.nl; adult/child €13.50/7.50; closed Mon)* are primarily geared to children, but parents might just feel like kids again, too.

The museum aces delivering facts in a fun way. Floors of exhibits present a motley crew of specimens, fossils and bones, ranging from insects to gargantuan skeletons like Ramo the Asian elephant. A lot is packed in without too many steps or spaces where you'll have to carry or chase little ones around. The collection aside, what's more enjoyable than that for parents?

EATING & DRINKING IN CENTRUM: OUR PICKS

Man Met Bril: The modern all-day brunch is a hit list of food trends, but everything's yummy. *7am-5pm Mon-Fri, 8am-6pm Fri & Sat* €€

Pierre: Modern, rustic interiors and sunny pavement seating. The long menu includes small or big plates of fish stew and beef bourguignon. *10am-midnight or later* €€

Biergarten: A sun-bleached labyrinth of wooden tables for sundowners: ice-cold pilsner, house-made lemonade and barbecue. *hours vary*

Bokaal: Boasts an all-day sunny space heaving with craft-beer sippers and food-truck action on summer nights. *11am-1am*

OLRAT/SHUTTERSTOCK

Het Park

ROTTERDAMMERS' SUMMER OF LOVE

Lotte Biesheuvel and **Tim Hölscher** are Dutch newlyweds living in Rotterdam. These are their favourite activities to do as a couple.

iKapitein Boats & Bites: Go to Delfshaven and explore the canals on a self-driving boat with your own food, drinks and music. *(ikapitein.nl)*

Kralingse Bos: The perfect park-lake combo for an afternoon of cycling. Before you go, eat at De Eekhoorn Kralingen or Pannekoekhuis De Nachtegaal. *(hetkralingsebos.nl)*

Het Park: After you go up the Euromast, walk around the park and have lunch on the lawn at Parqiet. We also love Old Scuola West, which has a terrace and proper Italian pizzas. *(hetparkinrotterdam.nl)*

Westen

Don't be put off by the fact that this neighbourhood lacks major tourist sights, because it compensates with one of the city's few 'Golden Age' enclaves (Delfshaven), a major cafe strip (Nieuwe Binnenweg) and the beautifully landscaped surrounds of Het Park. At the end of the day, local *bruin cafés,* a scattering of restaurants and good nightlife promise at least a full day of satisfying exploration.

Most of the action in Oude Westen, the pocket closest to the city centre, occurs along the major boulevards of West Kruiskade and Nieuwe Binnenweg – you'll have no problem sourcing a meal or coffee here. Nieuwe Binnenweg leads to the Delftshavenseschie, a canal going to the former entrepôt of Coolhaven, home to the excellent Museum Rotterdam. If you continue west from here, you come to the charming town of Schiedam, home to historic distilleries making *jenever* (Dutch gin).

Greenery for every desire

Landscaped in English-garden style, **Het Park** *(hetparkin rotterdam.nl)* was established in 1852 and is much loved by locals. Families come here to picnic and grill in the designated barbecuing area, and kids blow off steam swinging on low-branched trees and climbing frames. Cyclists and strollers abound. Beyond enjoying leafy spaces, you can grab a coffee to-go at the charming **Parqiet** *(parqiet.nl).* The cafe's deck chairs spread out on the lawn also invite sitting pretty.

Immediately east of the park is **Historische Tuin Schoonoord** *(tuinschoonoord.nl; free),* a small gated garden planted during the same period.

Centraal Station

The most used – and quite possibly best loved – building in Rotterdam, Centraal Station was designed by Benthem Crouwel, MVSA and West 8. Built between 1999 and 2013, it features a dramatically angled passenger hall with a pointed, stainless steel–clad roof that almost punches into the sky. Beyond being an artwork in itself, contemporary art is becoming a focus on Stationsplein square.

JESPER SOHOF/SHUTTERSTOCK

Striking Architecture

Rotterdam's reputation as a contemporary architecture powerhouse starts at its first point of arrival. Opened in 2014, Centraal Station is the angular result of a decade-long redevelopment project.

The sweeping steel structure does not take a single geometric form. From a full-frontal view on Stationsplein, the building's shape looks like a slanted, asymmetrical wave – maybe a pyramid as painted by surrealist artist Salvador Dalí. The crowning feature, a glass-and-steel roof, blesses transiting passengers with abundant natural light.

Gallery in Transit

The station is also a contemporary art gallery. Temporary exhibitions sometimes appear in collaboration with Sculpture International Rotterdam and others.

On Stationsplein, look up at **Moments Contained**. Nearly 4m tall, the bronze sculpture by British artist Thomas J Price depicts a Black woman standing casually, hands in her jeans pockets. The sculpture calls out a lack of diversity within public monuments and stays here until at least 2028. The sculpture was inspired by another Price work, *Reaching Out,* originally showcased in London. Here, the sculpted figure casually scrolls through her phone.

Sometimes Stationsplein also hosts festivals and markets.

TOP TIPS

● Long-distance trains and buses arrive at Centraal Station.

● Witte de Withstraat and Nieuwe Binnenweg are notable nearby walking streets.

● Find out about upcoming activities and events on the station's official website *(mijnstation.nl/rotterdam/activities)*.

PRACTICALITIES

● ns.nl/stationsinformatie/rtd/rotterdam-centraal
● free ● 24hr; shops 10am-6pm Mon-Thu & Sat, to 9pm Fri

COOL HUNTING IN CENTRUM

Cycling from Centraal Station, get a perfect taster of what Rotterdam does best: in-your-face architecture and hidden art finds.

START	END	LENGTH
Moments Contained	Markthal	5km; 1 hr

Stand on Weena and look back at Stationsplein for the perfect view of Centraal Station's distinctive stainless-steel-clad roof against the thought-provoking sculpture ❶ **Moments Contained** (p187). The bronze-cast Black woman reflects on historical power and representation.

Hop on your bike over to Weena-Zuid and turn down Poortstraat to see a crashed ❷ **Red BMW** (p182) protruding from a building. (It's art, obviously.) Turn right onto Delfsestraat and take the roundabout onto Coolsingel to ❸ **De Bijenkorf** (p182). The grand dame of Amsterdam School architecture is still impressive today, despite Rotterdam's modern heavyweights. Turn onto Oude Binnenweg and cycle until you reach Eendrachtsplein's controversial ❹ **Santa Claus** (p182) sculpture.

Continue onto Nieuwe Binnenweg and turn left onto Museumstraat, staying left onto Rochussenstraat to end up in front of the Dutch Functionalist icon ❺ **Huis Sonneveld** (p182). Go south on Westersingel for a peek at ❻ **Museum Boijmans van Beuningen** (p193), the city's major art gallery, in Museumpark.

Cycle back to Oude Binnenweg until Binnenwegplein and turn left onto Bulgersteyn to the ❼ **Markthal** (p191) entrance on Binnenrotte. From here, take in the full view of the Blaakse Bos development, some of Rotterdam's most distinctive buildings. Park your bike and wander inside the Markthal to snack on gourmet delicacies and rest your legs under an arched mural ceiling depicting fruits and vegetables.

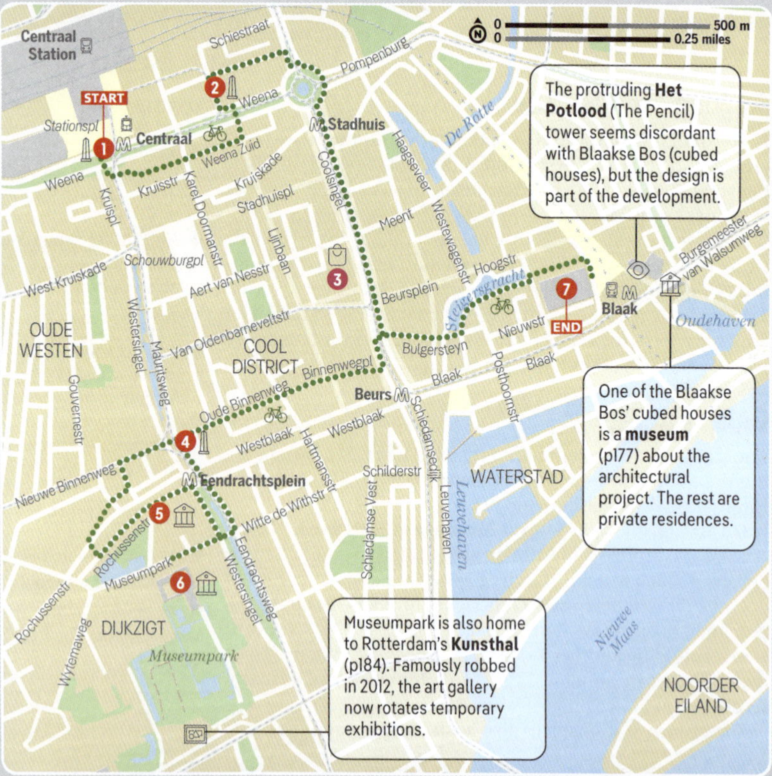

The protruding **Het Potlood** (The Pencil) tower seems discordant with Blaakse Bos (cubed houses), but the design is part of the development.

One of the Blaakse Bos' cubed houses is a **museum** (p177) about the architectural project. The rest are private residences.

Museumpark is also home to Rotterdam's **Kunsthal** (p184). Famously robbed in 2012, the art gallery now rotates temporary exhibitions.

Old Dutch mast(er)

Designed by HA Maaskant as a landmark and built between 1958 and 1960, the 185m-high **Euromast** *(euromast.nl; adult/child from €13/9)* might be ancient history as far as Rotterdam's modern architecture is concerned, but it's still hip. Located next to Het Park, the building offers unparalleled 360-degree views of Rotterdam from its 100m-high observation deck. Or you can go even higher: the rotating glass Euroscoop lift goes right to the top of the mast.

It's also possible to enjoy a drink or meal at the cocktail bar–brasserie underneath the observation deck or overnight in two hotel suites on the observation deck. Thrill-seekers can sign up for weekend abseiling and ziplining up and down the tower *(from €67.50; May-Sep)*.

A journey through Rotterdam's past

The '40-'45 NOW exhibition at **Museum Rotterdam** *(museumrotterdam.nl; adult/child €12.50/free; closed Mon)* provides deep insights into the most pivotal day of WWII for the city: the Rotterdam bombing on 14 May 1940 (p190), when the entire historic centre was destroyed. It reveals also what led up to the moment when 54 German aircraft dropped more than 1000 bombs in a mere 13 minutes.

Revamped factory

Built between 1925 and 1931, the modernist World Heritage–listed **Van Nelle Fabriek** *(vannellefabriekrotterdam.com)*, northwest of the city centre, is an icon of 20th-century industrial design. Often described as a steel and glass palace, the factory was a state-of-the-art coffee, tea and tobacco factory until the 1990s. It now houses creative industries.

Though closed to the public, architecture excursion agency **Urban Guides** *(urbanguides.nl)* runs one-hour guided tours of the building. These tours peek into the management area and electricity plant (the second built in Rotterdam) on a distinctive diagonal bridge. It ends in the tobacco factory's light-drenched spaces, twin stairways that workers separately scaled (one for each sex, preventing fraternisation), and a sprawling cafeteria.

Look east from the factory and spot the **De Schie Penitentiary**, a 1980s low bunker with a startling orange and blue colour scheme starkly contrasting with its dark function.

EUROPEAN JAZZ CAPITAL

Music dominates Rotterdam's year-round entertainment calendar, with plenty of festivals and venues on offer, but the **North Sea Jazz Festival** *(northseajazz.com)* reigns supreme. On the second weekend of July, the annual festivities harmonise hundreds of musicians across 15 stages and 150-some, genre-spanning performances. Impromptu, informal jam sessions are also known to pop up across clubs and bar stages.

In the weeks prior, the **North Sea Round Town fringe festival** also hosts a variety of jazz acts across public spaces and concert halls. Festival performances are truly a year-long affair, though; check the North Sea website for the full programme.

EATING & DRINKING IN WESTEN: OUR PICKS

Lilith: Neighbourhood favourite with a crowded terrace in sunny weather. Queuing for tables is not unknown, but the breakfast and lunch are worth it. *9am-5pm* €

Parqiet: Wildflowers in Kilner jars, terrace seating and striped deckchairs on the front lawn contribute to the charm of this cafe in a former coach house in Het Park. *9am-6pm* €

Pannenkoe Schiedam: The IHOP of the Netherlands is essentially this family-friendly pancake house. Good kids' menu. *11am-8.30pm* €

De Oude Sluis: This *bruin café* in Delfshaven has a terrace with views down the canal to a reconstructed 18th-century windmill. *noon-1am or later*

ROTTERDAM BLITZ

A single event has largely shaped modern Rotterdam. On 14 May 1940, near the beginning of WWII, a squadron of 90 Luftwaffe planes dropped more than 1000 bombs on the city, destroying buildings and setting off a firestorm that levelled the medieval city centre and many other neighbourhoods. When the fires eventually died down, Rotterdammers were faced with the immense task of surviving the war.

Germans controlled the city from 1940 to 1945, and Rotterdam suffered Allied attacks in and around the port. On 31 March 1943, one of these raids went horribly wrong when the US Air Force mistakenly bombed a residential area, killing hundreds. Only after Germany's defeat could locals begin to rebuild both the city and their lives.

Sip the nation's treasured spirit

Housed in an 18th-century distillery, the **Nationaal Jenever-museum Schiedam** *(jenevermuseum.nl; adult/child €15/10; closed Mon)* is dedicated to the industry that the town of Schiedam is best known for: the production of the traditional Dutch gin known as *jenever*.

In 1850, when the industry was at its height, hundreds of businesses distilled malt wine and added juniper to produce this liquor, which was shipped all over the world. The distillery's huge bins, cooling vessels and copper distilling kettles are still here, as are a number of upstairs exhibits about *jenever*-making.

Floating art in Vroesenpark

The leafy, locally loved **Vroesenpark** is a residential Westen favourite for its endless rolling greens and a small lake with a kooky surprise. *Het Badkonijn* (Bath Bunny) is a collaborative piece of public art and essentially the mascot of Westen. From March to October, people take turns painting the floating rubber-ducky-bunny mascot in every design imaginable. In the off-season, he gets a good scrub.

The bunny also shares the lake with another water-logged sculpture, *Hat of Lou Bandy,* a giant boater-style straw hat floating upside-down in the water (also removed in the off-season) commemorating a Dutch vaudeville entertainer. It's one of many unexpected art installations around Rotterdam designed by the Dutch pop-art group, Kunst en Vaarwerk (p182).

August is the perfect time to visit Vroesenpark when both sculptures are afloat amid the three-day **Duizel in Het Park festival** *(duizelinhetpark.nl),* full of literary events, exhibitions, theatre and live music.

Zuiden

It's not that long ago that the port areas south of the Nieuwe Maas were no-go zones for most Rotterdammers. These days, the situation couldn't be more different. Since city authorities initiated major programmes in the 1980s to redevelop both the docks at Kop van Zuid (South Bank) and the red-light district on the Katendrecht peninsula, this part of town has acquired cutting-edge architecture, a great restaurant and bar scene, boutique hotels, and a reputation as one of the city's must-visit neighbourhoods.

 EATING IN ROTTERDAM: FINE DINING

De Matroos en Het Meisje: Dutch fine dining in a spectacular setting with Delft Blue walls and chequered tablecloths. *6pm-midnight daily, plus noon-4pm Sat & Sun* €€€

François Geurds: The Michelin-starred tasting menus from Rotterdam's best-known chef are edible masterpieces. *6.30-8.30pm Wed & Thu, noon-1.30pm & 7-9pm Fri & Sat* €€€

Putaine: Trendy dishes on a Rijnhaven-docked pontoon. Floor-to-ceiling windows and a sunny terrace for fab lunches. *6pm-midnight Mon, from noon Tue-Sat* €€€

Zeezout: Rotterdam's fanciest seafood cuisine, modernly prepared with luscious foams and garnishes. *noon-2pm & 6-9pm Wed, Thu & Sat, to 8.30pm Fri* €€€

Markthal

Opened in 2014, Rotterdam's Markthal is one of the city's signature buildings. The extraordinary horseshoe-shaped market hall, costing €175 million to design, was dreamed up by the local starchitect firm MVRDV. Quite literally, it turns the traditional concept of European market halls upside down. It's not only an architectural stunner, but also one of the city's favourite foodie hubs.

NATTAWIT.SREE/SHUTTERSTOCK

Is This Surrealism?

Rotterdam's Markthal might be Europe's most unusual market hall. From the facade to interiors, it is, as one newspaper put it, perhaps the definitive 'Comic Sans of architecture'.

The hall forms a 40m-high arch that curves over the square, a radical, space-saving inversion of the rectangular market halls seen in most cities. Look up at the swooping monumental arch, fitted with glass facades, for a shimmering skylight effect. The entire thing is covered in a multicoloured, almost psychedelic mural of fruit and veg. Dotted between avocados and grapes, tiny windows reveal some 230 apartments and offices.

A Tasting Journey

Squeeze past the crowds at both entrances; there's a lot of good food and drink to get into here. Most stalls sell prepared dishes to eat on the spot rather than produce to take home, unless you count speciality shops for cheese, nuts and more. Some are even sit-down eateries with bar-stool seating at counters and upper-level 'terraces'.

Spanish *pinchos* (tapas), Greek souvlaki, Asian bowls and dumplings – the selection is immense. There are no huge standouts among them; here, variety is the spice of (market) life.

TOP TIPS

● Despite the name, One Hundred Restrooms always has long queues. Using the toilets at the Starbucks across Binnenrotte square is a better idea.

● In the parking garage, the free DeTijdTrap (*detijdtrap.nl*) exhibition displays excavated artefacts unearthed during Markthal's construction.

PRACTICALITIES

● markthal.nl ● free
● hours vary

BEST TOURS

Koloniaal Rotterdam: Download the app for self-guided routes exploring Rotterdam's colonial and slavery past.

De Rotterdam Tours: Walking tours combined with watertaxi rides. The coolest, the Floating City Tour, explores sustainable architecture and innovation. *(derotterdamweekendtours.nl)*

Urban Guides: Beyond the tour inside Van Nelle Fabriek (p189), excellent architectural walking tours on sustainable transformation and development. *(urbanguides.nl)*

S'Dam Tours: Walk or boat around the historic harbour and distillers' district, from old warehouses to distilleries and soaring windmills. *(sdam.nl)*

City Rotterdam Tours: Highlights include a guided architecture walking and cycling tour, as well as a Zuiden walk focused on migration stories. *(cityrotterdamtours.com)*

SHEREEN ALOU/SHUTTERSTOCK

Watertaxi

The neighbourhoods south of the Nieuwe Maas are easily accessible from Centrum and equally easy to explore. The main attractions of the area are its contemporary architecture and urban renewal projects, and, of course, the famous watertaxis. Walk over the Erasmus Bridge to admire the Kop van Zuid skyline and then west down Wilhelminakade to Hotel New York and then over to the SS *Rotterdam*. Or hop on watertaxis with a Tourist Day Ticket for unlimited rides.

Ahoi watertaxi!

Hands down one of the coolest experiences in Rotterdam is taking a local **watertaxi** *(watertaxirotterdam.nl)*. Flying down the Maas river in these zero-emissions e-boats is a wonderful peek into the commuter lifestyle. If you're travelling with kids (or perhaps just if you ask nicely), boat drivers will showboat by zigzagging, speeding up or hitting waves. (If you're paying by card, you can tip them.)

 EATING IN ZUIDEN: OUR PICKS

Fenix Food Factory: Almost everything in this vast former warehouse is made locally and sold by entrepreneurs. *hours vary* €

Foodhallen Rotterdam: Lively indoor food market fittingly converted from a former spice warehouse. *noon-1am Tue-Sat, to midnight Sun* €

Rolph's Deli: A haven off Otto Reuchlinweg, this deli offers all-day breakfasts and lunch options. *noon-2.30pm & 5.30-11pm Tue-Fri, 5.30-11pm Sat* €

CEO Baas van Het Vlees: Rotterdam's best steakhouse. Chefs in an open-kitchen cook spectacular cuts of beef perfectly to order. *5-10pm Tue-Sat* €€€

Depot at Museum Boijmans van Beuningen

In Rotterdam's Museumpark, Museum Boijmans van Beuningen is one of the Netherlands' most famous art institutions. Its preeminent gallery space is stellar and spans multiple periods and movements, with a roll call of major artists including Rembrandt, Monet, Van Gogh and Picasso. While the museum is closed, it's offering a 'backstage pass' viewing experience into its Depot storage facility.

YASEMIN OZDEMIR/SHUTTERSTOCK

Undergoing a Facelift

Established in 1849, Museum Boijmans van Beuningen holds a staggering trove of more than 151,000 masterpieces. While undergoing a massive renovation that's expected to finish in 2030, the museum is temporarily opening its art storage facility to the public.

Enter the Depot

The world's first open-access art storage facility, the **Depot** showcases the hidden facets of the repository, valued at €8 billion. Behind unlocked compartment doors lies behind-the-scenes enchantment: a temporary museum where priceless works are displayed against white grates and protective barriers. Visits are available by guided tours only.

The greenery-wrapped glass pavilion of adjoining restaurant **Renilde** is great for an espresso or light lunch.

Permanent Collection

The museum's complete anthology spans diverse periods and movements, with luminaries such as Rubens, Rembrandt, Monet, Degas, Van Gogh, Picasso, Miró and Bacon. Masterpieces like Jan van Eyck's *The Three Marys at the Tomb* (1425–35), Hieronymus Bosch's *The Pedlar* (c 1500), and Pieter Bruegel the Elder's *Tower of Babel* (c 1568) are highlights. These pieces are often among the 'backstage' access.

TOP TIPS

● All tickets must be purchased in advance on the website and are time-slot specific.

● Come after dark to see the Depot's facade illuminated with a light-and-video installation from the renowned Swiss experimental artist Pipilotti Rist.

PRACTICALITIES

● boijmans.nl ● adult/child €20/free ● 11am-5pm Tue-Sun

WHY I LOVE ROTTERDAM

Barbara Woolsey,
Lonely Planet writer

Once a fishing village and now Europe's busiest port, Rotterdam has come a long way. Fellow creative thinkers, this awesome maritime city is destined to become your kindred spirit. Across wacky art and innovative architecture, untamed creativity runs giddily amok. Still, the vibe stays laid-back and unpretentious, a tour de force of urban cool. Release your razzle-dazzle at summer festivals and investigate funky rhythms from jazz nests to warehouse raves. Find out why Rotterdammers are some of my favourite people to get to know and party with.

Cruise ship and Rotterdam skyline

The cost of the journey depends on the length of your ride. With river ports circumventing the city, watertaxis are great for sightseeing in the Zuiden (south) area, docking at iconic architectural landmarks, including the Erasmusbrug, Hotel New York (p217) and Maritiem Museum (p184).

What's especially enjoyable is how you hail a watertaxi. Just like requesting a regular taxi (or, at least, in the prehistoric era before Uber), call the hotline at *010-403 03 03*. Operators ask for key information, including how many people and where you're getting on and off, and give you a rough timeframe in which the boat will arrive.

You can also just wait at a dock and try your luck for the next available ride, though we don't recommend this – it's a popular service. The highest waiting times are during summer and school holidays. On weekends, you can buy a day pass for the Circle Line *(adult/child €10/5)*, a route that stops at all major highlights, essentially a hop-on, hop-off sightseeing service.

The **Tourist Day Ticket** *(touristdaytickets. com; €14.50)* is good for unlimited watertaxis and all other public transport.

ADDRESSING COLONIALISM

The 'Our Colonial Inheritance' exhibition at **Wereldmuseum Amsterdam** (p104) provides an excellent understanding of restitution and decolonialism broadly, which is shaping the future of museums and collections.

AVC PHOTO STUDIO/SHUTTERSTOCK

Scale the king of contemporaries

The city's most acclaimed contemporary building is easily **De Rotterdam** *(derotterdam.nl)*. Designed by OMA, whose star architect was Rotterdam-born Rem Koolhaas, this 'vertical city' is a castle of contemporary design across three Jenga-like interconnected towers. Completed in 2013 on the Zuiden waterfront, it's the coolest government building anywhere, comprising mostly city council offices but also apartments and a hotel where you can visit the cocktail bar.

The €340 million building was inspired by Koolhaas' love for movies; pre-starchitect, he considered a filmmaking career. He envisioned that when viewed from passing cars, diverse perspectives would unfold across the six storeys and interconnecting towers. In the original design, the towers didn't touch.

Stay on a retired cruise ship

The permanently moored, retired 1950s ocean liner **SS Rotterdam** *(ssrotterdam.nl)* is a lot of fun for a family stay with a difference, for a couple of days or so. The renovated cabins, abounding with contemporary kitsch decor from bright-yellow bathrooms to flowery curtains, are dark, and some have no portholes. (Those that do have nice watery views.)

There's much to explore aboard the 1958-built former flagship of the transatlantic Holland America Line, whose second life was as a cruise ship. Spiffily restored public spaces are museum-quality, with little historical displays throughout.

Audio guide tours *(adult/child €12.95/8; 10am-5pm)* allow you to explore the ship's history from bow to bridge and its below-deck machinery. The kids' tour keeps them busy with 'missions', and there's an escape room in the former storage area.

The downside of bunking at SS *Rotterdam* is that it's far from Centrum if you're not using watertaxis.

Amazing migration museum

Opened in mid-2025, **Fenix** *(fenix.nl; adult/child €15/free; closed Mon)* is a thoroughly modern museum that flawlessly weaves together global immigration history and art. In a converted harbour warehouse, Fenix showcases migration through deeply personal displays. There's the 'Suitcase Labyrinth', where visitors walk among 2000-some suitcases and listen to recorded audio from their owners. 'Family of Migrants' is a photojournalism archive sourced from more than 100 people.

Artworks by Hans Holbein the Younger and Steve McQueen, a Lampedusa-seized boat and a chunk of the Berlin Wall compile diverse diaspora narratives into a unified experience. The spiralling, double-helix Tornado staircase, a modern architectural feat, crowns Fenix as Europe's first museum designed by a Chinese architect (Ma Yansong).

BEST FOR UNDERGROUND CULTURE

Operator Radio: Watch DJs broadcasting live from the booth ('70s and '80s sounds are a local speciality) and a nice beer garden. *(operator-radio.com)*

WORM: Everything from media mashups to queer nights, film screenings, performance art and experimental music. *(worm.org)*

Maassilo: Industrial-cool grain silo in Zuiden turned Rotterdam's biggest club. *(maassilo.com)*

Toffler: In an old pedestrian tunnel in Centrum, this long, narrow club specialises in the dark arts of techno. *(toffler.nl)*

Cultuurpodium Perron: Graffitied former post office hosting legendary local DJs from Marsman to David Vunk spinning indie dance and techno. *(perron.nl)*

Beyond Rotterdam

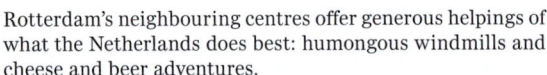

On a day trip from Rotterdam, discover Kinderdijk's creaky windmills and windswept dykes. Gouda is a gorge-worthy stop heading to Den Haag.

Places

Gouda p196

Kinderdijk p197

Waddinxveen p197

Biesbosch National Park p198

GETTING AROUND

Rotterdam connects to Gouda via cycling routes and regular train services. Walking around town is easy.

With the WaterShuttle (departing in front of the Erasmus Bridge), you can travel to the UNESCO-listed windmills of Kinderdijk in 30 minutes.

Kinderdijk is best explored by bicycle. The best plan is to hire your wheels in Rotterdam and bring them on the WaterShuttle for free. Ride off and away right after disembarking the ferry.

Rotterdam's neighbouring centres offer generous helpings of what the Netherlands does best: humongous windmills and cheese and beer adventures.

The nearby destinations of Gouda and Kinderdijk scratch the wanderlust itch for history, quaint cultural experiences and calorie-heavy indulgence. Some aspects are quite kitschy (what else would you expect from Gouda's famous pantomime-style cheese market?), but a visit to Biesbosch National Park offers a tranquil nature escape from the crowds.

If you're up for it, a deeper bite into Gouda shows the town is more than just its namesake export. Leave room for delicious Dutch sweets beyond the dairy. Kinderdijk's slow-motion windmills and polder (drained land) terrain offer a close-by counterpoint to lively Rotterdam.

Gouda

TIME FROM ROTTERDAM: 45MIN 🚆

Beyond the dairy

Gouda's fame is mostly weighed in dairy blocks, but the cheese doesn't stand alone. The historic centre, close to the town train station, has a cheesy staged market full of costumed mongers and maidens, but it's a nice stroll for quaint medieval architecture. **Sint Janskerk** *(sintjan.com; adult/child €11/free)* is the highlight, boasting the world's largest cache of in situ 16th-century stained glass and a chequered past. Previous incarnations burned down with immoral regularity about every century from 1361 until the mid-16th century. At 123m, it's the longest Dutch church.

Museum Gouda *(museumgouda.nl; adult/child €16/free; closed Mon)* houses artefacts and artworks in a medieval hospital building. The most alluring (and aromatic) of Gouda's many canal-side cheese shops, **'t Kaaswinkeltje** *(kaaswinkeltje.com; closed Sun),* has a tasty assortment of the specialty Gouda you won't find in regular supermarkets.

At the shop of the **Kamphuisen Siroopwafelfabriek** *(siroopwafelfabriek.nl; €11.50; closed Sun),* pick up a crispy *stroopwafel* (caramel-syrup-filled wafers) packed fresh from the production line. This traditional Dutch treat also originated in Gouda.

Chocolate factory library

Gouda's best-kept secret is its **Chocoladefabriek** (Chocolate Factory). The industrial building no longer churns out sweets but houses the town library. Peruse regional archives and a printer's workshop; it's also beloved by locals for the adjoining cafe **Kruim** *(kruimgouda.nl).* Relax on the patio with a slice of lemon meringue cake. The warm chocolate milk and brownies are divine, too.

Kinderdijk

TIME FROM ROTTERDAM: 1HR

Windmills and waterways

UNESCO World Heritage site **Kinderdijk** *(kinderdijk.com; adult/child €19.50/8)* is a beautiful polder landscape of empty marshes and waterways, above which 19 historic windmills (some brick, some timber) rise like sentinels. The mills are kept in operating condition, and some still function as residences. In summer, tall reeds line the two canals, lily pads float, and bird calls break the silence. It's a wonderful – and quintessentially Dutch – landscape to explore.

A pumping station has been repurposed as a **visitor centre**. There's a dual pedestrian and bicycle path between the canals, and boat cruises are also available.

Two of the windmills – the 17th-century **Nederwaard** and **Blokweer** – are museums offering insights into former miller families' lives. Several of the most important types of windmills are found here, including hollow posts and rotating caps. The latter are among the country's highest, built to optimally catch the wind.

The name Kinderdijk is said to derive from the horrible St Elizabeth's Day Flood of 1421, when a storm and flood washed a *kind* (child) in a crib up onto the *dijk* (dyke). Since then, efforts have strongly focused on flood protection and managing water levels. Kinderdijk is an excellent example of how the Dutch use windmills for water management and dykes to help reclaim land from water.

Waddinxveen

TIME FROM ROTTERDAM: 20MIN

Superyacht in the skies

It's a bird, it's a plane…it's a megayacht? Surprisingly, passing above the A12 motorway on the **Gouwe-Aqueduct**, that just may be what you see. On Gouda's outskirts, this engineering

A CHEESE ODYSSEY

Gouda's cheese-making history dates back to the 12th century, when local farmers sought to preserve excess milk. Over time, production evolved from humble beginnings into a thriving cross-European business.

Gouda is traditionally crafted from cow's milk, and aged from anywhere from four weeks (young/*jong*) to a year (aged/*oud*) or longer (extra-aged/ *overjarig),* transforming from semi-soft to hard, and becoming more savoury. Like many other aged cheeses, it's generally low in lactose and well-tolerated by those with dairy intolerance.

Smoked Gouda, still a favourite today, was aged in olden times on wheels near open flames. Traditionally, wheels were wrapped in protective wax; today, plastic is common.

EATING IN GOUDA: CHEESE & BEYOND

David's Gelato: This well-known ice cream parlour (watch the documentary about it) serves dairy-free sorbets. *noon-10pm Wed, Thu & Sat, 2-8pm Fri & Sun* €

Miss Nice Banana: Healthy vegan breakfasts and lunches, with everything plant-based and gluten-free, even the pancakes. *11am-8pm Thu-Sat, to 5pm Sun* €€

Brownies & Downies: Gouda's locale of a socially minded chain, with neurodivergent staff serving coffee and treats. *11.30am-5pm Mon, from 9.30am Tue-Sat* €

Koeien en Kaas: The twin specialities are in this rustic eatery's name (Cows and Cheese): steak and fondue from local cheese. *5-11pm* €€

EXPLORING WITH KIDS

Sophie van der Gugten-Verbree, a child psychologist living in Gouda, is also a mum of two. These are her top tips for entertaining little ones.

Keck: Train station–adjacent coffee stop with a playground. In nice weather, take your coffee to go and walk around Van Bergen IJzendoornpark. *(instagram.com/keckingouda)*

Kinderboerderij De Goudse Hofsteden: Petting zoo with a large playground and a flower and veggie garden. *(kinderboerderijgouda.nl)*

Barista Cafe: Heaven for parents with small kids. Good coffee for after sleepless nights and a toy-filled play corner. *(baristacafe.nl)*

Studio Kiewie: Nice secondhand children's clothes. *(studiokiewie.nl)*

Play Today LEGO Shop: A LEGO-lover's dream. *(playtoday.nl)*

marvel ingeniously allows barges and sailboats on the Gouwe River to skim the water passage running over a busy eight-lane road.

Constructed from 1975 to 1981, the 700m-long, 45m-wide structure was the answer to traffic jams as the A12 expanded. Formerly, a drawbridge would open and close for passing ships.

As you're departing Gouda, pay attention as you disappear beneath a cargo ship or luxury yacht making its way into Rotterdam. If you're lucky, it's a pretty weird, jaw-dropping spectacle on one of the Netherlands' most frequented aqueducts.

Biesbosch National Park

TIME FROM ROTTERDAM: 30MIN 🚗

Wildlife wonderland

Created when a large tract of polder land was submerged in the St Elizabeth's Day Flood, the 7100-hectare wetland of **Biesbosch National Park** *(np-debiesbosch.nl; free)* is Europe's largest freshwater tidal zone.

Along one of the Netherlands' largest natural expanses, preserved animal habitats abound across the Nieuwe Merwede's riverbanks. There are beavers (reintroduced to the park in 1988), deer and voles, along with scores of birds. Designated hiking routes sprawling across estuarine reed marsh and woodland offer chances to spot a white-tailed eagle or listen to a bluethroat's trilling songs that sound like bicycle bells.

The most scenic journey is arriving from Rotterdam via the nearest town of Dordrecht (a 15-minute train ride) and then cycling the 25km route into the marshland. Thanks to a large network of rivers, creeks and islands, canoe and guided boat tours make Biesbosch a special choice for outdoorsy adventure seekers.

CONNECTING WETLANDS TO COAST

Zeeland's **Delta Works**, one of the Netherlands' most controversial environmental projects, has had a direct impact on Biesbosch National Park. The reduction of tides is killing reeds that have grown in the park over centuries, though Zeelanders say saving their farms trumps reeds any day.

Den Haag

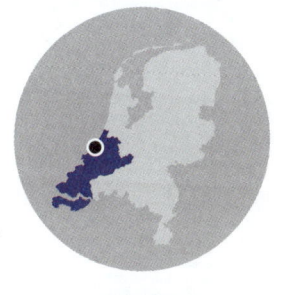

URBAN NATURE | MUSEUMS | WORLD DIPLOMACY

Den Haag (The Hague) is so much more than meets the eye. The popular perception of the Netherlands' third-largest city (the 'International City of Peace and Justice') is that it's stuffy thanks to bureaucrats and businesspeople. While this is true to some extent, that's a stereotype. The city's cultural scene is fiercely anchored by old and new. Palaces house spectacular art museums, such as the Mauritshuis, as well as important posts of governance (national and global) and Dutch royalty.

Meanwhile, the Spuiplein cultural precinct Amare packs modern panache. Entertainment has moved far past the embassy cocktail parties that once dominated. The culinary scene is replete with contemporary restaurants, and there's a lively music venue for every taste. Nightlife district Grote Markt proves that locals know how to party. Easy to explore on foot or by tram, Den Haag is a city that amply rewards those who stay for a few days.

GETTING AROUND

Trams and buses keep Den Haag's walkable city centre connected to neighbouring, less-busy districts. A night bus route runs from central Binnenhof to Scheveningen and all the way to Delft, but Uber is, of course, more convenient. In the city centre, walking gets you mostly everywhere, but long stretches abound. A trusty bicycle offers reprieve.

Urban National Park

Fresh green scene

Urban greenery doesn't get much better than Den Haag's 2024-unveiled **Koekamp**. Once a medieval cattle field, Koekamp is now a primly manicured entity joining up with Haagse Bos (Hague Forest) to form the new Hollandse Duinen National Park.

Strolling the park, ponds and canals unfold, and there's a pocket-sized nature reserve called **Stad en Duin** with a deer enclosure and stork-beloved meadow. In nice weather, locals waste no time in enjoying soft, clean grasses where blankets are wonderfully unnecessary.

Koekamp is now a green gateway to **Haagse Bos**, where 100 hectares of ancient woodlands keep surprises such as wild parakeets and the Dutch royal family's residence. Hire a bike and escape the city here for a bit.

☑ TOP TIP

Before you travel, check *denhaag.com* for major events on your desired travel dates and reserve your accommodation well before (at least three months in advance), as Den Haag's hotels and hostels are often fully booked. Checking home rentals via Airbnb *(airbnb.com)* or Kindred *(livekindred.com)* can be a good option.

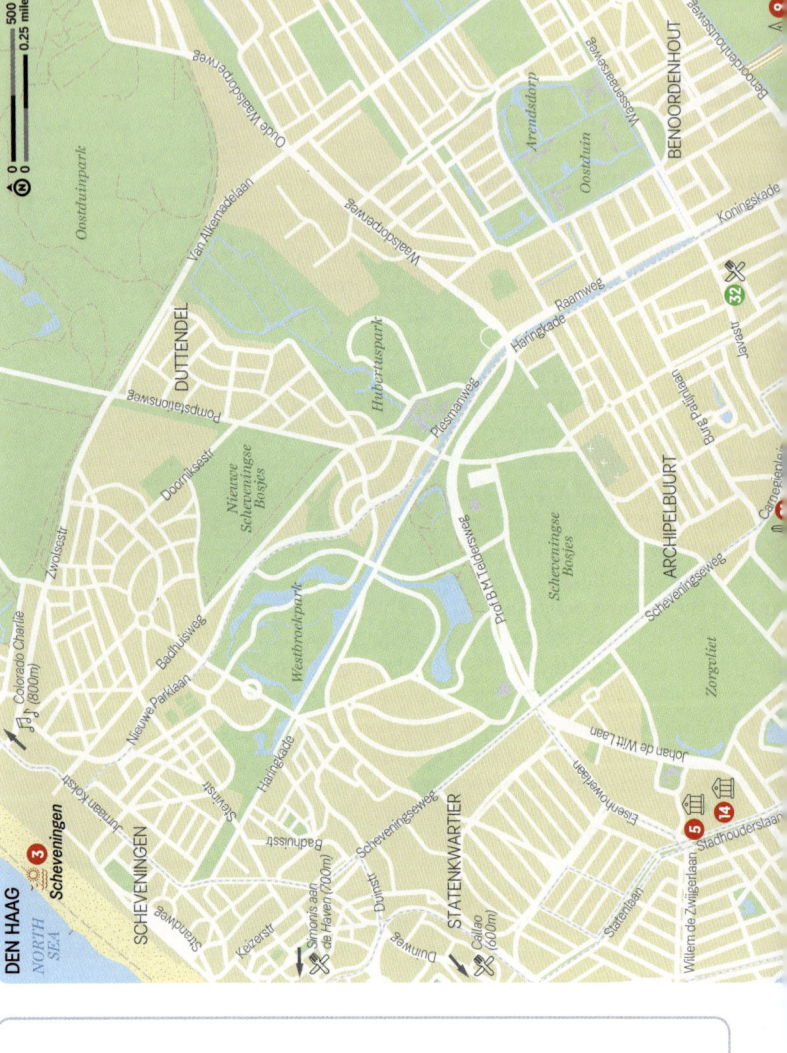

⭐ **HIGHLIGHTS**
1 Escher in Het Paleis
2 Mauritshuis
3 Scheveningen

● **SIGHTS**
4 Binnenhof
5 Fotomuseum Den Haag
6 Galerij Prins Willem V
7 Grote Kerk
8 Grote Markt
9 Haagse Bos
see 8 Haagse Harry
10 Haagse Jantje
11 Haagse Toren
12 Hofvijver
see 5 KM21
13 Koekamp
14 Kunstmuseum Den Haag
15 Paleis Noordeinde
16 Paleistuin
17 Plein
18 Postzegelboom
see 6 Rijksmuseum de
    Gevangenpoort
19 Van Kleef
20 Vredespaleis
21 World Peace Flame
22 Yi Jun Peace Museum

● **ACTIVITIES**
23 De Ooievaart
24 ProDemos

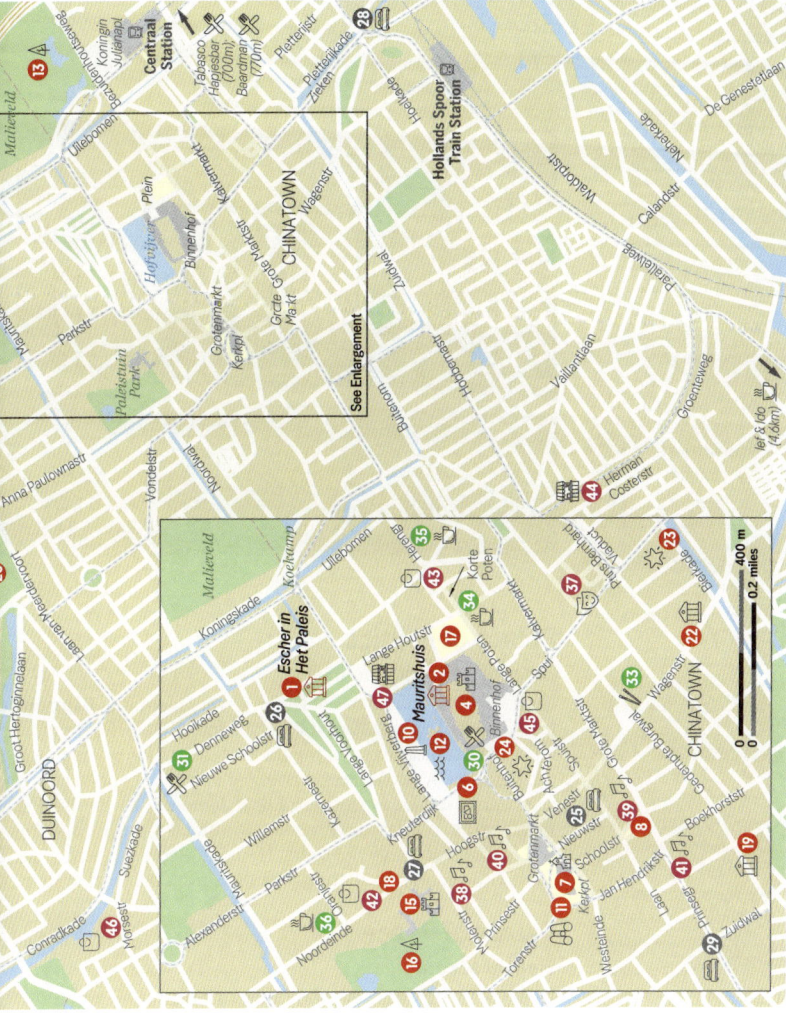

SLEEPING
25 Collector Hotel
26 Hotel des Indes
27 Hotel Indigo
28 Stayokay Den Haag
29 Will & Tate City Stay

EATING
30 Buitenhof Herring Stall
31 Dekxels
32 Fouquet
33 Little V

DRINKING & NIGHTLIFE
34 Bloem
35 Dutch Language Cafe
36 Lola Bikes & Coffee

ENTERTAINMENT
37 Amare
38 Café De Oude Mol
39 De Zwarte Ruiter
40 Muziekcafé De Paap
41 Paard

SHOPPING
42 Bookstor
43 De Bonte Koe
44 De Haagse Markt
45 De Passage
46 Kaiya Studios
47 Le Marie Marché

Officially known as 's-Gravenhage (the Count's Hedge), Den Haag, once a royal hunting lodge, is today the Dutch seat of government and monarchy. Before 1806, it was the Dutch capital, but that year, Louis Bonaparte installed his government in Amsterdam. When the French were ousted in 1814, the government returned to Den Haag, but Amsterdam remained the capital.

In 1899, the Permanent Court of Arbitration (PCA), the first global body for dispute resolution, was created out of the First Hague Peace Conference. More than 200 international legal and diplomatic organisations are headquartered here, making Den Haag a hub for humanitarian affairs.

INFOCUS.EE/SHUTTERSTOCK

Binnenhof

Palace of Politics

Heart of Dutch governance

Home to both houses of the Dutch government, the **Binnenhof**, adjacent to the Mauritshuis, is one of Den Haag's most beautiful scenes. Overlooking the Hofvijver (Court Pond), the medieval palace complex is arranged around a central courtyard once used for executions. Local democracy organisation **ProDemos** *(prodemos.nl)* conducts guided tours around the Binnenhof and inside the Dutch House of Representatives, detailing the complex's history and the Dutch political system.

Palace of Peace

Elegant accord

Home to the UN's Permanent Court of Arbitration and International Court of Justice, **Vredespaleis** *(Peace Palace; vredespaleis.nl; free; noon–5pm Wed-Sun)* is housed in a grand 1913 building donated by American steelmaker Andrew Carnegie. Its visitor centre has multimedia exhibits detailing

 EATING IN DEN HAAG: OUR PICKS

Little V: Trendy Vietnamese restaurant decked to the nines in Dutch *kabinet* (cabinet of curiosities) style. *noon-10.30pm Tue-Thu, to 11pm Fri & Sat* €€

Dekxels: Asian small plates with Mediterranean twists. The well-priced wine list trawls the globe. *5-10pm Sun-Thu, to 11pm Fri & Sat* €€

Fouquet: Multicourse market-fresh daily menus in an elegant restaurant with impressive presentation and service. *11am-6pm Wed, Sat & Sun, to 1.30pm Thu & Fri* €€

Baardman: Beautiful, minimalist bistro with a Mediterranean-inspired menu. Mains swim in decadent sauces. *11am-11pm Tue-Sat* €€

Scheveningen

On the outskirts of Den Haag, the unexpected resort town of Scheveningen boasts a 4.5km-long sandy beach that attracts nine million visitors per year. Though the water and sand are clean, it's still the North Sea coast, with strong winds and nippy tides making for a northern European (not Mediterranean) seaside experience.

VLADIMIR ZHOGA/SHUTTERSTOCK

Splash from the Past

Scheveningen's promenade keeps up a carnival-like quality. *Strandtenten* (beach bars), clubs and stands selling herring and soft ice cream elbow each other for space on concrete tiers. Despite its beginnings as a humble medieval fishing village, Scheveningen has been a seaside resort since the 19th century. From the weary aesthetic of the once luxurious Kurhaus, formerly a grand hotel, to the historic pier, Schevenginen's age is certainly apparent. A years-long, ongoing renovation project hopes to bring out a modern edge.

Sea, Sand & Surf

For travellers into watersports, the North Sea waves couldn't be more inviting. Shops hire out everything you need for surfing, kitesurfing or paddleboarding – also, wetsuits – and run lessons. Peak season is July and August, but you'll see someone attempting to catch breakers any time of year here.

Dune Country

Potentially even better than the surf are hillocks of dunes. Hype tapers off as you leave the harbour heading north into pristine dune territory. A series of WWII bunkers, once part of the Nazi Atlantic Wall defence, is an eerie reminder of the Netherlands' place in European history.

TOP TIPS

● Visit in April or May to admire the sand sculpture competition.

● Off-season strolling can be marvellous – and much less crowded than in July and August.

● A years-long redevelopment is modernising the pier and promenade. Some areas might not be open until it's fully completed in 2028.

PRACTICALITIES

● denhaag.com/de/tun/strande/scheveningen

● free ● 24hr; restaurants 10am-10pm, bar and club hours vary Mar-Oct

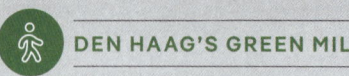

DEN HAAG'S GREEN MILE

No city delivers lush urban greenery better than Den Haag. On this self-guided tour, trace modern city life and leafy, open areas.

START	END	LENGTH
Paleis Noordeinde	Koekamp	2km; 1 hr

Begin your city-centre emerald tour outside the ① **Paleis Noordeinde** (p208), where King Willem-Alexander works and attends official functions. It faces a statue of his long-ago predecessor, William of Orange. The colossal horse chestnut tree, the ② **Postzegelboom** (p208), casts a grand silhouette and is highly revered locally. A bit further on, pop into the century-old bookshop and cafe ③ **Bookstor** (p208).

Cappuccino in hand, keep going northwest on Noordeinde, one of the city's most interesting shopping and cafe strips. Turn left on Hogewal. Walk along the water and, when the canal ends, turn left on Prinsessewal, continuing to walk along ④ **Paleistuin** (p206) behind the Paleis Noordeinde. It's known as the 'Secret Garden'.

After wandering around its hedges and flowerbeds, return to Prinsessewal and turn left onto Molenstraat, which takes you back to Noordeinde. Turn right. From Noordeinde, turn left onto Plaats and cross over the Buitenhof to walk along the shaded walking path snuggled left against the ⑤ **Hofvijver** (p208). One weekend per month, there's a market here along the large ornamental pond, flaunting the Binnenhof and Mauritshuis as a backdrop.

Continue straight to reach ⑥ **Koekamp** (p234). The pocket-sized nature reserve, boasting a deer enclosure and canals, is a perfect resting place or, even better, a jumping-off point for exploring Haagse Bos (Hague Forest).

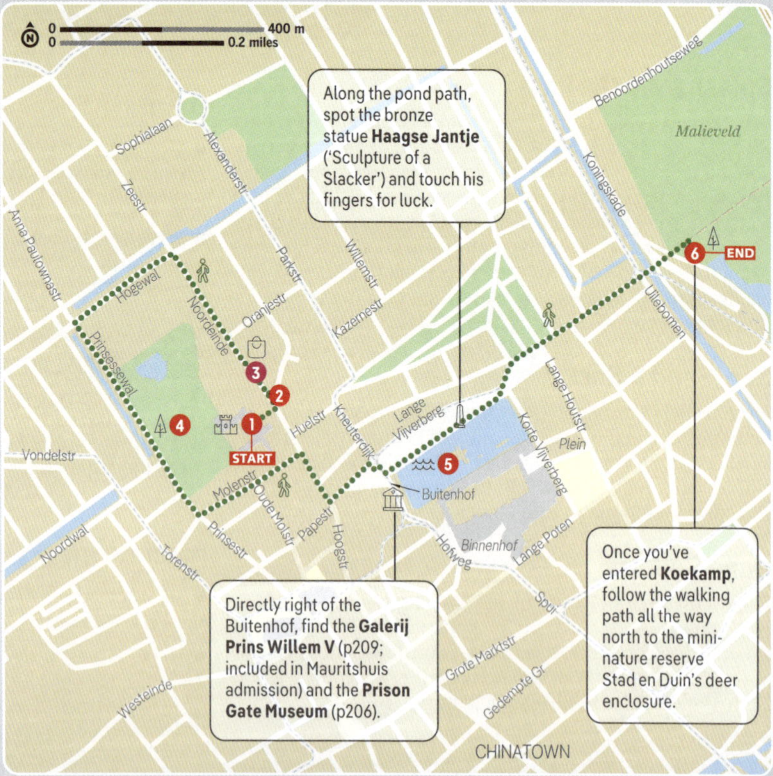

Along the pond path, spot the bronze statue **Haagse Jantje** ('Sculpture of a Slacker') and touch his fingers for luck.

Directly right of the Buitenhof, find the **Galerij Prins Willem V** (p209; included in Mauritshuis admission) and the **Prison Gate Museum** (p206).

Once you've entered **Koekamp**, follow the walking path all the way north to the mini-nature reserve Stad en Duin's deer enclosure.

the history of both the building and the organisations within; these are enjoyed in a free 30-minute audio guide tour.

Hour-long guided tours of the palace are also offered *(adult/child €16.50/free)*. Book ahead on the website to ensure your spot, though some are kept for walk-in visitors on the day (turn up at 10am to score one). A passport, EU identity card or driving licence must be shown upon entry.

A Model UN Garden
Eternal flame of unity

Nestled between the Peace Palace and the International Court of Justice, a modest flame has been burning within a stone pillar since 2002. Descending from a light ceremoniously ignited in Wales by the World Peace Flame Foundation in 1999, it is a quiet symbol of global unity.

The so-called **World Peace Flame** *(worldpeaceflame.org)* is poignantly surrounded by a small garden, comprising a stone from the 197 countries that the UN recognised in 2004. Along a circular path, each piece of native geology has been meticulously arranged next to an explanation of its origins.

Take a few moments for a sombre exploration of growing peace, from a Berlin Wall remnant to a fragment of the Robben Island prison where South African leader Nelson Mandela was held.

Monochrome Masterpieces
The enigma of Escher

Once home to members of the Dutch royal family, the 18th-century Lange Voorhout Palace now contains **Escher in Het Paleis** *(Escher in the Palace; escherinhetpaleis.nl; adult/child €13.50/7.50; closed Mon)*. Spooky, haunting works of Dutch graphic artist MC Escher (1898–1972) are showcased here among opulent interiors.

The permanent exhibition features notes, letters, photos, and plenty of woodcuts and lithographs from various points throughout his career, including everything from early realism to later phantasmagoria. Immersive multimedia conjures up a waking nightmare, blending black-and-white and greyscale, mathematical conjunctions and more WTF? moments. Delve deep into the artist's dark mind and leave with your own portrait simulated in his inimitable style (for an additional fee).

BEST FESTIVALS IN SOUTH HOLLAND

Grauzone Festival: Underground dance music and avant-garde art warm up Den Haag venues in February. *(grauzonefestival.nl)*

Motel Mozaïque: In Rotterdam, 'MOMO' ignites the city with art and live music in April. *(motelmozaique.nl)*

Rotterdam Architecture Month: Month-long June affair celebrating structural innovation with site visits, walking tours and workshops. *(rotterdamarchitectuurmaand.nl)*

North Sea Jazz Festival: Rotterdam's renowned jazz festival stages concerts from global acts. The weeks-long North Sea Round Town festival leads up to it with free performances. *(northseajazz.com)*

Ontzet: Leiden commemorates its 1574 'relief' from starvation and liberation from Spanish forces with annual festivities in October. *(3october.nl)*

 EATING IN DEN HAAG: SEAFOOD SMORGASBORDS

Buitenhof Herring Stall: Practise slurping herring like a local at this beloved seafood stall. Watch out for sneaky seagulls. *10am-6pm* €

Tabasco Hapjesbar: This restaurant wouldn't be memorable if it weren't for its €1.50 oysters on Saturdays. Availability varies; call ahead (070 889 0982). *3-11pm* €€

Simonis aan de Haven: Harbour canteen with eclectic bites: think lobster thermidor, salmon and herring on toast. *10am-8pm* €€

Callao: Modern Peruvian *cevicheria* (ceviche restaurant) in a cool, industrial-chic space. Killer small grilled plates. *5-10pm Mon, Wed & Thu, from noon Fri-Sun* €€€

Koekamp: A 15-minute walk from the train station, this pretty green lung leads into the greater Haagse Bos (p34). Together, they comprise a new Hollandse Duinen National Park.

Haagse Toren: Go up the medieval bell tower of Grote Kerk for amazing 360-degree panoramas from the balcony. *(dehaagsetoren.nl)*

Hofvijver: Picturesque pond overlooking the Binnenhof and Mauritshuis. Along the Lange Vijverberg waterside, there's sometimes also a market (p208).

Paleistuin: Behind Paleis Noordeinde, this paradisiacal urban park boasts flowerbeds and fountains.

De Ooievaart: Take a 1½-hour boat tour and see Den Haag's most interesting sights at canal level. *(ooievaart.nl)*

Prison Unpleasantries
Twisted crime and punishment

Situated paradoxically (or perhaps fittingly) within Den Haag, the 'International City of Peace and Justice', **Rijksmuseum de Gevangenpoort** *(Prison Gate Museum; gevangenpoort. nl; adult/child €15/7.50; closed Sun)* provides illustrations of dubious past approaches to maintaining peace and justice. Warning label: it's not kid-friendly.

Established in 1428, the Court of Holland's former prison primarily housed debtors and people awaiting interrogation and trial for plotting and disseminating dangerous ideas. Only in the 17th century did incarceration become a punishment via confining suspects in dim, cramped cells for months. The museum vividly recreates an oppressive atmosphere experienced by the likes of Cornelis de Witt, accused of plotting against the Prince of Orange.

In a torture chamber, chilling confession-extracting instruments are displayed among thin floors and ceilings that once amplified inmates' cries. Guided tours are available.

Cultural Core
Artistic meeting point at Amare

Spuiplein's striking, 2016-opened cultural complex, **Amare** *(amare.nl),* has brought the principals of the Netherlands' renowned performance scene together under one roof.

The grand, modern structure was architecturally inspired as a 'multiversum', with a facade resembling theatre curtains. Spanning 54,000 sq metres, its concert halls stage key performances by main cultural heavyweights. The Nederlands Dans Theater *(ndt.nl),* Koninklijk Conservatorium *(Royal Conservatory; koncon.nl)* and Residentie Orkest *(Philharmonic Orchestra; residentieorkest.nl)* are all based here.

Even between performances, the space stays lively with the comings and goings across a rehearsal hall, classrooms and studios. A sustainability-focused canteen is open to the public *(closed in summer),* and design elements include solar panels and bamboo walls, as well as birdhouses and bat roosts built into the facade.

Van Gogh's Genever
Bottom's up

Allegedly, Van Gogh found much creativity in the bottom of a barrel at this *genever* (Dutch gin) distiller.

 DRINKING IN DEN HAAG: BEST CAFES

Lola Bikes & Coffee: This cafe and cycling workshop has excellent coffee and cakes in a cute, shabby-chic seating area. *9am-6pm or later*

Bloem: Granny-style salon from high tea served on mismatched china to vintage armchairs, knick-knacks and needlepoint. *11am-5pm Thu & Fri, to 6pm Sat & Sun*

Dutch Language Cafe: Community cafe bringing together internationals for language exchanges, board games and meetups. *hours vary*

Ief & Ido: Modern coffee bar roasting its own beans weekly. Take a beginner's workshop. *10am-5.30pm Wed-Fri, to 5pm Sat & Sun*

MILOS RUZICKA/SHUTTERSTOCK

Kunstmuseum, Den Haag

Van Kleef *(museumvankleef.nl; tastings Sat & Sun €26.50; closed Mon),* Den Haag's only surviving *genever* producer, now works off-site, but keeps this stop for visitors to discover its historic distillery process. Compare heady 'old' *genever,* packed with herbs and spices (like Van Gogh once guzzled it), with its 'young' successor, a cheaper, more hasty concoction popular in WWII. If you're brave, there's also *Kruìde Baggâh,* a herbal bitter whose name means 'dirty herbs' – the name says it all. It's still punchy, except it's now made with safe, clean water that won't leave drinkers sprinting to the outhouse.

Displayed artefacts include *drankorgels* (liquor organs, a system of wall-hanging vessels, pipes and taps used by distillers before industrial barrelling), barrels tapped by patrons and Den Haag's first telephone book, where drinkers (maybe even Vincent himself) dialled 1 for the distillery's 'moonshine hotline'.

Fine Art Fusions

Genres and generation spanning

In a fabulous art deco haven, hit three separately curated visual powerhouses in one fell swoop.

Kunstmuseum Den Haag *(kunstmuseum.nl; adult/child €20/free; closed Mon),* a fine art museum, devotes an entire wing to eye-popping De Stijl (Neoplasticism). Its major drawcard is Piet Mondrian's unfinished *Victory Boogie Woogie* (1942–44), which the abstract painter worked on up until his death. Its 'Discover the Modern' exhibit encompasses early-20th-century works by Van Gogh, Picasso, Kandinsky and others, including Egon Schiele's exquisite *Portrait of Edith* (1915).

Adjoining, the **Fotomuseum Den Haag** *(fotomuseumden-haag.nl; adult/child €16/free; closed Mon)* mounts excellent snapshots (especially war photography), while **KM21** *(km21.nl; adult/child €16/free; closed Mon)* curates multidisciplinary, 21st-century installations.

INTERNATIONAL CRIMINAL COURT

Den Haag is the seat of the International Criminal Court (ICC). Since it was established in 2002, the UN-independent permanent tribunal for international justice has seen several political leaders stand trial for crimes against humanity here, including in relation to Kosovo and Democratic Republic of the Congo.

The ICC made international headlines in 2025 when the former Philippines President Rodrigo Duterte was arrested in Manila and brought to Den Haag. At the time of writing, he was being held in the ICC detention centre awaiting trial. More than 5000 supporters, mostly Filipino immigrants in Europe, came to Den Haag to protest and demand his repatriation. They have promised more rallies.

BEST SHOPS IN DEN HAAG

Bookstor: Century-old used bookshop a short walk from the Paleis Noordeinde. Its shelved interiors double as a cafe. *(bookstor.nl)*

De Passage: Magnificent, 19th-century glass-roofed shopping arcade. Boutiques for unique souvenirs. *(depassage.nl)*

De Haagse Markt: Among the Netherlands' largest outdoor markets, more than 500 multicultural stalls, including vendors from Suriname, Turkey and Morocco. *(dehaagsemarkt.nl)*

Kaiya Studios: Bright, airy ceramics shop and studio holding painting workshops. Check online for dates. *(kaiyastudios.nl)*

De Bonte Koe: Converted former butcher's shop now home to a Dutch chocolate maker selling bonbons, bouchées and bars. *(debontekoe.nl)*

RICHIE CHAN/SHUTTERSTOCK

Paleis Noordeinde

The King's Office

Gaze around the gates

The king's and queen's official quarters at **Paleis Noordeinde** are not open to the public, but it's worth a poke into and around the crested gates.

Members of the Netherlands' Orange Nassau monarchy have lived and worked here since 1595. Extensively rebuilt in the early 19th century, it now functions as King Willem-Alexander's workplace and state office.

Admire the building's classical facade through the barrier. The 19th-century equestrian statue out front depicts William of Orange. One of the most important figures in Dutch history, he led the revolt against the Spanish Habsburgs that set off the Eighty Years' War (1568–1648) and resulted in the formal independence of the United Provinces in 1581.

What's behind the statue is interesting. Locals call this leafy mammoth, a horse chestnut tree, the **Postzegelboom** (Stamp Tree) after the stamp collectors who've historically gathered here. Planted in 1883, the tree is so beloved in Den Haag that, in the 1930s, the foundation of the Paleis Noordeinde's Gothic hall was removed so that its roots could continue growing.

Courting the Court Pond

Attractive waterside stroll

Flanking the opposite side of the **Hofvijver** (Court Pond) from the Mauritshuis and Binnenhof, a shaded, waterside walking path (running parallel to Lange Vijverberg) makes for a lovely stroll. During the summer, the monthly **Le Marie Marché** *(11am-5pm Fri & Sat Apr-Aug)* sets up here and turns the gravel passage into something of an open-air museum as artists display their sculptures and other works on pedestals against the water. The market's far end (on the corner of Buitenhof) is where you'll find a food-truck extravaganza of Den Haag specialities selling everything from oysters to *frites* (fries), *stroopwafel* and wine by the glass.

Mauritshuis

Offering a wonderful introduction to Dutch and Flemish art, the splendid Mauritshuis is set in a 17th-century mansion built for wealthy sugar trader Johan Maurits. The 800-strong collection of paintings focuses on works from the 15th and 18th centuries. Several masterpieces are primed to lure you in, from Vermeer's *Girl with a Pearl Earring* to Rembrandt's *The Anatomy Lesson of Dr Nicolaes Tulp.*

MIKHAIL MARKOVSKIY/SHUTTERSTOCK

Paintings & Pop Culture

In 2003 and 2019, respectively, Dutch masterpieces Vermeer's *Girl with a Pearl Earring* (c 1665) and Fabritius' *The Goldfinch* (1654) became the centrepieces of riveting Hollywood blockbusters. In the world-renowned Mauritshuis, see both prolific paintings in real life.

The 1822-founded institution houses a huge collection of Dutch and Flemish art, once the Royal Picture Collection. Beyond its two big-screen starlets, intriguing works include Rembrandt's *The Anatomy Lesson of Dr Nicolaes Tulp* (1632), Van der Weyden's *The Lamentation of Christ* (c 1460–64) and Vermeer's *View of Delft* (c 1660–61), the most famous cityscape from the 'Golden Age'.

Beyond these Dutch greats, there are also multiple pieces by Anthony van Dyck, Peter Paul Rubens, Hans Holbein the Younger, Frans Hals, and Jan Steen, plus a swish modern art wing.

Bonus Gallery

Included in admission is the **Galerij Prins Willem V**, where William V's 18th-century art collection poses among crystal chandeliers and more 'Golden Age' opulence. Opened in 1774, the Netherlands' first public museum closed for almost two centuries after French occupiers seized works in 1794. Since 1977, works from Jan Steen, Peter Paul Rubens and Paulus Potter are on the walls again.

TOP TIPS

● Purchase your ticket (with an automatically chosen time slot) online to skip queues.

● Download the museum's free app for guided tours with a special focus. Particularly good are 'Johan Maurits and the Mauritshuis' on colonial history and 'The Women of the Mauritshuis'.

PRACTICALITIES

● mauritshuis.nl ● adult/child €20/free ● 10am-6pm Tue-Sun, from 1pm Mon, Galerij Prins Willem V noon-5pm Tue-Sat

BEST PERFORMANCE VENUES

Amare: Sprawling concert hall complex on Spuiplein. Home to the Nederlands Dans Theater, Royal Conservatory and Philharmonic Orchestra. *(amare.nl)*

Paard: The city's best live-music venue. Eclectic programming from jazz to metal and reggae. *(paard.nl)*

Café De Oude Mol: Cosy *bruin café* hosting intimate rock shows. *(facebook. com/DeOudeMol)*

Muziekcafé De Paap: Live bands from Thursday to Saturday in a delightfully energetic 'music cafe' pub atmosphere. *(depaap.nl)*

De Zwarte Ruiter: Hit the dance floor on weekends when bands and DJs fill up this cavernous *bruin café*. *(zwarteruiter.nl)*

Colorado Charlie: Seaside summer party venue hosting big-name electronic-music DJs in **Scheveningen** (p203). *(colorado charlie.nl)*

In the middle of the market, look for the bronze statue of *Haagse Jantje,* better known by its nickname 'Sculpture of a Slacker'. The sculpture is inspired by a Dutch children's song. Sometimes, people touch his fingers (pointing at the Binnenhof) for good luck, leaving them quite shiny.

Den Haag's Lively Chinatown
Delectable food, fascinating history

Den Haag's buzzy Chinatown unfolds along Wagenstraat. The area, once part of the Jewish district, remained desolate after the Holocaust until the 1970s, when neighbourhood redevelopment led to Chinese immigrants settling here.

Today, Chinatown is a bustling multicultural neighbourhood. Small restaurants serve well-priced soups and hotpots, and some stay open until late. Traditional shops also offer Chinese medicines and groceries, and during Chinese New Year, crowds spill onto Wagenstraat for fireworks and dragon dancing.

Among Chinatown's hidden histories is the **Yi Jun Peace Museum** *(denhaag.com/en/yi-jun-peace-museum; adult/child €5/free; closed Sun)*. In 1907, visiting Korean peace advocate Yi Jun was found dead in his hotel. A tiny museum delves into what became a newsworthy event in his homeland (at the time under Japanese rule).

Dining & Drinking Precincts
City centre at dusk

In central Den Haag, there are two good areas to know for evening pursuits: the historic squares of Plein and Grote Markt.

Start the night off at **Plein**, one of Den Haag's favourite after-work spots. Restaurants and pubs line the square, and their terraces get packed by early afternoon. (Before that, it's a ghost town.) Spots serve *borrelhapjes* (fried snacks), small seafood dishes and the like, but you're here more for the vibe than anything. The cobblestone centre has a statue of Willem the Silent, and often, modern murals and other installations from the Buitenkunst Den Haag, a local initiative that aims to turn the city into an open-air museum.

A 10-minute walk down Spuistraat leads you to the nightlife hot spot, **Grote Markt**. The streets aren't green and leafy like those north of the city centre, but they are colourful and attract a diverse crowd of students, international visitors and Hague-based bureaucrats. On these lively streets, ambassadors' mansions and office buildings seem worlds away.

Look out for **Haagse Harry**. From a comic strip about an everyday, working-class *Hagenaar* (Haag local), the statue is an unofficial mascot for the city. Bald, goofily grinning, pot-bellied and rocking a T-shirt that reads, 'Kap Nâh!!' ('Cut it out!!' in Haag dialect), he represents the other side of Den Haag: down-to-earth locals who aren't bureaucrats, politicians or ambassadors. Essentially, the kind of guy you might see drinking on Grote Markt.

Beyond Den Haag

From Den Haag, two iconic Dutch destinations, Leiden and Delft, are only a 15-minute train ride away.

Den Haag proves that day trips needn't be exhausting. Neighbours Delft and Leiden may be smaller, but they showcase South Holland's diverse character through great landmarks.

Delft offers an afternoon's worth of austere medieval magnificence and 'Golden Age' glory. Leiden is undoubtedly the more fascinating and worth perhaps even a couple of days to delve into how it became the 'City of Discoveries'.

A bit further afield, Lisse, a one-hour train ride from Den Haag, is home to Keukenhof Gardens, the world's biggest tulip show. Its short spring blooming season sees a torrent of more than a million visitors take over its fields. The rest of the year, a hibernation period keeps crowds away.

Places

Delft p211
Leiden p214
Lisse p216

GETTING AROUND

Frequent trains and trams from Den Haag Centraal Station go to Delft; an 11km bike ride is also possible. Delft's historic centre is walkable.

Exploring Leiden is easiest with a bicycle. The train station is 400m northwest of the centre. Attractions are decently spread out from one another.

In season, special buses link Keukenhof Gardens with Schiphol Airport and Leiden's Centraal Station (tickets combine transport and entry).

Delft

TIME FROM DEN HAAG: 15MIN 🚆

Visit the Markt

The centrepiece of delicate Delft is its **Markt**, one of Europe's largest historic squares. Some of South Holland's most culturally important – not to mention opulent – landmarks perch here, all enduring reminders of its serious golden-goose days.

Worth visiting is the **Nieuwe Kerk** *(New Church; oudeen nieuwekerkdelft.nl; adult/child €8.50/4)*. Completed in 1655, it's the grandiose final resting place of almost every House of Orange royal since 1584. William of Orange (Willem the Silent) lies here in an over-the-top marble mausoleum. Climbing the church's 109m-high tower, spiralling across 376 narrow steps, promises panoramic views of an exquisite landscape.

Beyond this, Delft's touristy square doesn't hold up the charm its diminutive streets do. Ceramics-flaunting souvenir shops enwrap the Markt – check out the **Royal Delft Outlet** *(royaldelft.com)*, where authentic but off-season or slightly imperfect stock is discounted (but remains rather pricey). **De Blauwe Tulp** *(bluetulip.nl; closed Sun)* also paints and sells its own Delftware in a studio-shop just off the Markt.

Medieval to modern

Delft may be tiny when compared with other Dutch cities by area and population (about 100,000), but it certainly proves that petite things can also be powerful. The town boasts

TILES OF GLORY

Given that the process of Delftware was first developed in China, it's ironic that the fake Delft Blue abounding in Dutch souvenir shops comes from there. During the 'Golden Age', Dutch traders imported Chinese porcelain and local artisans, unable to replicate it, began producing their own. Workshops flourished, especially after 1653 when De Koninklijke Porceleyne Fles (Royal Delft) standardised production and style.

The real stuff is harder to find in Delft these days, produced in limited quantities by a small circle. Royal Delft remains famous, but its earthenware factory is well outside the city centre, admission is expensive and tour groups of retirees off cruise boats swarm. The on-site shop, though vast, is also priced for them, too.

exuberant architecture and art from the 'Golden Age' and medieval eras – a wealth amassed through dainty, pretty pottery, among other treasures.

Delft's diminutive streets, weaved with brightly painted houses and exquisite canals, are quite an alluring trove to explore. Wandering here is a treat, especially if your only impression of 'Golden Age' canals has been in Amsterdam. In Delft, the canal scenery feels much more quaint and laid-back (though, on weekends, to describe the main waterside areas as 'uncrowded' would be a stretch).

Along Delft's historic canals, you'll find a few lovely surprises. Walking from Markt, **Gemeenlandshuis van Delfland**, one of the last medieval buildings left in Delft, sticks out like an aristocratic sore thumb. Constructed around 1505, its sandstone facade, adorned with finely detailed heraldic shields and symbolic carvings, is a rare, ornate example of a late-Gothic city palace in the country. Since 1645, the building has been the Delfland Water Board's headquarters.

On the canal's other side, a bit further north, **Voor de Kunst** (*uitdekunstdelft.nl*) is a rare example of modern (neither

EATING & DRINKING IN DELFT: OUR PICKS

Spijshuis de Dis: Fresh fish and soups served in bread bowls and nice outdoor tables on the Beestenmarkt for a lovely dinner. *5-10pm Tue-Sat* €€

Kek: Stylish cafe for freshly squeezed juices, fruit smoothies, and a tempting array of cakes, muffins, tarts and sandwiches. *8.30am-4.30pm Wed-Mon* €

Stads-Koffyhuis: When the sun's out, there's no better place to be than this cafe's terrace aboard a moored barge. *9am-5pm Mon-Sat, from 11am Sun* €

De Oude Jan: Popular *bruin café* opposite Oude Kerk, where occasional performances by live bands grace a charming courtyard's outdoor stage. *hours vary*

HENK VRIESELAAR/SHUTTERSTOCK

Gemeenlandshuis van Delfland

ceramic nor antique) art in Delft. Established in 2002 by Delft-born artist Tijn Noordenbos, it's an old-time telephone booth now housing the world's smallest contemporary gallery. Anyone can take a peek at changing sculptures and other mini, modern masterpieces inside.

Antiques canal show

These days, the best way to shop for Delftware is the old-fashioned way: a good old antiques rummage. Tucked between Oude Kerk and the Nieuwe Delft canal, Delft's **Antiekmarkt** *(9am-4pm Sat Apr-Sep),* sometimes also referred to as the 'Curiosa Market', is an excellent place to hunt for well-styled ceramics. More than 100 stalls set up here; come early for the best bargains.

Vermeer's legacy

Delft, with its time-capsule-like charm, remains remarkably unchanged since Johannes Vermeer painted *View of Delft* (c 1660–61) as a heartfelt expression of his birthplace.

 Vermeer Centrum Delft *(vermeerdelft.nl; adult/child €12/free)* pays tribute to the painter. Although none of his works remain in Delft, the centre provides insights into his life and work. There are reproductions of his paintings, a short film about his life, and displays on 17th-century painting techniques and materials that give context. Audio guides are free. The centre also sells a printed guide of the **Vermeer Cube Walk** *(€3)* at the information points around town.

VERMEER IN DETAIL

The Dutch master Johannes Vermeer (1632–75) lived in Delft, fathered 11 children and left behind fewer than 40 paintings. (The actual number is disputed.) Vermeer captured natural light in everyday settings in a way few others have accomplished, which is somewhat ironic, considering so little is known about his personal life. The 2003 film *Girl with a Pearl Earring* (based on the 1999 novel) speculated on Vermeer's relationship with his most famous portrait's subject.

 In 2004, a Vermeer painting once considered a forgery was confirmed authentic, adding an air of mystery. *A Young Woman Seated at the Virginals,* the first Vermeer auctioned in 80-plus years, sold for €24 million to an anonymous buyer.

AN ICONIC VIEW

Vermeer's best-known exterior work, *View of Delft,* is a brilliant, sentimental rendering of his hometown. Visit the location where he painted it, across the canal at Hooikade. The real painting hangs at **Mauritshuis** (p209) in Den Haag.

LEIDEN HISTORY

Leiden's university – the Netherlands' oldest – was a gift from Willem the Silent in 1575 for withstanding two Spanish sieges. Supposedly, the Spaniards left so quickly that they abandoned a kettle of *hutspot* (stew) – today the dish is heartily ladled up at Leiden's Ontzet festival commemorating the country's liberation.

Decades later, Protestants fleeing persecution arrived to a slightly warmer welcome. Among them was a group that later sailed into history as pilgrims aboard the *Mayflower*.

Wealth from the linen industry buttressed Leiden's growing prosperity, and during the 17th century, the town produced several brilliant artists, most famously Rembrandt. He remained here for 26 years before achieving fame in Amsterdam.

Leiden

TIME FROM DEN HAAG: 15MIN

Giant waterlilies and more botanics

Leiden's rich history of biology and horticulture science is in full bloom at the **Hortus Botanicus** *(hortusleiden.nl; adult/ child €11.50/4.50)*. Established in 1590, Leiden's botanical gardens are among the oldest in the world. The Dutch tulip obsession can be firmly traced back to the soil here when imperial botanist Carolus Clusius propagated tulip bulbs that could thrive in local conditions.

Tulips account for a petal of the 10,000-some plant species around Hortus Botanicus today. The obvious highlight is exploring a set of tropical greenhouses. Climate-controlled to a balmy 24°C to 28°C (wear layers you can shed) and abounding in tropical flora, it's a little Amazon rainforest in Europe. Trekking the dirt paths, overgrown with creepers, palmy leaves and lurking carnivorous plants, is an Indiana Jones–like experience. The favourite of many is the *Victoria amazonica,* enormous pink and white Amazonian water lilies (the world's largest flower), floating majestically on a 2m-wide pond. Every July, when the lilies are of prime size, parents can bring babies (no older than six months) for Anne Geddes–like photo shoots nestled inside of them, a tradition going strong for more than a century.

The sprawling grounds unfold across a world of landscaped areas, including an orangery and gardens specialising in ferns, alpine species and Chinese herbs. Wooden benches throughout invite staying for a while, so plan to come well before the 5pm closing.

Secretive gastronomic hot spot

Head inside the grand **Kroonvilla** (Crown Villa), a national heritage monument, where a wardrobe is a portal to the Narnia of modern eateries. **Paco Ciao** *(pacociao.nl)* is a fantasy realm of bohemian-chic design. From vintage armchairs to tropical plants, a planet-sized disco ball, chandeliers and drawstring curtains, the ambience changes within different rooms. No piece of decor is, seemingly, ever repeated – even the tableware is mismatched.

The menu comprises a miscellany of global food trends from bao burgers to sushi and pink pancakes. It's everything an Instagram influencer (or wannabe) dreams of, and you'll find them lurking here at night. During the daytime, though, the vibe stays relaxed, and the service is fast and friendly. Located on Stationsweg, it lies perfectly on the way to or from Leiden by train.

EATING & DRINKING IN LEIDEN: OUR PICKS

In den Doofpot: High-calibre, creative fine dining with luxe products; think ox tail and razor clams with sommelier wine pairings. *hours vary* €€€

Proeflokaal 1574: Cosy wine bar with European vino and lovely dishes, from colourful lunch salads to escargot and oysters for dinner. *hours vary* €€

Cafe de Vergulde Kruik: Snug old-world pub with a neat backstory: the Heineken star originated here. *hours vary*

Waag: Leiden's historic weigh station, now a bar, boasts sunny canal-side tables and vaulted interiors. *hours vary*

VLADIMIR ZHOGA/SHUTTERSTOCK

Pieterskerk

Intellectual worship

Crowned by its huge steeple, the now deconsecrated **Pieterskerk** *(pieterskerk.com; adult/child €8.50/2.50)* is often under some scaffolding, a good thing, as Leiden's oldest church has been prone to collapse since it was built in 1121. It hasn't been used as a place of worship for many years. It's now a public and community space for everything from concerts to art fairs; the website has a full schedule.

If this Gothic beauty isn't closed for private functions, there's much to explore. Also known as the Church of the Pilgrim Fathers (briefly, a Dutch refuge for *Mayflower* separatists), its distinctive features include an unusual marble and stone floor. However, its 'buried' scientific history is interesting.

On a central stone pillar, look for the displayed **gravestone of Ludolph van Ceulen**. The Dutch mathematician was renowned for spending 25 years calculating a method for the numerical value of pi. Not long after he died in 1610, Isaac Newton found a new method that made Van Ceulen's life's work obsolete, making him a somewhat forgotten character in the 'who's who' of maths books. Pieterskerk is also the final resting place of another great mathematician, Willebrord Snellius, who developed the fundamental physics law of refraction. The precinct includes the gabled **Latin School**, which – before it became a commercial building – was attended by a pupil named Rembrandt from 1616 to 1620.

BRAINIACS WELCOME

Leiden University *(universiteitleiden.nl)*, one of Europe's oldest and most prestigious institutions, has a rich history of scientific discoveries, from superconductivity to the electrocardiograph. Famous scholars who taught and studied here include Albert Einstein, Christiaan Huygens and René Descartes.

The sprawling, 40-hectare campus abounds with hidden histories, including a sink used by Einstein (now, bizarrely, in a lecture room) and a graffiti wall signed by legendary figures from Nelson Mandela to Winston Churchill. (Neither is publicly accessible.) Off-campus, the **Oude Sterrewacht** *(Old Observatory; universiteitleiden. nl/oudesterre- wacht; €5; English tours 2.30-3.30pm Wed-Sun)* and Hortus Botanicus (p214) are both publicly accessible.

BLOOM & BUST

The investment hysteria of the Netherlands' tulip craze (1636–37) ranks among the world's greatest booms and busts.

In the mid-1500s, Istanbul's Habsburg ambassador brought tulip bulbs (originating as wildflowers in Central Asia) back to Vienna, where imperial botanist Carolus Clusius propagated them. In 1590, Clusius became director of Leiden's **Hortus Botanicus** (p214), successfully cross-breeding tulips in the cool, damp climate and fertile delta soil.

Trickle-down wealth stoked flora exotica speculation. When bulb traders couldn't capture expected prices in 1637, the market's bottom fell out, and many went bankrupt. Still, the Dutch love of tulips endures. Today, the Netherlands is the world leader in tulip cultivation.

Poetic prose and equations

Keep your eyes peeled. More than 100 murals around Leiden celebrate its scientific and literary legacy.

Muurgedichten *(Wall Poems; muurgedichten.nl)* spans about 100 hand-painted poems adorning walls, bridges and more. Iconic prose in 30-some languages, from Shakespeare to e.e. cummings and Yeats, takes aesthetic shapes, such as tornadoes to waves.

With a little help from the Wall Poems website, Leiden's streets become an open-air gallery tour. Walking and cycling themed routes include one on foreign writing excerpts, including the oldest-known Dutch text by a Flemish monk c 1100, South Sulawesi (Indonesian) Buginese script and Mandelstam's 'Leningrad'. Photographs of the art feature audio and texts on interpretations and histories.

Meanwhile, not to be outdone by Lit 101, **Murrformules** (Wall Formulas) inspired by the *Muurgedichten* also decorate Leiden's cityscape. Started in 2015, 20-odd years after the Wall Poems, this initiative was spearheaded by a couple of Leiden University–affiliated physicists, and it realises mathematical equations as mural art. Einstein's field equations, Snell's law and other formulas linked to Leiden's academic legacy decorate facades. Hit them all on a walking tour *(tegen-beeld.nl)*. Leiden students have also developed an audio guide app *(izi. travel/en/netherlands/city-guides-in-leiden)*.

Lisse

TIME FROM DEN HAAG: 1 HR

Seven million flower bulbs

Once a rural retreat for wealthy city merchants, Lisse changed in the 19th century when its manor houses surrounded by formal gardens and forests were sold and the land was given over to what this pocket of South Holland is best known for: flower cultivation. Today, flowers and the tourists they attract are the town's major industry, and the main attraction, the **Keukenhof Gardens** *(keukenhof.nl; adult/child €20/9, return shuttle bus from Amsterdam €32; 8am-7pm Mar-May),* hosts more than a million visitors during the short bloom season. There are few reasons to visit at other times of the year, but a springtime trip (preferably in April) is a highlight of time spent in the Netherlands.

The 32-hectare Keukenhof is the world's largest bulb-flower garden, with more than seven million bulbs and 800 multi-coloured varieties of tulips, as well as daffodils and hyacinths in bloom.

Across the road, the grand **Kasteel Keukenhof** *(kasteelkeu kenhof.nl; guided tour €5)* can also be visited. The castle grounds encompass more than 80 hectares of woodland, meadows and flowering gardens.

In town, the small **Museum de Zwarte Tulp** *(Museum of the Black Tulip; museumdezwartetulp.nl; adult/child €10/5; closed Mon)* – with a name inspired by an Alexandre Dumas novel – displays myriad historical info, including about the mythical bloom that helped drive tulipmania in 1636.

Places We Love to Stay

€ Budget €€ Midrange €€€ Top End

Rotterdam p176

Centrum

CitizenM € A new-generation hostel encompassing modern capsule-like rooms and super-stylish common spaces and coworking areas.

King Kong Hostel € Hip hostel in Rotterdam's major party precinct with female and mixed-sex dorms and great facilities, including laundry and a communal kitchen.

Stayokay Rotterdam € Stay inside one of the iconic Blaakse Bos cube houses. Dorm beds, puzzled into oddly shaped rooms, are surprisingly comfy. Perfectly located for sightseeing.

Man Met Bril Koffie Hotel €€ A stay at the world's first 'coffee hotel' promises excellent breakfasts in bed from Rotterdam's original artisan roastery. Rooms, small yet warm and modern, are above the restaurant.

Haven Hotel €€€ Prime city-centre hotel stay for walking to museums and restaurants, and getting around Rotterdam quickly by watertaxi and metro. Chic contemporary rooms with harbour views.

Westen

Hotel Stroom €€ Designer rooms in a converted power station, ranging from studios to lofts with dining areas. Once trendy rooms are now a little dated, but they deliver an unusual, boutique stay for a group or family.

Zuiden

SS Rotterdam (p195) **€** On a retired 1950s ocean liner, pint-sized cabins restored with kitschy decor are fun (at least, for a couple of nights). The watertaxi station here is convenient.

Hotel New York €€ Rotterdam's most characterful accommodation option. A former Holland America passenger ship office (a listed monument) offers comfortable, well-sized rooms and watertaxis linking to the city centre.

Pincoffs €€ In an 1879-built customs house, Rotterdam's only truly boutique hotel, boasts generations-spanning art and cosy comfort.

Den Haag p199

Stayokay Den Haag € Frill-free but fine, just as the name says. Same-sex dorms, a bar and a sunny canal-side terrace offer cool factor.

Will & Tate City Stay € Boutique hostel mixing dorms (including one for women only) and a few private rooms, all adorned with different murals. Close to Paard and Grote Markt, the location is great.

Collector Hotel €€ Central hotel fully delivering on old-world charm. Elegant decor extends into a lovely Renaissance courtyard.

Hotel des Indes €€€ Built as a residence in 1858, it's been a luxury hotel since 1881. Den Haag's sleekest accommodation.

Hotel Indigo €€€ A clever transformation of the 1884 De Nederlandsche Bank headquarters on fashionable Noordeinde.

Delft p211

Delftse Hout € Wonderfully maintained campground for outdoor vibes with a city mindset. Amenities include a swimming pool, food truck and brasserie area.

Casa Julia € Boutique B&B in a 1920s building. Stylish, comfy and conveniently located rooms, though small, are well-priced.

Hotel Arsenaal €€€ Delft's classiest address. Former artillery warehouse transformed into sleek modern rooms.

Leiden p214

D'Oude Morsch €€ Stylish boutique hotel occupying the 1870 watchhouse of a former army barracks. It shares a canal bank with De Put windmill.

Ex Libris €€ Former bookshop and adjoining house near Pieterskerk. Five cute rooms up steep stairs.

Huys van Leyden €€ Stately canal houses home to characterful rooms plus a grand dining salon, sauna and Jacuzzi.

For places to stay in Friesland (Fryslân), see p237

RUDMER ZWERVER/SHUTTERSTOCK

Above: Frisian Lakes (p232); Right: Eise Eisinga Planetarium (p228)

Researched by
Sara van Geloven

Friesland (Fryslân)

PROUD LAND OF LAKES

This coastal province is rich with bountiful islands, a unique intertidal ecosystem and historic towns dotted around idyllic lakes.

The fertile fields of Friesland have drawn people for centuries, even though the waves of the Waddenzee (Wadden Sea) and Zuiderzee (which is now the IJsselmeer) washed over the land regularly. Industrious early inhabitants built *terpen* (mounds) onto which they could retreat with their livestock when the water came.

They erected dykes to eke out land and to protect increasingly busy centres of farming, fishing, shipbuilding and trade, and dug canals so these centres could be reached over water, which, for centuries, was much faster than travelling by muddy road.

City rights were awarded to 11 towns in the province because of their historical significance, not their size. These tiny, waterfront cities are all popular summertime destinations, and the lakes and waterways connecting them are still busy, now with pleasure crafts. If you do one thing in Friesland, take to the water to soak in the legendary views of big skies and serene farm fields by boat.

The Friezen are a proud, independent people with a language of their own. But there's a sense of humour, too, evident in the capital city of Leeuwarden's own Leaning Tower of Pisa. It's easy to spend a few days in the city's walkable centre, but don't miss the crowning jewel of the province: the Waddenzee, part of the world's largest intertidal system of sand and mudflats, and its four unspoilt Frisian Islands.

THE MAIN AREAS

LEEUWARDEN (LJOUWERT)
Creative provincial capital. **p222**

FRISIAN LAKES
Historic towns and water fun. **p232**

HARRY WEDZINGA/SHUTTERSTOCK

Find Your Way

This northern province, bounded by water to the north and west, can be driven across in an hour, while its idyllic Wadden Islands take a little longer to reach, but are all serviced by regular ferries.

CAR

The most comfortable way of exploring Friesland – having your own four wheels makes visiting remote towns and lakes a breeze. Consider an electric vehicle, as the charging infrastructure across the province is excellent.

TRAIN & BUS

Larger cities and towns like Leeuwarden, Harlingen and Sneek are well-connected by train, while most smaller towns are serviced by bus. Some have a reduced timetable in winter, as is the case for the ferries to the Wadden Islands.

Leeuwarden (Ljouwert), p222

The cosy, creative and walkable provincial capital makes a good starting point for visiting the Waddenzee and Frisian Islands.

Frisian Lakes, p232

This summer holiday hub of historic towns and 20 idyllic lakes is perfect for taking to the water.

WOLF-PHOTOGRAPHY/SHUTTERSTOCK

Leeuwarden (p222)

Plan Your Time

Combine a city trip with the delights of the countryside in this easily navigable province with stunning lakes and unspoilt islands.

Two Days to Explore

● Catch a train to Leeuwarden to take in its excellent **museums** (p224). Hop on a boat ride from **Blokhuispoort** (p225), a former prison, when it's sunny.

● After a good night's sleep, head back to the station and hop on a train to **Franeker** (p228) and **Harlingen** (p229), with just enough time to explore both historic towns.

A Week-Long Stay

● Spend a day in **Leeuwarden** (p222) and then catch a ferry to **Vlieland** (p230) from **Harlingen** (p229). Settle into an island rhythm and enjoy several days of long beach walks, bicycle rides and sheltering from the inevitable bouts of rain in cosy cafes.

● Back on the mainland, round off your trip with a tour of the historic towns around the **Frisian Lakes** (p232).

Seasonal Highlights

SPRING
With flowers in bloom everywhere, the historical towns are at their most attractive, while not yet as busy as in summer.

SUMMER
High season and the time to get out on the water, with the best chance of good weather. On the islands, the crowds disperse easily.

AUTUMN
Quiet and frequently wet, autumn is the time to enjoy hearty food in homely cafes and dive into culture and history in the museums.

WINTER
Dress warmly to brave blustery beaches and moody canal-scapes in sleepy towns. Ice skating (indoors or, if you're lucky, outdoors) is a must.

Leeuwarden (Ljouwert)

HISTORY | STREET ART | CULTURE

GETTING AROUND

The city centre of Leeuwarden is pedestrian-friendly – you can get everywhere within 15 minutes. The easiest way to travel to the city is by train, which takes about two hours from Amsterdam.

☑ TOP TIP

Hidden across the city are dozens of 'miniature people' – 2cm-tall figurines displayed on ledges and hidden in brick walls that depict scenes of local life. Keep an eye out for them.

The capital of Friesland has buckets of history, culture and urban renewal packed into its compact, walkable centre. Leeuwarden was built on three *terpen* ('ward' is an old word for *terp,* which means mound), one of which was already inhabited in Roman times.

The city's rich history is reflected in the cosy alleys and many old buildings around the centre, such as De Waag, built in 1597 for traders to weigh their wares, and the Oldehove, Leeuwarden's version of the Leaning Tower of Pisa.

Urban design hasn't stood still – the 115m-high, contemporary Achmeatoren now dominates the cityscape, joined by a growing number of cutting-edge buildings, such as the imposing, glass-fronted Fries Museum. A cultural renaissance of sorts has swept across Leeuwarden in recent years. The city has more than 200 works of street art, and many creative cafes and boutiques flank its canals and alleyways.

Walk the City with a Local

A free tour

The small-scale, free walking tours offered by **A Guide to Leeuwarden** *(aguidetoleeuwarden.nl)* have been going strong for more than a decade and are a fantastic way to get to know the city. Founder Henk Leutscher still leads many tours himself and has built a team of knowledgeable local guides. Some put more emphasis on historical stories, while others have a

 EATING IN LEEUWARDEN: BEST BRUNCH

Stek: Enjoy inventive brunch dishes in this cute cafe in a bridge house, with a terrace right on the canal. *hours vary by season* €

Fer Koffie: This colourful cafe is a local favourite. Its owner travelled halfway across the world to learn to brew. *9am-5pm Tue-Sat, from 11am Sun* €

Garage Modern: Fresh focaccia is the draw at this hip Italian spot. On the last Sunday of the month, join the boozy brunch with an Aperol spritz. *11am-midnight* €

Barrevoets: No-frills cafe that hits the spot with hot coffee, delicious house-made cakes and classic Dutch sandwiches. *10am-5pm Tue-Sat* €

LEEUWARDEN (LJOUWERT)

⭐ **HIGHLIGHTS**
1 Blokhuispoort
2 Fries Museum
3 Keramiek Museum
   Princessehof

🔴 **SIGHTS**
4 De Waag
5 Oldehove
6 Prinsentuin

🔴 **ACTIVITIES**
see 23 A Guide to Leeuwarden

7 Greenjoy

⚫ **SLEEPING**
8 Alibi Hostel
9 Boutique Hotel Catshuis
10 Hotel Vie Via
11 Post-Plaza Hotel

🟢 **EATING**
12 Barrevoets
13 Bistro Aragosta
14 Fer Koffie
15 Garage Modern
16 Lazy Lemon

see 11 Post-Plaza Grand Cafe
17 Sophias
18 Stek

🟢 **DRINKING & NIGHTLIFE**
19 Dr Watson
20 Proefverlof
21 Speciaalbier Café de Markies
22 Vino & Verder

🔵 **INFORMATION**
23 Visitor Centre

SPEAKING FRISIAN

You'll notice it as you enter the province: signposts showing two names for cities and towns, one Dutch and one Frisian. Friesland in Frisian is 'Fryslân', and Leeuwarden is 'Ljouwert'.

Frisian has a special status. It's an official language in the country – the only one besides Dutch and Dutch Sign Language – and is taught in schools and used by municipalities across the province. Almost all Frisians speak Dutch, but most are fluent in Frisian, too.

As a language, it's closer to English than Dutch. Pick up a few words, such as *tankewol* (thank you), *húske* (toilet) and *oant sjen* (goodbye). Start a conversation with a Frisian-speaking local and you might find that you can understand more than you'd expect.

passion for street art or local tales, but whichever guide you end up with, after an entertaining walk of 1½ hours, you'll know your way around Leeuwarden like a local.

English-language tours start outside the city's **Visitor Centre** *(visitleeuwarden.com),* across the square from the Oldehove every Saturday at noon (book ahead online). Although the tours are free, donations are encouraged.

Two Top-Tier Museums

Art, resistance and pottery

Leeuwarden's city centre is home to a duo of excellent museums. On the buzzing main square of Zaailand, the **Fries Museum** *(friesmuseum.nl; adult/child €17.50/free)* takes centre stage. This provincial museum occupies three floors of an imposing glass-fronted building. On the 1st floor, permanent exhibition, Ferhaal fan Fryslân, (Tale of Friesland) tells engaging Frisian stories via 100 objects from around the province – the museum holds the largest regional collection in the country. Through the objects, the exhibition answers questions like 'How Frisian are Frisian cows?', 'What were Vikings doing here?' and 'Why are some tiny towns in the province called cities?' The 2nd floor houses **Het Fries**

 EATING IN LEEUWARDEN: OUR PICKS

Post-Plaza Grand Cafe: A French-inspired eatery in the former red-brick post office, now a large contemporary space. *8am-11pm* €€

Sophias: Golden and flower ornaments adorn this stylish bar-restaurant with an open kitchen and urban garden out back. *10am-midnight* €€€

Lazy Lemon: This living-room–style restaurant with attentive staff serves up no-frills dishes inspired by different world cuisines. *9am-10pm* €€

Bistro Aragosta: Intimate bistro serving a chef's menu of Mediterranean dishes. The seafood is a standout and seasonal. *6-10pm Wed-Sat* €€€

MARC VENEMA/SHUTTERSTOCK

Blokhuispoort

Verzetmuseum, the moving WWII Frisian Resistance Museum, and the 3rd floor offers temporary modern art exhibitions, often with themes centred on fashion, textiles or archaeology, that can be big draws.

A combined ticket (€25) with nearby **Keramiek Museum Princessehof** *(princessehof.nl; adult/child €17.50/free)* is great value. This national ceramics museum is housed in a small but magnificent 18th-century palace, the former home of one of the king's ancestors. It contains an unparalleled selection of Delftware and international ceramics works, most notably Chinese, superbly displayed in the permanent exhibition 'From East to West'. Don't miss the small basement exhibition on the famous graphic artist MC Escher, who was born in the palace.

Former Prison Turned Creative Hub

Boats, boutiques and a quirky stay

The imposing, brick **Blokhuispoort** *(blokhuispoort.nl),* a former prison built in 1870, is worth a visit to explore the complex. Two courtyards and several of the former cells are freely accessible. Part of Cell Block H has been given a new lease on life as **Alibi Hostel** (p237), one of dozens of creative

FRYSLÂN BOPPE

Perhaps no other Dutch province has preserved its culture as strongly as Friesland. Many locals see themselves as Frisian first and Dutch second.

For years, Frisian skippers dominated the North Sea, and they founded trading posts as far afield as England, Germany and Sweden. There were mythical leaders, like King Redbad, who ruled Magna Frisia, which stretched along much of the Dutch coast. The Franks eventually defeated Redbad, and Friesland had to endure a long line of foreign rulers in between periods of self-rule. During the Dutch Republic, it was one of seven sovereign provinces.

By the late 18th century, Friesland was finally fully absorbed into the Netherlands, yet Frisians still proclaim, *Fryslân boppe!* (Friesland on top!).

DRINKING IN LEEUWARDEN: OUR PICKS

Proefverlof: Overlooking a canal and part of a former prison, this snazzy bar and restaurant is a fab spot for a cocktail. *11am-11pm Tue-Sun*

Speciaalbier Café de Markies: A cosy brown cafe with 12 craft beers on tap and more than 200 in bottles. Ask for the local draft Grutte Pier. *4pm-1am Tue-Sun*

Vino & Verder: Tucked away down a side street, this excellent wine bar with a terrace surrounded by street art is worth a detour. *3pm-midnight Wed-Sun*

Dr Watson: A speakeasy fronting as a doctor's office, this rowdy basement bar has a wide selection of excellent cocktails. *8pm-1am Wed-Sat*

THE GREAT DUTCH RACE(S)

Ice skating in the Netherlands is synonymous with the *Elfstedentocht* (11 Cities Tour), a 200km skating competition across frozen canals. The record time for completing the gruelling race is just under seven hours. Because of climate change, the chances of a cold-enough winter to hold the race are ever-diminishing; the last race took place in 1997.

Frisians have gotten creative with alternative tours that aren't as reliant on weather. There's an annual rowing and SUP competition, a five-day walking tour and a cycling race on Whit Monday. The latter is most popular, with starting tickets given out via a lottery system. If you're interested in cycling (part of) the 265km route, you can also do this at your own pace year-round.

businesses now occupying the premises. From artisan gift shops to a jewellery workshop and a vinyl record press company, there's no shortage of creativity in between the thick walls.

Hear incredible stories about the history of the prison and some of its infamous inmates on a **guided tour** *(leeuwardencityevents.nl; €10)* led by a retired prison guard. They take place every Saturday and Sunday – reserve ahead online and request a tour in English.

Afterwards, enjoy a bite and a drink in trendsetting **Proefverlof** (p225) with canal views. Next to the restaurant's wooden deck, several electric sloops of **Greenjoy** *(greenjoy.nl)* are docked, which you can hire by the hour via a handy online booking system for a self-drive tour of the city's waterways (no sailing experience needed).

The Leaning Tower of Oldehove
A climb up slanted stairs

In medieval times, several Dutch cities were in competition to build the country's highest tower. Groningen's 97m-tall Martinitoren (p242) got close, but it was Utrecht's 112m Domtoren (p154) that took the prize.

Sadly, Leeuwarden's **Oldehove** *(oldehove.eu; adult/child €3.50/1.50)* never got further than 39m. Shortly after construction started in 1529, things went wrong as the tower started to tilt, and it was never finished. In the centuries since the fiasco, Leeuwarders have embraced their version of the Leaning Tower of Pisa.

Climb the 183 steps to the rooftop (or there's a lift to take you halfway). At the top, you have a panoramic view of the city and the nearby **Prinsentuin**, a lovely park for a picnic with a view of the tower.

Ice Skating with the Locals
Winter delights

In winter, there's no activity more quintessentially Frisian than strapping on some ice-skates. Because of climate change, the chances of a long stretch of frost and the canals freezing over for ice skating are increasingly slim. To join locals on the ice for guaranteed wintry fun, head to contemporary indoor **Elfstedenhal** *(elfstedenhal.frl; Oct–Mar)*, named after the famed and gruelling ice skating race across 11 cities in the province.

Thankfully, this large ice-skating rink has the perfect conditions for a leisurely skate throughout autumn and winter. Hire skates and helmets – if you're confident, go for the speed skates with long blades, the Frisian skate of choice. Before heading out on the ice, check for the speed lanes and the slower lanes, and be sure to bring gloves because you're not allowed on the ice without them.

After several rounds, your toes are likely to start tingling with cold, so when you're ready to warm up, hand in your skates and head to **11SCafé** for a steaming cup of hot cocoa with whipped cream.

Beyond Leeuwarden

Leeuwarden is your springboard to a crescent of idyllic islands, floating a few kilometres off the dyke-ringed Waddenzee coast.

Much of the land around Leeuwarden was reclaimed from the sea and is a fertile farm region. To the west lie two of the 11 cities: tiny Franeker, once a university town and home to the world's oldest working planetarium, and Harlingen, the province's main harbour, with a large fleet of historic ships.

To the north, a connected system of ancient dykes provides a barrier to the tidal mudflats of the Waddenzee, an incredible ecosystem that can be hiked across at low tide with a guide. Across this shallow sea awaits a quartet of Frisian Islands with magnificent dune-scapes, picturesque villages and sweeping white-sand beaches that have made them popular holiday destinations with the Dutch and Germans.

Nationaal Park De Alde Feanen

TIME FROM LEEUWARDEN: 20MIN

Sail the wetlands of a watery national park

In the heart of the province lies a water wonderland. **Nationaal Park De Alde Feanen** *(np-aldefeanen.nl; free)* was once an impenetrable peat bog, heavily excavated for years, but now offers 2000 verdant hectares of canals, streams and lakes to explore at your leisure.

Hire a SUP board, canoe or electric boat with a free route leaflet at **De Twirre** *(detwirre.nl)* in the park's sole village of Eernewoude (Earnewâld), and enjoy the pastoral views.

Ameland

TIME FROM LEEUWARDEN: 2HR

Watersports and island bicycle rides

Multicoloured kites zipping across a blue sky dotted with clouds is a common sight greeting visitors to the island of Ameland, reached by a 50-minute ferry ride across the Wadden Sea from the tiny harbour town of Holwerd on the mainland.

Two wheels are best for exploring. Hire a bicycle or e-bike at **Kiewiet Fietsverhuur** *(fietsenopameland.nl)* and head to Nes, the island's largest village, a cute collection of brick

Places

Nationaal Park De Alde Feanen p227

Ameland p227

Franeker (Frjentsjer) p228

Harlingen (Harns) p229

Vlieland p230

Terschelling p231

GETTING AROUND

Reach De Alde Feanen and Holwerd, where the Wagenborg ferry to Ameland departs, by bus from Leeuwarden, but hiring a car gives you more freedom, especially if you plan to visit more places in the region or want to take your car to Ameland or Terschelling (book well ahead for this).

Franeker and Harlingen, where the Doeksen ferries to Vlieland and Terschelling depart, are easily reached by train from Leeuwarden. Vlieland is car-free for visitors.

SEAFLOOR HIKES

At low tide, water is forced through the tidal inlets between the Wadden Islands to the North Sea, leaving the Waddenzee nearly dry, allowing for hikes across the seafloor to Ameland (10km) and Schiermonnikoog (18km).

Wadlopen (mudflat walking) is a thrilling way of exploring the mudflats, to be undertaken only with an expert guide. Sturdy stretches of sand are rare as you traverse thick mud and wade through creeks and gullies.

Crossings take place in summer and are gruelling, but it's possible to do shorter tours year-round. The islands' tourist offices have details, and, on the mainland, the villages of Paesens-Moddergat and Pieterburen are *wadlopen* hubs. **Oan 'e dyk** *(oanedyk. nl)* in Friesland and **Landgoed Wilgenheerd** *(p; wilgenheerd.nl)* in Groningen province offer excellent tours.

houses and cobbled streets. Just before the village, you pass the **Tourist Office** *(vvvameland.nl)*, offering activities such as seal-spotting tours and nature excursions.

Continue north through the village to the wide North Sea beach, where you can head out on the waves with a surfboard or race across the sand in a blokart (sail buggy) at **Ameland Adventure** *(amelandadventure.nl)*. Cycling east through the dunes past the village of **Buren** leads to a sprawling nature reserve, **Natuurgebied 't Oerd**.

Past the westernmost village of **Hollum** stands the red-and-white banded **Bornrif Lighthouse** *(amelandermusea.nl; adult/child €7/5.50)*. If you've got some strength left in your legs, climb the 236 steps for sweeping island views.

Franeker (Frjentsjer) TIME FROM LEEUWARDEN: 15MIN 🚌

The oldest working planetarium

Picturesque but tiny Franeker, one of the 11 cities, squirrels away the world's oldest working planetarium. **Eise Eisinga Planetarium** *(eisinga-planetarium.nl; adult/child €6/5)*, designated a UNESCO World Heritage site in 2023, is named after its builder, an 18th-century wool comber with a serious sideline in mathematics and astrology.

DRINKING ON AMELAND: OUR PICKS

Sjoerd: A beautiful beach bar with a cosy fireplace and a large terrace sheltered from the wind. *10am-6pm*

Nobels Proeflokaal: A tasting room with different varieties of the signature island liqueur, Nobeltje. Ask about its heady origin tale. *10am-6pm*

Sunset: Perched on a narrow strip of sand, this beach bar has smashing sea views, most strikingly at – you guessed it – sunset. *11am-sunset*

Amelander Bierbrouwerij: Order a tasting flight of craft beers made in this at-home brewery, best enjoyed in the large garden. *11am-5pm Wed-Sun*

SVETLANA TERTYSHNAYA/SHUTTERSTOCK

Harlingen

Inspired by books from the nearby university (closed by Napoleon), Eisinga single-handedly built a moving scale model of the solar system, powered by a pendulum clock. It's still accurate, and at any time of day, it can tell you the exact phase of the moon, the time of sunrise and the position of the planets. Several rooms in Eisinga's former house and an adjoining building contain displays about the cosmos, but it's the turquoise planetarium that's the showstopper.

Harlingen (Harns)

TIME FROM LEEUWARDEN: 25MIN

Scenic harbour town

A 10-minute train journey west of Franeker lies the only one of the historic Frisian ports that retained its connection to the sea after the Afsluitdijk was built.

Harlingen, another of the 11 cities, is a lovely town to explore for a few hours before catching a ferry to Vlieland or Terschelling. Its protected centre has quaint canal houses, narrow alleys and historic boats docked in several marinas. Head to the old, industrial waterfront buzzing with creative cafes and breweries like **Het Brouwdok** or enjoy sea views from beach bar **Strandpaviljoen 't Zilt**.

AN ENGINEERING MARVEL

Perhaps the most impressive of the Dutch structures built to keep out the water is Afsluitdijk, a 32km-long barrier dyke so vast that it's visible from space. The dam was constructed in 1932 and effectively sealed off the Zuiderzee (South Sea), which eventually became the freshwater lake IJsselmeer.

On the Frisian side of the dam, 15km from Harlingen, the futuristic **Afsluitdijk Wadden Center** *(afsluitdijkwadden center.nl; adult/ child €5/3)* offers a captivating, interactive exhibit about the construction of the dyke and its ecological impact. Learn more about its fascinating history and future via an English-language mobile audio tour, included in the ticket price.

EATING & DRINKING IN HARLINGEN: OUR PICKS

San Marino: Local staple with standout staff who serve Italian comfort food and a signature side salad across two bright and cosy floors. *1-9pm Wed-Sun* €€

Strandpaviljoen 't Zilt: A wooden pavilion on the beach with a big terrace, an unassuming menu and front-row seats at sunset. *11am-8pm* €€

Skom: Part of the Afsluitdijk Wadden Center, this modern cafe offers fresh sandwiches and unobstructed IJsselmeer views. *9am-5.30pm Wed-Sun* €

Het Brouwdok: This glass-fronted, cosy taproom overlooking the harbour has craft beers brewed on-site and tasty snacks. *3-10pm Tue-Sun*

WHY I LOVE VLIELAND

Sara van Geloven,
Lonely Planet writer

I have fond memories of summers spent camping on Vlieland in my teenage years, my hair tied back in a ponytail, salty from all the swims in the sea. My worries always seemed to disappear the second I stepped aboard the ferry in Harlingen.

I still love the 1½-hour ride across the Waddenzee, but I often choose to visit in winter now. The pace is even slower, and accommodation is available at the last minute (with some great deals). After a freezing walk on the beach, I like ducking into **Gestrand** in the village to warm up and watch the sky, at its most dramatic when a curtain of rain sweeps across the steely grey Wad.

Vlieland

TIME FROM LEEUWARDEN: 2¼HR 🚗 + 🚢

Island delights

This small, westernmost Frisian Wadden island packs a punch. The main street of Vlieland's sole village is lined with boutiques, cosy hotels and historic brick houses. The ferry from Harlingen docks right in the centre and, in summer, brings crowds in droves, as the island's particularly popular with Amsterdammers, who've dubbed it 'Vliebiza'.

Thankfully, wide open space is abundant. Vlieland has perhaps the most beautiful stretch of beach of all the Wadden Islands. Head past the marina for a walk across a crescent of white sand to **Oost**, a contemporary shoebox of a beach pavilion serving up fresh seafood. Back south through the dunes, you'll pass contemporary brewery **Fortuna** (*fortunavlieland. nl; tour €17.50*), open daily for tasting tours in summer (book ahead online).

Days on the island are a succession of simple delights: bracing bicycle rides, battling the salty breeze past fields of blooming heath and stumbling across island gems, such as **De Kaasbunker** (*zeewierkaas.nl*), a former WWII bunker now used to ripen cheeses from a local maker. Take a late-afternoon dip in the chilly waves of the North Sea, followed by a warming drink in the setting sun at buzzing beach bar **'t Badhuys**.

The west side of the island is desolate, a vast sand plain partly used by the military for training. You can explore it by hopping on a large expedition truck, **Vliehors Expres** (*vliehors-expres.nl; adult/child €29.50/22*), which in summer runs alongside a ferry service from the westernmost point of the island to Texel (*waddenveer.nl; adult/child €42.50/32.50*).

MORE WADDEN DELIGHTS

The peaceful Frisian island of **Schiermonnikoog** (p228), to the east of Ameland, is reached by ferry from Lauwersoog in Groningen.

EATING & DRINKING ON VLIELAND: OUR PICKS

Bakkerij Westers: Family-run bakery serving coffee and pastries. *Suikerbrood* (sugar loaf) is a regional favourite. *8am-noon & 1.30-5pm Mon-Sat* €

Gestrand: A bright interior, Waddenzee views and a no-nonsense menu make this all-day restaurant across from the ferry dock a winner. *10am-10pm* €€

Oost: The trek across the sand is worth it for the fresh seafood in this small, contemporary beach pavilion with a terrace. *10.30am-7pm Tue-Sun Mar-Sep* €€€

't Badhuys: This spacious beach bar with an open kitchen is the island's best spot for a cocktail with a view of the North Sea. *10am-10pm*

Terschelling

Island delicacies and dark skies

Terschelling offers the most well-rounded island experience of the Frisian quartet. It's the largest, with a string of villages filled with hotels, campgrounds, restaurants and merry bars. The ferry from Harlingen docks in the centre of **West-Terschelling**, the main village that's home to the iconic brick **Brandaris Lighthouse** (still in use, not open to visitors). Hire an e-bike – you'll appreciate the boost for the distances between villages – at **Tijs Knop Fietsverhuur** (*tijsknop.nl*) and set out to explore the island, west to east.

Start at quirky beach pavilion **De Walvis**, with a popular terrace and a view of **De Noordsvaarder**, a nature reserve. From here, 60km of cycling trails zigzag northeast through the dunes. Whichever trail you pick, you're sure to encounter an interesting pitstop before long, from **De Bessenschuur** (*terschellingercranberries.nl; free*), dedicated to the island's wild cranberries, to the **Bunker Museum** (*bunkermuseum terschelling.nl; free*), a well-preserved WWII complex.

The wild and uninhabited east side of the island, nature reserve **De Boschplaat**, is best explored on foot. Stay after sunset to see the Milky Way appear overhead – the reserve is one of just two Dark Sky Parks in the country.

An immersive island festival

For 10 days each June, the entire island of Terschelling is turned into a stage. Theatre performances take place among the dunes, stretches of beach are turned into works of art and live music is played in remote farm sheds. A ticket to **Oerol Festival** (*oerol.nl; adult/child €66/13.50*) gets you access to festival areas and most concerts, while theatre shows have to be booked separately. Book online well in advance for tickets and accommodation.

SAILING ON THE WADDENZEE

Tsjerk Hesling Hoekstra is skipper of the Dutch clipper *Willem Jacob*, part of the *bruine vloot*, the largest sailing fleet of historical ships in the world. He shares what makes the Waddenzee so special.

@klipperwillemjacob
'I've sailed on tall ships from Norway to South Africa, but, for me, nothing beats the Waddenzee. Everything is always changing in this place. Almost as soon as sea charts are printed, they're outdated again. We've got big, blazing skies, and because it's a shallow sea without large waves, the water can turn into a mirror or blend with the sky in 50,000 shades of grey. It's a place where heaven and Earth share the same stage.'

 EATING & DRINKING ON TERSCHELLING: OUR PICKS

't Lokaal: Colourful deli with local treats, great coffee and fresh sandwiches to eat at the tiny terrace or take away. *10am-5pm* €

De Walvis: Soak in the views from the broad porch of this beach bar that has been going strong since the 1960s. *10.30am-6.30pm*

Eilandbistro de Boschplaat: A French-inspired eatery with top seafood and wine pairings in the island's easternmost village. *5.30-11pm Tue-Sat* €€€

Pura Vida: This buzzing living-room–style restaurant serves street-food–inspired shared dishes with fresh flavours. *10am-midnight Tue-Sat* €€

Frisian Lakes

IDYLLIC LAKES | WATERSPORTS | HISTORIC TOWNS

GETTING AROUND

Sneek, Workum and Hindeloopen are all connected by Arriva railway from Leeuwarden, and trains run regularly. A bus runs to Woudsend from Sneek, but a hire car might be more convenient, especially if you want to visit multiple villages and lakes.

☑ **TOP TIP**

In 2018, 11 international artists created fountains for each of the 11 cities. All these contemporary artworks incorporate themes from the towns where they were placed, such as the lions from the city crest in Workum and animal motifs in Hindeloopen. Spot seven of the fountains in the Frisian Lakes area.

The Friese Meren (Fryske Marren) region is the Netherlands at its most idyllic. More than 20 lakes are scattered among verdant fields, not unlike the spots on the black and white cows that are so numerous here. They were formed over centuries through peat extraction and natural flooding, which gradually turned the low-lying landscape into a network of interconnected lakes and waterways once essential for transporting goods and now crowded with pleasure crafts. A scattering of historical towns offers marinas, no-frills restaurants (often specialising in seafood), campgrounds and quaint holiday homes for rent.

Waterpret (*wetterwille* in Frisian, meaning water fun) is what this region is all about. From kitesurfing on the IJsselmeer and standup paddleboarding on the canals in Sneek to cycling around lakes and driving a blissfully silent, electric boat along canals, the aquatic lifestyle is easy to fall in love with.

Bicycles, Boats & Booze in Sneek

Explore Friesland's aquatic heart

Sneek (Snits) is Friesland's aquatic heart. Surrounded by lakes, and the largest of the 11 cities after Leeuwarden, it's home to many marinas and boating companies.

Start your day at the iconic 15th-century **Waterpoort** in the centre, the only one of the city gates left standing. Hire two wheels at **Bike Totaal Rodenburg** (*fietsenverhuursneek.nl*) and cycle across the centre to the **Fries Scheepvaart Museum** (*friesscheepvaartmuseum.nl; adult/child €11/5.50*). This superb nautical museum is spread across five monumental buildings and displays intricate ship models. Don't miss the exhibitions on the seafaring history of Friesland and Elfstedentocht, a famous ice-skating race (p226). Kids love the children's section, where they can learn to tie knots.

A few doors down from the nautical museum sits the enchanting vintage liquor shop and distillery **Weduwe Joustra** (*weduwejoustra.nl*). For more than 150 years, the aromatic,

FRISIAN LAKES

0   10 km
0   5 miles

★ **HIGHLIGHTS**
1 Jopie Huisman Museum
2 Weduwe Joustra

● **SIGHTS**
see 2 Fries Scheepvaart Museum
3 Museum Hindeloopen
see 2 Waterpoort
4 Woudagemaal

● **ACTIVITIES**
5 JFT Watersport

● **SLEEPING**
6 Camping Vrijhaven
see 3 De Hinde
see 2 Hotel Stadsherberg Sneek

● **EATING**
7 Beachclub Sneek
8 Café de Watersport
see 3 De Hinde
see 2 De Koperen Kees

● **SHOPPING**
see 3 Roosje Hindeloopen

● **TRANSPORT**
see 2 Bike Totaal Rodenburg

slightly bitter drink *beerenburg* has been distilled (using *jenever,* Dutch gin, and a secret mix of herbs) and sold here. Tours of the distillery have to be booked well in advance, but visitors to the shop are invited to peruse the storage room out back, full of antique knick-knacks, and head up to the attic for a free tasting (small donation encouraged) of a wide selection of *beerenburg* bottles – be careful on the stairs down!

Of course, no visit to Sneek is complete without taking to the water. Hop back on your bike for a 10-minute cycle to **JFT Watersport** *(jft-watersport.nl),* a family-run outfit offering SUP boards, sail dinghies and motorboats to sail to Sneeker-meer, the nearby watersport hub.

A Walk Through History in Hindeloopen
Where water and crafts rule

Of all the 11 cities, **Hindeloopen** (Hylpen) is perhaps the most charming. It's surrounded by the IJsselmeer on three sides, with a church tower and a forest of masts visible from afar. The historic centre has been well-preserved, with narrow streets interlaced by canals, flower-filled gardens and a multitude of bridges. Around every corner, you'll find a new vista that seems to have jumped straight from a postcard.

✺ EATING NEAR THE FRISIAN LAKES: BEST SPOTS WITH A VIEW

De Koperen Kees: Modern brasserie with perfectly executed dishes. A terrace overlooks one of Sneek's canals. *5-10pm Mon, from 11.30am Tue-Sun* €€€

Beachclub Sneek: Enjoy a cold drink and a fried snack with your feet in the sand on the terrace with a view of the Sneekermeer. *11am-10pm* €€

Café de Watersport: This Woudsend staple serves generous portions, and its terrace is a prime boat-watching spot. *10am-11pm Wed-Mon* €€€

De Hinde: A fine seafood restaurant with rooms and picture-perfect views of Hindeloopen's marina. *11am-10pm Mon, Tue & Fri-Sun* €€€

BEST SAILING FESTIVALS

Sneekweek: Time your visit to Sneek on the first Saturday in August to join the ultimate sailing party. Sneekweek is the largest sailing event on Europe's inland waters. Expect thousands of small sailboats, lots of racing on the Sneekermeer and parties in the streets. *(sneekweek.nl)*

Skûtsjesilen: Each summer, historical cargo barges called *skûtsjes* travel across the province for several weeks of sailing competitions. The fleet sails from one town to the next, and it's a marvellous sight to see the graceful ships with brown and white sails battle it out on the lakes.

When the IJsselmeer was still the Zuiderzee, Hindeloopen was an important trade town on the route from Amsterdam to Scandinavia and beyond. Traces of this heritage can still be seen around town. Visit the small **Museum Hindeloopen** *(museumhindeloopen.nl; adult/child €11/6.50)* in the former town hall (1683), also home to the visitor centre, to learn more about Hindeloopen's rich history through the stories of Hylpers, including a housewife – for months at a time when the men were at sea, women ran the show in the city.

Walk across town (which takes all of five minutes) to see how traditions are kept alive at **Roosje Hindeloopen** *(roosjehindeloopen.com),* a family-owned boutique and workshop where furniture is still painstakingly hand-painted with colourful motifs of flowers and animals. **De Hinde** (p233), around the corner and overlooking the harbour, is the spot for a pick-me-up, with exquisite seafood and, in winter, the best *snert* (traditional pea soup) around.

Workum's Utterly Unique Museum

Paintings of broken things

In the historic centre of **Workum** (Warkum), one of the 11 cities, sits a wonderful museum shaped like a steel-fronted church, dedicated to a single painter. Jopie Huisman, who passed away in 2000, was a prolific self-taught artist with a

Woudagemaal

HOW THE LAKES CAME TO BE

After the last Ice Age, rising sea levels turned southwest Friesland into a vast bog. Over time, a thick layer of peat built up, rich fuel for excavation. From the Middle Ages onwards, people dug long, narrow plots to cut peat for turf, and farm settlements sprang up alongside.

As the peat oxidised, the ground sank, and the lowest parts filled with water again, creating the lakes. Unlike in North Holland, the Frisians never reclaimed the land by creating polders (areas of drained land). The sandy soil wasn't suitable for farming, and the region was never densely populated. With few roads linking the villages, travel by boat was far more practical. The waterways still connect all 24 of the Frisian Lakes today.

love of depicting Frisian peasant life. He's best known for his remarkable lifelike paintings of rags.

By painting 'broken things', as he called them, he made them beautiful. After three of his works were stolen from a gallery, Huisman never lent out his works again. The **Jopie Huisman Museum** *(jopiehuismanmuseum.nl; adult/child €12.50/free)* is the one place where you can see the originals and hear their stirring stories. Ticket prices include an English-language audio tour.

The Power of Steam in Lemmer

How feet are kept dry

A tall chimney stands out in the otherwise flat landscape around **Lemmer**, the gateway to the Frisian Lakes from the south. It belongs to the **Woudagemaal** *(woudagemaal.nl; adult/child €11/6.50),* the largest steam-powered pumping station in the world that's still in operation. The impressive red-brick building was constructed in 1920 (then the picture of progress) in an area where windmills and sluices had for centuries managed surplus water. Today, it's a UNESCO World Heritage site that's still fired up occasionally to let visitors see the intricate pump system in action and to help keep Frisian feet dry when water levels rise.

A SELF-DRIVE SUMMER BOAT TOUR

Head out from picture-perfect Woudsend, which sits between two of the largest Frisian Lakes, for a boat ride.

START	END	LENGTH
Jachthaven de Rakken	Café de Watersport	9km; 2 hr

Hire an electric boat at ❶ **Jachthaven de Rakken** (book ahead online via *sloeptehuur.nl or happywhale.nl*). After a quick explanation of the vessel – an easy-to-drive, silent electric sloop, some 3D-printed and built right here in the village – you're off.

Turn right as you exit the marina and at the next crossway, steer left and head into the lake Noorder Ee and then turn left again into the Nauwe Wijmerts. Enjoy the views of farm fields and spotted cows until you come to the Johan Frisokanaal crossing. Go straight, but watch for other boats.

Take a left on the Hegemar Far and steer past the marina into the heart of the historical town of ❷ **Heeg**. ❸ **Restaurant d'Ald Wal** is a great coffee pit stop. Afterwards, cast off and follow the canal to the Heegermeer. ❹ **Eiland van Heeg** sits in the middle of the lake and is a fine spot for a swim.

Follow the marked channel south across the lake to the small inlet of the ❺ **Woudsenderrakken**, a reed-lined, meandering canal. Follow it until you reach the marina, moor your boat and walk to ❻ **Café de Watersport** (p233) in Woudsend to toast to a successful outing on the water.

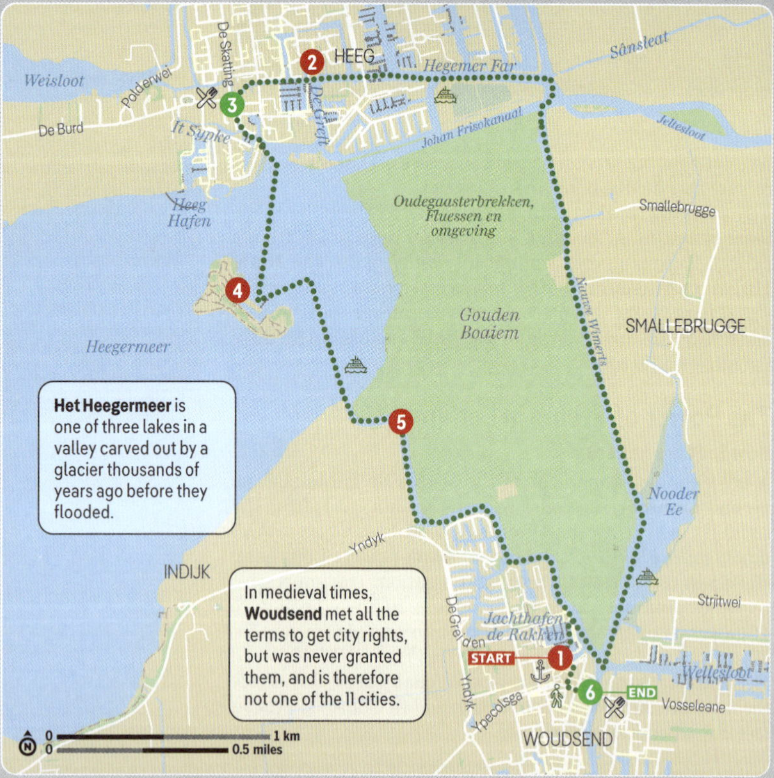

Het Heegermeer is one of three lakes in a valley carved out by a glacier thousands of years ago before they flooded.

In medieval times, **Woudsend** met all the terms to get city rights, but was never granted them, and is therefore not one of the 11 cities.

THE GUIDE

FRISIAN LAKES **FRIESLAND (FRYSLÂN)**

0   1 km
0   0.5 miles

Places We Love to Stay

€ Budget €€ Midrange €€€ Top End

Leeuwarden (Ljouwert)
p222

Alibi Hostel € A hostel inside Blokhuispoort, a former prison. Sleep in private or dorm rooms, all refurbished cells. (Don't worry, you get a key!)

Hotel Vie Via €€ Bright and colourful rooms with a massive rain shower and a contemporary, communal lounge. Self check-in.

Boutique Hotel Catshuis €€ This family-owned, small-scale hotel in a historic residence has beautiful rooms and stand-out staff.

Hotel Post-Plaza €€ An urban-chic spot inside the 19th-century post office and a former bank, perfectly blending old and new.

Ameland
p227

Camping Duinoord € Pitch a tent or rent a bell tent or chalet to camp in the dunes and fall asleep to the sound of rolling waves.

Van Heeckeren Hotel €€ Stays start right with a welcome drink at this central, quiet hotel with tasteful rooms and rental apartments.

Vlieland
p230

Camping Stortemelk € A sprawling campground in the dunes with a homey bar, rental tents and cabins, and direct beach access.

Badhotel Bruin €€ In the centre of the village, this boutique hotel delights with bright, comfortable rooms.

Terschelling
p231

Camping De Kooi € This small-scale campground with an orchard is car-free and comfortable, with rental tents and a cosy all-day restaurant.

Stayokay € Standout chain hostel with an environmental focus, simple dorms and private rooms, some with top sea views.

Frisian Lakes
p232

Camping Vrijhaven € This campground with native trees sits right on the water near Heeg and has quirky tiny houses to rent.

Hotel Stadsherberg Sneek € Monumental hotel with snug rooms a stone's throw away from Sneek's top sights.

De Hinde €€ Two tastefully decorated rooms with a view of the marina occupy the 1st floor of this Hindeloopen staple.

UWE ARANAS/SHUTTERSTOCK

Hotel Post-Plaza

Researched by
Sara van Geloven

Northeastern Netherlands

A DYNAMIC CITY, QUIET PARKS AND DEEP HISTORY

One of the country's buzziest cities is hemmed by the enigmatic Waddenzee (Wadden Sea) to the north and blissfully crowd-free national parks to the south.

Remote Groningen has one of the oldest universities in the country, and the city's cultural influence still reaches far and wide. A historic city centre coupled with a young student population has created a heady mix of well-preserved traditions, urban renewal and thriving bar scene.

The city likes to celebrate. On 28 August, a culinary fest and firework display commemorate the defeat of invading troops led by 'Bommen Berend' (the Bishop of Munster) in 1672, while new, innovative festivals have taken pride of place in both summer and winter party calendars.

The seemingly empty countryside around the provincial capital is a treasure trove of surprises. Across the Waddenzee lies the idyllic island of Schiermonnikoog, with forests, dunes and beaches begging to be explored by bicycle. Hugging the German border in the east is one of the best-preserved fortifications in the country, 16th-century Bourtange.

Bucolic Drenthe, south of Groningen, has three magnificent national parks (more than any other Dutch province), interspersed with attractive medieval towns, ancient forests and fields grazed by sheep. The land was steamrolled by glaciers 100,000 years ago and, at the end of the last Ice Age, moulded by rivers to form sandy ridges and valleys with meandering rivers.

In this epic landscape, now a UNESCO Global Geopark, early farmers built the mysterious *hunebedden* (megalithic prehistoric burial chambers). Fifty-two of these 5000-year-old burial chambers can be explored across the province.

PHOTODIGITAAL.NL/SHUTTERSTOCK

THE MAIN AREAS

GRONINGEN
Buzzing student city. **p242**

DRENTHE
The country's garden. **p252**

For places to stay in Northeastern Netherlands, see p257

SANDER VAN DER WERF/SHUTTERSTOCK

Left: Dwingelderveld National Park (p253); Above: Martinitoren (p242), Groningen

Find Your Way

The northernmost province of Groningen has its namesake capital city at its heart. From here, it's about a 40-minute drive to both the Waddenzee and the German border. Rural, landlocked Drenthe is idyllic driving country, with most sights no more than 45 minutes apart.

Groningen, p242

This handsome Hanseatic city with a young heart and innovative pulse is the best starting point for exploring Groningen province, as well as Drenthe.

TRAIN & BUS

Groningen and Assen are well connected by train, and a regular bus service links to Schiermonnikoog ferry timetables. Regional train lines and buses reach most villages in both provinces, but service can be sporadic.

CAR

A car is ideal for visiting the remote towns and parks in Drenthe and the countryside around Groningen. Consider an electic vehicle, as the fast-charging infrastructure in both provinces is excellent, and rental options are numerous.

Drenthe, p252

A great garden with shifting tableaus of sheep pastures, marshlands and fascinating *hunebedden*.

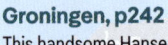

Noordpolderzijl

GERMANY

Roodeschool

Pieterburen   Uithuizen

Bierum

Emden

Loppersum

Bedum   Appingedam   Delfzijl

Ten Boer

Garmerwolde

Groningen   Forum   GRONINGEN

Groninger Museum

A7   A7

Hoogezand Sappemeer   Winschoten

Eelde

Veendam

Midlaren

Annen   Vlagtwedde

A28   Bourtange

Assen   Drents Museum   Stadskanaal

Smilde   Hunebedcentrum

Borger

Beilen   Drenthe   Odoorn

N371   Westerbork   Klijndijk

Dwingeloo   A28   Orvelte

Dwingelderveld National Park   Emmen

Ruinen

Hoogeveen   A37

Coevorden

OVERIJSSEL   GERMANY

FRIESLAND

Eems Kanaal

0 ——— 20 km
0 ——— 10 miles
N

Bourtange Fortress (p250)

Plan Your Time

Allow for enough time to sample the many delights of Groningen city and then head north to Schiermonnikoog, south to Drenthe or both.

Three Days by Transit

● Pull into **Groningen**'s (p242) grand train station and explore the **historic centre on foot** (p247). Visit the rooftop of the **Forum** (p242) and then try the city's **best bars** (p243).

● Explore the **Groninger Museum** (p246) or head to **Lauwersoog** (p249) and hop on the ferry to idyllic **Schiermonnikoog** (p250).

A Week for a Road Trip

● Enjoy buzzing **Groningen** (p242) and then drive to **Lauwersoog** (p249) and take the ferry to **Schiermonnikoog** (p250).

● Back on the mainland, set off on a coastal road trip. From fortress town **Bourtange** (p251), cross into Drenthe to drive the **Hunebed Highway** (p252). Round off your visit with a stay in nature near the heathlands of **Dwingelderveld** (p253).

Seasonal Highlights

SPRING

The fields in Drenthe turn tennis ball green, while in Groningen, the terraces start to come out, as do many flowers across the city gardens.

SUMMER

Groningen is at its busiest and prettiest. Cyclists and hikers head to Drenthe and Schiermonnikoog in droves.

AUTUMN

Wet and windy, autumn is the season to explore without the crowds and warm up in blissfully comfy bars between bracing walks and bicycle rides.

WINTER

Christmas lights and festivals brighten dark days in Groningen city, while Drenthe's national parks sparkle under a blanket of frost.

Groningen

NIGHTLIFE | CULTURE | CAFES

GETTING AROUND

Thanks to careful urban planning, Groningen's centre is almost entirely pedestrianised. You can get from one side to the other in less than 15 minutes. For destinations a bit further out, hiring a bike or taking the bus might be more convenient. The easiest way to get to the city is by train, which takes about two hours from Amsterdam.

☑ **TOP TIP**

Summer is when the city's at its most attractive, with picnics among the trees in the Nooderplantsoen and evenings spent on the sun-soaked terraces. To experience the buzz when all the students are in town, visit during the academic year (September to June).

Looking at a map of the Netherlands, Groningen seems a long way from anywhere, but this vibrant, youthful city is among the country's most progressive urban metropolises, with a 50,000-strong student population injecting bags of creative zest into its lively cafes, hedonistic nightlife and flourishing cultural scene.

The Hanseatic city has an opportune location. It was built on the outliers of the Hondsrug hills and for centuries also had a direct connection to the sea. It was already an independent city-state and key trading centre by the late Middle Ages.

Despite heavy fighting in WWII, many historic buildings have been well-preserved, including the iconic Martinitoren, the tallest structure in the city. No new development is allowed to top it, but the cityscape has been modernised in recent years by the addition of fresh icons such as the Forum. There's no better base for exploring the north.

The Best View of the City

Visit a contemporary cultural centre

Impossible to miss is the modern, 45m-tall structure rising like an upside-down, sandstone-coloured mountain close to the central square, Grote Markt. **Forum** *(forum.nl; free)* is the city's premier cultural centre and houses the tourist office, library, an arthouse cinema, **Storyworld** *(storyworld. nl; adult/child €10.50/7.50)* museum, restaurant **Nok** *(nok groningen.nl)* and a rooftop terrace with spectacular views of the city, most strikingly the neighbouring **Martinitoren**. During the day, you can head up the building's zigzag escalators to visit the rooftop for free. In summer, there are rooftop cinema nights.

WOLF-PHOTOGRAPHY/SHUTTERSTOCK

Vismarkt (p248)

Bar Hop Through the City

Visit buzzing bars and a brewery

No visit to a Dutch student city is complete without a late-afternoon or early-evening bar hop. Start at **Café de Sigaar**, a bruin café (traditional pub) on the Hoge der Aa with a (rare in Groningen) lovely canal-side terrace. Next, head down a few backstreets to tiny Belgian cafe **De Pintelier**, which has 23 beers on tap and an inviting summer terrace. If you're already feeling peckish, student hangout **De Uurwerker** across the square serves delicious, wood-fired oven pizzas.

Now it's time for a little detour, depending on your tastes. Whisky fans will feel right at home at **Café de Toeter**, which has a staggering offering of 350 single malt whiskies and a fun pub quiz on Wednesday and Sunday evenings. Wine lovers will be happier at celebrated wine bar **Barrel Wijnlokaal**, where the *kleine proeverij* (small tasting) is great value. Back to beer: microbrewery **Brouwerij Martinus** lies somewhat hidden down a side street, but it's well worth tracking down, as is speakeasy **The Stockroom**, the spot for a high-end cocktail. At Oosterstraat 24-1, look for the door with a blow-up drawing of a rowdy bar.

Around the corner are Poelestraat and Peperstraat, where, if you're so inclined, a collection of all-night cafes can keep you entertained into the wee hours.

BEST FESTIVALS IN GRONINGEN

Noorderzon: For 10 days in August, the Noorderplantsoen hosts this performing arts meets summer fest with free entry. Enjoy live music, food trucks and top-bill, paid performances. *(noorderzon.nl)*

Winterwelvaart: This magical, floating Christmas market spills across the Hoge and Lage der A waterfront for a weekend in December, with food and art stalls, mulled wine, and ships hosting live music, often with free entry. *(winterwelvaart.nl)*

Eurosonic Noorderslag: An ubercool pop-music showcase festival in January. Tickets are in high demand, but there's also a free fringe festival held in bars across town. *(esns.nl)*

DRINKING IN GRONINGEN: BEST ALL-DAY BARS

Mr Mofongo: This bar is a treasure trove of curiosities, with tables topped with travel memorabilia and a robot arm that pours house-made gins. *11am-midnight*

Drie Gezusters: Possibly the biggest bar in the country, these interconnected historical cafes along Grote Markt's south side are pretty as a picture. *11am-1am*

Dot: A massive, orb-shaped and hip gastrobar with a sprawling terrace and city beach that's a popular swimming spot in summer. *3-10pm Wed-Sat, from 10am Sun*

Werkman: Inspired by the namesake local artist, this contemporary bar has an eclectic interior, striking glass facade and three floors to choose from. *11am-midnight*

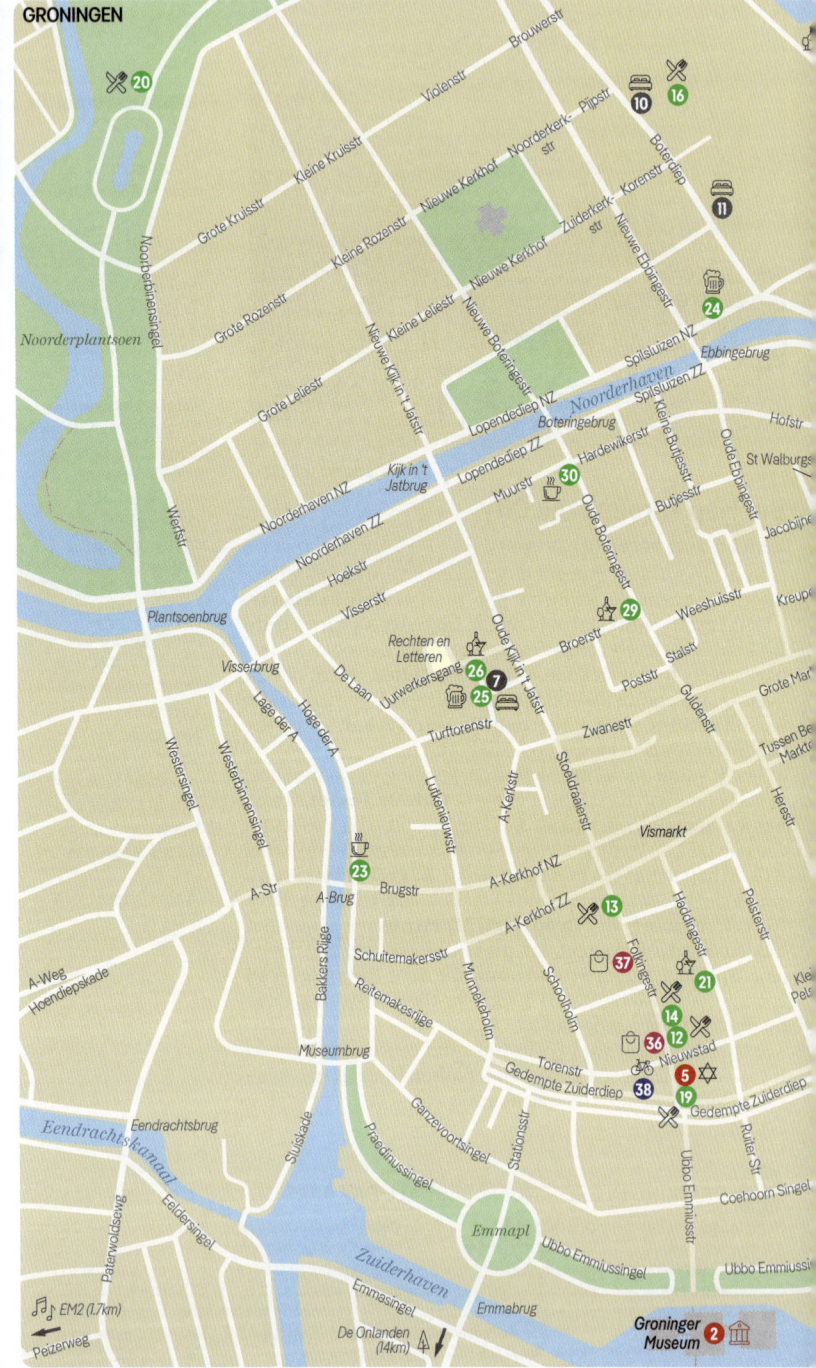

GRONINGEN

Noorderplantsoen

Brouwerstr

Violenstr

Kleine Kruisstr

Grote Kruisstr

Noorderbinnensingel

Grote Rozenstr

Kleine Rozenstr

Noorderkerkstr

Pijpstr

Korenstr

Nieuwe Ebbingestr

Boterdiep

Kleine Leliestr

Nieuwe Kerkhof

Zuiderkerkstr

Nieuwe Kijk in 't Jatstr

Grote Leliestr

Nieuwe Boteringestr

Lopendediep NZ

Boteringebrug

Spilsluizen NZ

Noorderhaven

Ebbingebrug

Spilsluizen ZZ

Hofstr

Kijk in 't Jatbrug

Lopendediep ZZ

Muurstr

Hardewikerstr

Kleine Butjesstr

Oude Ebbingestr

St Walburg

Werfstr

Noorderhaven NZ

Noorderhaven ZZ

Oude Boteringestr

Butjesstr

Jacobijne

Plantsoenbrug

Hoekstr

Visserstr

Broerstr

Weeshuisstr

Kreupe

Rechten en Letteren

Uurwerkersgang

Poststr

Stalstr

Grote Mar

Visserbrug

De Laan

Lage der A

Hoge der A

Turftorenstr

A-Kerkstr

Zwanestr

Stoeldraaierstr

Guldenstr

Tussen Be Marktr

Westersingel

Westerbinnensingel

Lutkenieuwstr

Vismarkt

Herestr

A-Str

Brugstr

A-Kerkhof NZ

A-Kerkhof ZZ

Haddingestr

Pelsterstr

A-Brug

Bakkers Rijge

Schuitemakersstr

Munnekeholm

Schoolholm

Folkingestr

Kleie Pels

A-Weg

Hoendiepskade

Reitemakersrijge

Torenstr

Nieuwstad

Museumbrug

Sluiskade

Ganzevoortsingel

Gedempte Zuiderdiep

Gedempte Zuiderdiep

Rutter Str

Eendrachtskanaal

Eendrachtsbrug

Praediniussingel

Stationsstr

Ubbo Emmiusstr

Coehoorn Singel

Paterswoldseweg

Leldersingel

Zuiderhaven

Emmapl

Ubbo Emmiussingel

Ubbo Emmiussi

♫♪ EM2 (1.7km)

Emmasingel

Emmabrug

Emmabrug

Groninger Museum

← Peizerweg

De Onlanden (14km)

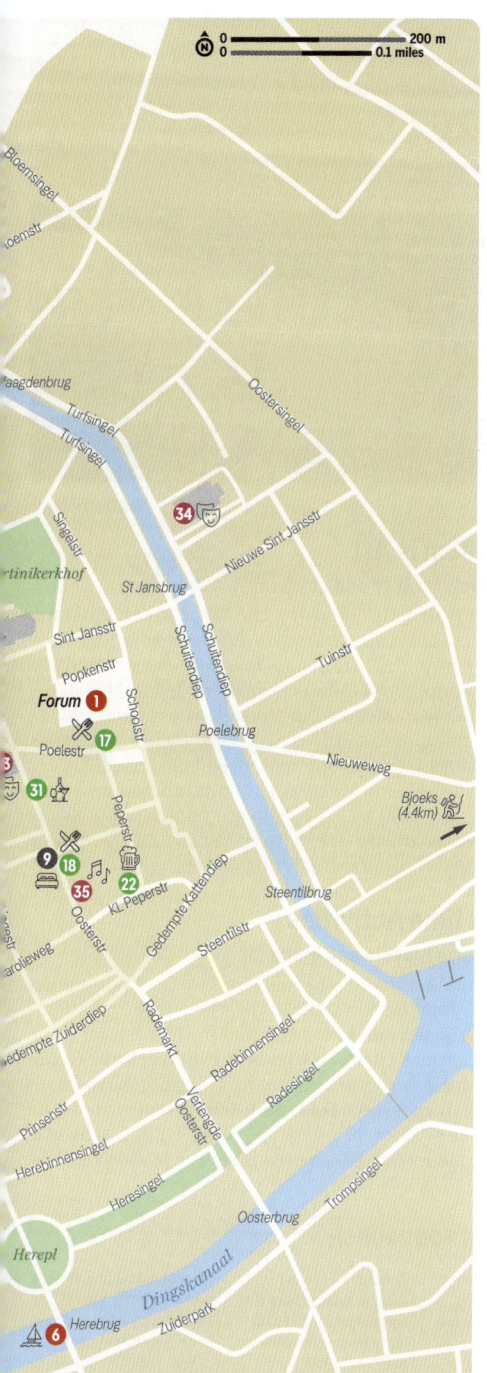

⭐ HIGHLIGHTS
1 Forum
2 Groninger Museum

● SIGHTS
3 Grote Markt
4 Martinitoren
see 1 Storyworld
5 Synagogue

● ACTIVITIES
6 beDRIJFNAT

● SLEEPING
7 Happy Traveler
8 Market Hotel
9 PJs Hostel
10 Simplon Hostel
11 Social Hub

● EATING
12 Ariola
13 Bar Barrie
14 Bistro Boys
15 De Oude Tijden
16 Florentin
see 33 Gustatio
17 Het Concerthuis
see 1 Nok
18 Olijfboom Greek Canteen
19 Toet
20 Zondag

● DRINKING & NIGHTLIFE
21 Barrel Wijnlokaal
22 Brouwerij Martinus
23 Café de Sigaar
24 Café de Toeter
25 De Pintelier
26 De Uurwerker
27 Dot
28 Drie Gezusters
29 Mr Mofongo
30 Spaak
31 Stockroom
32 Werkman

● ENTERTAINMENT
33 Grand Theatre
see 10 Simplon
34 Stadsschouwburg
35 Vera

● SHOPPING
36 Beauties
see 14 Klinkhamer
37 Le Souk

● TRANSPORT
38 Fietsverhuur Groningen

SANDER VAN DER WERF/SHUTTERSTOCK

De Onlanden

TOP TIPS FOR FOLKINGESTRAAT

Minke Felix is the co-owner of natural cosmetics salon **Beauties** (p248) in Folkingestraat. She shares some of her favourite food spots. *@beauties.groningen*

'All the shopowners in the street know each other. On my lunch break, I often go to **Le Souk** *(winkellesouk. nl)*, a family-run North African grocer where my go-to is freshly made *mhadjeb*, a delicious savoury pancake. Or I head to **Ariola** *(facebook. com/AriolaFolkinge)* for Italian comfort food. This tiny deli is more than 30 years old and the owner knows the names of all her regulars.After work, I like paying a visit to **Bistro Boys** *(bistroboys.nl)*. The food is fantastic: shared dining with dishes that are always a hit. I love the community we have here and the support that's there for small, independent shops like ours.'

Art Museum Is Art

Eclectic architecture and celebrated exhibitions

The striking structure housing the **Groninger Museum** *(groningermuseum.nl; adult/child €19.50/free)* is known to stop passersby in their tracks. Its four psychedelic pavilions were each crafted by a different architect, led by Italian designer Alessandro Mendini in 1994. This explains why, to many, the museum has little consistency.

Inside, things are quite different. Bright colours add life to the excellent permanent exhibition halls, and natural light seeps in from all angles. The temporary art exhibitions are often big international draws (from Versace to the Rolling Stones) – check the current offering online.

Summertime Activities

On water, on a bicycle and in the air

Both students and *stadjers* (Groningers) love heading outdoors in summer. Join them in some of their favourite activities.

By bicycle, you're out of the city and in the pastoral countryside in no time. Hire two wheels at **Fietsverhuur Groningen** *(fietsverhuurgroningen.com)* and explore the wetlands of nearby nature reserve **De Onlanden** or venture out a bit further to the picturesque *wierde* (mound) town of **Garnwerd**.

If racing bikes sounds like even more fun, coffee and bike

 EATING IN GRONINGEN: BEST FOR BRUNCH

Het Concerthuis: The Sunday hangover brunch is a local favourite at this living room-style restaurant with a sunny terrace. *10am-1am* €

Toet: Colourful, cheery cafe known for fresh sandwiches, delectable cakes and all-day desserts. *10am-5pm* €

Zondag: Casual bites and a large terrace make this a popular lunch stop in leafy Noorderplantsoen. *10am-10pm* €€

Florentin: Middle Eastern and Mediterranean dishes served with unlimited cava in a hip former factory. *6-11pm Tue-Sun, brunch hours vary* €€€

A STROLL THROUGH GRONINGEN'S OLD TOWN

See the city's main historic sights and get your bearings on this one-hour jaunt.

START	END	LENGTH
Grote Markt	Prinsentuin	4km; 1 hr

① **Grote Markt**, the central square, is dominated by the 96m-tall medieval Martinitoren and adjourning Martinikerk. Head west past the imposing **②** **Stadhuis** (Town Hall) and the intricate 17th-century **③** **Goudkantoor** to the **④** **Academiegebouw**, the University of Groningen's main building, which is particularly stunning when lit up at night.

Head south via **⑤** **Vismarkt** and walk past the neoclassical **⑥** **Korenbeurs**, once used for the grain trade and now home to the Dutch supermarket icon Albert Heijn. Pass medieval church **⑦** **Akerk** to Brugstraat and turn right on the Hoge der A, flanking one of the city's canals.

Notice that the opposite bank sits much lower, a remnant from the time when city water levels changed with the tides of the Waddenzee. From the **⑧** **Visserbrug**, you have a picture-perfect view of the city skyline.

Next, walk past the houseboats of Noorderhaven to **⑨** **Noorderplantsoen**, once the site of defensive ramparts and now a park. The sprawling terrace of **⑩** **Zondag** (p246) is a fine spot for a coffee. Head south through Hortusbuurt, with pretty houses and hidden gardens and then turn left when you reach the canals and enter the **⑪** **Prinsentuin**, a peaceful walled garden open to the public. Enjoy the smell of roses and herbs.

The **Vismarkt** (fish market) is the city's second square and hosts a bustling produce market on Tuesdays, Fridays and Saturdays.

In WWII, despite fierce fighting along the north and east sides of the Grote Markt, both the **Martinitoren** (p242) and **Martinikerk** miraculously survived.

247

BEST PERFORMANCE VENUES

Stadsschouwburg: Built in 1883, this grande dame of the arts has one of the fairest theatre halls in the country.

Vera: Club and pop stage that books a roster of up-and-coming artists (U2, Nirvana and Dua Lipa all played here before going supernova).

Simplon: Intimate pop stage with punk movement origins, now best known for its hip-hop and electronic music programming.

Grand Theatre: Originally built as an art deco cinema, nowadays the performing arts centre of the city.

EM2: City oasis on the grounds of a former sugar factory, with weekend club nights and concerts.

shop **Spaak** (*spaak.cc*) organises a free, active tour every Saturday and Sunday. Gather at 9.30am and BYOB (bring your own bike).

Are heights more your thing? Climbing centre **Bjoeks** (*bjoeks.nl*) has one of the tallest climbing towers in the world, and real daredevils are invited to camp out at the top.

Want to take it a bit easier? **beDRIJFNAT** (*bedrijfnat.nl*) rents standup paddleboards, canoes and electric boats in the city centre for you to explore the canal ring at your own leisure. If you choose the boat, order a snack plate and a tasting flight of local beers, sit back and enjoy the summer vibes in the city.

Folklore in Folkingestraat
Jewish history and independent shops

Folkingestraat is the main thoroughfare of what was once the Jewish quarter in the city. Dotted along the street are subtle artworks commemorating Jewish life here. A Moorish-inspired **synagogue** from 1906 tucked away at the end of the street is the most visible reminder of the once thriving community that was decimated during WWII. Very slowly, Jewish culture blossomed again in the years after the war, and a section of the synagogue is still used for worship. A permanent exhibition about Jewish culture and history in Groningen is open to the public, and there are also regular tours of the **former Jewish quarter** (*synagogegroningen.nl; adult/child €5.50/free*).

Today, the car-free Folkingestraat is buzzing, a strong contrast to the traditional main shopping streets in the city (and across the country) that struggle with empty shopfronts. Folkingestraat is crammed with independent shops, cafes and bistros. The products on offer range from fresh produce and colourful dresses to a mind-boggling selection of teas and handmade jewellery. Some stores, like antique shop **Klinkhamer** (*klinkhamerantiek.nl*), have been going strong for decades, while newer additions like **Beauties** (*instagram.com/beauties.groningen*), selling natural cosmetics and treatments, ensure the street will thrive for years to come.

EATING IN GRONINGEN: OUR PICKS

Bar Barrie: This charming neighbourhood bar does walk-ins only, with a small menu of inventive and delicious dishes to share. *noon-10pm Wed-Sat €*

Gustatio: This intimate Italian spot serves creative, house-made pasta dishes. It's popular, so book ahead. *1-10pm €€*

De Oude Tijden: A cosy, living room-style local favourite with big windows and a chef's menu celebrating local produce. *5-11pm €€€*

Olijfboom Greek Canteen: Laid-back, modern canteen dishing up fresh Greek flavours. The filled pitas are great value. *noon-9pm Tue-Sat €*

Beyond Groningen

North and east of Groningen appear to be a whole lot of nothingness at first glance, but the countryside is full of surprises.

Before dykes were built to keep the waves of the Waddenzee at bay, early inhabitants drawn to the fertile land built *wierden* (mounds) to keep their farms, and later entire villages, safe and dry. You'll find these peppered among the otherwise flat farm fields spilling out towards the Waddenzee.

To the northwest, the waters of the former Lauwerszee have been tamed after the sea was closed off in 1969, transforming into the Lauwersmeer, now a national park and birding paradise. Harbour Lauwersoog is home to a seal hospital and it's also where ferries to Schiermonnikoog depart – one of the smallest and most authentic of the Wadden Islands. Elsewhere in the province await stylish manor houses and an impressive 16th-century fortress town.

Lauwersmeer National Park

TIME FROM GRONINGEN: 30MIN

Birding paradise and starry nights

Lauwersmeer National Park *(np-lauwersmeer.nl; free)* is a half-hour drive from Groningen city, and it's a different world. Fertile grasslands, patches of forest and reed-filled islands surrounding a large lake provide a sanctuary to more than 100 species of birds that nest here, creating a bird-watcher's paradise.

Nature centre **Lauwersnest** has a free bird exhibit and excursions with rangers. It's the starting point of several hikes, some best undertaken at night under a starry sky – Lauwersmeer became a Dark Sky Park in 2016.

Lauwersoog

TIME FROM GRONINGEN: 45MIN

See seals and feast on seafood

It's best known for the ferry to Schiermonnikoog, but fishing harbour Lauwersoog, on the strip of land between the Lauwersmeer and Waddenzee, is worth a visit in its own right. It's home to the **Wadden Experience Centre** *(zeehondencentrum.nl; adult/child €22.50/13.50)*, a striking wooden building, opened in 2025, with an interactive exhibition about the UNESCO World Heritage site on its doorstep, the largest system of intertidal sand and mudflats in the world.

Places

Lauwersmeer National Park p249

Lauwersoog p249

Schiermonnikoog p250

Noordpolderzijl to Bourtange Fortress p250

GETTING AROUND

You can get to both Lauwersmeer National Park and harbour Lauwersoog by bus from Groningen's train station in about an hour. The bus service connects to the ferries to Schiermonnikoog, which depart multiple times per day. On Schiermonnikoog, catch a bus to the sole village or, better yet, hire a bike. On the mainland, two regional train lines take you to several small towns, but a hire (electric) car gives more freedom to explore.

SUMMER ISLAND HOPPING

From April to September, **Eilandhopper** *(eilandhopper.nl),* an eco-conscious sailing ferry, operates between the Wadden Islands.

Two graceful, century-old clippers hop from one island to the next. Guests can step aboard for a crossing or stay for one night or more. A cook whips up three delicious meals every day, and the crew loves showing guests the ropes (no sailing experience necessary). It's a marvellous way to see the UNESCO-listed Waddenzee and, if you're lucky, you might even get to experience *droogvallen* (deliberately running aground at low tide to spend several hours on the seafloor).

Willem Jacob sails from Lauwersoog and *Minerva* from Harlingen.

Get acquainted with the Wadden's most famous inhabitants in the on-site state-of-the-art seal hospital. Feeding time is a joy to behold through a floor-to-ceiling submerged window in one of the seal basins, and you can catch regular talks by scientists. Feeling peckish yourself? Feast on fresh seafood at quirky slow-food restaurant **'t Ailand** *(ailand.nl)* across the harbour, run by local fishers, or go for a quick deep-fried fish snack at cafeteria-style **Vishandel Sterkenburg** *(vis handelsterkenburg.nl).*

Schiermonnikoog
TIME FROM GRONINGEN: 2HR
An island escape

The smallest of the Frisian Wadden Islands is also the least developed, and that's precisely why many Dutch and German visitors return to Schiermonnikoog via the ferry from Lauwersoog year after year. Just like on Vlieland, drivers have to leave their cars parked on the mainland and get around the island by electric bus, on foot or, best yet, by bicycle. Hire one at **Soepboer Rijwielverhuur** *(fietsenverhuurschiermon nikoog.com)* at the ferry pier.

From the single village that's still home to a small monastery – the *schiere monniken* (grey monks) gave the island its name – a network of cycling paths fans out in the national park that covers the majority of the island. Nature rules here, and it's the perfect place to get away from a screen. On an immense beach, brave a chilly dip in the waves of the North Sea, bike across rolling dunes or go for a spot of bird-watching.

The excellent village **visitor centre** *(vvvschiermonnikoog. nl)* has info on bike routes, excursions with guides and a free interactive exhibit about the island.

Noordpolderzijl to Bourtange Fortress
TIME FROM GRONINGEN: 30MIN
A drive back in time

North and east of the city of Groningen lies unspoilt land with many surprises. Head out on a day trip along the coast to the German border.

Drive north from the city, between flat fields peppered with several *wierde* villages. First stop is **Noordpolderzijl**, a tiny harbour smelling of salt and soil overlooking the mudflats, surveyed by an old inn, **'t Zielhoes** *(zielhoes.nl),* that serves coffee and pie at seemingly the world's end.

EATING & DRINKING ON SCHIERMONNIKOOG: OUR PICKS

Wad Anderz: Spectacular views of the Waddenzee mudflats and creative dishes featuring garden produce. *10.30am-9.30pm Tue-Sun €€*

De Marlijn: Cosy beach bar with a large terrace in the dunes – the place to warm up after a dip in the sea. *10am-8pm €€*

Spaghetteria: With perfectly cooked pasta and a lively vibe, this Dutch chain pasta bar is a worthy island addition. *5-10pm €€*

4 Dames: Wood-clad wine bar with a generous European wine selection and a leafy terrace in a quiet part of the village. *10am-10pm*

MARLIES DE BUCK/SHUTTERSTOCK

Lighthouse, Schiermonnikoog

Next, visit the lavish moated estate **Menkemaborg** *(men kemaborg.nl; adult/child €11.50/3.50),* with well-preserved rooms detailing 17th- and 18th-century aristocratic life. From here, it's a 40-minute drive southeast to **Punt van Reide**, where you can spot seals in their natural habitat from behind a viewing wall. From May to September, park at the **Visitor Centre Dollard**. Keep going east and pull over just before the border with Germany to find outer-dyke bird-watching hut **De Kiekkaaste**, with panoramic views of the Dollard bay.

Follow the border south past fields of golden grain for about half an hour to reach the final and most impressive stop of the road trip: **Bourtange Fortress** *(bour- tange.nl; fortress free to visit, museums adult/ child €11/6),* a star-shaped, reconstructed 16th- century town complete with ramparts, canals and drawbridges.

HIKE THE LENGTH OF THE COUNTRY

Pieterpad *(pieterpad. nl),* the Netherlands' most famous multiday walking trail, starts in the tiny town of Pieterburen and legs it all the way south from the Groningen clay to the hills of the Sint-Pietersberg in Limburg.

The path is the brainchild of two women: lifelong friends Bertje from Groningen and Toos from Tilburg, who felt the country could do with a long-distance path. Together, they walked the length of it from 1978 to 1983 to map out the ideal route. They created a walking guide for friends and family, which, to their surprise, soon became wildly popular. More than 40 years on, tens of thousands of hikers still traverse the 500km route every year.

MORE WADDENZEE ADVENTURES

There are four more idyllic Wadden Islands in the Netherlands: **Texel** (p135), **Vlieland** (p137), **Terschelling** (p231) and **Ameland** (p227), the latter of which you can trek to with a guide at low tide, which is possible to Schiermonnikoog as well.

Drenthe

NATIONAL PARKS | MEDIEVAL TOWNS | RICH HISTORY

GETTING AROUND

This region has limited public transport, so an (electric) hire car is best for exploring. Only Assen is easily accessed by train from Groningen and Zwolle, and buses are sporadic.

The national parks have ample parking, including at the start of hiking trails. If you prefer cycling, find hire shops in the bigger villages bordering national parks, such as Dwingeloo, Ruinen and Appelscha. You can use the excellent *fietsknooppunten,* numbered markers at every bike path crossing, to guide you around. It's easiest to find or create routes via a free app or planner *(anwb.nl)*.

Lesser visited than its northern neighbours of Friesland and Groningen, the province of Drenthe still feels pleasantly under the radar. With no sea access or big cities to call its own, it is as Vincent van Gogh described it in 1883: 'Here is peace'.

Drenthe has three magnificent national parks (more than any other Dutch province) and well-preserved medieval towns with village greens like Dwingeloo and Orvelte that have retained their historic connection to the surrounding landscapes. The forests that protected village farms from shifting sands still stand, while sheep flocks graze on adjoining heather fields.

It's a place where history comes alive, from the moving Westerbork Memorial, a former WWII transit camp, to the colonies of the Maatschappij van Weldadigheid (Society of Humanitarianism), where tens of thousands of the country's poor were sent in the 19th century. In the hilly east await 52 mysterious *hunebedden* (megalithic prehistoric burial chambers) that are even older than England's Stonehenge.

Rocking it Down the Hunebed Highway

A road trip to ancient dolmens

Drive on the provincial road N34 and you'll notice a retro-looking sign pop up among the verdant fields and forests. Welcome to the **Hunebed Highway**, where it's all about the dolmens. The 60km-long road following the Hondsrug, an elevated, sandy ridge formed during the ice ages, borders no fewer than 47 *hunebedden,* prehistoric burial chambers constructed with massive boulders.

A road trip along the Hunebed Hwy is a fun way to explore them, although you have to get off it to actually see the Neolithic marvels. The impressive **Hunebedcentrum** *(hunebedcentrum.eu; adult/child €14.50/7.50)* in **Borger** is a great starting point and home to the largest *hunebed* in the country, while most are completely free to visit, like the duo D53 and D54 in **Havelte**.

DRENTHE

0 — 10 km
0 — 5 miles

Veenhuizen
Assen
Drents Museum
Stadskanaal
Smilde
Appelscha
Borger
Hunebedcentrum
Beilen
Westerbork
Dwingeloo
Odoorn
Orvelte
Klijndijk
Dwingelderveld National Park
Emmen
Ruinen
Hoogeveen
Coevorden

⭐ **HIGHLIGHTS**
1 Drents Museum
2 Dwingelderveld National Park
3 Hunebedcentrum

🔴 **SIGHTS**
4 Bosbergtoren
5 Drentsche Aa National Park
6 Drents-Friese Wold National Park

7 Gasselterveld
8 Kamp Westerbork
9 National Prison Museum
see 7 't Nije Hemelriek

⚫ **SLEEPING**
see 9 Bitter & Zoet
10 Camping Buitenland
11 De Jufferen Lunsingh
12 D'Olde Kamp

13 Landgoed Mariahoeve

🟢 **EATING**
see 9 Bitter & Zoet
14 De Bospub
15 De Strohoed
16 Tea Time

🟢 **DRINKING & NIGHTLIFE**
see 9 Brouwerij Maallust

Fens, Forests & Sheep in Dwingelderveld

Drenthe's wildest heathland

Dwingelderveld National Park is one of the largest wet heathlands in Europe. It was shaped by ice and wind; during the penultimate Ice Age, glaciers ground the land, leaving a dense, stony layer, later covered by drifting sands. This layer prevents rainwater from draining away, creating the damp, nutrient-poor conditions in which rare plants and animals thrive. Thanks to limited human interference, the park has been incredibly well preserved.

More than 60km of hiking trails and several beautiful cycling routes lace through misty moors, verdant forest and pink heather (in bloom in August). The central park area is a massive, wide-open field, where silence is disturbed only by the occasional bleating of sheep. The park has two sheepfolds, and shepherds take their flocks out every day. One of them is in the southwest corner of the Dwingelderveld, where you'll also find the **visitor centre** (*natuurmonumenten.nl; free*)

BEST NATURE EXPERIENCES

Renate Sanders, host at Visitor Centre Dwingelderveld, shares her favourite ways to enjoy nature in Drenthe. *natuur monumenten.nl*

'We've got three spectacular national parks together in one small province. There's a network of cycle paths to explore, but I personally prefer hiking. I love soaking up a landscape slowly. Here in the Dwingelderveld, it unfolds itself while you're walking: the vastness, the silence, the little larks. Even though the parks are close to one another, each one is unique. I live in the **Drentsche Aa** (p255) area and love walking past the farm fields near the river. The **Drents-Friese Wold** (p255) is rougher and wilder, especially the centre. We're blessed to have all this nature around us.'

CYCLING LOOP ACROSS THE DWINGELDERVELD

Hop on a bike for a cycling tour away from busy roads in one of the country's best spots for it.

START	END	LENGTH
Dwingeloo	Lhee	30km; 2 hrs

Hire a bike at ❶ **Reiber Rijwielen** in Dwingeloo and follow the Drift road southwest to head into Nationaal Park Dwingelderveld. Pause at tiny garden shed ❷ **De Kleine Koffiestop** (blink and you'll miss it), great for a pick-me-up. From here, take a left and then a right and follow the bike path southeast into a forest with several small hills and ❸ **Theehuys Anserdennen**, a cafe with a pretty terrace in a forest clearing. Follow the bike path until you hit a bigger road, Witteveen. Take a right here and head onto Benderse to ❹ **Visitor Centre Dwingelderveld** (p253).

Backtrack slightly and then enter the wide-open field that forms the park's heart. Keep going straight past the heath and then turn north onto Heidepad. Follow this until you reach the ❺ **radio telescope** at the edge of the forest. Set your phone to aeroplane mode in its vicinity to not disturb readings. Follow the Davidshoeve road east past the sheepfold and keep your eyes peeled for its fluffy inhabitants.

Continue east until Koelevaartsveen and then turn onto a bike path to the ❻ **Boslounge**, a small info centre. Head northeast and then west through a forested area and past Zandveen glen before joining up with the Lheebroekerzandweg on the edge of the park. Follow the road to the village of ❼ **Lhee**.

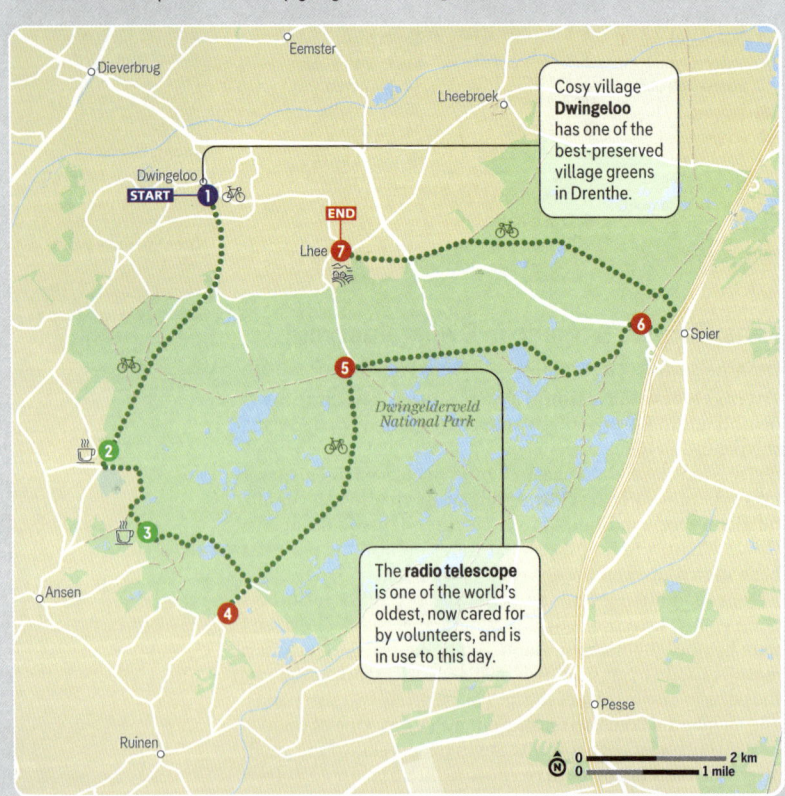

Cosy village **Dwingeloo** has one of the best-preserved village greens in Drenthe.

The **radio telescope** is one of the world's oldest, now cared for by volunteers, and is in use to this day.

with a large, green roof and an accessible natural play area for kids. Pick up a hiking or cycling map here before heading out to explore.

Harrowing History at Kamp Westerbork
Important and moving WWII stories

More than 100,000 Jews, several hundred Sinti and Roma, and dozens of resistance fighters were deported from Nazi transit **Kamp Westerbork** *(kampwesterbork.nl; adult/child €13.50/6.75)* in WWII. Of those who were put on the fateful transport to Auschwitz, Sobibor and other concentration and death camps, including Anne Frank, only 5000 were to return.

There is little to see here today. After the war, the barracks were used to house Moluccan refugees for more than 20 years and then were demolished. But there are several moving monuments, and you can listen to the harrowing stories of life in the transit camp and the dreaded moment of the announcement of the transport list, either through an English-language audio tour or a tour with a volunteer guide. Both are organised from the excellent museum that sits 2km from the camp and is reached by shuttle bus (included in the entry ticket) or a pensive walk through the forest.

A Marvellous Art Museum in Assen
What makes us human

The compact capital city of **Assen** is widely known for two things: the annual TT motorbike fest and the magnificent **Drents Museum** *(drentsmuseum.nl; adult/child €17.50/free)*. This jewel of the province is housed in a collection of historic and new buildings, all interlinked. Temporary exhibitions are displayed in the dazzling white underground contemporary wing topped with a garden, while the permanent collection presentation 'Labyrinthia' is spread across 15 rooms and is well worth a visit.

Each room has a distinct theme, from 'Why do we collect?' to 'What is taste?' and 'What would you do when threatened?', and tries to answer what makes us human through art, sounds and even smells. Wander through the maze-like, kaleidoscopic corridors – some part of a former monastery, others a splendid mansion – to discover a surprise around every corner, or pick up a metro-inspired map next to the museum shop to find your way to the top pieces, ranging from the oldest canoe in the world, the bog body Yde Girl and one of Vincent van Gogh's Drenthe paintings.

☑ **TOP TIP**

Without many flashy, famous sights, visitors can be inclined to rush through Drenthe, but the beauty of this province is in slowing down. Head out on an extended bicycle ride or hike and stay in nature for a night or two for the full experience.

WHO CRIED WOLF

It had been more than 150 years since a wolf was last seen in the country when, in 2015, locals were shocked to spot one in Drenthe. The sighting marked the start of the species' return. Conservationists hailed it as the reward for decades of European efforts to protect habitats, while critics questioned whether there was enough space in such a small country. Farmers worried for their sheep, which soon proved to be a favoured prey.

Protective measures followed, from electric fencing to compensation schemes. In the decade since that first sighting, more than 100 wolves have settled in the Netherlands. The chances of spotting one are still slim, but it's clear that the wolf is here to stay.

TWO MORE NATIONAL PARKS

Besides Dwingelderveld, Drenthe is home to two more national parks. **Drentsche Aa** has its namesake river at its heart, which meanders through a varied landscape of farm fields, heather and ancient forests. Traces of early human settlement are visible in various *hunebedden* and burial mounds.

Drents-Friese Wold borders Drenthe and Friesland and is one of the largest parks in the country. Its wild centre is a haven for animals, and its open-drift sands and dense forests are prime hiking and cycling territory.

Climb the steel tower **Bosbergtoren** *(appelscha.nl; €2.50)*, which rises like a mega pine tree trunk from the forest, for a panoramic view of the park.

Go Behind Bars in Veenhuizen

A social experiment

In the 19th century, the village of **Veenhuizen** was constructed as the largest of seven 'colonies of benevolence' (Koloniën van Weldadigheid). These sites were created to house the poor, vagabonds and orphans and remake them into 'model citizens' through hard work.

Life in these villages was rule-ridden and its reality complex. When funding for the social experiment dried up, the Veenhuizen was officially turned into a prison and remained completely self-sufficient and closed off to the outside world. It was only in 1983 that the village finally opened its doors to the public.

Today, it's a UNESCO World Heritage site and a fascinating place where normal village life plays out in buildings that are still clearly tied to the past. There's the former grain mill, now home to **Brouwerij Maallust**, a small brewery and tasting room serving a flight of craft beers to enjoy in the garden. On the other side of the village, **Bitter & Zoet** is a hotel and restaurant spread across the former stately homes of the prison's medical staff.

The centre of the village is home to the main former colony residences from 1823, now the captivating **National Prison Museum** *(gevangenismuseum.nl; adult/child €14/7.50)*. The museum tells the stories of former colony residents, some of whom came to build a better life, while others were forced to live here. The second part of the museum is dedicated to the history of the penal system in the Netherlands, from its earliest beginnings to modern-day prisons, where visitors get to weigh in on the penitentiary of the future.

A Wild Swim in Gasselterveld

A lake with a touch of Scandinavia

Perfect soft sand from the Hondsrug has been excavated across Drenthe for many years, leaving behind deep lakes. Some, like **Gasselterveld** *(hetgasselterveld.nl; free),* have strikingly clear water with bright blue hues on sunny days. With an unspoilt, white beach fringed by pine trees, the place feels more like Scandinavia than the Netherlands.

The northeast side of the lake, near the car park (paid in summer), is the best spot for a swim and also where you'll find the shallow pond **'t Nije Hemelriek**, ideal for kids to splash around. Too chilly for a dip? Take the scenic 5km walk around the lake instead.

 EATING IN DRENTHE: OUR PICKS

De Strohoed: Family-run spot with its own secret recipe for sweet or savoury Dutch pancakes. *noon-8.30pm Wed-Sun* €€	**Tea Time:** Enjoy a scrumptious afternoon tea at this villa with an English aristocratic theme. *11am-7pm Wed-Sun* €€€	**De Bospub:** This cosy cabin with a large terrace in the woods has a no-frills pub food menu and often hosts live music. *11am-9pm* €€	**Bitter & Zoet:** A heritage restaurant and hotel with an orchard that serves Dutch set-course menus celebrating organic produce. *noon-3pm and 5.30-11pm* €€€

Places We Love to Stay

€ Budget €€ Midrange €€€ Top End

Groningen p242

PJs Hostel € Contemporary hostel with luxurious bathrooms and dorms with cocoons (enclosed beds with a curtain) for a more private sleeping experience.

Simplon Hostel € Straightforward but creatively designed budget hostel, affably operated by staff being trained to reenter the workforce.

Social Hub €€ Welcoming and playful chain hotel with comfortable rooms and a trendy bar, bordering the city centre.

Happy Traveler €€ This quirky travel-themed hotel has a prime location in the university district right next to several fun bars (earplugs provided).

Market Hotel €€€ State-of-the-art, luxury hotel that couldn't be more central. Its stylish cafe is on the Grote Markt.

Lauwersoog p249

Schierzicht €€ Contemporary hotel where big windows bring sweeping harbour and sea views straight to your bed.

Schiermonnikoog p250

Hotel van der Werff €€ This island institution feels like a step back in time, beginning with the ferry pick-up in a vintage bus. Reservations by phone only.

Hoogeland

Landgoed Wilgenheerd €€ A serene, small-scale campground with rental tents and rooms in an adjoining farmhouse. The welcoming hosts offer excellent *wadlopen* (mudflat walking) tours.

Drenthe p252

Landgoed Mariahoeve €€ Large, quirky campground in the woods near Drentsche Aa National Park and Gasselterveld with rental bell tents and fairground wagons tucked away in quiet corners.

D'Olde Kamp €€ Small-scale campground on the edge of the Dwingelderveld with traditional peat cabins for rent and free-range farm animals.

Camping Buitenland €€ Creative stays ranging from a school bus to tiny cabins dot this buzzing campground with firepits and pink bathrooms.

Bitter & Zoet €€ This heritage hotel's pretty rooms and apartments nod to the building's past as lodging for Veenhuizen's prison hospital staff.

De Jufferen Lunsingh €€€ Elegant rooms in this historic manor house overlook the gardens, with a renowned restaurant on-site.

RONALD WILFRED JANSEN/SHUTTERSTOCK

Hotel van der Werff

257

For places to stay in Central Netherlands, see p277

NANCY PAUWELS/SHUTTERSTOCK

Above: Jachthuis Sint Hubertus (p268), Hoge Veluwe National Park (p267);
Right: Weerribben-Wieden National Park (p273)

Researched by
Abigail Blasi

Central Netherlands

NATURAL AND CULTURAL SPLENDOUR

This area has some of the Netherlands' most rolling scenery, its 'Venice', WWII sites associated with Operation Market Garden and extraordinary art museums.

The central area of the Netherlands feels like a well-kept secret. Despite the region's national parks, which cover a forested ridge, heath and dunes, the main reason international visitors come here is for its WWII history. The towns of Arnhem and Nijmegen played crucial roles in WWII as key battlegrounds during the ill-fated Operation Market Garden, their leafy, hydrangea-lined streets forming an incongruous backdrop to ferocious fighting as Allied forces attempted to seize key bridges and create a route into Germany.

Today, these towns still bear the scars of war, with museums, cemeteries and monuments alongside a vibrant student life and cultural attractions. The Dutch love this area for its holiday parks,

ANTON HAVELAAR/SHUTTERSTOCK

each a collection of cabins, from rustic to plate-glass creations, with shared amenities such as pools and playgrounds. North of Arnhem are two especially splendid national parks, with rolling countryside and forest, plus the second-largest collection of Van Gogh paintings in the world.

To the north is the tourist-magnet village of Giethoorn, dubbed the 'Dutch Venice', which has canals instead of roads, still enchanting despite the hordes of tourists lured by social media reels of its flower-laden waterways. To the south, the IJssel river is dotted by the handsome towns of Kampen, Deventer and Zwolle, whose defensive canals and grand 17th-century buildings evoke their heritage as members of the Hanseatic League.

THE MAIN AREAS

ARNHEM
Operation Market Garden museums and WWII sites. **p262**

GIETHOORN & WEERRIBBEN-WIEDEN NATIONAL PARK
Picturesque canal village and protected area crisscrossed by waterways. **p271**

Find Your Way

Arnhem and Nijmegen have excellent rail links with Amsterdam and elsewhere, while buses cover more rural parts. To explore some of the smaller places, a car is useful.

TRAIN & BUS

The area is well connected by affordable trains and buses. Amsterdam to Arnhem takes one hour by train. For Hoge Veluwe National Park from Arnhem, take the train to Ede and then a bus.

BICYCLE

Cycling is the best way to explore Dutch cities. Oosterbeek is a short ride from Arnhem, while Hoge Veluwe takes 30 to 40 minutes. The 230km LF3 national long-distance cycling route links major towns.

Giethoorn & Weerribben-Wieden National Park, p271

Glide through canals past flower-laden houses and teeming birdlife in this beautiful canal village and nature reserve.

Arnhem, p262

Dive into the history of WWII's Operation Market Garden through vivid museums, and visit the country's largest open-air museum. Nearby are national parks and the superb Kröller-Müller Museum.

0 — 50 km
0 — 25 miles

GERMANY

GRONINGEN

DRENTHE

Emmen

Assen

FRIESLAND

Steenwijk

Meppel

Giethoorn & Weerribben-Wieden National Park

Dedemsvaart

Ootmarsum

Oldenzaal

TWENTE

Almelo

A1

Enschede

Hengelo

Diepenheim

E30

OVERIJSSEL

Staphorst

Zwartsluis

Zwolle

Kampen

Olst

IJssel

Deventer

Twente Kanaal

Zutphen

GELDERLAND

A1

Bocholt

Nederlands Openluchtmuseum

A18

A12

A35

Elburg

E232

A28

Harderwijk

Apeldoorn

A50

E30

A1

Ede

Hoge Veluwe National Park

Veluwezoom National Park

Arnhem

Airborne at the Bridge

Eusebiuskerk

Nijmegen

A12

Rhenen

Rijn

Lek

Waal

Maas

A15

E25

A2

Zaltbommel

UTRECHT

Amersfoort

Hilversum

Almere

Lelystad

FLEVOLAND

IJsselmeer

Enkhuizen

Hoorn

NOORD-HOLLAND

Markermeer

ZUID-HOLLAND

NORTH SEA

Deventer (p275)

Plan Your Time

Distances are small, so you can fit in a lot in a few days, but allow enough time to explore and relax in the countryside.

Pressed for Time

● Around Arnhem, explore Operation Market Garden sites, including **John Frost Bridge** (p262) and the superb **Airborne Museum Hartenstein** (p266), which brings alive the brutal history of the conflict in this part of the country.

● Don't miss the excellent **Nederlands Openluchtmuseum** (p264) and **Hoge Veluwe National Park** (p267), with one of the world's great art museums hidden at its centre.

A Few Days to Explore

● To explore this rural neck of the woods, anchor yourself in the picture-postcard Hanseatic town of **Deventer** (p275) or provincial capital **Zwolle** (p275).

● Mooching north, explore the landscape created by the graft of peat workers in serene **Weerribben-Wieden National Park** (p273). Stay in the northern part of the village and travel around by e-boat in the village of **Giethoorn** (p271).

Seasonal Highlights

SPRING

Spring flowers bedeck the countryside. Canoe and kayak outfitters usually start their seasons in April.

SUMMER

The rural Netherlands is at its best in summer when the fields are verdant, the waters are swimmable and the nights are long.

AUTUMN

You can still hire canoes and kayaks, usually until September. National parks are filled with autumn colour, and accommodation is good value.

WINTER

Winter is *gezellig* (cosy), with skating on canals. Arnhem has a twinkling Christmas market, and Deventer dresses up Victorian-style for its **Dickens Festival** (p275).

Arnhem

WWII HISTORY | MUSEUMS | PANORAMAS

GETTING AROUND

Cycle, walk or take a bus around the city centre, which has some large, traffic-heavy roads. To reach the sites beyond Arnhem, a bus or bicycle will take you there, though a car gets you there quickest. Parking must be paid for at Hoge Veluwe National Park.

With its centre all but levelled during WWII, Arnhem has been rebuilt to become a prosperous town with fine museums, leafy parks and handsome townhouses: some original, others reconstructed. Its medieval city walls were destroyed in the 19th century, leaving only the Sabelspoort gate (1357).

The town is (in)famous as the heart of Operation Market Garden, the failed 1944 Allied attempt to seize the Nederrijn bridges. The Battle of Arnhem raged here, particularly in Oosterbeek; it's hard to imagine in this peaceful, leafy suburb.

Around town are violet and gorse-yellow heaths, ancient forests, paddy-flat wheat fields and meandering dykes. North of Arnhem is the Nederlands Openluchtmuseum, the largest open-air museum in the country, with many historic reconstructed buildings. A few kilometres further is forested Hoge Veluwe National Park, cut through with walking, cycling and driving trails, and harbouring its extraordinary Kröller-Muller Museum.

A Bridge Too Far

Famous focus in WWII

The infamous 'bridge too far' dramatised in the all-star 1977 film, **John Frostbrug** is a replacement for the original road bridge here and was built after the war in 1948. Operation Market Garden was an audacious attempt by British Major General John Dutton Frost (1912–93), who led the only battalion to reach the bridge, which it held for four days against all odds. Head down to the riverbank just west of the bridge, where a series of broad granite shelves provides a good vantage point and popular sunset hangout.

Next to the bridge is the small, waterside **Airborne at the Bridge** *(airbornemuseum.nl; adult/child €16/11),* a museum positioned in a watchtower-style building overlooking the river. It's a companion museum to the much larger **Airborne Museum** (p266) in Oosterbeek, but it's similarly vivid, telling

☑ **TOP TIP**

It's nicer to stay in the countryside around Arnhem rather than in the city centre. Check out the small towns around Hoge Veluwe National Park.

ARNHEM

Hoge Veluwe National Park

HIGHLIGHTS
1 Airborne at the Bridge
2 Eusebiuskerk
3 Nederlands Openluchtmuseum

SIGHTS
4 Airborne Museum Hartenstein

5 Arnhems Oorlogsmuseum
6 John Frostbrug
7 Oosterbeek War Cemetery
8 Oude Kerk Oosterbeek
9 Sabelspoort

SLEEPING
10 Drijfpaleis

11 Hotel Modez
12 Stayokay Arnhem

EATING
13 Brasserie de Borderij
14 De Watermolen
15 Foodhall Arnhem
16 Het Arnhemsje Bakkertje

the story of the operation and battle, with views over the river. The museum uses audiovisual displays to evoke the events as seen from the perspectives of three soldiers – Dutch, British and German – each giving a different viewpoint of the events as they unfolded. Thoughtfully curated and immersive, the museum offers a poignant reminder of the human stories behind the history.

Memorabilia at Arnhem War Museum

Operation Market Garden artefacts

The first thing you notice at **Arnhems Oorlogsmuseum** *(arnhemsoorlogsmuseum.com; adult/child €20/15; closed Mon)*, a rural war museum, is the T-34 Russian tank outside. It's an

263

OPERATION MARKET GARDEN

This area is synonymous with the failed WWII incursion codenamed Operation Market Garden. 'Market' was an attack from the air, with three parachute divisions (two American, one British) dropped, intending to capture bridges at Eindhoven, Nijmegen and Arnhem. 'Garden' was the ground offensive by the British XXX Corps, intended to reinforce the other divisions.

Fierce Axis resistance and bad weather conditions contributed to the mission's failure. The 1946 film, *Theirs Is the Glory,* was a reenactment of the battle acted by several key characters, and Richard Attenborough's *A Bridge Too Far* (1977) was based on the ultimately disastrous events.

Eusebiuskerk

incongruous sight because the Russians didn't make it here, but it turns out on closer inspection that the Germans had snaffled this specimen for their own use, and it saw some action in Arnhem. After the liberation, Canadian forces captured it and took it back to Canada. It was later returned to Arnhem.

There are no whizzy effects at this museum, but it's full of incredible memorabilia gathered together over the 80-plus years since Operation Market Garden.

See Living History at the Openluchtmuseum

The Netherlands' largest open-air museum

Just north of Arnhem's centre is the largest of the Netherlands' wonderful open-air museums, covering 44 hectares. At the **Nederlands Openluchtmuseum** *(openluchtmuseum.nl; adult/child €19/16),* houses from different eras were moved brick by brick to a rural setting to preserve and educate visitors about the history of the Netherlands and how people lived. All over the site, which has a windmill at its centre, you can explore the lovingly recreated interiors of houses. The area was formerly a large country estate, with a manor house and outbuildings, several of which (the white farmhouse and labourers' cottages) now form part of the exhibits. A steam tram takes visitors around the large, wooded site. Allow a full day to experience it.

Museum staff in period costumes are ready to chat and demonstrate traditional skills, such as spinning and weaving flax, milling flour, forging iron, farmhouse cooking and brewing. This museum is more than 100 years old, founded in the early 20th century because of concerns that old ways of life were disappearing. It welcomed its first visitors in 1918, just after WWI.

The museum has a large car park (fee payable). By public transport, take bus 3 or 8 from Arnhem Central Station, which takes about 15 to 20 minutes, followed by a five- to 10-minute walk. It's 4km from Arnhem, so it takes 15 to 20 minutes to cycle here.

Going Up

Eusebiuskerk's glass lift

It's worth visiting Arnhem's Catholic **Eusebiuskerk** *(euse bius.nl; adult/child €16.50/7.75)* to take the glass-sided lift up its 73m-tall spire. On the way, you can gawp at Europe's biggest carillon, featuring 54 bells, at 60m. At the top, step into a dizzying glass box for a magnificent city panorama, offering sweeping views over Arnhem, the River Rhine and the surrounding countryside.

The church is named after St Eusebius, who continued to preach despite having his tongue torn out while being tortured. The church was built between 1452 and 1570. It was heavily bombed during the Battle of Arnhem in September 1944 and was restored in the 1960s, when many of the flying buttress statues were added. The panoramic glass box was a 2018 addition. Three nephews of William of Orange are entombed in the crypt.

Thrilling WWII Museum

The last Allied holdout

Only 5km west of central Arnhem is the leafy suburb of **Oosterbeek**, with grand, elegant villas built by moneyed Dutch returning from the colonies in the 18th and 19th centuries and pristine gardens full of hydrangeas, an extraordinarily incongruous setting for some of the fiercest fighting during the Battle of Arnhem.

On 17 September 1944, the British 1st Airborne Division began its ambitious mission to capture the bridge at Arnhem, landing west of the city. However, strong and unexpectedly swift German resistance, combined with worsening weather, communication breakdowns, disrupted supply lines and a critical lack of reinforcements, forced Allied troops to retreat

BEST CYCLE ROUTES AROUND ARNHEM

Liberation Route Arnhem: Part of the Liberation Route Europe, the path Allied soldiers tried to take to cross the Rhine in 1944.

Posbankto: If you cycle towards Veluwezoom National Park, you hit unusual terrain: hills. Aim for the Posbank, a whopping 90m-high point that gives you views of Germany.

Hoge Veluwe National Park: This park has more than 40km of mostly flat cycle paths.

Roman Limes Route: Follows the northern border of the Roman Empire, passing through Arnhem and Nijmegen.

Tour of Holland: Starting and ending in Arnhem, this national route is a 1385km path around the country.

EATING IN ARNHEM: OUR PICKS

Het Arnhemsje Bakkertje: Back-in-time bakery selling delicious bread and cakes since 1904. *8am-4pm Tue-Sat* €

De Watermolen: North of Arnhem, in Velp, this 600-year-old water mill has Mediterranean-accented fine dining. *noon-10pm Tue-Thu, from 5pm Mon, Fri & Sat* €€€

Foodhall Arnhem: Riverside food and drink stalls with Chinese, Thai, Indian and more. *noon-10pm Sun-Thu, to 1am Fri & Sat* €€

Brasserie de Borderij: The 'Farm Brasserie' is in Sonsbeek Park and serves top-notch French cuisine. *11am-10pm Sun-Thu, to midnight Fri & Sat* €€

AUDREY HEPBURN'S ARNHEM

Arnhem was home to Hollywood icon Audrey Hepburn as a teenager in the 1930s. She moved here with her Dutch mother, who thought it would be safer than their former home in Brussels.

Audrey's grandfather was Arnhem's mayor. Her mother, separated from her feckless English father, was a fan of Hitler in the early days, an association that was difficult to shake when she later had a change of heart.

Far from being the haven they hoped, Operation Market Garden and subsequent famine were traumatic events in the film star's youth. The story of her time during WWII is told in *Dutch Girl*, a book by Robert Matzen.

Oude Kerk Oosterbeek

and regroup in Oosterbeek. There, under relentless attack, they continued to hold the line for eight desperate days, until a strategic withdrawal was ordered on 25 September.

The excellent **Airborne Museum Hartenstein** *(airbor nemuseum.nl; adult/child €16/11)* is an essential port of call on any WWII trail. Housed in the former Allied headquarters, this interactive museum powerfully evokes the events of Operation Market Garden. In a vast underground bunker beneath the gardens, the Airborne Experience presents an immersive nighttime scene complete with sound, light and motion, vividly recreating the chaos and intensity of the Battle of Arnhem (recommended for over eight years only).

There's an outdoor cafe in the gardens and an excellent shop.

See Iconic Oosterbeek WWII Sites

Operation Market Garden memorials

Oude Kerk Oosterbeek *(oudekerkoosterbeek.nl; free; 1-4pm Wed, Thu & Sun May-Sep),* still pocked by bullets, dates from the 10th century. It was a scene of intense fighting in September 1944, when Allied forces held the church for eight days before retreating.

To the north of the suburb is the peaceful **Oosterbeek War Cemetery** *(cwgc.org),* 500m east of Oosterbeek train station, containing row upon row of white gravestones, markers for the 1691 Allied troops killed during Operation Market Garden.

Beyond
Arnhem

Visit rolling countryside, an astounding Van Gogh–packed art museum and iconic WWII sites.

North of Arnhem is the Veluwe, a forested ridge of low hills. This area is partly encompassed by the soft hills and forests of Hoge Veluwe National Park, which harbours the Kröller-Müller Museum, home to the world's second-largest collection of works by artist Vincent van Gogh.

A pristine web of cycle paths runs across the park, accessible thanks to free-with-your-ticket white bicycles to borrow. Only 20 minutes by train to the south of Arnhem lies the oldest city in the Netherlands, Nijmegen on the Waal River, a former Roman settlement and key location during WWII, with Operation Market Garden sites. It's a buzzy place, famous for its annual music and arts festivals.

Hoge Veluwe National Park

TIME FROM ARNHEM: 35MIN

Cycling and hiking in the park

Free white bikes stand at every entrance to **Hoge Veluwe National Park** *(hogeveluwe.nl; adult/child €13.40/6.70)*. Hop on one and glide through pine forests and past unexpected open-drift dunes, relishing the endless-seeming space (55 sq km). The national park was once the hunting grounds of Anton and Helene Kröller-Müller, rich industrialists who bought the area in 1909.

The park has more than 40km of signposted hiking and biking trails. Substantial populations of wild boar, rams and red deer roam wild.

You have to pay to enter the park, at booths at the three entrances – Schaarsbergen (south), Hoenderloo (east) and Otterlo (west, the busiest of the three) – which have basic information and helpful park maps for a fee. There are paid car parks at each.

Masterpieces in the forest

Cycle or walk to the glorious treasury of art in the centre of Hoge Veluwe National Park. The **Kröller-Müller Museum** *(krollermuller.nl; museum incl park entrance adult/13-18/6-12 yrs €26.90/20.15/6.70; closed Mon)* has the greatest collection of Van Gogh's works – almost 90 paintings and 180 drawings – outside Amsterdam's Van Gogh Museum (p94). It allows you to see the development of his art, from his tentative early

Places

Hoge Veluwe National Park p267

Veluwezoom National Park p269

Groesbeek p269

Nijmegen p269

GETTING AROUND

Driving is the most convenient way to get around this region, but you need to pay for parking at Hoge Veluwe National Park and in Nijmegen. Public buses serve the areas around Arnhem, offering a budget-friendly alternative, though getting between multiple sights this way can be time-consuming.

For the most scenic and ecofriendly option, consider cycling. Arnhem and Nijmegen have excellent, well-maintained bike paths and bike hire, as do smaller towns.

GATHERING THE VAN GOGHS

German Helene Müller, from a family of wealthy industrialists, married Dutchman Anton Kröller, who worked in their business, in 1888. She began art appreciation classes with art critic and painter HP Bremmer in 1905 and began collecting art under his guidance, buying her first Van Gogh the following year.

Van Gogh had died in 1890, when he was beginning to receive some recognition for his art. After a life-threatening operation, Helene vowed to create a museum for her collection that would be appreciated for years to come.

works to his later masterpieces. The collection includes *Place du Forum* (1888), painted in southern France, and fabulous portraits, including the bearded Arles postman, Joseph Roulin. The rest of the collection is equally superb, with works by Renoir, Monet, Manet, Picasso and Mondrian.

The sculpture garden has 160-odd alfresco works by Barbara Hepworth, Henry Moore and others peppering its 25 hectares of pea-green lawns and woodlands. Most thrilling is *Jardin d'émail* by Jean Dubuffet, which you can climb into via a small internal staircase *(May-Oct)*.

The museum is about 3km from the park entrance in Otterlo, 4km from the Hoenderloo entrance and 10km from the Schaarsbergen entrance. The museum has indoor/outdoor cafe-restaurants.

Art nouveau hunting lodge

The Kröller-Müllers' dream house, the stolid lakeside **Jachthuis Sint Hubertus** *(hogeveluwe.nl; adult/child €6/3; closed Mon Nov-Mar)* can be visited by guided tour (in Dutch, but participants get a multilingual audio guide).

The interiors of the lodge are high-concept art nouveau. Dutch architect Hendrik Petrus Berlage (1856–1934) designed every element, from the floor tiles to the stained-glass windows, in the V-shaped mansion, built between 1915 and 1920. It was inspired by an English country manor with its separate quarters for each family member, a smoking room, a ladies' drawing room and a billiard room. Upon the request of the Kröller-Müllers, a tower was added to ensure sweeping bird's-eye views.

Berlage left the project in a huff when Helene Kröller-Müller tinkered too much with his vision. Ironically, the couple used to stay more regularly at the more modest, thatched Het Klaverblad ('the Cloverleaf'), as they felt the finished vision was a little austere.

Bat walks and moonlit tours at a retro radio station

To the north of Hoge Veluwe National Park is an extraordinary cathedral-like former transmitting station, **Radio Kootwijk** *(hierradiokootwijk.nl; adult/child €6/3)*, used to broadcast long-distance to Dutch colonies. National architect Julius Luthmann designed the art deco structure, constructed from concrete without any wood or iron. There are regular walks, moonlit walks and tours of the magnificent interior.

 EATING IN HOGE VELUWE: OUR PICKS

De Wever Lodge Bistro: Quirky brunch and bistro dishes, with a terrace overlooking a garden and woodlands. *10am-11pm* €€

Brasserie Otterlo: Informal French and international classics in Otterlo village. Book ahead. *11am-10pm Wed-Sat* €€

Cèpes: High-end dining at a parasol-shaded terrace overlooking flowery gardens and grassy fields. Adults only. *noon-2pm & 5.30-7.30pm* €€€

Ijs van Co: Gourmet artistry at this ice-cream parlour, serving up scoops since 1938 in Hoenderloo, a 10-minute stroll from the park entrance. *11.30am-8.30pm* €

R. DE BRUIJN PHOTOGRAPHY/SHUTTERSTOCK

Veluwezoom National Park

Veluwezoom National Park

TIME FROM ARNHEM: 30MIN

Enjoy the hills

Veluwezoom National Park *(natuurmonumenten.nl; free)* protects the southeast section of the forested ridge, Veluwe. Hire a bike, e-bike or scooter from the park visitor centre to explore these unusually undulating slopes. The park has wild horses, deer, badgers and lots of birdlife, as well as especially magnificent heather.

Groesbeek

TIME FROM ARNHEM: 30MIN

Visit a parachute-shaped WWII museum

A short trip from Arnhem or Nijmegen, the **Vrijheidsmuseum** *(Freedom Museum; freedommuseum.com; adult/child €18.50/9)* resembles a parachute. It's almost on the German border. The interactive displays bring the experience of WWII and liberation to life and pose the question: How would you have responded to Nazi occupation?

Nijmegen

TIME FROM ARNHEM: 20MIN

Discover Nijmegen's historic centre

Wearing the weight of history lightly, Nijmegen is a buzzy university town with a medieval heart and a 16th-century riverside. Start your exploration at Nijmegen's sweeping market square, **Grote Markt**, unscathed by WWII. Open-air markets still take place here each week on Saturdays and Mondays. The ornate Dutch Renaissance **De Waagh** (1612), once the town's all-important weigh house, is now a cafe.

WHY I LOVE HOGE VELUWE NATIONAL PARK

Abigail Blasi, Lonely Planet writer
Hoge Veluwe is not what you think of the Netherlands. It doesn't have canals or windmills, but dunes, wind-scoured heath, fuzzy heather, tall pine forests that slice the sunlight and a good chance of spotting a red squirrel.

What's even better is that one of the world's greatest art collections is hidden away in the middle of the forest, and the main way you can reach it is by bicycle. Hopping on a white bike, pedalling the gentle pathways, exploring the museum and then hopping back onto your bike to explore some more, has to be one of my favourite travel experiences.

OPERATION MARKET GARDEN IN NIJMEGEN

On the banks of the Waal River, Nijmegen is the Netherlands' oldest city, with Roman roots. Like Arnhem, it was central to WWII's Operation Market Garden campaign. The Allies took the bridge here, the scene of furious fighting.

The city is almost in Germany, with a restored medieval historic centre focused on its Grote Kirk, and its location is why it received most damage close to the end of the war, as American forces bombed it by mistake. The city was repaired and is now full of life, with festivals including the annual **Four Days Marches** *(4daagse. nl)* hiking fest and **Zomerfeesten** *(vierdaagsefeesten.nl)* music festival.

WOLF-PHOTOGRAPHY/SHUTTERSTOCK

Diners, Nijmegen

From Grote Markt, duck beneath the ornate Gothic **Kerkboog** (1542; Church Arch) – which originally had a cattle grid and pit beneath to prevent pigs from the marketplace escaping into the churchyard – to see **Sint Stevenskerk** *(stevenskerk. nl)*, built between the 13th and 15th centuries and restored post-WWII destruction. A hike up the 183 steps in the **tower** *(adult/child €5/2)* offers big views. The **Skywalk** *(adult/child €15/7)* is a bridge across the rooftop for even more thrills.

East of Grote Markt, the **Stadhuis** (Town Hall) is a much-restored fairy tale in stone that dates from the 16th century; the octagonal turret with onion dome was built in the 1950s, however.

Close to the river is the impressive **Nationaal Fietsmuseum Velorama** *(velorama.nl; adult/child €15/free),* with everything from penny farthings to a recreated 19th-century bicycle workshop.

Charlemagne ruins and Valkhofpark relics

Nijmegen's wooded **Valkhofpark** contains the romantic remains of a ruined palace begun by Charlemagne in the 8th century and continued by Emperor Frederick Barbarossa from 1155. It was destroyed in 1796, and all that remains is the 16-sided Sint Nicolaaskapel, a rare example of Byzantine architecture in the Netherlands, and the ruined Sint Maartenskapel.

Beside the park is the **Valkhof Museum** *(valkhofmuseum. nl),* with Roman relics, reopening after several years of restoration in 2026.

 EATING IN NIJMEGEN: OUR PICKS

De Hemel: Relaxed restaurant with seating inside under wood beams and outside in the cobbled courtyard. *noon-midnight Sun-Thu, to 1am Fri & Sat* €€

Fresca: A superbly cosy cafe with a leafy terrace and superb breakfasts, pancakes, super-food bowls, salads and cakes. *8am-6pm* €€

De Pelgrim: Tables outside in a lovely leafy square and international dishes from salads to pho. *5pm-midnight* €€

Café de Plak: Laid-back organic *eetcafé* (cafe serving food) with lots of tasty vegetarian choices. *noon-11pm* €€

Giethoorn & Weerribben-Wieden National Park

BOATING | ARCHITECTURE | COUNTRYSIDE

Giethoorn and its surrounding countryside are enchantingly pretty, with thatched cottages fronted by hydrangea-filled gardens. This area is Weerribben-Wieden National Park, the largest freshwater wetland in northwestern Europe. Its 10,000 swampy hectares contain centuries-old peatlands, bogs, reed beds dotted with different orchid varieties, forest and a treasure trove of wildlife. It's cut through with canals and is a wonderfully tranquil place to spend a few days.

Giethoorn, a small village that has waterways instead of streets, is world famous – something of a surprise for a small, central Netherlands village. Yes, it's incredibly picture-perfect, and the 'goat horn' village even appears on the international Monopoly board, thanks to a strong fan base in Asia. Every year, thousands of tourists come here from all over the world. A quieter town to base yourself in is Sint Jansklooster, which is also home to the national park visitor centre.

Boating in Giethoorn

Thatched cottages and flower-framed canals

Every other house or business lining the canals in the southern part of the village hires out boats. They're very similar, so it's worth shopping around a bit on price. A reliable, friendly place is **Boothuren Giethoorn** *(giethoornbootjehuren.nl),* close to one of Giethoorn's car parks.

Lots of outfits offer canal cruises, with an hour-long guided tour, or you can take a private tour on a traditional sloop boat. Much more fun, however, is to hire your own self-drive boat, for two to 10 people. The waterways get busy: it almost feels like a lazy river as boats glide along one after the other.

GETTING AROUND

The closest railway station to Giethoorn is Steenwijk, reachable in 15 minutes by bus. Buses also link small towns and villages.

Zwolle is the nearest major rail junction and the transfer point for trains further north. Deventer also has a train station. All sizeable towns offer bike hire.

☑ **TOP TIP**

Find accommodation in the northern part of Giethoorn for a more atmospheric and tranquil stay, where the architecture is more traditional and there are picturesque bridges. The busiest area is the southern part of the village, which has most restaurants and bars.

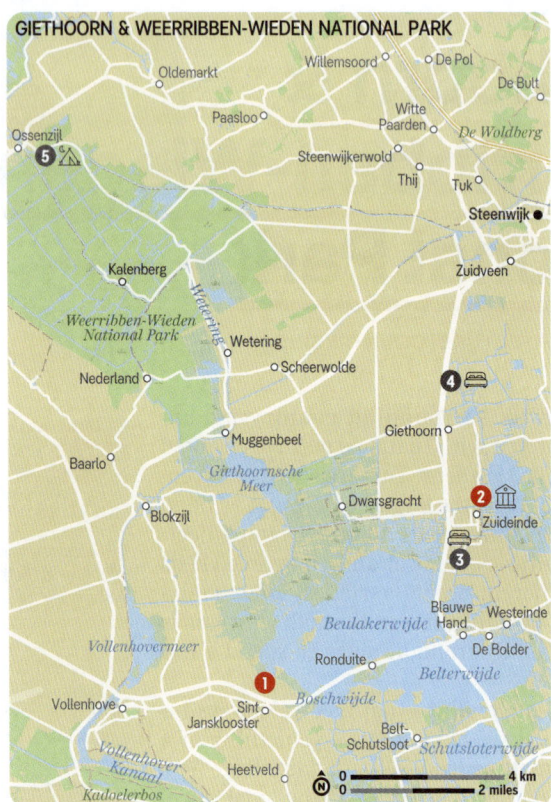

GIETHOORN & WEERRIBBEN-WIEDEN NATIONAL PARK

⭐ **SIGHTS**

1 De Wieden Visitor
   Centre
2 Museum Giethoorn
   't Olde Maat Uus

🔴 **ACTIVITIES**

see 2 Boothuren Giethoorn

see 1 Eco WaterLiner

⚫ **SLEEPING**

3 Black Sheep Hostel
4 Hotel de Harmonie
5 Recreatiecentrum
   De Kluft

It's one-way traffic through the main village canal, which reduces the likelihood of chaos, and there are four different looped routes to choose from, all taking you through lush, reed-fringed countryside. The shortest loop is two hours and goes around the main village and then across the broad **Bovenwude** lake. The longest loop takes four hours and visits the pretty canalside village of **Dwarsgracht**, which is much less touristy.

Discover Local Life & History

Historic house and peat farm

In the southern part of Giethoorn, the small **Museum Giethoorn 't Olde Maat Uus** *(museumgiethoorn.nl; adult/child €7.50/2.50; daily Apr-Oct, closed Mon & Tue Nov-Mar)* is housed in a former farmhouse, with reconstructed interiors showing the life of a peat farmer in the 19th century. Explore its rooms and boathouse. In the summer, costumed volunteers bring the setting to life.

Boating, Cycling & Walking in Weerribben-Wieden National Park

Wetland wonderland

Weerribben-Wieden National Park is a glorious escape for lovers of nature, birds and boats. There's a watercolour scenery of canals, ponds and lakes. Its fields are uncannily flat and cut through with canals, so you'll frequently see the entertaining sight of a boat seeming to float through a field. Warblers, bitterns, western marsh harriers and purple herons nest in the national park, much to the joy of bird-watchers, who flock here to absorb its rich array of species from a traditional sloop boat or along one of the park's many scenic cycling and hiking trails.

Base yourself either in quieter **Sint Jansklooster** or busy – but with more restaurants and boat businesses – Giethoorn. **De Wieden Visitor Centre** *(natuurmonumenten.nl)* in Sint Jansklooster has information boards on the landscape and wildlife of the region, plus a teahouse with a pleasant terrace. A number of walks and cycle routes start from here, and boat hire is also available. Immediately behind the centre, a fine 1km boardwalk trail threads through the reeds, a good place to spot black terns.

Eco WaterLiner *(visitweerribbenwieden.com; day pass adult/child €9/5; May-Sep)* runs two small watercraft between Giethoorn and Blokzijl via the visitor centre (1½ hours). As you glide along lily-pad–strewn canals that open into lakes, you might get a glimpse of the reed harvesters at work. You can take your bike aboard *(extra €6)* so that you can combine cycling and cruising.

THE GOAT

A group of settlers called the Flagellants founded the first settlement at Giethoorn in 1230. They named it after the goat horns they found when building here, relics of goats that died in the flood of 1170.

The canals were dug out later, in the 17th century, as workers dredged peat that could be used as fuel. It was transported along the canals on punts. The hamlet still has few roads or cars. Local farmers even used to move their cows around in row boats filled with hay.

Beyond Giethoorn & Weerribben-Wieden National Park

Wealthy Hanseatic towns punctuate the lush riverbanks of the IJssel.

Places

Kampen p274
Zwolle p275
Deventer p275
Twente p276

GETTING AROUND

Trains run to Kampen, Zwolle and Deventer, with regular connections to Amsterdam, Rotterdam, Utrecht and beyond. The trip between Amsterdam and Zwolle takes an hour.

Combining train and bike is an ideal way to explore the area. However, a car is useful if you want to see a lot of the area quickly. Parking is usually available only for a fee, but is easy to access via the Easypark app.

The majestic IJssel is a shimmering, serpentine distributary of the Rhine that winds its way through the eastern Netherlands. It forms the natural western boundary of the province of Overijssel, meaning 'across the IJssel'.

Along the river lie some of the Netherlands' best-preserved historic towns: Kampen, Zwolle and Deventer. These cities were once part of the Hanseatic League, a powerful medieval alliance of trading cities that dominated northern Europe. The league's legacy remains in the impressive 16th- and 17th-century architecture of grand gabled houses, sturdy merchant buildings and monumental weigh houses, reflecting when the IJssel was a vital artery of economic power. Today, these Hanseatic towns are full of historical buildings and fine museums and galleries.

Kampen

TIME FROM GIETHOORN: 30MIN

Renaissance gates, towers and art

Set on the mirrorlike IJssel river, Kampen feels stuck in time. The damming of the Zuiderzee put a stop to the busy port's development. Three out of the former seven city gates remain standing: the sturdy 14th-century **Koornmarktpoort** (the towers were added a century later); the **Broederpoort**, with four slender towers; and the rectangular **Cellebroederpoort** (Celle Brothers' Gate, named after a local monastery). Broederpoort and Cellebroederpoort were built in 1465 and rebuilt in Renaissance style around 1615.

Dominating Kampen's skyline is 17th-century **Nieuwe Toren** *(10am-5pm select days in summer only)*. Its 48-bell carillon gets a regular tinkle by the city carillonneur.

The small **Stedelijk Museum** *(stedelijkemuseakampen.nl; adult/child €5.50/free; closed Mon)* contains winter scenes by 16th-century painter Hendrick Avercamp, born deaf and unable to speak, and is known as *de Stomme van Kampen* (the mute of Kampen).

Kamper Kogge *(kamperkogge.nl; free)* is a medieval-style cargo ship moored in the harbour. You can visit the shipyard, including a lovingly reconstructed medieval fisher's cottage, carpentry workshop and smithy.

Zwolle

TIME FROM GIETHOORN: 30MIN

See Hanseatic architecture

Ringed by a star-shaped canal, medieval Zwolle, the capital of Overijssel, is a 10-minute train ride from Kampen. It was a major Hanseatic port with monumental buildings, including its **Grote Kerk** *(closed Sun & Mon)*, built between 1370 and 1452. Its tower was the Netherlands' highest until it was struck by lightning in 1682.

Visit the 15th-century **Sassenpoort** *(sassenpoortzwolle.nl; 11am-5pm Wed & Sat)*, a crenellated gatehouse, whose steps spiral up four floors past the original prison, complete with trap doors to pour burning oil on prisoners. Zwolle's **Stadhuis** consists of the stately old council chamber and adjacent new wing, in front of which stands a statue of *Adam* (1881) by French sculptor Auguste Rodin.

Zwolle's most distinctive church is **Onze Lieve Vrouwe Basiliek** *(peperbus-zwolle.nl)*, nicknamed the *peperbus* (peppermill) and built from 1394 to 1452. Climb 234 steps up its 75m-tall **tower** *(adult/child €2.50/1)* for great views.

Zwolle by boat

To take to the water, hire canoes, boats, standup paddleboards or even a doughnut at **Hiawatha Actief** *(hiawatha-actief. nl)*. It's next to Nieuwe Havenbrug (New Harbour Bridge).

Modern art in a neoclassical courthouse

Housed in a neoclassical courthouse is the **Museum de Fundatie** *(museumdefundatie.nl; adult/child €17/free; closed Mon)*, stages large-scale temporary exhibits by contemporary artists. There's a cocoon-like contemporary extension on the rooftop.

Deventer

TIME FROM GIETHOORN: 1HR

Wander Deventer's 16th-century streets

Deventer is a beguiling town of gingerbread-like houses set on the banks of the silvery IJssel. Already a bustling port by 800 CE, it became an important printing city in the 15th century. It holds a **Dickens Festival** *(dickensfestijn.nl)* every Christmas.

On the vast, elongated main square, the **Brink** is an extravagant red-brick 16th-century weighing house. It was once busy with merchants coming to weigh their wares and now contains the local history museum, the **Museum de Waag** *(museumdewaag.nl; adult/child €9.50/free; closed Mon)*. You get to explore the oldest part of the building, the cellar, dug out in 1528. In front, look for a 15th-century cauldron hanging on the wall, where counterfeiters were boiled alive. To the east, the bohemian **Bergkwartier** bristles with beautiful, restored Hanseatic-era buildings.

BEST SHOPS IN ZWOLLE & DEVENTER

Waanders in de Broeren: A bookshop and cafe in the church of a 15th-century Dominican convent in Zwolle.

Zwolle Balletjeshuis: At this centuries-old Zwolle sweet shop, try the house speciality, *Zwolse balletjes* (pillow-shaped boiled sweets).

Bussink Deventer Koekwinkel: Purveyor of Deventer *koek* (dense, spiced gingerbread) in vintage red tins.

Appel & Ei: Stocks quality vintage and new clothing for men and women.

Zwolle Market: Zwolle's market spreads through Melkmarkt, Oude Vismarkt and the star-shaped centre on Friday mornings and all day on Saturdays.

HANS ENGBERS/SHUTTERSTOCK

DEVENTER'S BEST HISTORICAL STREETS

Polstraat: Centuries-old wall carvings and window decorations.

Walstraat: Look for a female figure hanging by a sheet on the wall at No 20 – a reminder of its former use as a women's prison – and Charles Dickens murals.

Bergstraat: Lined with Hanseatic houses, including a lovely Gothic-style model at No 29.

Kleine Poot: Has the oldest stone house in town on a side alley, originating from 1100 CE.

Roggestraat: The former Jewish ghetto. The Etty Hillesum Centre, in a former synagogue, is devoted to the extraordinary diarist who died in Auschwitz.

Ootmarsum

Yorkshire-born St Lebuinus founded the **Grote of Lebuïnuskerk** *(lebuinuskerk.nl)* in 738, but today's structure is 15th-century Gothic. Its wall paintings, whitewashed by Protestant mobs in 1580, were later restored. Climb the tower *(€3.50)* for panoramic views.

Twente

TIME FROM GIETHOORN: 1¼HR

Local history

Ootmarsum is a lovely windmill-shaded village in the area, with an open-air museum. **Openluchtmuseum Ootmarsum** *(openluchtmuseumootmarsum.nl; adult/child €9/free)* brings alive rural farm life, and your ticket combines a peek into how the other half lived at local manor house **Drostenhuis**, a short walk away.

Cycling around a nature reserve

The Twente region combines peat bogs, marshes, heather fields and golden-sand river beaches.

Lutterzand *(lutterzand.nl)* nature reserve stretches across 750 hectares, encompassing pine forests and flat moorland beyond. The tiny hamlet of **De Lutte** is the starting point for a 35km circular cycling trail (closed when river water levels are too high), and walkers can enjoy five marked trails (3km to 7km long).

Thought-provoking Enschede

The university town of Enschede is Twente's largest. It's worth the trip for **Rijksmuseum Twenthe** *(rijksmuseumtwenthe. nl; adult/child €12.50/free; closed Mon)*, where contemporary works are hung against historic ones in a thoughtful dialogue. This purpose-built 1930 museum was created by textile manufacturer Jan Bernard van Heek and his brother, both passionate art collectors, and it centres on a courtyard garden.

De Museumfabriek *(demuseumfabriek.nl; adult/child €8.50/7.50; closed Mon)* is a hands-on museum made to inspire curiosity, where you can make your own coral or design a fossil.

Places We Love to Stay

€ Budget €€ Midrange €€€ Top End

Arnhem
p262

Stayokay Arnhem € On a wooded hill 2km north of town, this hostel is inconvenient for the centre but good for Hoge Veluwe National Park.

Drijfpaleis €€ Glorious multicoloured boho houseboat with work-of-art, muralled rooms and terraces overlooking the water.

Hotel Modez €€ Fabulous hotel with each room styled by a different designer.

Hoge Veluwe National Park
p276

De Houtkamp € Pristine, verdant farm with animals, three doubles in a 1930s farmhouse and a self-catering cottage sleeping six to 10 guests. Only 350m from Hoge Veluwe's Otterlo entrance.

De Wever Lodge €€€ Enchanting small hotel with rooms scattered through the forest, about 1km from the Otterlo entrance.

Hotel de Serrenberg €€€ Designer countryside retreat close to the park entrance, with a lush top-end restaurant and wellness centre.

Nijmegen
p270

Hotel Credible € A townhouse with bright white rooms of various sizes and some fun, quirky touches, such as foosball in the family room. Has a good restaurant.

Boutique Hotel Straelman €€ Contemporary rooms in 50 shades of beige in a handsome old townhouse.

Giethoorn & Weerribben-Wieden National Park
p271

Black Sheep Hostel € Flower-filled canal-side garden, boats for hire and daisy-fresh dorms at this top Giethoorn hostel that's close to the action but out of the mayhem.

Recreatiecentrum De Kluft € Campground that has 275 tent pitches, cabins, four-person waterfront lodges with decks directly on the water, and a small hotel. Bike and boat hire are available, plus canoe and SUP lessons.

Hotel de Harmonie €€ Some of the simply decorated, comfortable rooms at this hotel in the peaceful northern part of Giethoorn have balconies, and views are over the canal or parklands to the rear. There's boat hire and a good restaurant.

Kampen
p274

Boetiek Hotel Kampen € Grand riverside townhouse hotel, with 11 rooms with decorative ceramic tiling and sweeping river views.

Hotel van Dijk € Super-cheery welcome at this simple hotel with 18 rooms, a locked bike room and an excellent breakfast that includes fresh fruit and house-made jam.

Zwolle
p275

Hotel Staatsman €€ In a glorious neogothic former government building built by architect Jacobus van Lokhorst in 1895, this hotel has beautiful tiling, stained glass and well-appointed rooms.

De Librije €€€ Top-notch flamboyant luxury, with rooms in strong hues that err on maximalism. It's hard to believe this building was once the city's prison.

Pillows Grand Boutique Hotel Ter Borch €€€ A former police station in a wedding-cake mansion, with luxurious, high-ceilinged rooms and a conservatory restaurant.

Deventer
p275

Camping de Worp € This small, rustic and leafy campground is a lovely spot to pitch up and enjoy elegant views of the Hanseatic town on the opposite riverbank. The ferry into town is a five-minute walk.

Finch Hotel €€ In a historic building in the centre, with lots of art on the walls and hipster touches such as record players in the rooms.

Twente
p276

Het Meuleman € Seven-hectare old-school camping, partly protected by the Lutterzand nature reserve, close to the beach and blissfully peaceful. Cottages and hikers' huts are available.

Little Monkey Hostel € Curtained pods that give you a sense of private space or gleamingly clean double rooms at this cheerful boutique hostel in Enschede's centre.

For places to stay in Southeastern Netherlands, see p299

IVO ANTONIE DE ROOIJ/SHUTTERSTOCK

**Above: St Janskerk and St Servaasbasiliek (p297), Maastricht;
Right: De Draak (p286), Den Bosch**

Researched by
Mark Elliott

Southeastern Netherlands

'BURGUNDIAN' JOIE DE VIVRE

Grab a beer glass and a big appetite for this heady mix of historical gems and post-industrial cities set amid fields and forests.

The Netherlands' predominantly Catholic south is famed for an exuberance that's unusual by Dutch standards. This is particularly evident in the boisterous pre-Lenten carnivals that occur in major industrial and post-industrial cities, such as Eindhoven and Tilburg, as well as in artsy Den Bosch, party-loving Breda and originally Roman Maastricht.

The people's epicurean reputation for rich food and fun times is embodied in the concept 'Bourgondisch' (Burgundian). That can seem a little confusing in today's world, where Burgundy is associated with a fairly limited geographical region of east-central France. However, in the 15th century, Burgundy was a major European power encompassing most of the Low Countries. The ancient counties of Brabant and Limburg, which now give their names to provinces here, were within the 'Burgundian Netherlands', which became a major unit within the Habsburg Empire.

In the early 16th century, Henry III of Nassau brought power and wealth to Breda, the dynastic centre for what would later become the Dutch royal lineage of Orange-Nassau. However, the whole southeast was devastated during the Eighty Years' War, when the areas controlled by the Spanish and Dutch alternated, with Den Bosch often in the way.

Fast forward to the 19th century, and from 1830, newly created Belgium initially tried to grab the whole of Limburg, but Maastricht held out, ensuring that the Netherlands would have at least one small area of hills.

IVO ANTONIE DE ROOIJ/SHUTTERSTOCK

THE MAIN AREAS

DEN BOSCH
Synonymous with medieval surrealism. **p282**

MAASTRICHT
Life-affirming indulgence overlays Romanesque roots. **p295**

Find Your Way

The region's main centres are all handily accessed from Den Bosch or Tilburg. Additionally, Breda makes an easy stop between Rotterdam and Antwerp (Belgium). Maastricht is nearer to Liège (Belgium) and Aachen (Germany) than to other major Dutch cities.

Arnhem

Rotterdam

Geldermalsen GELDERLAND

A15

Gorinchem Nijmegen

ZUID-HOLLAND A50

Woudrichem

Dordrecht Cuijk

Heusden Binnendieze Oss

Bergse Maas St Janskathedraal

Willemstad A16 Den Bosch Jheronimus Bosch
A59 Art Center

A4 Kaatsheuvel Overloon

A17 Breda Tilburg A2 Venray

Bergen op A58 Meersel- A58 Helmond A73
Zoom Roosendaal Dreef Baarle- Eindhoven
Zundert Nassau NOORD A67 E34
Essen BRABANT Venlo

A4 A67 A2 LIMBURG

Turnhout Weert

BELGIUM Hamont Roermond

Thorn

GERMANY

Sittard

St Servaasbasiliek Heerlen

Onze Lieve Kerkrade
Vrouwebasiliek

Maastricht Margraten Aachen

Liège

Charleroi

Den Bosch, p282

The mind-bending art of Hieronymus Bosch comes to life as you cruise the city's partly under-ground canals.

Maastricht, p295

Brimming with joie de vivre, the Nether-lands' second-oldest yet least Dutch city has Roman and Romanesque heritage, tunnels and – yes – hills.

TRAIN & BUS

Although Maastricht might appear relatively detached from the region's other hubs geographically, fast direct train connections regularly run from Den Bosch and Utrecht via Eindhoven and Roermond. Regular buses serve Efteling from Den Bosch and Tilburg.

CAR

Having a car is problematic in cities but useful for visiting some of the region's appealing villages and small towns, such as Thorn, while zipping quickly past industrial complexes or monotonous agricultural swathes.

0   50 km
0   25 miles

Eindhoven (p294)

Plan Your Time

Intercity transport is frequent and efficient, so no matter where you base yourself, it's easy and quick to access the region's other highlights.

Short on Time

● First up, head to **Den Bosch** (p282), a delight for medieval history buffs. Those in interested in history and food might prefer **Maastricht** (p295).

● A great choice for families is **Efteling** (p290) theme park, which combines rides with fairy-tale enchantment.

● Try fun-loving **Breda** (p292) for partying, or **La Trappe Brewery** (p291) near Tilburg for beer tastings. If you have time, head to **Eindhoven** (p294) to explore its technology links.

A Southeast Week

● Combine most of the above, basing yourself initially in either **Den Bosch** (p282) for quirky, well-appointed accommodation or **Tilburg** (p291) for hostels. Visit **Breda** (p292) and **Efteling** (p290) from either.

● Cycle or drive to the lovely villages of **Heusden** and **Woudrichem** (p291) and then stop in **Eindhoven** (p294) en route to **Maastricht** (p295), which is well worth a couple of days.

Seasonal Highlights

SPRING

Maastricht, Tilburg, Breda, Den Bosch and Eindhoven all claim their Lenten carnavals are the best. Expect merry mayhem for the five days culminating on **Mardi Gras**.

SUMMER

For much of July, every hotel room in Maastricht is booked solid for the **André Rieu concerts** (p297) which pack the city's main square.

AUTUMN

Fine deciduous forests south of Breda and east of Maastricht turn russet gold. Eindhoven hosts **Dutch Design Week** in October.

WINTER

11e van de 11e (11 November) is nicknamed the 'Day of the Crazy People' as each city announces next year's Prince of Carnaval. Expect drunken revelry.

IURII DZIVINSKYY/SHUTTERSTOCK

Den Bosch

SURREALISM | HISTORY | BOAT RIDES

GETTING AROUND

The bus station and train station are close together, a short walk west of the Uilenburg nightlife district.

On arrival, consider hopping aboard the free, eight-seater blue micro-bus known as **De Blauwe Engelen** (gastvrij-shertogenbosch. nl). Its 10-stop loop around the city centre gets you close to most sights and main hotels and is great for orientation. It runs every 15 minutes from 10am to 4.15pm on Tuesdays to Saturdays. This drops to half-hourly on Sundays and all operational days between November and March. No service on Mondays.

Cycling and walking trails lead into the 202-hectare meadowlands of the Bossche Broek right from the city centre.

Fortunately for visitors, the historic city that's officially written as 's-Hertogenbosch (Duke's Forest) is generally abbreviated to its far less challenging short-form, Den Bosch ('the forest'). It's the birthplace of 15th-century artist Jheronimus van Aken, far better known by the pen name Hieronymus (or Jeroen) Bosch, who is famous for his instantly recognisable hell scenes.

As well as many sights linked to his legacy, the historical core also boasts fascinating tunnel-canals, a gigantic statue-festooned cathedral and a vast triangular market square, the Markt.

Long contested by warring forces, the city has retained many of its sturdy fortifications and its protective 'moat' of diverted rivers. These didn't stop many a medieval battle, with Den Bosch suffering especially during the Eighty Years' War. Today, the growing city has a comfortably wealthy vibe and a wonderful array of buzzing bars and convivial eateries. Even the graffiti-daubed Tramkade wharf area is now a trending regeneration zone.

15th-Century Surrealist

Hieronymus Bosch's hometown

For sheer impact, few museums trump the **Jheronimus Bosch Art Center** (jheronimusbosch-artcenter.nl; adult/child €12/5), housed in a grand, century-old church. It has reproductions of all 29 known Bosch paintings, plus dangling 3D sculptures, an astronomical clock and a basement recreation of the artist's studio. Many Monty Pythonesque elements are taken from details on Bosch's classic surrealist canvas The Garden of Earthly Delights, a fabulous triptych completed in 1510 and now housed at Madrid's Prado museum. Plenty more such figures have been turned into **public sculptures** dotted around town and in some of the canals.

WOLF PHOTOGRAPHY/SHUTTERSTOCK

Markt

On the Markt, a **statue of Bosch** turns his back on the house where his family first arrived in 1462. The future artist was 12, and the building was already more than a century old. Amazingly well preserved, it is now the excellent, intimate museum **Het Huis van Bosch** *(hethuisvanbosch.nl; adult/child €12/6)*.

A series of engaging audiovisuals illustrates Bosch's biography and the lives of 15th-century townsfolk more generally. Upstairs, compare a 1545 painting of the Markt with today's view from the window: the market square has changed surprisingly little in nearly 500 years.

Aged 30, Jeroen moved to a bigger, more luxurious house at **Markt 61** (now the Levi's shop), having married the daughter of a major landowner and member of the 'Swan Brotherhood'. It's still an influential charitable institution with royal connections. Their lavish mansion HQ, the **Zwanenbroedershuis** *(adult/child €8/4)*, can be visited on a tour, four days a week at 2pm. Buy tickets from Kring Vrienden (p287).

> ☑ **TOP TIP**
>
> Combination tickets are available for several of the city's attractions, and some options include various canal tours. **Kring Vrienden** (p287) organises walking tours and visits to otherwise closed spots, such as the cathedral tower and city hall.

 DRINKING IN DEN BOSCH: OUR PICKS

Coffee Lab: Big, buzzing den for coffee, breakfast and cannoli. Handy for the train and bus stations. *7am-6pm Mon-Fri, from 8am Sat & Sun*

Café Bar le Duc: Eccentric pub-cafe serving the full range of Kolleke beers brewed around the corner. *2pm-2am Mon, from 11am Tue-Sat, noon-1am Sun*

Wijn bij Stijn: Classy wine bar with enthusiastic staff keen to explain the vintages you're tasting. *5pm-late Mon, Wed & Thu, from 1pm Fri-Sun*

Bobby's Bar: If you thought a cocktail bar had to be suave and sparkly, Bobby's fun, merrily grungy approach will make you think again. *4pm-2am Wed-Sun*

DEN BOSCH

Bolwoningen
(4.4km)

Willem van Nassau

Orthenseweg

Citadellaan

Veemarktweg

Boschdijkstr

Boschveldweg

Magistratenlaan

Koninginnenlaan

Havensingel

De Dommel

Emmapl

Buitenhaven

Smalle Haven

Jan Heins Str

Zuid-Willemsvaart

Zuid-Willemsvaart

Tolbrugstr

Burgemeester
Loeffplein

**Train
Station**

Stationsweg

Visstr

Lepelstr

Eerste Korenstr

Binnendieze

Hooge Steenweg

Karenstr

Pensmarkt

Markt

Kerkstr

Gasselstr

Hinthamerstr

Nassaulaan

St Janssingel

Molenstr

Kruisstr

Schapenmarkt

Snellestr

Riddersr

Achter Het Stadhuis

Fonteinstr

Verwersstr

Lombardpad

Lange Pad

Julianapl

Postelstr

Uilenburg

Willemsplein

Mayweg

Koningsweg

Van Der Does De

Westwal

Vughterstr

De Mortel

Spinhuiswal

Parklaan

De KASerne
(1km);
Fort Isabella
(2.3km);
Fusilladeplaats
(5.9km);
Nationaal Monument
Kamp Vught (6.3km)

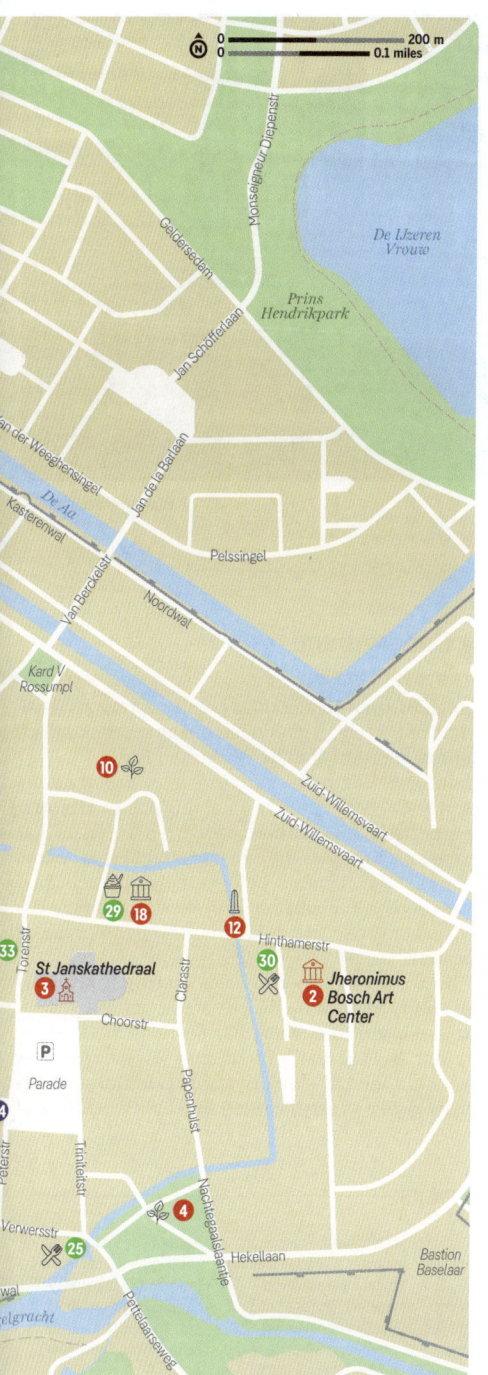

⭐ HIGHLIGHTS
1 Binnendieze
2 Jheronimus Bosch Art Center
3 St Janskathedraal

🔴 SIGHTS
4 Casinotuin
5 Citadel
6 De Draak
7 Design Museum Den Bosch
8 Heraldic Wellhouse
9 Het Huis van Bosch
10 Jeroentuin
11 Kruithuis Museum
12 Man-Eating Bug
13 Markt 61
14 Noordbrabants Museum
see 8 OLV Huisje
15 Stadhuis
16 Statue of Hieronymus Bosch
17 Willem Twee
18 Zwanenbroedershuis

🔴 ACTIVITIES
19 Zelfvaren Den Bosch

⚫ SLEEPING
20 CubaCasa
21 De Bossche Kraan
22 Rental Houseboats
23 't Keershuys
24 Uylenhof

🟢 EATING
25 Anne&Max Cafe
26 Auberge de Veste
27 Dit
28 Fishmongers' Vans
29 Gelateria Davide
30 Het Viswijf
31 Jan de Groot
32 Korte Puutstraat
33 Pilkingtons

🟢 DRINKING & NIGHTLIFE
34 Bobby's Bar
35 Bossche Brouwers
36 Café Bar le Duc
37 Coffee Lab
38 Wijn bij Stijn

🔵 INFORMATION
39 Tourist Office

🔵 TRANSPORT
40 Bolwerk St-Jan
41 Bus Station
42 De Blauwe Engelen
43 Denboschoutdoor
44 Kring Vrienden
45 Train Station

GREAT SCULPTURES

Man-Eating Bug: A favourite among the many statues inspired by Bosch's *Garden of Earthly Delights*. To see it, look down from the railings beside Hinthamerstraat 146.

Jeroentuin: In a quaint corner of the centre, this garden has a surrealist mural evoking Bosch, watched through the gates by a Bosch-style figure of a naked man riding a bird sidesaddle.

Casinotuin: This garden has sculptures of contrasting styles, including a tall, horned giraffe taken from Bosch. Look into the canal from either access bridge to see two more.

De Draak: A shimmering golden dragon built as the von Draakensteen family memorial. Also underlines Den Bosch's nickname, *Moerasfraak* (Marsh Dragon).

Binnendieze canal

CAMILA FRANCO E/SHUTTERSTOCK

Cruising Underground

Canal tours beneath the city

The Den Bosch **Binnendieze** canals aren't as pretty as those of Amsterdam or Utrecht, but uniquely, many sections cut beneath buildings and tunnel under the urban fabric.

Three main boat-tour routes *(dagjedenbosch.com; adult/child €12/6; Apr-Oct)* leave from two starting points. **Historical Route** tours leave several times hourly, but use boats that are a little too long to access the most memorable part of the network: the Hellegat. That's a 'hell' section of tunnel-canal where almost complete blackness is broken by a mesmerising audiovisual surprise that takes you through purgatory and into heaven.

Coming this way four times daily, the **Vesting Route** tour has a commentary focused on the city walls, and you disembark to explore one of the triangular bastions. Both of the above start from Molenstraat, with tickets sold just a minute's walk away within the low-slung riverside cafe **Bolwerk St-Jan**, which looks like a rusty beached ship hulk when viewed

EATING IN DEN BOSCH: OUR PICKS

Korte Puutstraat: A whole street that's shoulder to shoulder with restaurant and bar terraces, a stone's throw from the cathedral. *hours vary* €€

Anne&Max Cafe: Great balcony perch overlooking the Binnendieze boat turn spot. The menu includes plenty for vegans and vegetarians. *8am-5pm* €€

Het Viswijf: Fresh fish dinners. Create a sharing meal from assorted starters, choose catch of the day (most under €30) or go for a 'surprise menu'. *5-10pm Wed-Sun* €€

Auberge de Veste: Evolving gourmet menus from €59.95 in a pretty canal-side house that's served food since 1849. *6-8pm Mon, Tue & Thu-Sat* €€€

from the roadside. Within the cafe–ticket building is a short section of city wall, complete with a few historical panels, interactive displays and archaeological finds that you can peruse while waiting.

An alternative boat-tour option incorporating the Hellegat and adding an extra video stop is the **Jeroen Bosch Route**. This makes an up-and-back excursion through refreshing greenery, passing several surreal Bosch-based statuettes along the waterway. For this tour, board the boat opposite Anne&-Max Cafe (p286) – wait beneath the trio of metal umbrella statues. You can buy tickets from Bolwerk-St Jan or from **Kring Vrienden** on Peperstraat.

Movements on Markt
The charms of market day

The centre of any Dutch or Flemish city is the Markt, or marketplace. Den Bosch's **Markt** remains active, notably on Wednesday mornings and all day Saturdays, with Fridays also seeing a slightly smaller array of stalls focusing on regional organic products.

Each market day is made jollier by the barrel organ that is pulled around the square. On any day except Mondays, you'll find **fishmongers' vans** selling bargain seafood snacks while the campanile bell on the **Stadhuis** rings out the hours – watch the horses go round! To take a breath, there's comfy seating in the helpful **tourist office**, housed in a 13th-century 'city castle'.

The square has two eye-catching centrepieces, both faithful copies of medieval originals. One is a **heraldic wellhouse**, and the other is **OLV Huisje**, a Madonna statuette in a kind of cage on a stick. The latter's cost, as well as the decision to leave her with a missing arm (as per the original), has led to some lively press mockery.

Soaring Spirit
Gothic greatness of St Jan

From outside, the vast 1550 **St Janskathedraal** is a strange architectural mongrel that lacks the awe of Breda's Grote Kerk (p292). However, within it is one of the Netherlands' finest churches with some fine late-Gothic stained-glass windows and giant ribbed columns. The atmosphere is especially spiritual in 'Mary Month' (May), when a much-revered

BURGUNDIAN EXUBERANCE

Den Bosch sees itself as heir to the indulgent *gezelligheid* (conviviality) traditions of its Burgundian forbears, the dukes of Brabant.

Friday and Saturday nights are cacophonous around **Korenbrugstraat**'s drinking holes and the jam-packed restaurant strip on semi-hidden **Korte Puutstraat** (p286).

Big festivals include the lively **Oeteldonk Carnaval** (*oeteldonk. org*) in February or March and **Jazz in Duketown** (*jazzinduketown. nl*) around Whitsun. Year-round local indulgence is most famously typified by a distinctive culinary creation: the *Bossche bol,* a grapefruit-sized pastry filled with sweetened cream and coated in chocolate. They're made by the **Jan de Groot bakery**, but also sold from many more atmospheric cafes.

EATING IN DEN BOSCH: CHEAP EATS

Gelateria Davide: Contemplating the cathedral facade while savouring deliciously tangy Italian ice cream. Founded in 1932. *noon-10pm* €

Fishmongers' Vans: For the best snack deals in town, buy a pre-fried fish (from €2/3.50 with/without bones) or have a fish sandwich made up. *10am-6pm Tue-Sun* €

Pilkingtons: Modern brasserie with garden seating and a special takeaway window for its trademark apple crumble. *10am-6pm Sun-Wed, to 10pm Thu-Sat* €€

Dit: Fun, funky and imaginative cafe food with vegan options. *noon-9pm Mon, 10am-9.30pm Tue-Sun* €€

LESSER-KNOWN ATTRACTIONS IN DEN BOSCH

Noordbrabants Museum: Imaginative, if sometimes slightly confusing, museum combining city history and an art collection so remarkable that its 10 Van Gogh canvases are by no means the only highlights. *(hetnoord brabantsmuseum.nl)*

Design Museum Den Bosch: Stylish museum with cutting-edge design-based exhibitions. *(designmuseum.nl)*

Willem Twee: Contemporary art in a spacious former cigarette factory. Exhibitions change regularly, and most are free. *(willem-twee.nl)*

Kruithuis Museum: A rare surviving armoury building where an exhibition tells the story of the 1629 siege of Den Bosch, albeit mostly in Dutch.

Madonna and Child statue is moved from a side chapel to mid-transept. Here, it becomes the focus of major pilgrimages with countless worshippers lighting candles.

For city views, you can climb to the parapet of the cathedral's brick clock tower on **guided tours** *(dagjedenbosch. com; €8)* that run four times most days, starting from the outside southwest corner. If you don't book online, try for a last-minute ticket at Kring Vrienden.

Tramkade Regeneration

Offbeat hangout for activities and good vibes

North of the train station, across the water from the star-shaped fortress **citadel**, is a compact district called Tramkade. Once an area of 20th-century post-industrial dreariness, it has now been partially transformed into an arty regeneration zone. You'll still find graffiti-enhanced silos and car repair garages, but there's a whole lot more to discover with craft workshops, a jazz studio, a 'Pixel Arcade' games space, cinema and cafe-bars in half-decayed buildings.

Come here if you want to take to the water under your own steam rather than on a piloted cruise, using small boat rental outfits like **Zelfvaren Den Bosch** *(zelfvarendenbosch.nl),* though note that you can't take the subterranean routes. You can also do e-scooter tours with **Denboschoutdoor** *(denbo schoutdoor.nl)* and sleep on a **houseboat** *(thecoon.nl, ho teldebootel.nl, wikkelboat.nl).* There's even a disused crane turned B&B, **De Bossche Kraan** *(debosschekraan.nl).*

CLAIRE SLINGERLAND/SHUTTERSTOCK

St Janskathedraal (p287)

In one of the former eyesore warehouses, don't miss **Bossche Brouwers** *(closed Mon & Tue)*, a microbrewery that makes inventive beers beneath old grain-delivery chutes. Its dark quadruple is deceptively quaffable, and it makes a delightful ginger-lemongrass triple.

Dark Memories

Vught's WWII horrors

A waterside cycle ride 6km southwest of Den Bosch takes you along the Drongelen Canal, past the former **Fort Isabella** barracks and to the **Nationaal Monument Kamp Vught** *(nmkampvught.nl; adult/child €12/6)*, infamous in WWII as a labour and transit camp.

Some 32,000 captives passed through, including 12,000 Jews, almost all of whom were later transported to death camps. Today's affecting museum is set amid the buildings of what's still an active prison and powerfully documents the personal experiences of both prisoners and Nazi SS commanders. Drab architecture and stark barbed wire are all part of the thought-provoking atmosphere.

From there, the Lunettepad walk continues southeast through woodlands past fortress remnants. On one of the lunettes (fortified islets) is **Fusilladeplaats**, an eerie memorial spot where 329 men were summarily executed by firing squad during 1944. By that stage, camp deportations had become impossible because of Allied advances.

EXPERIMENTAL BALLS

In the late 1960s, with modern architecture tending towards harsh brutalism, the Dutch government decided to create a grant for creating something more interesting and experimental. The most famous result was the 1977 set of cube houses in Rotterdam (p176), which are now a landmark attraction in that city.

Far less known, and the last project funded in this way, was a 1984 set of 50 white spheres in a riverside park in an obscure northern suburb of Den Bosch. They're small (55 sq metres of living space), hard to clean and tend to overheat in summer, but these **Bolwoningen** are still used as social housing, and residents report loving their community of urban ball-dwellers.

Beyond
Den Bosch

Crisscrossed by major waterways, this green region of Brabant is essentially flat, its fields and forests punctuated by historical and post-industrial cities.

Places

Efteling p290
Tilburg p291
Breda p292
Eindhoven p294

GETTING AROUND

Excellent transport connections make it easy to base yourself in any of the area's cities and commute, with the railway generally the easiest option.

At Eindhoven, local Sprinter trains give you the option of getting off directly at Strijp-S (for the urban regeneration zone), as well as the main station. Efteling is accessible by buses 300 and 301 from both Tilburg and Den Bosch. In both cases, the bus and train stations are beside one another.

The attractions around Den Bosch are a real pick-and-mix assortment whose appeal varies according to your interests.

The enchanting Efteling theme park is by far the top draw, especially for families. Eindhoven and Tilburg are both places whose industrial reputations tend to mask their potential as tourist destinations. Nonetheless, both have a gamut of attractions.

Eindhoven is both a model of urban regeneration and home to the sci-fi masterpiece Evoluon. Student city Tilburg has an artistic side and makes an alternative hub for those visiting the region on a budget. Photogenic Breda is the dynastic centre of the Dutch royals, but it's also a joyful gateway for cycling and hikes in the forest and heathlands directly south.

Efteling

TIME FROM DEN BOSCH: 40MIN

Family wonderland

Efteling *(efteling.nl; entry €38-53)* is the Netherlands' foremost theme park. It's an entrancing melange of fairy-tale innocence and high-adrenaline rides in a vast site that's remarkable for its mature woodland setting.

Start by surveying the extent of the park in the ascending **Pagode**, a gently rotating 'temple' climbing high above the forest. Fry your senses on the toe-curling **Vogel Rok** 'dark' ride or **Baron 1898**, a roller coaster that includes a death-defying free-fall drop.

Contrastingly low-key **Fabula** is a 4D film (well, 3D plus air-jets), taking a friendship-themed metamorphic journey through the animal kingdom. **Symbolica** waltzes through a colour-suffused series of 'secret' rooms. **Danse Macabre** seats you for a concert and then whirls you around in a kind of haunted house meets mechanical waltz. The amusement park has much more, including boat rides and calming strolls through the delightful **Fairy Tale Forest**. Download the app for detailed tips and live wait times.

Staying overnight on-site is pricey, but rooms usually sleep a whole family, and rates include park entry (on arrival and departure days too), with a half-hour head start to beat the crowds to some popular rides. You also save the €15/day parking and pay only €12.50 for the magical **CARO** evening show.

MARK ELLIOTT/LONELY PLANET

Tilburg

TILBURG TIPS

Gabriella Zarod: Anglo-Polish barista and global nomad, has fallen in love with Tilburg. Here's what she recommends

Poppodium013: This impressive music venue brought me to Tilburg in the first place.

Kempentoren: This gravity-defying spiral viewpoint tower rises like a skeletal trumpet in Spoorpark. Things go crazy around here during King's Day celebrations.

Indie shops on Nieuwlandstraat: I love Boekhandel Livius and Ananda for 'spiritual living'. There's a vinyl record store, a vegan deli and Cool Bananas for games.

Cul-de-Sac: Good-energy bar/nightclub, the sort of place where people dance like there's nobody watching.

Piushaven: Cool off while paddleboarding.

Tilburg

TIME FROM DEN BOSCH: 15MIN 🚆

A Trappist brewery you can visit

The Benelux countries have seven active Franciscan monasteries where monks oversee the brewing of Trappist beers. You can visit **La Trappe Brewery** *(latrappe.nl)* of Koningshoeven Abbey, in fields near Tilburg. The 80-minute visitor experience *(adult/child €17.50/10)* is guide-led but interactive with elements of stand-up comedy. It's available in English at 11am on Tuesdays, Thursdays, Fridays and Saturdays.

On more-frequent Dutch-language tours (typically at 2pm), non-Dutch speakers will miss some of the jokes but can still follow key details through booklets and video subtitles. Bus 141 runs hourly from Tilburg station, or it's a pleasant 30-minute cycle ride.

Making the most of Tilburg

Don't expect medieval beauty in the sprawling university city of Tilburg. **Hostel Roots** (p299) offers regionally rare backpacker accommodation near the five-way junction of the city's coolest streets. Here, semi-attractive early-20th-century houses meet independent shops and cafes.

Bicycle shop **Guill van de Ven** *(guillvandevenfietsen.nl; closed Sun & Mon)* offers bicycle hire *(€10 per 24hr)*, ideal for reaching La Trappe Brewery or the superb **Textile Museum** *(textielmuseum.nl; adult/child €16/6)*, which celebrates Tilburg's weaving heritage with working machinery and changing exhibitions.

En route, drop into the excellent **De Pont Museum** *(de pont.nl; adult/child €16/free)* for an art fix. Even when it's closed, you can still see Anish Kapoor's entrancing 2017 *Sky Mirror* outside the entrance, cleverly turning passing clouds into works of art.

BRABANT VILLAGES

These two gorgeous rustic getaways make appealing destinations for a quick drive or longer riverside outing by bicycle from Den Bosch.

Heusden has an almost perfectly preserved star-fort layout, including triangular ravelins (island bastions) in its river moat. A mini bridge and picturesque inner yacht harbour add character.

Woudrichem is a citadel village ringed by grassy medieval rampart banks. Its small harbour is filled with old-world fishing boats. Relatively intact Hoogstraat is lined with 17th-century houses, and an 'on call' mini-ferry takes pedestrians across the creek towards **Slot Loevestein** *(adult/child €17.50/12),* a 14th-century moated castle complex with B&B rooms (p299).

Breda

TIME FROM DEN BOSCH: 35MIN 🚆

Put on your party hat

Breda loves to party. The restaurants on Veemarktstraat and the countless terrace cafes on Grote Markt and Havermarkt always seem to be buzzing, and on summer evenings, there's plenty more merriment along the waterfront at Haven.

For the full effect, come on the Ascension Day weekend when, for four foot-tapping days, the mostly free **Breda Jazz Festival** *(bredajazzfestival.nl)* fills more than 20 stages with live music. Venues include the cafe of the patchily interesting **Stedelijk Museum Breda** *(stedelijkmuseumbreda.nl; adult/child €14.50/6.50)* and the church beside the sweet little **Begijnhof**.

Just over a week later, on Whit Monday, comes **Nassaudag** *(bredanassaustad.nl),* with exhibitions, open days for otherwise closed buildings and a lunchtime parade of costumed characters evoking the Nassau dynasty, who were fundamental to Breda's rise to prominence. It was the Nassaus who built Breda's gigantic 1509 **Grote Kerk** *(grotekerkbreda.nl; free),* arguably the Netherlands' finest church. It has a glorious 97m belfry tower that looks especially photogenic from across the **Hoge Brug** with a foreground of canal boats.

Take a breath in Breda's green lung

At the southern edge of the city lies **Mastbos**, the perfect

EATING IN BREDA: OUR PICKS

Den Boerenstamppot: A Breda institution for no-frills meals: veg-and potato mash topped with your protein of choice. *4-7pm Mon-Sat* €

Foodhall: More than a dozen different street-food stalls in a world of different styles, so it's hard to choose. More than 30 different beers, too. *noon-9pm Tue-Sat* €€

Suikerkist: Large, inclusive bistro-cafe-bar whose triangular terrace has the perfect view of Grote Kerk. The toilets have a Banksy-esque twist. *noon-late* €€

Pellens: Low-key lunches and superb dinners, often using house-grown veg and flowers. *4-11pm Wed & Thu, from noon Fri-Sun* €€€

HUNG CHUNG CHIH/SHUTTERSTOCK

Grote Kerk

antidote to all that partying. Crisscrossed by footpaths and cycleways, it's a beautiful woodland of beech, birch, large oaks and especially giant Scots pine, originally planted in 1515 as masts for future ships. The area also has ponds, sandy spaces and marshy areas with boardwalks.

Bus 6 (hourly, not on Sundays) gets you to the eastern edge, leaving many possible walking options. For the shortest quick taster, start at the small but picture-perfect moated castle called **Bouvigne** (*landgoedbouvigne.nl; free; closed Sat & Sun*). Visit the formal gardens and then strike out into the forest and loop back in about 20 minutes to the village-like suburb of **Ginneken** on the forest's northeast tip. A picturesque triangular square here has three inviting cafe-bars.

For a longer adventure, hire a bicycle. Some hotels can help, and **Explore Breda** (*explorebreda.com/en/city-surroundings/practical-information/bike-rental-parking*) lists hire outlets on its website. Start by skirting Mastbos following the banks of the Mark River to **Meersel-Dreef** (13km). Only an 1843 border marker post beside the cycle path alerts you to the fact that you've actually crossed into Belgium.

In the village, visit a Lourdes-style **grotto garden** and refresh yourself beside the abbey-church **Kapucijnenkerk** in the simple tavern **Bij de Paters**. Return via Galder, and cross the whole Mastbos from south to north.

A GEOGRAPHICAL ABSURDITY

Conjoined towns Baarle-Nassau (Netherlands) and Baarle-Hertog (Belgium) form a ridiculous geopolitical jigsaw with the world's most complex border. **Baarle-Hertog** consists of 22 miniature Belgian exclaves, within which are seven further enclaves of the Netherlands. This utterly bizarre arrangement can be traced back to an 1198 agreement in which the Duke of Breda (later Nassau) was given the village of Baarle. However, the surrounding farmland was retained by the Hertog (Duke) of Brabant. Centuries later, Breda became Dutch, southern Brabant Belgian and a smuggling era began. Today, sitting on the terrace of **Hotel Brasserie Den Engel**, you can have one foot in either country.

 DRINKING IN BREDA: OUR PICKS

Café & Brouwerij de Beyerd: Old-world beer specialist dating from 1843. Try the double IPA. *10am-1am Mon, Thu, Fri & Sun, from 2pm Sat*

Cafe Vulling: The most atmospheric of countless terraced cafe options that line Grote Markt. Has board games and an old-school pinball machine. *10am-midnight*

Botanist: Known for its G&Ts and hand-crafted lemonades but a relaxing place to sip any drink beside the canal. *11am-midnight*

Kamu: A range of bean origins and grinds for your barista coffee in a large bicycle shop. *9am-5pm Mon-Wed, to 8pm Thu-Sat, 10am-6pm Sun*

Eindhoven

TIME FROM DEN BOSCH: 25MIN

Philips town

For decades, the city of Eindhoven has been synonymous with Philips, a global corporate giant famed for 20th-century innovation in home electronics. Today, you're more likely to know Eindhoven for its soccer team **PSV**, but that itself stands for Philips Sport Vereniging. The team plays at **Philips Stadium** *(psv.nl/en/museum-tours/home)*, which has a PSV **museum** *(adult/child €7.50/5)* for which admission is included if you do a stadium tour *(adult/child €21/18.50)*. Prebooking is essential.

Amid otherwise faceless architecture around the stadium lies a nearly quaint century-old neighbourhood known as **Philipsdorp**, built as company housing.

Along with the superb art gallery, **Van Abbemuseum** *(va nabbemuseum.nl; adult/child €16/free)*, central Eindhoven's most unmissable attraction is the **Philips Museum** *(philips .nl/en/a-w/philips-museum; adult/child €12.50/6)*, telling the company's story in suitably high-tech fashion. The top floor focuses on AI and the way Philips uses it in cutting-edge medical equipment.

One train stop north, the whole former Philips industrial quarter known as **Strijp-S** is now a model of urban regeneration, centred around the huge Philips Clock building, **Klokgebouw**. While far from beautiful, it's a lively hub for a series of art spaces, a rock school, music venues, **Area 51** (a giant indoor skatepark), **Enversed** (VR experiences) and some hip cafe-restaurants.

Climb into a UFO

Shaped like a concrete flying saucer, the 1966 **Evoluon** was once the epitome of futurism.

Pop into the foyer *(free)* to admire a *Back to the Future* DeLorean car or spend a couple of hours in **Next Nature** *(next nature.org; adult/child €16/4.50)*, an imaginative, unsettling and occasionally frustrating experience that nostalgically examines past notions of the future from many angles. Interactive 'Deep Dive' illustrates infinities of scale by looking ever closer into a giant photograph. Eco-warnings are given by a harrowing doomsday clock. A 'fractal forest' questions our addiction to technology, albeit sometimes in ways that are baffling without an explanation.

For an extra €6, a VR time machine ride takes you to the end of the universe and back. Don't forget to watch your hands as you speed towards an unembodied dimension.

PHILIPS INVENTIONS & INNOVATIONS

Light bulbs: From 1891, the Philips family mass-produced carbon-filament light bulbs, unlocking a step-change in home lighting.

X-rays: During WWI, Germany cut off supplies of Röntgen tubes, needed for hospital X-rays. Philips repaired old ones and then began making its own.

Rotary electric shavers: Invented and trademarked in 1939 as 'Philishave'.

Audio recordings: Pioneered global standards for hand-size cassette tapes in the 1970s and then, with Sony, developed the world-standard format for CDs.

Record label: Between 1953 and 1976, Philips-label artists included Dusty Springfield, Frankie Vaughan and Shirley Bassey.

 ## EATING & DRINKING IN EINDHOVEN: OUR PICKS

Grand Café de Lichttoren: Lively, expansive brasserie in the Witte Vrouw, a white 1923 former factory building. *11am-11pm Tue-Sat, 10am-5pm Sun* €€

Restaurant 1910: Sophisticated salad and sandwich lunches or multicourse dinners featuring lamb, sweetbreads and lobster bisque. *11am-9.40pm* €€€

Rabauw: A fun, slightly hidden Strijp-S brewpub with board games, fuzzy walls and good food, some of it made with beer. *3-11pm Wed-Sat*

Biergarten Eindhoven: Drinks and decent nibbles on Strijp-S's central square. *3pm-late*

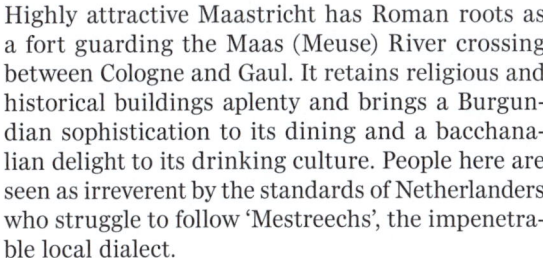

Maastricht

ROMANESQUE CHURCHES | TUNNELS | FEASTING

Highly attractive Maastricht has Roman roots as a fort guarding the Maas (Meuse) River crossing between Cologne and Gaul. It retains religious and historical buildings aplenty and brings a Burgundian sophistication to its dining and a bacchanalian delight to its drinking culture. People here are seen as irreverent by the standards of Netherlanders who struggle to follow 'Mestreechs', the impenetrable local dialect.

The fact that the city is Dutch at all is because of military commander Bernardus Dibbets, who in 1830 refused to accept an ultimatum to let Maastricht become part of Belgium. The city withstood a siege and, for nine years, was a disconnected exclave before the Netherlands reclaimed connecting land (the 'Limburg appendix'). It remains hemmed in on three sides by Belgium and Germany, perhaps explaining why Maastricht was chosen for the signing of the February 1992 treaty that paved the way for the EU and the Euro common currency.

☑ TOP TIP

The concerts of André Rieu's Strauss Orchestra put intense pressure on Maastricht hotel beds for much of July. If you're not here for the waltzes, avoid the city at that time because there's no room at the inn.

Saints & Sinners

History and revelry on the Vrijthof

The **Vrijthof** is Maastricht's finest square, with many attractive facades, pollarded plane trees, a grand **theatre**

 GETTING AROUND

The train station and bus station are across the river from the old centre in the Wyck district, an area of charm in its own right, with plenty of dining options. Bus 4 links the station and Vrijthof, but it's almost as fast to walk.

When taking a train, be careful to check in and out using the correct fare-charging pillar. Yellow is for NS trains, blue for private

Arriva services, such as those to Valkenburg. International short-hop buses to Hasselt (Belgium), Aachen (Germany) and elsewhere leave from the west side of the station. Long-distance Flixbus services and Flibco buses to Charleroi Airport use the International Bus Stop on the east side of the rail tracks.

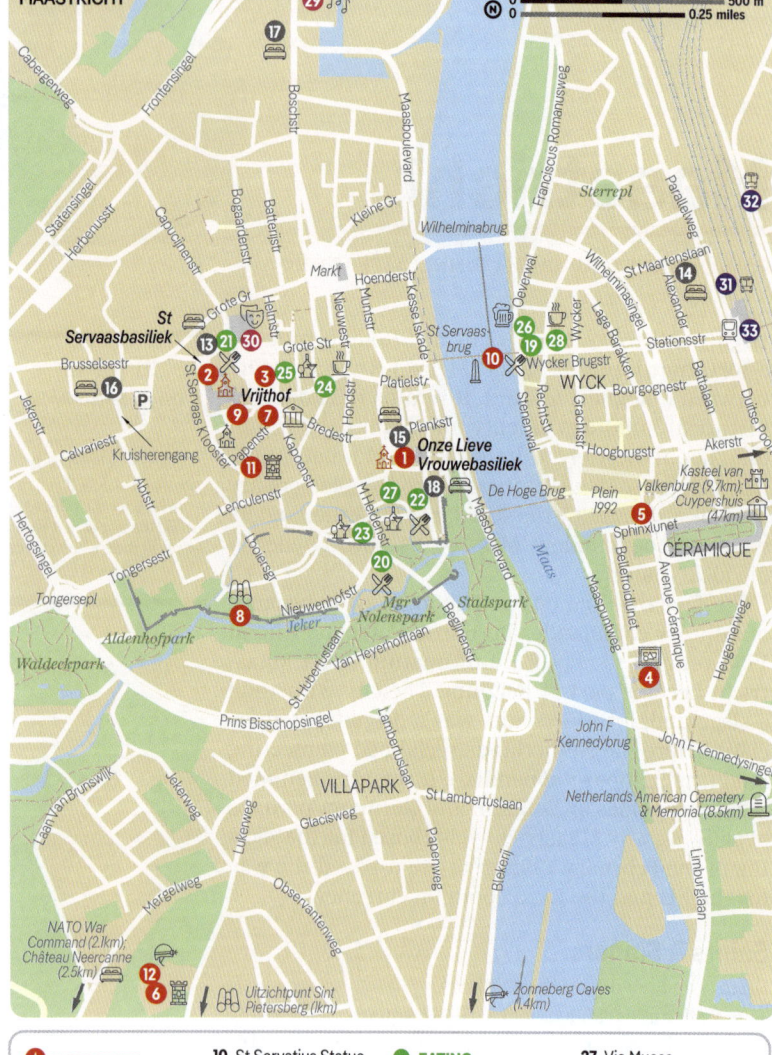

MAASTRICHT

⭐ **HIGHLIGHTS**

1 Onze Lieve
Vrouwebasiliek
2 St Servaasbasiliek
3 Vrijthof

🔴 **SIGHTS**

4 Bonnefantenmuseum
5 Centre Ceramique
6 Fort St Pieter
7 Fotomuseum
Aan Het Vrijthof
8 Nieuwenhofpoort
9 St Janskerk

10 St Servatius Statue
11 University Law
Faculty Tower

🔴 **ACTIVITIES**

12 Maastricht
Underground

⚫ **SLEEPING**

13 B&B de Hofnar
14 Green Elephant
15 Hotel Derlon
16 Kruisherenhotel
17 Social Hub
18 Zenden

🟢 **EATING**

19 Bouchon d'en Face
20 Café Sjiek
21 Pitology
22 Witloof

🟢 **DRINKING &
NIGHTLIFE**

23 Cafe de Pieter
24 Fretz
25 Somewhere
in the Middle
26 Stadsbrouwerij
Maastricht

27 Via Mucca
28 Zondag

🔴 **ENTERTAINMENT**

29 Muziekgieterij
30 Theater aan
het Vrijthof

🔵 **TRANSPORT**

31 Bus Station
32 International
Bus Stop
33 Train Station

(theatervrijthof.nl) and the small **Fotomuseum Aan Het Vrijthof** *(fotomuseumaanhetvrijthof.nl; adult/child €14/7)*.

During **Carnaval** in February or March, it's on Vrijthof that the clog-footed *Mooseif* (Cabbage Woman) is hoisted at 12.11pm on the Sunday before Lent. Three big parades follow, and the open-air finale party on Tuesday night is again on the Vrijthof. For much of July, local-born waltz-king **André Rieu** fills the Vrijthof with wildly popular orchestral concerts of light classical music *(andrerieu.com)*. In late August, the square becomes one vast dinner party during **Preuvenemint** *(preuvenemint.nl)*, the Netherlands' biggest food festival.

At calmer times, come to enjoy the square's strip of cafe-terraces or to survey a signature gaggle of **towers**. A surreally pointed 20th-century one that is partly hidden from here belongs to the **university law faculty**.

The other towers belong to two great churches. Painted ox-blood red to prevent erosion is the Protestant **St Janskerk** *(stjanskerkmaastricht.nl)*, whose tower can be climbed in 280 steps *(adult/child €4/2)*. Next door is one of Maastricht's Romanesque religious masterpieces, **St Servaasbasiliek** *(sintservaas.nl; adult/child €7/free)*. Now mostly a museum, the basilica is built over the tomb of Armenian-born bishop St Servatius (Servatius of Tongeren), whose death here in 384 CE led the city to become a major medieval pilgrimage centre. His skull is encased in an eerily human-looking gilt reliquary, the most precious object in the vast treasury collection.

St Servatius' stern likeness appears in various forms all over the city, including as a **statue** on the central bridge that carries his name.

Roman & Romanesque

Maastricht's archaeological fragments

Nijmegen (p270) might be the Netherlands's oldest city, but Maastricht is the oldest to have been continuously inhabited. One of the most offbeat ways to discover the city's Roman heritage is to stay at the 1870 **Hotel Derlon** *(derlon.com)*. Its breakfast room has tables dotted about archaeological remnants of a Roman piazza, with museum-like display cases of artefacts also on show. Non-guests have to pay €5 to take a look.

On the same tree-shaded cafe-square, look inside **Onze Lieve Vrouwebasiliek**, with its broodingly dark interior and candle-crammed shrine space piously honouring Mary 'Star of the Sea'. The church itself is not Roman but Romanesque, its regional Mosan style made that much more 'authentic'

DAY TRIPS FROM MAASTRICHT

Valkenburg: Gently quaint tourist town with forested hills, a castle ruin and a Pierre Cuypers replica of some Roman catacombs in an old limestone mine.

Netherlands American Cemetery & Memorial: Thought-provokingly vast WWII cemetery behind a white chapel-monolith.

Roermond: Hometown of architect Pierre Cuypers, whose former home and workshop form a fascinating museum, the Cuypershuis. Munsterkerk and Sint-Christoffel-kathedraal are fine churches restored after WWII.

Thorn: Picturesque village that was once the smallest principality of the Holy Roman Empire – and run by women. Almost every house is painted white and has been since the 1790s.

EATING IN MAASTRICHT: OUR PICKS

Pitology: Grand mansion turned mellow, student-friendly stop for hot Greek wraps. Of 15 varieties, five are veggie. Linden-shaded terrace. *noon-9pm Wed-Mon* €

Witloof: Classic Belgian dining: great mussels, rabbit with wine sauce and ham-wrapped chicory. What a beer cellar! *5.30-9.30pm Wed-Sun* €€

Bouchon d'en Face: Old-world place for traditional French cooking. Good-value set menu. *5.30-10pm daily, plus noon-4pm Fri & Sat* €€

Café Sjiek: The place to go for *zuurvlees* (sour meat stew). Summer tables on the grass opposite. *5-9.30pm Wed-Mon* €€

WHY I LOVE MAASTRICHT

Mark Elliott, Lonely Planet writer

I love Maastricht's joie de vivre: tree-shaded cafe terraces like **Fretz**, Sunday night jazz at grungy **Cafe de Pieter**, bigger gigs at **Muziekgieterij** or seeing what's new in the dynamically reimagined post-industrial Sphinx-kwarteier.

I also adore the city's quiet corners: spotting a heron from the city wall at **Nieuwenhofpoort**, the competing sounds on Heksenstraat with Conservatorium piano practice counterpointed by the De Reek waterwheel, pétanque played beneath the lime trees near Bousquetplein, fine art at the **Bonnefantenmuseum** or escaping rain in the comfortable if outwardly ugly **Centre Ceramique** library-museum with its full-scale model of the city.

thanks to prolific 19th-century star-architect Pierre Cuypers, of Rijksmuseum fame. Fragments of city wall from various eras add fascination to random walks around the city centre, most visibly beside the narrow Jeker River.

Getting Deep

Don't wander off underground

'If you get lost in here', quipped the guide with brutal humour, 'you'll probably die'. Over the centuries, some 230km of quarry tunnels were dug into the hills of the St Pietersberg Massif south of Maastricht. About 80km still exist, mostly unlit. Various tours run by **Maastricht Underground** *(exploremaastricht.nl/en/maastricht-underground)* visit different sections so that you can see charcoal murals and hear stories linked to the tunnels' creation, their Napoleonic history and their use as a virtual city for hiding the population during WWII bombardments.

One daily **North Caves** tour includes a visit to the 'secret' vaults in which a trove of the nation's art treasures (including Rembrandt's *The Night Watch*) was squirrelled away for three war years in specially regulated conditions. Another lets you inside a once top-secret **NATO War Command**. The **Zonneberg Caves** are wide enough to visit by scooter!

Prebooking online is advisable, or buy remaining tickets from a booth within the 1701 **Fort St Pieter**, itself an impressively hefty five-sided earthworks set within a deep-cut dry moat. Further guided tours enter the fort and its own tunnels, but you might prefer to peer briefly at the ramparts and then walk 1km south to the **Uitzichtpunt Sint Pietersberg**, which is a viewpoint platform suspended dramatically above the deep ENCI Quarry.

PIERRE CUYPERS

Master architect Pierre Cuypers 'antiquified' the **Onze Lieve Vrouwebasiliek** in Maastricht, and his house-studio is preserved in **Roermond**, but he's best known for the **Rijksmuseum** (p90) and **Centraal Station** (p61) in Amsterdam. The flamboyant **Kasteel de Haar** (p164) in Utrecht is essentially his creation.

DRINKING IN MAASTRICHT: OUR PICKS

Zondag: Sociable spot that blurs the lines between cafe, lunch place and drinking hole. *10am-2am*

Via Mucca: Friendly, intimate but unpretentious wine bar on a convivial lane of other cafes and eateries. *3-11pm Wed-Sun*

Stadsbrouwerij Maastricht: City brewery pub with 16 beers on tap and hard-to-beat terrace seats on the riverside. *noon-midnight Tue-Sun*

Somewhere in the Middle: Subterranean speakeasy cocktail bar in a cellar beneath Vrijthof (access beside Momus). *6pm-1am Wed-Sat & Mon, 5-11pm Sun*

Places We Love to Stay

€ Budget €€ Midrange €€€ Top End

Den Bosch p282

't Keershuys €€ Immaculate accommodation above a local bistro in a half-timbered 1450 building slap-bang in the city's buzzing bar zone. Superb breakfast.

CubaCasa €€ Four Latin-themed B&B rooms in a canal-facing house towards the station with a musical artist owner. Read the small print regarding arrival times.

De KASerne €€ Stylishly starkly modernist rooms with super-comfy beds, a 10-minute walk from the old town. Easy but payable private parking.

Uylenhof €€€ Pamperingly well-equipped luxury apartments in a pair of historic buildings accessed across the canal.

Efteling p290

Hotel 't Pepperhuis €€ Neat and clean if somewhat generic. Free parking, and you're just 2km from the Efteling entrance. Family rooms sleep up to five.

Efteling Wonder Hotel €€€ Revamped in 2024, the hotel is a playful attraction in itself, with a 'floating castle' theme and in-costume characters entertaining kids during breakfast. Includes park entrance from a private gate.

Efteling Grand Hotel €€€ Opened in 2025, the Grand's colour-themed rooms aim for a Vegas-sophisticated look. The key attraction is being the only hotel inside the park (entry fees included).

Tilburg p291

Hostel Roots € This cult hostel in central Tilburg has a few rough edges but remains the standout backpacker option in this part of the Netherlands.

Breda p292

Hotel Mastbosch €€ Nostalgic old-time hotel beside Mastbos forest with a grand cafe and easy parking. No-frills rooms are well-maintained but little changed for decades. Hire a bicycle for €16.

Hotel Nassau €€ Maze of rooms within three interconnected historic houses. Breakfast is served in a large stone chapel.

Bliss Hotel €€€ Nine individually designed suites with working fireplaces and old-world style furniture that stylishly create a neoclassical feel through tripod lamps and bookcases.

Heusden & Woudrichem p291

In den Verdwaalde Koogel €€ Simple but pleasant rooms in a step-gabled old building on the main square of lovely Heusden.

Slot Loevestein €€€ Smart B&B rooms in outbuildings of the 14th-century museum-castle complex that lies across the (unbridged) river from romantic Woudrichem village.

Maastricht p295

Green Elephant € Choose a 'tiny dream house' to pay hostel prices but receive a degree of privacy in a keypad lockable box-room with air-con.

B&B de Hofnar € Super-central, basic rooms, some with separate toilets. The automated check-in system helps keep prices for the cheapest rooms below €60.

Social Hub €€ Industrial chic hotel, social spaces and coworking rooms in a revamped former factory in the Sphinxkwartier. Has a gym, bike hire and a rooftop bar.

Zenden €€ Boutique rooms spread over three city-centre houses, giving a bleached sense of otherworldliness, which is either stylish or antiseptic according to your taste.

Kruisherenhotel €€€ A 1483 monastery complex converted into a design-statement hotel. Each room is individually decorated, and some are a little small, but the overall ambience is a delight.

Château Neercanne €€€ Majestic 17th-century castle with baroque gardens, a cave cellar event room, Michelin-star restaurant and five-star luxury suites, 5km south of the centre.

TOOLKIT

The chapters in this section cover the most important topics you'll need to know about in the Netherlands. They're full of nuts-and-bolts information and valuable insights to help you understand and navigate the Netherlands and get the most out of your trip.

Arriving
p302

Getting Around
p303

Money
p304

Accommodation
p305

Family Travel
p306

Health & Safe Travel
p307

Food, Drink & Nightlife
p308

Responsible Travel
p310

LGBTIQ+ Travellers
p312

Accessible Travel
p313

Sustainable Shopping
p314

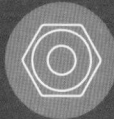

Nuts & Bolts
p315

Language
p316

De Wallen (p52), Amsterdam
ARCADY/SHUTTERSTOCK

Arriving

Conveniently near both Amsterdam and Rotterdam, Schiphol International (AMS) is the Netherlands' main airport and the second-busiest in the EU, served by most major airlines. The airport is like a small city, with a huge shopping centre and neighbouring airport hotels. Low-cost airlines fly into two more airports, Rotterdam The Hague Airport (RTM) and Eindhoven Airport (EIN).

Visas

In late 2026, new EU entry rules will require nationals from 60 visa-exempt countries, including the US, UK and Canada, to apply and pay for travel authorisation (€7) before entering the Schengen area.

Border Crossing

If you're already in the EU's Schengen area, or free-movement zone, crossing borders is visa-free. There are no passport controls when entering from neighbouring countries.

SIM Cards

Prepaid SIM cards can be purchased at airport kiosks and used on GSM phones. The EU has abolished costs for data roaming and local calls within its member states.

Wi-Fi

Schiphol's free wi-fi network is called 'Airport_Free_Wifi'. The network stays connected in four-hourly increments, and you can continuously rejoin the network.

	AMS to Amsterdam	RTM to Rotterdam	RTM to Den Haag
TRAIN	€5.70 35 mins	€3.28 30 mins	€5.50 45 mins
BUS	€60 **20 mins**	€35 **15 mins**	€50 **20 mins**
TAXI	€45 20 mins	€20 15 mins	€35 20 mins

AIRPORT UNCERTAINTY

Since 2023, a back-and-forth on government plans has left the future of air travel to and from the Netherlands in a state of limbo. Initially, the government was expected to introduce a cap of 452,500 yearly aircraft movements at Schiphol Airport (down from the current maximum of 500,000) to reduce noise pollution. In 2025, the cap slightly increased to 478,000. This could mean fewer flights to Schiphol, but not necessarily thanks to a new terminal expected to open in 2027. The airport in Lelystad, 50km east of Amsterdam, was expanded in 2025 and commercial flights could be routed from here.

CLOCKWISE FROM TOP LEFT: FUSE/GETTY IMAGES, GEORGE MDIVANIAN/EYEEM/GETTY IMAGES, SOOS JOZSEF/SHUTTERSTOCK

# Getting Around

There are no domestic flights within the Netherlands, but you learn quickly that doesn't matter. Most cross-country journeys are so short that you could be in a new town before your next meal.

TRAVEL COSTS

Car hire
from €35/day

Petrol
approx €2.29/L

EV charging
€0.30 to €0.35/ kWh

Train ticket from Den Haag to Amsterdam
approx €14.60

Train

Dutch trains are efficient, fast and comfortable. Service is frequent and regular across domestic destinations, sometimes running five or six times an hour. It's an excellent system and possibly all you need to get yourself (and even your bicycle) anywhere in the country. Pay ticket fare by tapping your credit card or phone's digital wallet to check in and out of platform turnstiles

Car

Dutch freeways are extensive but prone to congestion. Those around Amsterdam, the A4 south to Belgium and the A2 southeast to Maastricht are especially known for rush-hour jams. Smaller roads are well maintained, but wide bike lanes, speed bumps and frequent construction can make cruising less fun.

TIP

Public transport in Amsterdam is electronic-only. Only some trams have staffed booths for buying tickets. Contactless payment via card or smartphone is possible. Don't forget to tap out!

USING PUBLIC TRANSPORT

Purchase a reusable OV-chipkaart (anonymous/ personalised €8.50/7.50) at train stations and supermarkets. Charge it with credit (minimum €10/20 buses/trains) at ticketing machines. When entering transport, hold against the reader. When exiting, check out or you'll pay the highest fare. Leaving the Netherlands, request leftover credit at station counters or online (ovshop.nl) for a €2.50 fee. Without an OV-chipkaart, you automatically receive disposable tickets from machines (€1.50 fee plus fare).

DRIVING ESSENTIALS

Drive on the right.

50

Speed limits range from 50km/h (cities) to 120km/h (motorways).

.05

Blood alcohol limit is 0.5%.

Bus

Buses are a vital service primarily for regional transport where trains are less frequent or nonexistent, particularly in the Netherlands' northern and eastern parts. Some regions have good day passes. Don't be shy: ask a driver to recommend your journey's best option – they speak great English and are usually happy to help.

Bicycle

Dedicated cycling routes go virtually everywhere – in fact, most Dutch towns are blanketed with nicely paved paths. The Netherlands' extremely bicycle-friendly culture (p37) includes abundant parking facilities and two-wheeler train compartments. Destinations are usually within a one- to two-hour ride from each other, so get your pedal on.

Boat

Year-round passenger ferries connect the mainland with the Frisian Islands, and seasonal inter-island ferries link the most populous ones. Elsewhere, services range from the South Holland fast-service Waterbus (waterbus.nl) to minor routes linking shores across myriad canals and waterways.

Money

CURRENCY: EURO (€)

Cash Machines

Cash machines can be found at most banks, airports and train stations. Money changers are available at airports, though they don't necessarily offer better rates.

Credit & Debit Cards

Credit cards such as Visa and Mastercard are widely accepted, but American Express is less frequently accepted at independent businesses. Use any of the three for public transport tickets and at supermarket chains. Increasingly, many businesses, such as trendier cafes and restaurants in Amsterdam, have gone cash-free.

Supermarket Discounts

Albert Heijn's discounted prices are calculated into the final payment only if you have a loyalty card. Supermarket employees will happily let you scan theirs.

Tipping

The Dutch are modest tippers. Service charges and taxes must be included in menu prices, and your bill's total amount should reflect this.

Hotel porters €1 to €2

Hotel housecleaning €1 to €2 per night

Restaurants round up to the nearest euro (or 5% to 10%)

Taxis 5% to 10%

HOW MUCH FOR A...

Three-hour small boat hire
€120

Public toilet
€1–2

Train ticket from Amsterdam to Rotterdam
€32.30

I amsterdam Card
€65 (24hr)

HOW TO... Save a Few Euros

Staying entertained on the cheap is easy in the Netherlands. Free events abound across an all-year calendar of festivals. In Amsterdam and Rotterdam, catch free-entry entertainment at jazz cafes and prebooked **Concertgebouw** (p93) lunchtime shows. In summer, parks offer free entertainment, from performances in **Vondelpark** (p86) to **Oosterpark** (p106) tango nights.

CURRENCY SLANG

Dutch people love slang, and when it comes to money, several colloquialisms hark back to medieval guild (*gulden*) days. Common slang from merchant trading includes *tientje* ('little ten') for €10 and *vijfje* ('little five') for €5, reflecting guild notes going up in physical size by denomination. Orange-yellow €50 notes are called *geeltje* ('little yellow ones') after 50-guilder notes. Meanwhile, *dubbeltje,* once a 10-cent, tiny silver guilder coin, now refers to small change. Loose coinage is sometimes called *poen,* a 17th-century Yiddish term with the same meaning. Paper money is colloquially called *flappen* for being flappy, of course.

LOCAL TIP

In Amsterdam Noord, catch artists at work. Inside and around the former shipbuilding warehouse **NDSM Loods** (ppage 118) and **Straat** (ppage 118), murals and installations are always in the works.

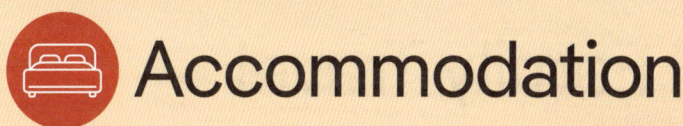

Accommodation

B&Bs

Bed and breakfasts are excellent for getting to know friendly locals and scoring their insider tips. Discovering the weirdest, wackiest and most wonderful of Dutch interior designs is simply an added perk. While B&Bs are not abundant in cities, the countryside is awash with them. Check in with tourist offices or peruse online booking portals.

Camping

The Dutch live for camping across their countryside. Campgrounds range from wild and remote to self-contained communities with shops and swimming pools. A typical campsite is for two people and a tent; caravans and cars cost extra. Bungalows, cabins or luxury tents with shared bathroom facilities are also available. Head to the Frisian Islands for plentiful campgrounds with stunning sea views.

Coworking Stays

Modern coworking accommodation, offering rooms and a workspace (usually a cafe/bar), is abundant. It ranges from budget hostels with laptop-friendly public spaces to luxury havens with well-designed, laptop-friendly lounges for hunkering down, cocktail in hand. Take advantage of networking opportunities here. Not only digital nomads but also many locals relish changing up their work scenery.

Hostels

Affiliated with Hostelling International (HI), the Dutch hostel association goes by the banner Stayokay *(stayokay.com)*. Not all are new builds, but they have a good variety of dorms as well as private rooms, and impressive facilities provide comfy visits overall. Some, such as **Stayokay Rotterdam** (ppage 217), are even in architecturally significant buildings. Indie hostels (cutting-edge to shambolic) abound in cities but are scarcer outside urban areas.

HOW MUCH FOR A NIGHT IN A...

Hostel dorm
€45

Campsite
€30

Coworking hotel
(private room)
€150–300

Hotels

Any Dutch hotel with more than 20 rooms is considered large. The plus is a boutique-y feel, with rooms and spaces boasting individualistic flair, plus plentiful accommodation that is independently run. Overall, expect your room to be on the snug side and not necessarily with a view to cherish. At canal-side accommodation, prepare to scale winding, narrow staircases carefully.

FINDING CHEAPER ACCOMMODATION

'Star' plaques out front of every Dutch hotel display ratings by the Nederlandse Hotel Classificatie (NHC; national hotel classification system). The stars (from one to five) indicate facilities, not quality. That means two-star hotels might offer better stays (though fewer facilities) than hotels of higher rank. Consult online reviews to find out.

Consider booking a hotel in a 'second city', such as Haarlem (instead of Amsterdam) or Delft (instead of Rotterdam). Prices are cheaper and you can reach both cities in under 30 minutes by train.

CLOCKWISE FROM TOP LEFT: UNVERDORBEN JR/SHUTTERSTOCK, DUTCHMEN PHOTOGRAPHY/SHUTTERSTOCK,
TUNEDIN BY WESTEND61/SHUTTERSTOCK, ERMAN GUNES/SHUTTERSTOCK

Family Travel

The Netherlands is one of Europe's most kid-friendly countries. The famous Dutch tolerance extends to children, and locals are exceptionally welcoming towards them – and parents, too. Most museums put effort into a tailored experience for younger visitors. Enduring icons such as castles, windmills and open-air museums captivate all ages. National parks make for excellent family holidays with summer activities on offer.

Dining Out

Children are welcome in all but the most formal restaurants. In fact, the trend towards stylish bistro-style eateries with high ceilings and a slightly raucous atmosphere is all the better for little ones. Overall, folks are quite understanding of kids and any chaos they bring along. You'll see Dutch families enjoying meals in restaurants or sitting in parks sharing *frites* (fries).

Child Ticket Prices

There's no rule on how much and from what age children pay. Some attractions are free to under-18s, others to under-17s and some only for under-5s. Child admission is usually half (or slightly less) of the adult price. Take advantage of good-value family passes combining sightseeing and public transport. Some attractions offer small discounts (€2 per ticket) for prebooking online.

Accommodation

Few hotels have a 'no kids' rule. Countrywide, family rooms sleeping four are common, and most hotels can add an extra bed for a minimal extra cost, or a baby cot for free. Check out new-wave design-driven hostels providing private rooms that sleep up to six.

Getting Around

Most bicycle-hire shops stock trailers, child and baby seats for bikes, and kid-sized wheels. In summer, it's best to book whatever you need before you arrive. Few offer helmets (for any age), so consider bringing your own.

KID-FRIENDLY PICKS

SS Rotterdam (p195) Converted cruise ship offers kid-friendly tours. Get here on a thrilling watertaxi ride.

Vondelpark (p86) Space-age slides, playgrounds and duck ponds in Amsterdam's biggest park.

Hortus Botanicus (p214) Leiden's botanical garden's tropical greenhouse is a colourful, canopied walking adventure.

Castellum Hoge Woerd (p163) Renowned Utrecht archaeological museum with a petting zoo and a bee conservation garden.

Zuid-Kennemerland National Park (p131) Explore lakes and a white-sand beach near Haarlem.

WHEN TO GO

The Netherlands is an all-year-round affair, although families may most appreciate the warmer, drier months – from Easter to September – for outdoor action from beaches to sailing or simply park frolicking. Windmills, open-air museums and canals galore offer fresh-air fun in all seasons. During winter, kids love skating rinks at the Christmas markets that spring up in many cities and towns.

The Dutch festival repertoire is a key planning consideration. Cold, wet February ushers in kid-friendly street parades during carnival season. Sinterklaas brings presents to kids on 5 December, while summer has a bonanza of fun (and free) festivals and sporting events.

 # Health & Safe Travel

MEDICATIONS

Unlike most other Western European countries, over-the-counter medications like aspirin are available at chemists and supermarkets in the Netherlands, not just at chemists. Pharmacies are widely available in cities and towns. For prescription medications, you generally need to get one by visiting a local healthcare provider. Pharmacies only fill medications; they don't write them.

NIGHT PHARMACIES

Dienstapotheek (night pharmacies) are available outside regular hours. Pharmacies take turns opening at night. Search online by city.

Prescriptions

Some commonly prescribed medications in the US, including those for anxiety and pain, are illegal narcotics in Europe. Their possession is taken seriously. Bring a signed and dated doctor's note in English, stating your name, prescription and condition, and make sure bottles are clearly labelled in their correct and original packaging.

Seeing a Doctor

If you don't live in the European Economic Area, expect to pay for medical treatment up front and seek reimbursement from travel insurance later. Keep all receipts and documentation. Dutch healthcare professionals speak great English. For non-emergency medical issues, such as minor illnesses or injuries, visit a *huisartsenpost* (out-of-hours doctor's service) before the emergency room on evenings and weekends.

SWIM SAFELY

Red flag
No swimming

Yellow flag
Caution

Green flag
Safe to swim

Orange wind sock
No inflatables.

Checkered flag
Water sports zone (no swimming)

Tap Water

Bring a refillable water bottle to stay hydrated. The Netherlands' tap water is clean, drinkable and well-filtered. Drinking fountains are widely available across parks, campgrounds, tourist areas and transport hubs. In restaurants, feel free to ask for tap water *(kraanwater),* which is usually free of charge.

INSURANCE CARDS

For necessary medical treatment in the Netherlands, citizens of the EU, Switzerland, Iceland, Norway and Liechtenstein receive free or reduced-cost, state-provided (not private) health-care coverage with the European Health Insurance Card (EHIC). Pay directly for treatment and claim refunds later by form (generally about 70% of the treatment costs). Each family member needs a separate card.

Food, Drink & Nightlife

HOW TO...

Order Fries Like a Local

Patatje or *frites* are one of the simplest yet most satisfying pleasures you can enjoy in the Netherlands. Traditionally served in a tall paper cone and eaten with small wooden forks, they make for the perfect on-the-go snack. Almost every *friteshuis* has a minimum of 10 sauces, and locals love to mix and match. Classic is *frietsaus*, (sometimes spelt *frietessaus*), a creamy, slightly sweet mayo-like sauce. Order this by saying *frites met* ('fries with'). Real mayo is only carried at Belgian-style stands.

Other sauces include satay (peanut), *joppiesaus* (tangy curry-based) and *andalouse* (sweet-spicy tomato-pepper). Combinations include *oorlog* ('war fries'), with satay, *frietsaus,* chopped raw onions, and *Speciaal* (the same but with ketchup or curry ketchup instead of satay).

You don't need to order *patatje* double-fried – that's the Dutch standard and what makes them crispy on the outside and fluffy on the inside.

Where to Eat

Bakkerij Bakery selling bread and pastries.

Bruin café Brown cafe; traditional drinking den with fried snacks called *borrelhapjes* (so-called 'brown fruit').

Coffeeshop *Not* a cafe but a cannabis shop; sometimes serves small snacks.

Eetcafé Traditional pub-cafe serving meals.

Markt Town square or market.

Koffiehuis Espresso bar or cafe (distinguishable from a coffeeshop).

Slagerij Butcher.

Kaaswinkel Cheese shop.

Kroeg Pub or bar serving drinks and often snacks.

Vijshandel/ Viswinkel Fish delicatessen/monger.

Wijnhuis Traditional wine tavern.

Wijnhandel Wine shop.

MENU DECODER

Menukaart Menu

Voorgerecht Starter

Hoofdgerecht Main

Bijgerecht Side dish

Borrelhapjes Bar snacks

Nagerecht Dessert

Ontbijt Breakfast

Middageten Lunch

Avondeten Dinner

Vegetarisch Vegetarian

Frites or frietjes Fries

Soep Soup

Salade Salad

Groenten Vegetables

Vis Fish

Kip Chicken

Vlees Meat

Rundvlees Beef

Varkensvlees Pork

Vatbier Draft beer

Fles Bottle

Glas Glass

Sap Juice

Met ijsblokjes With ice

Wijn Wine

Mousserende wijn Sparkling wine

Koffie Coffee

Bruisend water Sparkling water

Kraanwater Tap water

Taart Cake

Dagelijks menu Daily special

Een portie One portion

Zelfbediening Self-service

Reservering Reservation

Bestelling Order

Hier eten Dine in

Om mee te nemen Takeaway

Huisgemaakt Homemade

Zoet Sweet

Zout Salty

Pittig Spicy

Warm Warm

Koud Cold

Lactosevrij Lactose-free

Glutenvrij Gluten-free

Alcoholvrij Alcohol-free

Rekening Bill

Fooi Tip

Wachttijd Waiting time

Table Etiquette

Sitting down to eat, the Dutch keep dining polite. It's customary to say, *'Eet smakelijk'* (enjoy your meal) before digging in and to wait for the host or hostess to start eating first. When toasting, say *'Proost!'* and maintain eye contact. To show you're finished, place your knife and fork parallel on your plate.

_{FROM LEFT: PAULISTA/SHUTTERSTOCK, ANNA MALOVERJAN/SHUTTERSTOCK}

HOW MUCH FOR...

Small frites to go
€3

Michelin-starred dinner
€150–200

Cappuccino
€3.50

200g of cheese
€4

Pint of beer
€4

Craft beer
€6

Shot of jenever (gin)
€4

Order of bitterballen
€6

HOW TO...

Go Dutch with a Group

It's customary for whoever's inviting to pay for the meal – unless you're dining in a group, then expect to 'go Dutch', where everyone splits the bill. In many sit-down establishments, when you ask to pay up, servers ask upfront if it should be separate bills (*aparte rekening*) or one (*één rekening*) altogether. The fastest way of paying in a group is by splitting the bill evenly among the number of diners. Tipping is customary, but not obligatory. Typically, people round the bill up or leave a small tip, so if you're paying up in a group, make sure to discuss your approach (does everyone decide their own tip, or, if you're splitting the bill evenly, should it be calculated on top already?), so servers get their fair due.

A History of Fair Finance

The practice of 'going Dutch' supposedly originated during the 17th-century hostilities of the Anglo-Dutch Wars. Dutch merchants, taking an egalitarian approach, evenly shared expenses with trading partners to foster goodwill.

If you're going Dutch, it's always good to have a few euros on hand (in different denominations) for paying up, too. One person might pay the whole bill and have everyone pay them back. In case this person has paid with a Dutch PIN card, handing over cash makes paying them back easy. Another popular option is settling up over PayPal. An increasing number of establishments accept digital payments only and might not be able to split bills. Mobile payment apps like Tikkie and Splitwise can be a solution for keeping track of shared costs.

BRUIN CAFÉ CULTURE

Better experienced than defined, *gezelligheid* describes the uniquely Dutch concept of conviviality and cosiness. No scene carries this cultural trademark quite like its famous *bruin cafés* (brown cafes), named for their aged, tobacco-stained walls from centuries past. These 'neighbourhood living rooms' boast buzzing pub culture at its prime. While some *bruin cafés* are rowdy with live-music stages and dance floors, more commonly they're teensy and intimate: friends huddled around tables conversing deeply over beer, flickering candles and small platters of *borrelhapjes* (deep-fried snacks).

Pub-going crowds spotlight the Netherlands' concept of egalitarianism, typically counting a wonderful potpourri of *stamgasten* (regulars), locals and travellers of all ages. However, it may be harder than expected to strike up conversations with fellow guests; the norm is mostly about keeping to your own group. Rocking up in free-flowing later hours or sitting among the barstool congregators brings better luck, as do themed nights for pub trivia and karaoke. Overall, cold winter nights and a few pints bring out the truly social creatures that the Dutch are – once they've warmed up to new folks.

Bruin cafés are a tradition dating back as far as the 16th century, and proprietors take great care to preserve their original flair, maintaining antique furniture and affordable prices. In recent years, a new trend has seen new *bruin cafés* modelled with old-timey charm. At first sight, differences may not even be apparent, although they'll never replace the rich history and anecdotes of their elders.

Responsible Travel

Climate Change & Travel

It's impossible to ignore the impact we have when travelling; Lonely Planet urges all travellers to engage with their travel carbon footprint, which will mainly come from air travel. While there often isn't an alternative, travellers can look to minimise the number of flights they take, opt for newer aircrafts and use cleaner ground transport, such as trains. One proposed solution—purchasing carbon offsets—unfortunately does not cancel out the impact of individual flights. While most destinations will depend on air travel for the foreseeable future, for now, pursuing ground-based travel where possible is the best course of action.

The **UN Carbon Offset Calculator** shows how flying impacts a household's emissions

The **ICAO's carbon emissions calculator** allows visitors to analyse the CO_2 generated by point-to-point journeys

Europe's biggest flea market, **IJ Hallen** (ppage 118) in Amsterdam is a wonderland for shopping for pre-loved goods. In colder months, the market moves inside Amsterdam's **NDSM** (ppage 118), a former shipyard warehouse.

Afloat Amsterdam's Singel, quirky **Poezenboot** (cat boat) has been a sanctuary for stray cats since 1966. Fifty-plus cats prance around looking to be adopted. Admission is free, but donations are welcome.

Green Transport

Flat Dutch terrains and fast-charging infrastructure make the Netherlands a prime place for EV driving. Electric transport (vehicles, scooters, mopeds, bicycles, boats) is readily available. Look for pay-per-use providers, often billed by kilometre or minute.

Stop Overtourism

Help Amsterdam with its big overtourism problem by visiting smaller cities, such as Rotterdam, Utrecht and Den Haag. You're bound to love the pace of local Dutch life here, maybe more so than in Amsterdam.

Climate-Friendly Dining

Sustainable dining isn't exclusive to gourmet restaurants. Find plant-based cheeses, natural wines and zero-waste cooking in unexpected places. Amsterdam's **Café de Ceuvel** (p118), sustainable down to its compost toilets, is an obvious standout.

Conscious Canal Cruises

Take a canal cruise without racking up emissions, from pedalos to electric boats. **Plastic Whale** *(plasticwhale.com)* runs 'plastic fishing' trips cleaning polluted waterways aboard boats made from retrieved and recycled plastic waste.

Green Lungs

From one 'Dam to another, manicured parks buzz with local live entertainment. Delight in free summer concerts, like Vondelpark's **Openluchttheater** (p87), plus ponds and wading pools, as well as the usual picnic spots.

Decolonising Tourism

Addressing the Dutch colonial legacy is becoming an important initiative in the Netherlands' museums and galleries. The 'Our Colonial Inheritance' exhibition at **Wereldmuseum Amsterdam** (p104) explores the subject against topical themes such as immigration and identity.

Sleeping Green

Sustainable stays abound at all price points. Conscious Hotels *(conscioushotels.com)* has locations across Amsterdam, including in Vondelpark. Especially cool are stays in repurposed buildings like church-turned-pod-hotel **Bunk** (p121). Look for Green Key *(greenkey.nl)* eco-certification.

Eco-Boating

Discover Friesland on a self-guided electric boat tour from **Jachthaven de Rakken** (p236) in Sneek. Vessels are easy to drive and silent, and some are even 3D-printed right in the village.

Urban Greenery

Opened in 2024, **Koekamp** (p199) is a green expanse in the heart of Den Haag. The park has ponds, a deer enclosure and endless pretty flora with access to cycling and walking paths in the Haagse Bos forest.

Leiden's **Hortus Botanicus** (p214) hosts programmes and exhibitions on sustainable urban gardening and keeps rare, endangered plants.

On **Rederij Lampedusa** (p115), hear immigration stories aboard a former refugee boat.

Green Transition

The Sustainable Development Report ranks the Netherlands in 23rd place worldwide. The country aims for a circular economy by 2050. Prompted by the climate crisis and overtourism, Amsterdam is emerging as an impressively sustainable city.

RESOURCES

amsterdam.nl/en/policy/policy-tourism
Amsterdam's policy addressing overtourism.

government.nl
Info on national sustainability goals.

nederlandfietsland.nl
Netherlands Cycling Country's route planner.

FROM LEFT: ANNASTUDIO.UK/SHUTTERSTOCK, ALEXANDER GAFARRO/SHUTTERSTOCK

LGBTIQ+ Travellers

The Netherlands was the first country to legalise same-sex marriage (in 2001) and is touted as one of the LGBTIQ+ community's favourite destinations, especially Amsterdam, which boasts a year-round calendar of celebrations and awareness events. To say it's a queer hot spot is an understatement. Beyond the capital, rainbow flags fly proudly from homes across the country.

Pride Month

Dutch Pride parades truly encompass the Netherlands' diversity, with all ages, kinds and characters revelling as allies.

Amsterdam Pride, a water-borne spectacle, is also one of the world's biggest, packing hundreds of thousands of revellers around its canals. The second-largest is Rotterdam Pride, though roaring street celebrations take place everywhere from Maastricht and Eindhoven to Groningen and Utrecht. No two Prides happen simultaneously, so hitting all of them is possible. In 2026, World Pride, the premier world event for LGBTIQ+ awareness, promises the biggest party yet.

GAYBOURHOODS

Amsterdam's LGBTIQ+ scene is among the world's largest. During the 1980s, Reguliersdwarsstraat, Amsterdam's gay-bar strip, was established and has been hosting epic booze cruises ever since, though gentrification is increasingly leading to fewer LGBTIQ+ establishments overall. In Nieuwmarkt, pick up all types of fetish wear from boutiques, or stay at an S&M hotel furnished to fulfil bondage needs.

LGBTIQ+ HISTORY

Homomonument

In 1987, Amsterdam established the world's first publicly gay memorial, the **Homomonument**. Dedicated to LGBTIQ+ victims of Nazi persecution, its three large pink granite triangles symbolically resemble the badges forcibly worn in that era. During King's Day, hundreds gather for a proudly queer open-air festival.

Gain historical knowledge on a walking tour of LGBTIQ+ history in Amsterdam (*specialamsterdamtours. nl*). At Pink Point, Amsterdam's official LGBTIQ+ information kiosk (next to the **Homomonument** (ppage 312)), pick up gay and lesbian publications, and plan your visit by perusing party and event flyers.

SEX-POSITIVE SHOP

Amsterdam's **Condomerie**, the world's first condom specialty shop, was inspired as an initiative to increase safe sex awareness during the 1980s AIDS epidemic. Today, the Red Light District stop is mostly for average, wide-eyed kinds of tourists. Still, it stocks a wide selection of vibrantly coloured, multi-sized condoms for men and women, plus many more things for experimental play times.

Iconic Gay Bar

Around for more than a decade, **Cafe Kalff** (ppage 161) is a nightlife institution for Utrecht's LGBTQI+ community. The canal-facing pub is open late from Tuesdays to Sundays and regularly hosts events.

Accessible Travel

Most travellers with reduced mobility will find the Netherlands moderately equipped to meet their needs. Budget and midrange hotels, especially in central Amsterdam's older buildings, are limited because of steep and narrow stairwells.

Sightseeing

Most museums and attractions are wheelchair accessible, having lifts or ramps, plus accessible toilets. Noticeable exceptions include **Anne Frank Huis** (p67), **Westerkerk** (ppage 66) and some canal tour boats in Amsterdam.

Accommodation

Many budget and midrange hotels have limited accessibility, especially those canal-side. Older buildings generally have steep, narrow stairs and no lifts, a challenge for travellers of all levels of mobility. Airbnb has limited options.

Airport

Reduced Mobility Rights (*reducedmobility.eu*) is a fabulous resource on accessibility in the EU, including passengers' rights and airline and airport info. Schiphol Airport's website (*schiphol.nl*) also has information on passenger assistance for travellers with reduced mobility.

ROAD TRIPS

Hand-controlled vehicles and vans with wheelchair lifts are available from hire companies at no additional cost. Reserving well in advance is advised. Motorway service stations usually have accessible toilets and designated disabled parking.

TRAINS

Call the service centre for Nederlandse Spoorwegen (NS, Dutch Railways) at 030 235 7822 or visit a service desk to book free, 24/7 boarding and disembarking assistance. Reserve at least 48 hours in advance.

Dining

Restaurants tend to be on ground floors, though 'ground' sometimes includes a few steps and outdoor cobblestones. Particularly in smaller, older establishments, toilets might not be wheelchair accessible or fitted with rails.

Transport

Most train stations have ramps, lifts and accessible toilets. Wheelchairs, scooters and specialised bicycles (including tandem and e-bikes) are allowed onboard for free, but must meet size and weight requirements.

RESOURCES

gvb.nl Wheelchair-accessible public transport info.

accessibletravel.nl Downloadable guide to restaurants, sights and transport routes.

reisinfo.gvb.nl Journey planner including tram, train maps.

wheelmap.org Initiative mapping accessible facilities and toilets.

mobilista.eu Blog for wheelchair-friendly European travel.

mobilityequipment hiredirect.com Hire scooters, walkers and wheelchairs.

wheelchairtravel .org/amsterdam Comprehensive Amsterdam travel guide.

dcdd.nl Dutch Coalition on Disability and Development.

ongehinderd.nl Reviews cross-country points of interest, including museums (Dutch only).

Founded in 2018 by Amsterdam local Josephine Rees, Able Amsterdam (*ableamsterdam.com*) is the most comprehensive accessibility travel guide for a capital city you'll find. She started the blog to address a lack of English-language mobility resources online.

Sustainable Shopping

Antiques, art and attire from vintage to environmentally made and recycled – the Netherlands is fabulous for eco-friendly shopping. The country aims to ensure all textiles are either recycled or sustainably produced by 2050. Take your pick from boutiques embracing green and organic wares, plus circular and pre-loved fashion.

Trendy Shopping Strip

Haarlemmerbuurt (p70), a long neighbourhood thoroughfare of former shipyards, breweries and warehouses, is increasingly emerging as Amsterdam's 'sustainable shopping avenue'. Peruse independent food and fashion boutiques selling everything from slow fashion to natural cosmetics and homeware. You won't find any kitschy souvenirs here, but rather unique take-homes made with love (and to last). Vintage clothing shops also overflow throughout the area.

Sleek Antiques

Amsterdam's antique houses are a dream for maximalism enthusiasts and sustainably minded shoppers alike. The greatest treasure troves of antiques, art and vintage decor are found along the cobblestone streets of the **Spiegel Quarter**. In generations-old shops such as **Kramer Kunst & Antiek**, you'll find everything from paintings to Dutch heritage items like antique Delftware at specialty shops and depots. Indoor markets, for example, the **Antiekcentrum Amsterdam**, are also known for dealing in high-quality finds and rarities.

Flea Markets

The Dutch adore flea markets – the one in Amsterdam's **IJ Hallen** is among Europe's biggest. **Waterlooplein** is a downtown favourite where vendors sell secondhand and artisan-made goods. Fill up a whole bag of secondhand clothes from high piles and racks for just a few euros (bring a reusable bag to avoid plastics). The capital's **Westermarkt** also has over 150 stalls selling clothing and textiles. Haggling for small discounts politely isn't frowned upon.

Secondhand Clothing

Most Dutch cities have their fair share of secondhand stores; even smaller places will have at least one. In Amsterdam, you'll find the highest concentration of well-curated, pre-loved fashion shops around the **Negen Straatjes** area, and especially along Berenstraat. Head to **Figo Vintage** in the Noord neighbourhood–situated in a 1000sqm industrial warehouse, Amsterdam's largest vintage clothing store is a one-stop shop for high-quality items. Popular secondhand chains with locations across several Dutch cities include Vintage Island (vintageisland.nl), Episode (episode.eu) and the non-profit Salvation Army's excellent Reshare (reshare.nl) stores.

Innovative Fashion

Aimed at reducing the amount of textile production and waste, the Dutch government offers good support to sustainable designers and startups. You'll find a lot of stylish home-grown fashion brands with low carbon footprints. Especially in the capital Amsterdam, look out for backpacks, jackets and sneakers made with innovative processes using recycled plastics and even pineapple leather. The Dutch Sustainable Fashion Week (early October), hosting events in various cities across the Netherlands, is the scene's highlight.

CHANGING THE INDUSTRY

The Netherlands is emerging as Europe's leader in creating a more sustainable fashion supply chain. Through the Dutch government's 'Policy Programme for Circular Textile 2025–2030', textile production is becoming increasingly regulated. Since 2023, clothing producers must offer free options for customers to return old textiles (for example, by providing drop-off containers). Anything newly produced must be made from materials that are sustainable, bio-based, fossil-free or recycled.

Nuts & Bolts

OPENING HOURS

We provide high-season opening hours. Hours generally decrease in the shoulder and low seasons.

Banks 9am to 4pm Monday to Friday (sometimes Saturday mornings)

Bars Noon to 1am Sunday to Thursday, to 3am Friday and Saturday

Museums 10am to 5pm daily; some close on Mondays

Post offices 8.30am to 6pm Monday to Friday (sometimes until 8pm and on Saturdays in busier areas)

Restaurants Lunch 11am to 2.30pm, dinner 6pm to 10pm

Shops 10am or noon to 6pm Tuesday to Friday (many shops to 9pm on Thursdays), 10am to 5pm Saturday and Sunday, 1pm to 5pm Monday (if at all).

Supermarkets 8am to 8pm

Smoking

Smoking (any substance) in bars or restaurants (not coffeeshops) is illegal. Since 2024, supermarkets cannot sell tobacco, so cigarettes are usually found only at specialist tobacco shops (*tabakszaken*).

Canal Safety

Most canals have no fences or barriers; people and bicycles regularly fall in.

Public Toilets

Public toilets are uncommon, apart from Amsterdam's 'pee curls' (freestanding public urinals) in high-traffic areas. Plan to duck into cafes, pubs or department stores (ask first!). The standard fee is €1. HogeNood (*hogenood.nl*) maps toilets by location.

GOOD TO KNOW

Time zone
Central European Time (GMT/UTC+1)

Country calling code
31

Emergency number
112

Population
18 million

Electricity
230V/50Hz

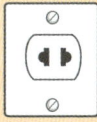

PUBLIC HOLIDAYS

Most museums adopt Sunday hours on public holidays (except Christmas and New Year). Many people treat Remembrance Day (4 May) as a day off. Carnaval is enthusiastically celebrated with huge parties during spring in the Catholic south.

New Year's Day 1 January

Good Friday The Friday before Easter

Easter Sunday in March or April

Easter Monday The Monday following Easter

King's Day 27 April (26 April if the 27th is Sunday)

Ascension Day 40th day after Easter

Whit Sunday/ Pentecost 50th day after Easter

Whit Monday 50th day after Easter Monday

Christmas Day 25 December

'Second Christmas'/ Boxing Day 26 December

Language

As a member of the Germanic language family, Dutch has many similarities with English. If you read our pronunciation guides as if they were English, you'll be understood just fine. It's a rarity for foreigners to make the effort to speak Dutch so if you do, you'll win friends quicker than you can say 'Nederlands' (Dutch).

Basics

Hello. Dag./Hallo. *dakh/ha·loh*
Goodbye. Dag. *dakh*
Yes. Ja. *yaa*
No. Nee. *ney*
Please. Alstublieft. (pol) *al·stew·bleeft*
Please. Alsjeblieft. (inf) *a·shuh·bleeft*
Thank you. Dank u/je. (pol/inf) *dangk ew/yuh*
Excuse me. Excuseer mij. *eks·kew·zeyr mey*
Sorry. Sorry. *so·ree*
What's your name? Hoe heet u/je? (pol/inf) *hoo heyt ew/yuh*
My name is … Ik heet … *ik heyt …*
Do you speak English? Spreekt u Engels? *spreykt ew eng·uhls*
I don't understand. Ik begrijp het niet. *ik buh·khreyp het neet*

Directions

Where's …? Waar is …? *waar is …*
What's the address? Wat is het adres? *wat is het a·dres*
Can you please write it down? Kunt u dat alstublieft opschrijven? *kunt ew dat al·stew·bleeft op·skhrey·vuhn*
Can you show me (on the map)? Kunt u het mij tonen (op de kaart)? *kunt ew het mey toh·nuhn (op duh kaart)*

Signs

Ingang Entrance
Gesloten Closed
Open Open
Uitgang Exit
Toiletten Toilets

Time

What time is it? Hoe laat is het? *hoo laat is het*
It's (10) o'clock. Het is (tien) uur. *het is (teen) ewr*
Half past (10). Half (elf). *half (elf)* (literally: half eleven)
am (morning) 's ochtends *sokh·tuhns*
pm (afternoon) 's middags *smi·dakhs*
pm (evening) 's avonds *saa·vonts*
yesterday gisteren *khis·tuh·ruhn*
today vandaag *van·daakh*
tomorrow morgen *mor·khuhn*

Emergencies

Help! Help! *help*
Leave me alone! Laat me met rust! *laat muh met rust*
I'm sick. Ik ben ziek. *ik ben zeek*
Call a doctor! Bel een dokter! *bel uhn dok·tuhr*
Call the police! Bel de politie! *bel duh poh·leet·see*

Eating & Drinking

What would you recommend? Wat kan u aanbevelen? *wat kan ew aan·buh·vey·luhn*
Cheers! Proost! *prohst*
Delicious! Heerlijk/Lekker! *heyr·luhk/le·kuhr*

NUMBERS	
1	**één** eyn
2	**twee** twey
3	**drie** dree
4	**vier** veer
5	**vijf** veyf
6	**zes** zes
7	**zeven** *zey·vuhn*
8	**acht** akht
9	**negen** *ney·khuhn*
10	**tien** teen

DONATIONS TO ENGLISH

buoy, cookie, cruise, dock, landscape (among many others)

WIDESPREAD ENGLISH

Some 90% to 97% of Dutch citizens speak conversational English.

What's in a Name?

Dutch words in street names and on signs are often combined into a single long place name, which can be tricky for a foreigner to decipher (eg *Derde Leliedwarsstraat* means 'third lily-cross-street').

Hold Your Vowels

Most vowels have a long and a short version, which simply means that you hold vowels for a greater or lesser length of time. It's important to make the distinction between long and short versions, as they can distinguish meaning – eg *maan* means 'moon' but *man* means 'man'.

Local Talk

Hey! He daar! *hey daar*
Great! Fantastisch! *fan·tas·tis*
Sure. Natuurlijk. *na·tewr·luhk*
Maybe. Misschien. *mi·skheen*
No way! Geen sprake van! *kheyn spraa·kuh van*
Go ahead! Doe maar! *doo maar*
Just a minute. Een minuutje. *uhn mee·new·chuh*
Just joking! Grapje! *khrap·yuh*
It's OK. In orde. *in or·duh*
No problem. Geen probleem. *kheyn proh·bleym*
All's OK! Alles kits! *a·luhs kits*

Distinctive Sounds

The pronunciation of Dutch is fairly straightforward. Some vowel sounds are a bit trickier for English speakers as they have no equivalent in English. Most common are *eu* (nasal *eu*, similar to the French vowel sound in *heur*) and *ui* (*oey*, similar to the French vowel sound in *oeil*). For consonants, note that *kh* is a throaty sound, similar to the 'ch' in the Scottish loch, *r* is trilled and *zh* is pronounced as the 's' in 'pleasure'.

WHO SPEAKS DUTCH?

Dutch, along with its variants including Flemish (Vlaams) in Belgium and Arfrikaans (in South Africa), is spoken by between 20 and 25 million people worldwide.

Flanders (Belgium) has the same written language but spoken dialects of Flemish (Vlaams) have considerable differences.

Spoken Afrikaans is a somewhat simpler, mutually intelligible form of Dutch. Written forms look more different.

Netherlands
Flanders
Aruba
Suriname
South Africa

STORYBOOK

Our writers delve deep into different aspects of Dutch life

A History of the Netherlands in 15 Places

Shaped by the constant battle with water and a spirit of enterprise and trade.

Abigail Blasi

p320

Meet the Dutch

Fond of a good discussion, the Dutch always tell it like it is – sometimes at their own expense.

Sara van Geloven

p324

Reclaiming Land from Water

Dive into the love and hate relationship that the Dutch have with water

Sara van Geloven

p326

Proud Dutch Rainbows

The first country to legalise same-sex marriage set the 'rainbowprint' for LGBTIQ+ rights progressing.

Barbara Woolsey

p330

Gedogen: The Blind-Eye Principle

The peculiarly Dutch art of tolerance: balancing rules and reality with pragmatism and compromise.

Abigail Blasi

p333

Beyond the Randstad

To understand the Netherlands, you need to look both to the country's powerhouse cities and the provinces that frame them.

Sara van Geloven

p336

Under the (Dutch) Influence

How the Dutch spread their creativity, innovation and influence across the centuries.

Abigail Blasi

p338

Maastricht (p295)
FOTO PARA TI/SHUTTERSTOCK

HISTORY OF THE NETHERLANDS IN
15 PLACES

The Netherlands takes its name from its low-lying topography. More than a quarter of the country sits below sea level, and 17% of its land has been reclaimed from the sea. Its history has been shaped not only by the constant battle with water, but also by a spirit of enterprise and trade. By Abigail Blasi

BOUNDED TO THE east by Germany and to the west by the North Sea, with Belgium (formerly part of the Netherlands) to the south, this mostly horizon-flat country has a key position at the heart of northern Europe. Being at the centre meant the Netherlands was beset by invaders for centuries, with Vikings from Denmark and power-grabbing leaders from France and Germany looking to extend their empires.

The Dutch, with their long maritime and trading history, built prosperity over centuries. The rationalism of the Dutch created optimal conditions for commerce. The Dutch were not averse to conquest either, extending their reach globally during the period known as the Dutch Golden Age, not so golden for those whose death or labour allowed merchants, colonialists and slave owners to accrue enormous wealth. After overstretching themselves so much that the homeland was left vulnerable, the Dutch retreated, withdrawing from overseas territories they had claimed. The country later suffered greatly during Nazi occupation in WWII, with the starving population reduced to eating tulip bulbs. Postwar, the Netherlands slowly rebuilt into a nation where cooperation and pragmatism were paramount, an outlook that has been rocked in recent years as migration and the boundaries of tolerance have become key political issues.

1. Hunebedden, Drenthe
NEW STONE AGE

Hunebedden, megalithic prehistoric burial chambers in today's Drenthe province, supply the earliest evidence of occupation in the Netherlands and are the country's oldest structures. They were built on higher sandy land by farming settlers who came here around 4400 BCE, and the little that's known about their lives has been discerned from the pottery remains. The boulders used to build the structures weigh about 40 tonnes apiece. They're called *hunebedden* because in the past, local people believed the megaliths could only have been built by a race of giants that they called Huynen.

For more on the hunebedden, see p252.

2. DOMunder, Utrecht
CENTURIES OF ROMANS

In the 1st century BCE, the Romans made their move, extending their empire under Julius Caesar and settling here for over four centuries. They conquered a wide region along the Rijn (Rhine) and its tributaries by 59 BCE. Celtic and Germanic tribes initially bowed to Caesar's rule, and Utrecht became a main outpost of the empire. Towns still bear the outlines of Roman occupation, but the most extensive remains are in Utrecht. At the underground site of DOMunder, visitors can trace a few millennia of history through the archaeological remains dating from when there was a Roman fortress here.

For more on DOMunder, see p154.

3. Valkhofpark, Nijmegen
CHRISTIANITY AND THE FRANKS

As the Roman Empire began to wane, the Franks (a Germanic tribe) stepped into the breach. By the 8th century, they had conquered the Low Countries and began forcing the local populace to convert to Christianity in a most un-Christian way. Charlemagne, the first in a long line of Holy Roman emperors, was the most successful Frankish king. He built a palace at Nijmegen, on the site of a former Roman fort, now in the lush Valkhofpark. The empire fell apart after Charlemagne died in 814, and the ruins here are from a later fortress, built by Frederick Barbarossa in the 12th century.

For more on Valkhofpark, see p270.

4. Sassenpoort, Zwolle
HANSEATIC LEAGUE ASCENDANCE

Over time, local lords began to gain power, and by the beginning of the 12th century, Dutch towns with sea access, such as Deventer, Kampen and Zwolle, joined the Hanseatic League, a group of power-ful trading cities. Canal-ringed Zwolle's magnificent Sassenpoort, a crenellated gatehouse, dates from 1409, during this well-preserved medieval town's heyday. The dukes of Burgundy gradually took over the Low Countries, ushering in a period of stability under Duke Philip the Good, who ruled from 1419 to 1467. The 15th century was a prosperous time, booming on the back of shipbuilding and trade.

For more on Sassenpoort, see p275.

5. Oude Kerk, Amsterdam
CATHOLICS VS PROTESTANTS

Oude Kerk, a 13th-century former Catholic church, survived the fire of 1452, which led to new building laws decreeing that only brick and tile be used in future. Not a disciple of the trend of Dutch tolerance, Philip II of Spain, sovereign of Holland in the mid-16th century and an enthusiastic supporter of the Inquisition, cracked down on Protestants. In 1566, Calvinists pillaged Catholic churches in response, stripping them bare, hence the stark appearance of many Dutch church interiors, including this one. Following the revolt, Philip counter-attacked, launching the Eighty Years' War. Various Dutch provinces proclaimed their independence in 1581.

For more on Oude Kerk, see p60.

6. Museum Willet-Holthuysen, Amsterdam
A PROSPEROUS 'GOLDEN AGE'

Despite the turmoil of the 15th and 16th centuries, Dutch merchant cities thrived. Even at the peak of the rebellion, the Spanish had to use Dutch boats for transporting their grain. As peace finally settled, a period of economic prosperity and cultural fruition came to be known as the 'Golden Age', a term that is now thought of as problematic because it ignores the trafficking, slavery and poverty on which vast fortunes were built. Amsterdam's Museum Willet-Holthuysen preserves a beautiful townhouse dating from the end of this period, with lavish interiors hidden behind the handsome but typically unshowy canalside facade.

For more on Museum Willet-Holthuysen, see p79.

Hunebedden, Drenthe (p252

R. DE BRUIJN_PHOTOGRAPHY/SHUTTERSTOCK

7. Wereldmuseum Amsterdam

THE DUTCH EMPIRE

The Dutch East India Company, formed in 1602, quickly monopolised shipping and trade routes to become the largest trading company of the 17th century. It became almost as powerful as a sovereign state, with the ability to raise its own armed forces and establish colonies. Its sister, the Dutch West India Company, traded with Africa and the Americas. Wereldmuseum Amsterdam (the 'World Museum') preserves artefacts from all over the globe, including from former colonies, such as Suriname and Indonesia. A French invasion at home in 1672 was the beginning of the end of the Dutch Empire.

For more on the Wereldmuseum Amsterdam, see p104.

8. Fort St Pieter, Maastricht

NAPOLEON AND NEW DUTCH MONARCHY

Fort St Pieter was built in 1701 to defend against the regular attacks from the French. When a series of struggles between the House of Orange and its democratic opponents led to a civil war in 1785, the French once again seized an opportunity to exploit the infighting. Napoleon renamed the territory the Kingdom of Holland and installed his brother, Louis Bonaparte, as king in 1806. However, Napoleon's failed Russian invasion gave the Dutch the opportunity to establish their own monarchy. Prince Willem VI was crowned King Willem I in 1814, beginning a monarchy that continues to this day.

For more on Fort St Pieter, see p298.

9. Jachthuis Sint Hubertus, Hoge Veluwe National Park

FRUITS OF SOCIAL MOBILITY

King Willem II instigated a constitution that celebrated democratic ideals, which remains the foundation of the Dutch government. No longer a global power, the Netherlands stayed out of WWI, but the country profited by trading with both sides. In the 1920s, the growing affluence of the middle class led to greater social mobility, and the Netherlands embarked on innovative social programmes that targeted poverty and promoted equality. A prominent family during this period, the new-money Kröller-Müllers, had an art nouveau hunting lodge built in their huge private park, with its architecture far more influenced by English aesthetics than the more curvaceous interpretations elsewhere in Europe.

For more on Jachthuis Sint Hubertus, see p268.

10. Batavialand, Lelystad

LAND FROM THE SEA

The Dutch began land reclamation as far back as the 13th century, using dykes, polders (low-lying areas reclaimed from the sea) and drainage. They stepped up the pace during the 17th century, as windmills could be used to pump out water to create new farmland. The most ambitious project came in the 20th century, when the Zuiderzee was dammed, leading to the creation of Flevoland, the world's largest artificial island. Batavialand is a hands-on museum where you can try your hand at building dykes, operating locks and seeing how a polder works, as well as visit the reconstructed 17th-century ship *Batavia*.

For more on Batavialand, see p322.

11. Anne Frank Huis, Amsterdam

WWII OCCUPATION

The Dutch tried to remain neutral during WWII, but in May 1940, the Germans invaded. The advancing Nazis levelled much of central Rotterdam, forcing the Dutch to surrender. The Germans put Dutch industry and farms to work. By 1944, famine took hold in the country, especially in the west and north. Dutch resistance grew during the course of the war, gaining momentum when thousands of Dutch men were taken to Germany and forced to work in Nazi factories. A far worse fate awaited the country's Jews, one of whom was teenager Anne Frank. A visit to the rooms where Anne's family hid before their eventual betrayal is quietly devastating.

For more on the Anne Frank Huis, see p67.

12. Airborne Museum Hartenstein, Oosterbeek

BATTLES IN LEAFY SUBURBS

The British-led Operation Market Garden, an attempt to seize strategic bridges in Axis territory, was a disaster. The Allies were beaten back in the leafy suburb of Oosterbeek, where the fascinating Air-

Z JACOBS/SHUTTERSTOCK

Vondelpark (p86), Amsterdam

borne Museum Hartenstein sits in their former headquarters. Afterwards, the Germans ravaged the country, and mass starvation ensued. Canadian troops finally liberated the country in May 1945. After the war, the Netherlands was shattered economically and spiritually. War trials ensued, in which 66,000 were convicted of collaboration, a fraction of those who were involved. However, many Dutch also risked everything to help Jews during the war.

For more on Airborne Museum Hartenstein, see p266.

13. Euromast, Rotterdam

POSTWAR REBIRTH

During the 1950s, a prosperous country began slowly to reemerge following the destruction of WWII. After disastrous flooding in Zeeland and the southern Netherlands in 1953, a 40-year campaign began to reshape the land and keep the sea forever at bay, with robust defences called the Delta Works. There was also rebuilding on land. Rotterdam's city centre had been largely destroyed by the Luftwaffe, and over the postwar decades, new architecture revitalised this important port city. Its extraordinary Euromast was built in 1960 for the Floriade, a horticultural festival, and has offered panoramic views over the glass-and-steel new city ever since.

For more on the Euromast, see p189.

14. Vondelpark, Amsterdam

SQUATS, HIPPIES AND EQUALITY

The social upheavals of the 1960s were deeply felt in the Netherlands, as they were across much of Europe and North America. Amsterdam became a magnet for hippies and countercultural movements throughout the 1960s and '70s. Amid a severe housing shortage, speculators left properties vacant, leading to a widespread squatting movement. Authorities even designated Vondelpark as a temporary open-air shelter. The country's pragmatic drug policy emerged during this period, when enforcing prohibitions became unrealistic. The rational Dutch were also early adopters of progressive social values. The Netherlands was a pioneer in LGBTIQ+ rights, becoming the first country to legalise same-sex marriage, in 2001.

For more on Vondelpark, see p86.

15. Het Scheepvaartmuseum, Amsterdam

SHAPING THE NETHERLANDS

Migration and the sea have long shaped Dutch society and fuelled the Netherlands' economic growth. In recent decades, however, migration has tested the country's self-image as open and tolerant. The 2002 assassination of anti-immigration politician Pim Fortuyn, and the 2004 killing of filmmaker Theo van Gogh by a Moroccan-Dutch extremist, shocked the nation. In 2023, a right-wing coalition led by Geert Wilders won the election, with political instability since driven by disputes over migration. For a deeper look at the Netherlands' maritime past and colonial legacy, and their impact today, visit Amsterdam's Het Scheepvaartmuseum (Maritime Museum), known for its thought-provoking exhibitions.

For more on Het Scheepvaartmuseum, see p110.

MEET
THE DUTCH

Fond of a good discussion, the Dutch always tell it like it is – sometimes at their own expense. SARA VAN GELOVEN introduces her people.

THE NETHERLANDS IS a small country – by car, you can cross the length of it in four hours and drive from Amsterdam to the German border in less than two. Yet there are 18 million of us, making the place rather cramped. Even in the less inhabited provinces like Drenthe and Zeeland, you'll pretty much always find the next farm or village a stone's throw away.

Living so close together, we've had to become good communicators. Dutch people tend to be direct, and we never shy away from a disagreement. We talk things out until we reach a consensus or, likelier, a compromise. We even have a term for it: *polderen,* named after the reclamation of land from water that necessitated people from all backgrounds to come together to construct dykes back in medieval times.

Often, getting to a compromise can take a while. Considering how small a country it is, it seems a little over the top to have more than 15 political parties. Some of these parties still carry a Christian identity, but the Netherlands is now one of the most secular countries in Europe, with its capital city, Amsterdam, also one of the most multicultural. That diversity is something that's celebrated in our food. Dutch cuisine not being the most exciting, we take pride in our ever-expanding offering of international restaurants.

Age Is Just a Number

The number of people aged 65 or older has increased tenfold in the last century, to make up one in five of the population. It's estimated that in 2040, almost five million Dutch people will be aged 65 or older.

Blessed with a passport that's consistently ranked as one of the top in the world and a general proficiency in English, we also pride ourselves on being internationally oriented and have a long history of flourishing trade and travel. This has a dark side, too – it's only recently that we've started addressing our colonial past, the horrors of slavery in what for years was called our 'Golden Age', and the structural racism that sadly exists in our society to this day. Some important steps are being taken, such as the king issuing a formal apology and ongoing decolonial efforts, but there is a long way to go.

Despite our fair share of other challenges, such as the nationwide shortage of housing, excess of nitrogen and polarisation crises (and that's not to mention rising sea levels because of climate change), we're also some of the luckiest people on Earth because we get to live here.

The Dutch consistently rank high in international reports on wealth and happiness. We love getting out and about in our bike-friendly cities and towns, and are always in for *gezelligheid* (conviviality). Whatever challenges the future holds, we know how to celebrate the good life, from one of the biggest Pride parades to King's Day, where everybody joins in the revelry whether they're a monarchist or not.

CLOCKWISE FROM TOP LEFT: ARCADY/SHUTTERSTOCK, MILA SUPINSKAYA GLASHCHENKO/SHUTTERSTOCK, JAN KRANENDONK/SHUTTERSTOCK, FOKKE BAARSSEN/SHUTTERSTOCK

THE MORE I TRAVEL, THE MORE I APPRECIATE MY COUNTRY

After spending the first 20 years of my life in the northern city of Groningen, I couldn't wait to get out and see the world. I was bored with the flat fields, sheltered culture and having to fill in a form for everything. I was ready for an adventure.

Over the next 15 years, I travelled to every continent except Antarctica to test how far my good English would get me and where my passport could take me (pretty much anywhere), and I came to appreciate how very privileged I am to have been born Dutch.

Even though I still love to travel, I now appreciate my country so much more, from the neat roads where bikes are king to the cities that are green and liveable. I may have even grown a little fond of all those annoying forms.

Clockwise from top left: Cyclists, Amsterdam (p47); Dutch couple; Boating, Giethoorn (p271); Carnival dancer, Rotterdam (p176)

RECLAIMING LAND FROM WATER

Dive into the complicated relationship that the Dutch have with water: it's a love and hate affair. By Sara van Geloven

THINK OF A Dutch landscape and chances are your imagination conjures up a flat field, covered in lush grass or tulips, criss-crossed with straight canals and towered over by a windmill or two. It's a land largely shaped by water and likely for many years wasn't land at all.

Keeping Feet Dry

Not so long ago, much of the Netherlands consisted of peat bogs, and the sea had free range. Floods regularly washed over the land at high tide. Early farmers built artificial mounds from clay and sod to re-treat to with their livestock when the water came. Roman author Pliny the Elder wrote: 'Twice a day, the sea floods a large part of their territory, so it's unclear wheth-er it should be counted as land or sea. The pitiful people build hills just high enough to keep their houses dry. At high tide, it looks like they are shipwrecked'.

These mounds are called *terpen, wierden or werven,* and they were numer-ous. In the northernmost provinces of Friesland and Groningen, the flat, pasto-ral landscape is still dotted with ancient towns that are noticeably elevated. Some even formed the basis of cities, such as Leeuwarden. It was the start of the Dutch moulding the land to fit their needs. What came next would change the shape of the Netherlands – literally meaning the low-lying lands – forever.

Creating New Land

More than 2000 years ago, the first *dijken* (dykes) – long walls or embankments – were constructed to protect patches of land from rivers and the sea. But they weren't numerous yet. That would change after the 11th century, when more dykes were painstakingly constructed using clay, sand, wooden stilts and grass until almost the entire coastline of the Netherlands was embanked around the year 1300.

But peat bogs remained. On large swathes of land where so much peat had been excavated, the ground level had sunk, sometimes metres beneath the water lev-el of the large rivers in the south and the North Sea to the west. This caused flood-ing, so a solution had to be found.

In the 14th century, people started build-ing inland dykes around an area near Gouda and, via an intricate system of waterways and sluices, moved the surplus of water to the nearby rivers. Because the rivers were embanked as well, the water could not flow back. Thanks to the sluiceway sys-tem, the water levels within the drained area could now be controlled – the first polder was created.

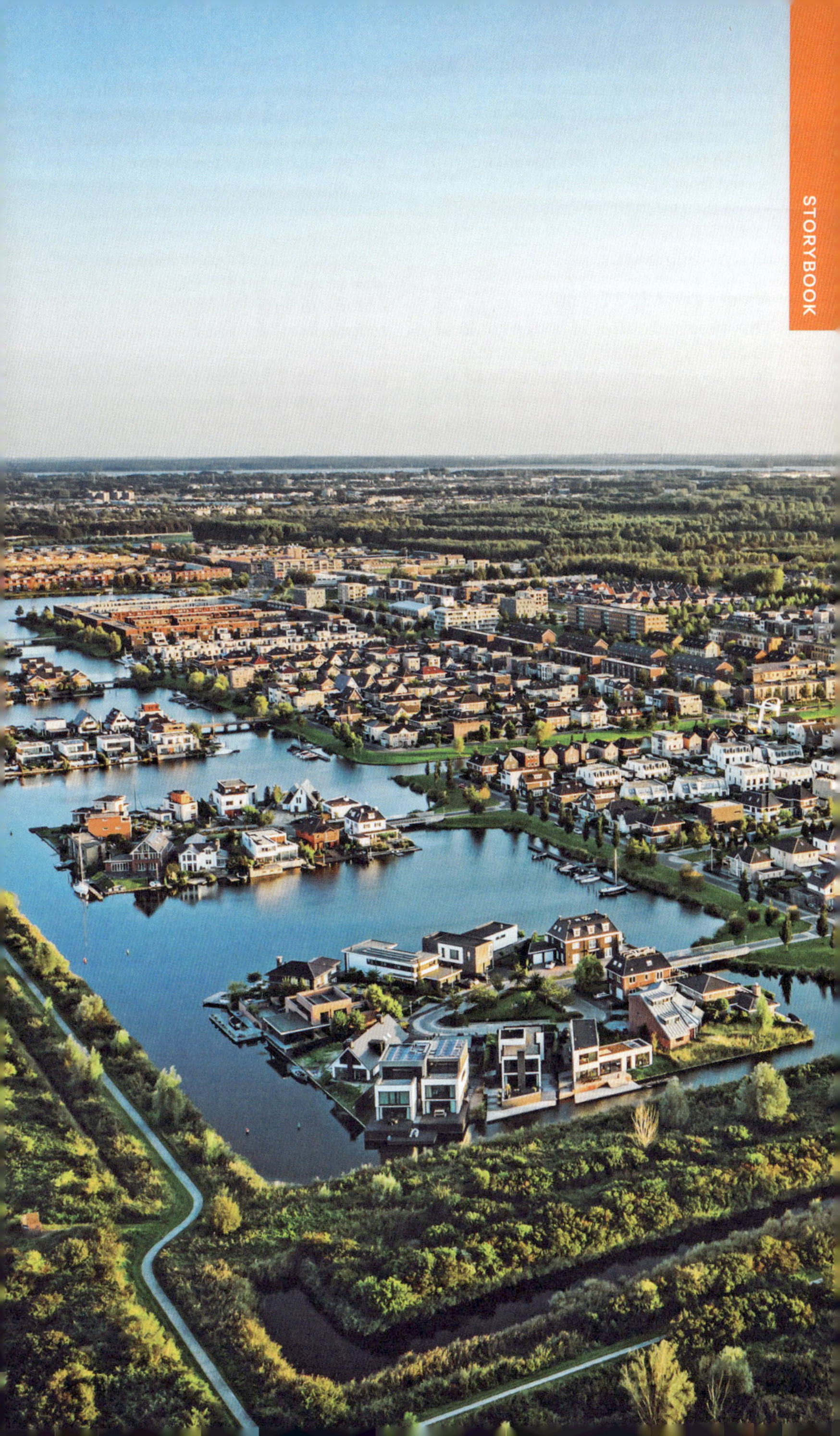

It wasn't long before the sluices were aided by windmills that could pump large amounts of water. Often, many windmills were placed in a row, each one a little higher than the other, so water could be transported from lower to higher elevation. It allowed the Dutch to not only drain swamps easily, but also to reclaim fertile land from metres-deep lakes.

Water as an Ally & Enemy

This precise control of water could also be used as a military defence strategy, by flooding strategic sections of land with enough water to make it impenetrable for soldiers and horses, but not deep enough for boats to cross. The strategy was used in multiple places, most famously in the Nieuwe Hollandse Waterlinie and Stelling van Amsterdam.

From 1815 to 1940, 200km of inundation channels, sluices, dykes, forts and castles were connected to form one big defence line of Holland (the most populous western provinces of the country). It was used as an effective deterrent in WWI, when the Netherlands was allowed to remain neutral, but when it was activated on the eve of WWII, the system proved hopelessly outdated – German planes could simply fly over it. Today, the remnants of the Nieuwe Hollandse Waterlinie and Stelling van Amsterdam are UNESCO World Heritage sites.

Despite the great degree of control of water levels, the threat of flooding remained. Throughout the centuries, there have been many dyke breaches. The dykes enclosing the Zuiderzee, a former sea extending about 100km inland between North Holland and Friesland, proved especially susceptible to storm surges and floods. As early as the 17th century, plans were drafted to build a massive barrier dam to close off the Zuiderzee. But to attempt such an undertaking was beyond the technology of the time.

Draining the Zuiderzee

In the late 19th century, the plans were revisited when a new invention, the steam engine, was used to successfully drain the large Haarlemmermeer. At the turn of the century, civil engineer Cornelis Lely set out by boat across the Zuiderzee to carry out tests of the seabed to see which parts were viable as arable land. He drafted a detailed plan to build a barrier dam and create new polders of a size that were unlike anything attempted before. There was just one problem: the costs would be astronomical. The plans didn't convince the government and were archived.

Several years later, in 1916, a powerful winter storm hit the country, and many of the Zuiderzee dykes burst. It led to a renewed call for the government to act. Conveniently, there was also a new Minister of Transport and Water Management with inside knowledge: none other than Cornelis Lely himself. He dusted off the plans he'd created years earlier and advocated once more for the creation of a barrier dam and multiple new polders. This time, he was successful.

Work started on the long dam to connect the provinces of Noord-Holland and Friesland, and in 1932, the Afsluitdijk was finally completed, turning the Zuiderzee into the freshwater lake IJsselmeer. Lely didn't live to see it – two years before, he passed away while working at his desk. His name lives on in Lelystad, the capital of the province Flevoland that was built entirely out of polders and completed in 1968. An astonishing 20% of the Netherlands today is reclaimed land.

Feats of Civil Engineering

The 32km-long Afsluitdijk is a sight to behold and so are the Deltawerken (Delta Works), recognised as one of the Seven Wonders of the Modern World by the American Society of Civil Engineers. They're some of the biggest flood protection systems on Earth and were part of the Delta-plan, created after a terrible storm hit the country in 1953, leading to the worst floods in recent history: the Watersnoodramp.

That winter, a dangerous cocktail of spring tide and a northwesterly storm made the seawater level rise to almost 5m above the mean. The dykes were not made to withstand this, weakened by a lack of maintenance during and following WWII, and they burst at more than 150 sites in the southern provinces of Zeeland, Zuid-Holland and Noord-Brabant. The floods came in the middle of the night and without warn-

Afsluitdijk (p229)
STEVE PHOTOGRAPHY/SHUTTERSTOCK

ing. Some 1863 people lost their lives, and 70,000 more were displaced.

The Deltaplan was created to drastically decrease the chances of a disaster like the Watersnoodramp happening again. Central to the plan was to shorten the coastline by 700km. This project was realised by building surge barriers and sluice gates that can be closed when a high tide is expected. The 9km-long Oosterscheldekering in Zeeland, built in 1986, is the biggest and most famous of the Deltawerken. On average, it's closed as a precaution about once per year.

Preparing for an Uncertain Future

In the years since building the Delta Works, coastal protection has continuously been improved, with dykes being raised (the country's tallest measures 11.5m) and keeping the natural dune landscapes healthy. The Dutch are now trying to work with nature instead of against it. In 2023, a migration river for fish was opened at the Afsluitdijk, restoring the connection between the Waddenzee (Wadden Sea) and IJsselmeer, so salmon and eel can migrate to rivers again.

In the delta that covers much of the south of the country, where some of Europe's biggest rivers reach the North Sea, floodplains have been created to give the rivers enough room. Meanwhile, the many waterways in the country are still used for drainage. Pumps run continuously to help keep feet dry.

This water management is taken seriously, and the Dutch even vote for the *waterschappen* (water council) in regional elections. Many decisions that the water management bodies have to make are political. For example, do you keep the water level low so that fields are relatively dry and farmers can plough them more easily, or do you make it higher to protect fragile vegetation better and help prepare for longer periods of drought?

These decisions are even more important now that the effects of climate change are increasing. Extreme rainfall in summer 2021 led to serious floods in the southernmost province of Limburg. With heavy rain and storms predicted to happen more often and the sea level rising, while one-quarter of the country already lies below it, the Dutch have their work cut out for them. But if its long history of innovation in water management is any indication, this country is ready to rise to the challenge.

PROUD DUTCH RAINBOWS

In 2001, the Netherlands became the world's first country to legalise same-sex marriage, setting a blueprint (or rather, 'rainbowprint') for progressing LGBTIQ+ rights. By Barbara Woolsey

THE NETHERLANDS IS renowned as the world's best host – both Amsterdam and Rotterdam are famous for their jam-packed, all-year calendars of festivals spanning music, performance and fashion across grand venues and parks. But one event has been designed to encompass these elements and more. The country's most fabulous celebration takes the (rainbow) cake: the annual Amsterdam Pride.

Dutch society has long believed that 'love is love'. In 2001, the Netherlands became the first country to legalise same-sex marriage, and Amsterdammit, they're proud of that. The capital's Pride is among the world's biggest, and flaunts the only waterborne parade. Taking place in late July and early August, the spectacle sees 500,000 revellers rejoicing on downtown canals. In 2026, Amsterdam Pride is putting on its most bedazzling performance yet, hosting WorldPride. Splashier entertainment and doubled attendance numbers promise an incredible energy.

A Spectacle of Inclusivity

Aside from seas of rainbow flags, Amsterdam Pride serves everything you'd expect: 80-some multi-sized boats and dinghies, decorated to the nines, float across canals blaring disco, drag lip-syncs and eye candy (including shirtless 'seamen').

The best part is that Amsterdam Pride – and other Prides across Dutch cities – are enjoyed by everyone. Locals, known for festooning their windows with rainbow flags year-round, make this party. Residents spectate from canal homes, adding a special, irreplicable charm. Groups huddle on tiny balconies, and everyone seems a little tipsy – more so after raising glasses

for merry toasts with cheering street passersby. Public displays of drunkenness are common, but Pride is as family-friendly as a street party can get; abundant pee curls (special Dutch public urinals) are a fine example. The day after the parade, the city centre's cobblestone streets are almost eerily clean, giving no hint of a thousands-strong orgy of sequins, sparkles and feathers.

How the Dutch do 'True Freedom'

The Netherlands' LGBTIQ+ history started long before legalising same-sex marriage. Dutch culture is shaped by what's known as 'true freedom', a value for open-mindedness, acceptance and tolerance that informs the legal framework and, therefore, society. For example, sex work and cannabis are not only allowed, but also are highly visible and integrated aspects of public life.

Unprejudiced views on diverse LGBTIQ+ lifestyles make sense in such a social fabric, but it wasn't always that way. Mostly, homosexuality has been illegal. Tolerance has been historically cultivated by a national obsession with discovering other cultures. That said, the colonisation of faraway places is part of a dark past. Today, colonialism has created a vibrant, multicultural population, though it displays that seafaring Dutch open-mindedness was not universal, at least regarding non-white and non-European people.

Rather, the bulging purse strings of the Dutch merchant class saw great wealth funnelled into developing highbrow European culture, fuelling national affinities for visual art and science. Flamboyant intellectuals, from Impressionist painters to physicists, expanded a cultural respect for zany creativity and diverging perspectives.

Still, homosexuality was a public offence and punishable by execution, mainly for religious reasons. In 1579, the Union of Utrecht made the Netherlands an unprecedented stronghold for religious diversity in Europe, and hundreds of pilgrims began voyaging to the United States from here, fleeing religious persecution in England. While Calvinism was the official religion, other Protestant denominations, Jews and Catholics freely practised their faith, and all agreed that homosexuality was corrupt.

The rules changed with French annexation, and the adoption of the Napoleonic Code decriminalised homosexuality in 1811. For about a century, sodomy laws stayed off the books until recriminalisation in 1911. Still, an underground LGBTIQ+ movement emerged, and in the early 20th century, Amsterdam's first gay bars were established.

WWII brought in 'new management' again with the 1940 Nazi invasion. While the Netherlands tried to remain neutral, only observing the oppression of Jews, homosexuals and intellectuals across the border, the government was given an ultimatum: surrender or be destroyed. They chose the former, but air-borne bombers were already en route.

Postwar, the LGBTIQ+ rights movement, like much of the Netherlands itself, had to rebuild. The reconstruction of buildings in the 1950s and '60s dovetailed with a redesigning of attitudes, and homosexuality became legal, this time to stay. An important remodelling of legal frameworks began, with the biggest change being the 1971 repeal of Article 248bis. Homosexuality was no longer to be treated as a mental illness, and a military ban on homosexuals was lifted.

From Persecution to Celebration

The 1980s were the heyday of LGBTIQ+ visibility, primarily with Reguliersdwarsstraat, still Amsterdam's happening gay-bar strip. In 1987, Amsterdam established the world's first publicly gay memorial about 1km away: the Homomonument, three large pink granite triangles, is dedicated to victims of Nazi persecution for sexual orientation. It's the home of a vivacious queer open-air festival on the Netherlands' favourite public holiday, King's Day.

The Netherlands continued to make strides in LGBTIQ+ rights, from movement towards banning conversion therapy to granting refugees asylum based on sexual orientation and gender identity. In 1993, parliament enacted a landmark anti-discriminatory Equal Rights Law before the 2001 legalisation of same-sex marriage. Since 2023, sexually oriented discrimination is prohibited by law. In 2015, the ban on blood donations from gay men was lifted.

Despite this, challenges to LGBTIQ+ advocacy persist, particularly in substantiating current legal frameworks to reflect diverse rights for transgender and intersex individuals. The Netherlands' robust base of Conservative Christian parties and their long-time voters, while opposing LGBTIQ+ discrimination, is a clear stumbling block. The Netherlands' autonomous overseas territories also don't share the same set of beliefs. Aruba and the Netherlands Antilles, highly influenced by the Roman Catholic Church, initially resisted recognising same-sex marriages. In 2007, the Dutch Supreme Court ruled that marriage documents from one part of the kingdom should be accepted throughout, leading to a begrudging recognition in Aruba.

On the World Stage

In 2026, Amsterdam's first time hosting WorldPride dovetails with important Dutch LGBTIQ+ rights history: the 25th anniversary of legalised same-sex marriage, 30 years of Amsterdam Pride and 80 years of COC Netherlands, the Netherlands' LGBTIQ+ advocacy organisation. Started in 1997, WorldPride is coordinated by the Interpride organisation and takes place every few years in a different city (past hosts have included Rome, Toronto, Washington, DC and Madrid). Cities bid for hosting duties and are chosen by a globally representative committee.

The special event will see Pride celebrations in Amsterdam extend pageantry from one week to two and encompass a girthier cultural programme, including a music festival and a pop-up WorldPride Village for activist and scholarly meets. A million attendees (possibly more) ensure a once-in-a-lifetime party atmosphere.

GEDOGEN:
THE BLIND-EYE PRINCIPLE

The peculiarly Dutch art of tolerance: balancing rules and reality with pragmatism and compromise. By Abigail Blasi

COFFEESHOPS SELLING MARIJUANA in various forms reflect the Dutch concept of *gedogen:* tolerating technically illegal acts that don't harm society. Euthanasia and prostitution are legal and strictly regulated. Far from being unusually permissive, the Netherlands often adopts a pragmatic approach: permitting certain behaviours while maintaining control through clear legal frameworks.

Tolerance Is Big Business

Gedogen as a conceit for coexistence can be traced back to various roots, one being the schism between Catholics and Protestants during the Reformation in the 16th century, the other the 80 Years' War with the Spanish. During those years of turmoil, trade continued to boom in the country, with this peculiarly pragmatic approach helping to oil the wheels of commerce.

During the 17th and 18th centuries, Calvinist, Huguenot and Jewish traders and refugees fleeing persecution came to the Dutch Republic to live, and they were broadly tolerated. The Calvinist majority banned public worship by Catholics, but turned a blind eye to hidden churches. One of these remains as a museum in Amsterdam, the Museum Ons' Lieve Heer op Solder (Our Lord in the Attic). Over time, the Calvinist Protestants came to dominate the north, while the Catholics remained in the south, which in 1830 became Belgium.

Philosophical Roots

Baruch Spinoza, the most enduringly influential of the Dutch philosophers, was Dutch-Portuguese, born in Amsterdam in 1632. His thinking on religion and state provided a solid backdrop to this uniquely Dutch approach to life's knottier problems. He wrote in his *Tractatus Theologico-Politicus* that it's impossible to seek to control individuals because they will end up doing what they want to in any case: 'Everyone is by absolute natural right the master of his own thoughts, and thus utter failure will attend any attempt in a commonwealth to force men to speak only as prescribed by the sovereign despite their different and opposing opinions'.

The Polder Model

The concept of *gedogen* is adjacent to the polder model, a political term coined at the end of the 20th century and named after areas of drained land to describe the consensus-based process of negotiation through compromise and discussion, and accepting that no one is going to be completely happy with the outcome. If you're

333

living among polders, it is essential to work together to maintain the protective dykes to survive. The challenge of living in areas prone to flooding is also thought to be among the sources of the famous Dutch directness. You can't mess around with hidden meanings if you have flooding to keep at bay.

Coffeeshops

Perhaps the most significant example of *gedogen* is the rise of Dutch coffeeshops, which openly sell and permit the consumption of cannabis under a policy of tolerance rather than full legalisation. This approach began in the 1970s in response to growing countercultural movements, particularly in Amsterdam. Authorities concluded that prosecuting people for cannabis use was not effective and that a tolerated cannabis market might prevent marijuana from acting as a gateway to harder drugs.

For decades, Dutch drug policy has focused on harm reduction, with notable results. As of 2023, the Netherlands had approximately 64.6 prisoners per 100,000 inhabitants, making it one of the countries with the lowest incarceration rates in Europe.

Coffeeshops operate under strict conditions: they may sell up to 5g per customer per day, cannot admit or sell to minors, must not sell hard drugs or cause public nuisance, and are limited to a maximum stock of 500g at any given time. In recent years, there have been increased efforts to limit the number of coffeeshops, especially in Amsterdam during its struggles with overtourism. In Amsterdam, the number of coffeeshops has declined from around 350 in the 1990s to about 165 in 2024.

While coffeeshops help keep cannabis users out of the criminal justice system, they are still required to obtain their stock from illegal sources. This ongoing reliance on the black market has fostered links to organised crime. In recent years, this issue has become a growing concern, prompting the launch of a government-run experiment to create a regulated cannabis supply chain, with pilots in select municipalities.

The Future of (In)tolerance

In recent decades, the Dutch principle of *gedogen* has faced growing challenges. A series of political assassinations in the early 2000s rocked the country's tolerant self-image. Right-wing politician Pim Fortuyn was shot dead by an environmental activist in 2002. Two years later, filmmaker Theo van Gogh was murdered by an Islamist extremist over his film *Submission,* which criticised the treatment of women in Islamic societies.

The Netherlands has a long history of migration. In the 1960s, the Netherlands encouraged immigration as manufacturing boomed, inviting temporary guest workers from Spain, Portugal, Greece, the former Yugoslavia, Türkiye and Morocco. But the tide of public opinion began to turn in the early 21st century. Politicians such as Fortuyn and later Geert Wilders stoked anti-immigrant sentiment. Tolerance, it seemed, was possible only if people didn't feel their lives might be affected. In the years since, polder model coalition governments have overseen the implementation of some of the most restrictive immigration laws in Europe.

At the same time, a deluge of cheap flights has led to the explosion of short-haul partying tourists and a rise in antisocial behaviour focused on Amsterdam's Red Light District. Left-wing Amsterdam Mayor Femke Halsema plans to move the district to an 'erotic centre' on the outskirts of the city. In favour of drug decriminalisation and rights for sex workers, she is also battling to reduce overtourism and improve conditions for residents. Coffeeshops have come under increased restrictions, and since 2011, only locals showing a 'weed pass' are allowed to buy marijuana at shops outside Amsterdam. Since 2017, coffeeshops must be at least 350m from a school, and this has led to the closure of 10% of the country's coffeeshops.

As the Netherlands adapts to 21st-century pressures, *gedogen,* the hallmark of Dutch pragmatism, still defines its culture and governance. But will this tradition of tolerance continue to make room for far-right, restrictive ideas instead of the liberal values it once upheld?

Coffee shop, Amsterdam (p46)

TUPUNGATO/SHUTTERSTOCK

BEYOND
THE RANDSTAD

To understand the Netherlands, you need to look both to the country's powerhouse cities and the provinces that frame them. By Sara van Geloven

HALF OF THE Dutch population lives in just a quarter of the country. The Randstad is home to the four biggest cities: Amsterdam, Den Haag, Rotterdam and Utrecht. It's the country's political and cultural centre, and where most visitors head. But in recent years, the appeal of life outside the Randstad has grown.

A Country of Cities

The Netherlands has, for a large part of its history, been markedly urban. For centuries, its wealth was built on a network of trading towns and cities, clustered around rivers and the Zuiderzee (now IJsselmeer), connecting them to the trade routes of the North Sea. To this day, medium-sized cities dot the map, rarely more than half an hour apart. Unlike countries with a single dominant metropolis, the Netherlands consists of a patchwork of cities and towns

not unlike the spots on the black-and-white cows that are so numerous here.

This landscape bred both cooperation and rivalry. Cities competed to see who could build the tallest church tower, and fought over trade rights and, more recently, jobs. Between 1960 and 1990, government services were deliberately moved to cities outside of the Randstad to provide more employment.

The Heart of the Randstad

The Randstad – literally meaning 'edge' or 'rim city' – got its name in the 1930s, when Albert Plesman, an aviation pioneer and later the director of KLM, flew over Holland (the provinces of Noord-Holland and Zuid-Holland). He described how he saw a ring of urban areas wrapped around a largely rural interior, *Het Groene Hart* (the green heart). Today, you can still see this horseshoe form on a map when you look at the urban centres that form the Randstad: Den Haag and Rotterdam to the southwest, Amsterdam and Almere to the north, and Utrecht to the east. All these cities are interlinked by railways and motorways, making travel between them a breeze.

Schiphol Airport and the country's busiest railway hubs sit squarely in the region, which is also home to some of the Netherlands' biggest draws: Amsterdam's canals and parks, Den Haag's parliament buildings and museums, Rotterdam's modern skyline, and Utrecht's medieval old town. So it doesn't come as a surprise that it's estimated that more than two-thirds of international visitors to the Netherlands never even leave the region.

A Tale of Two Countries

But the Netherlands doesn't stop at the Randstad's edge, and people outside it often use the term with a note of bitterness or mockery. Bitterness because residents outside the region, in what is sometimes called *de provincie* (the provinces), say that national media (located in Hilversum, in the Randstad) and Den Haag seat of the Dutch government have forgotten about them. The argument's not without merit. Much investment and infrastructure flows to the four biggest cities, while other cities feel left behind. In Groningen province, earthquakes as a result of lucrative natural gas fracking were ignored for many years while they caused significant damage to the homes of the people living there. In 2024, drilling was finally ended.

In recent years, provincials have started to speak up, as farmer protests gripped the nation and right-wing populist party BBB (the Farmer-Citizen Movement) sent shockwaves through the country with an unexpected victory in provincial elections in 2023; thus, somewhat tying into the stereotype expressed by some Randstedelingen that everyone in the provinces is a farmer (only 2% of the population actually works in agriculture). Meanwhile, the provincials mock people living in the Randstad for being out-of-touch *havermelkelite* ('oat milk elite') who don't have a clue where their food comes from and pay a ridiculous amount in rent to live in cramped flats far removed from green spaces.

Life Beyond the Ring

Yet it's not all hard feelings. People outside of the Randstad pride themselves on being self-sufficient and more in touch with what makes life worth living, boasting better social coherency, more time spent in nature and less *haasten* (rushing) all the time. Those are all attractive qualities for visitors, too, who venture outside the Randstad more and more. They come for the bountiful green spaces, such as the forests of the Veluwe and Brabant, Drenthe's three serene national parks, or for a scenic cruise on the bountiful canals and lakes in Friesland or Overijssel's Weerribben-Wieden National Park. Of course, travellers also come to visit the splendid provincial capitals, such as Groningen, Den Bosch and Maastricht, all of which pack big-city energy without the crowds.

Shifting Perspectives

More Dutch people have begun to appreciate the surrounding provinces. Affordable housing and pandemic-era work-from-home policies have started to entice many to relocate to the north, east and south. On social media, these 'import provincials' gush about the availability of fresh produce, leafy parks and cosy markets. It's a welcome influx for regions threatened by an aging and declining population, but there are side effects, too, such as the inflation of local house prices.

Coincidingly, the Dutch tourism board has launched campaigns to spread visitors more evenly, encouraging trips to places outside of the Randstad to relieve pressure on Amsterdam, which is struggling to deal with its rising visitor numbers. Of course, iconic places like the country's capital will remain a first port of call on many itineraries, but it's a shame to stop there when a train ride north, east or south across flat farmland brings so many surprises.

The Netherlands being as compact as it is also means that Randstedelingen and provincials are more alike than they care to admit. They might snipe at each other across the invisible border, but together they form a country where contrasts are never more than a few hours apart.

FROM LEFT: TRAVEL WITH CO/SHUTTERSTOCK, HANOHIKI/SHUTTERSTOCK

UNDER THE (DUTCH) INFLUENCE

A small country with a big footprint: how the Dutch spread their creativity, innovation and influence across the centuries. By Abigail Blasi

DESPITE ITS MODEST size, the Netherlands has had an outsized global impact, from artists like Van Gogh and Rembrandt to its colonial legacy and world-changing inventions. Den Haag is the home of international justice, while Dutch innovations range from gin to Bluetooth. Even the humble orange carrot owes its modern form to the Dutch.

Foreign Influence

The Dutch were ruthlessly effective colonisers, driven by commerce, maritime expertise and business acumen. In 1602, the Dutch East India Company (VOC), considered the world's first multinational corporation, expanded Dutch interests in Asia. It soon established a powerful and often violent presence in what is now Indonesia, including Java, Sumatra and Bali. The spice trade brought huge prosperity at home, but it relied on systems of exploitation, forced labour and military dominance. Dutch rule in Indonesia lasted until the 20th century, leaving a deep and complex legacy still felt today.

A few decades later, the Dutch began exploring the Atlantic. The Dutch West India Company played a major role in the transatlantic slave trade, establishing colonies in the Caribbean, along the West African coast and in the Americas. In North America, the Dutch founded the colony of New Netherland, with its capital New Amsterdam on what is now Manhattan. Though the British seized it in 1664 and renamed it New York, Dutch influence endures in names like Harlem (from Haarlem), Brooklyn (Breukelen) and Flushing (Vlissingen). Even Wall St is named after a Dutch-built defensive wall.

Elsewhere, Dutch explorers and cartographers scattered Dutch names across the globe. New Zealand was named after Zeeland, Mauritius after Prince Maurice of Nassau, and Cape Horn after the city of Hoorn.

In 1652, the VOC established a supply station at the Cape of Good Hope, which grew into the Cape Colony. Dutch settlers (Boers, meaning 'farmers') gradually moved inland, displacing Indigenous communities. Their 17th-century vernacular Dutch evolved into Afrikaans, now one of South Africa's official languages, but the settler structures they helped establish laid the foundations for apartheid centuries later.

The Protestant Orange Order, still active in Northern Ireland today, was named after William of Orange, a Dutch Protestant prince who became King of England. The Order's annual marches commemorate its 1690 victory over the Catholic King James II at the Battle of the Boyne, a legacy of religious and colonial conflict that continues to stir political tensions.

From global migration patterns and place names to language, religion and politics, many countries around the world bear the imprint of the Dutch influence overseas.

Art

The Netherlands' 17th-century boom had another side effect: patronage of the arts. As the Catholic Church and the princely states in Italy were able to fund the great art of the Renaissance, so Dutch merchants, citizens and middle-class citizens bankrolled their artists. The type of art they wanted was different, however. The art that flourished here was portraiture, domestic scenes and still lifes. During the 17th century, artists Rembrandt, Vermeer and Hals produced works that offered psychological depth, everyday realism and technical brilliance.

In later centuries, Dutch painting deeply influenced European and American artists. Vermeer's quiet, intimate compositions inspired 19th- and 20th-century painters and photographers alike. Rembrandt's use of light and shadow (chiaroscuro) and psychological depth influenced artists from Goya to Van Gogh, and Hals' brushstrokes foreshadowed the work of the Impressionists.

VAN GOGH'S (1853–90) GENIUS CAUGHT THE WORLD'S IMAGINATION.

Van Gogh's (1853-90) genius caught the world's imagination. The emotional intensity of his work shaped the expressionist and Fauvist movements and beyond, while his life, intimately documented in letters to his brother Theo, was that of the ultimate 'tortured artist'. Piet Mondrian, working in the 20th century, developed grid-like paintings and was likewise hugely influential, a pioneer of abstract art.

Architecture

In Indonesia, South Africa and the Caribbean, Dutch colonial architecture endures as a visible reminder of a complex past, often blending European design with local materials and climatic adaptations. In Curaçao, the UNESCO-listed capital Willemstad has distinctively Dutch gabled buildings in brilliant Caribbean hues.

In more recent decades, the Netherlands has become a global leader in contemporary sustainable architecture. Innovative firms like OMA (Office for Metropolitan Architecture), founded by Rem Koolhaas, and MVRDV are internationally recognised for reimagining urban spaces, with a playful yet practical aesthetic informing buildings such as the CCTV Headquarters in Beijing and BLOX in Copenhagen.

Inventions

The Dutch are renowned for their collaborative and practical approach to problem-solving, which often places them at the forefront of innovation. Nowhere is this more evident than in water management. The Netherlands pioneered dyke systems and polders, tracts of land reclaimed from the sea and kept dry through drainage systems.

In the 17th century, the Dutch 'Golden Age' saw a burst of innovation. The Dutch were major drivers of modern capitalism, introducing the first stock exchange. The VOC issued the first publicly traded shares.

Meanwhile, there were advances in technology. Cornelis Drebbel, a Dutch engineer and inventor, was the first to build a navigable submarine and is credited with inventing the compound microscope. As you sip your gin and tonic, raise a glass to the Dutch, who invented gin as a medicinal drink known as *jenever,* fragrant with juniper berries.

More recent ways the Dutch have impacted the world include the development of wi-fi technology (developed with NCR Corporation and AT&T in 1991) and Bluetooth, invented by Dutch engineer Jaap Haartsen at Ericsson in 1994.

Carrots

Carrots originated in Persia, coming in varieties of red, purple and yellow. The orange carrot we know today is the result of selective breeding in the Netherlands during the 16th and 17th centuries. It's believed that this was to honour the Dutch royal family, the House of Orange-Nassau. What began as a horticultural curiosity and a patriotic gesture has become one of the most recognisable and betacarotene-rich vegetables in the world.

INDEX

A

accessible travel 313
accommodation 305
activities 40-1
    Alkmaar water activities
        134
    Ameland Adventure 228
    Area 51 294
    Chocoladefabriek 197
    Eise Eisinga Planetarium
        228
    Elfstedenhal 226
    Free Movement 130
    Frisian Lakes 232
    giant swing 116
    Hollandsche Manege 96-7
    JFT Watersport 233
    Kanoverhuur Amster-
        damse Bos 103
    Kiewiet Fietsverhuur 227
    Seafloor hikes 228
    skatepark 93
    Skywalk 270
    Supflow SUP Haarlem 130
    Wadden Experience
        Centre 249
Alkmaar 132, 134
Ameland 227, 228
Amersfoort 22, 166, 168, **168**
Amsterdam 46-121, **48-9**,
    see also individual neigh-
    bourhoods
    accommodation 120-1
    itineraries 50-1
    travel within
        Amsterdam 48-9, 61
Amsterdam Noord 116-19, **117**
    accommodation 121
    drinking 119
    eating 118
    travel within
        Amsterdam Noord 116

animals 43, 255
Anne Frank Huis 67-9, 322
architecture & design 16-17,
    102, 338-9
Afsluitdijk 229
Arcam 115
Bridges 82
De Rotterdam 195
ex-squats 92
gable stones 84
Gable Stones 74
Gouwe-Aqueduct 197
Groninger Museum 246
Haarlemmerpoort 71
Het Muizenhuis 62
Oost-Indisch Huis 115
Plan Zuid 100
Proeflokaal de
    Ooievaar 62
Rotterdam 182-3
Royal Delft 212
Sint Janskerk 196
St Janskathedraal 287
Stadhuis 126
Arnhem 262-6, **263**
    cycling 265
    food 265
    travel within Arnhem 262
art galleries & installations,
    see also museums
    Amsterdam in Motion 77
    Beurs van Berlage 61
    Cuyperspassage 61
    Depot at Museum
        Boijmans van Beuningen
        193
    Drents Museum 255
    Fabrique des Lumières 77
    Fish, The 87
    Foam 83
    Frans Hals Museum 129
    Groninger Museum 246
    H'ART 82
    Jheronimus Bosch
        Art Center 282
    Kalverpassage 61
    Kunstinstituut Melly 184
    Muurgedichten 216
    NDSM 118
    Red BMW 182
    Santa Claus 182
    Stedelijk Museum 133
    Utrecht Lumen 158

Vermeer Centrum
    Delft 213
    Spiegelkwartier 84
Artis Zoo 112
ATMs 304

B

B&Bs 305
Batavialand 322
beaches 8-9
    Strand IJburg p111
    Bloemendaal aan Zee 131
Bennebroek 132
Binnenhof 202
boat travel 303
boating 40-3, 273, see also
    boat travel, watertaxis
    Boothuren Giethoorn 271
    Eilandhopper 250
    pedal boats 158
    Rederij Volendam Marken
        Express 144
    Sailing on the
        WADDENZEE 231
books 33
border crossing 302
Breda 292-3
bus travel 303

C

camping 305
canals 18-19, 71, 315, 326
    Amersfoort canals 167
    Amsterdam Oersoep 61
    Binnendieze 286
    Boaty 101
    De Boswinkel 103
    Haarlem Canal Tours 130
    Nieuwegracht 155
    Oudegracht 155
    Rederij Lampedusa 115
    Schuttevaer Canal
        Tours 158
car travel 303
cash machines 304
castles & forts
    Bourtange Fortress 251
    Bouvigne 293

Den Bosch
    citadel 288
    Fort bij Vechten 163
    Fort Kijkduin 138
    Fort Pampus 146
    Fort St Pieter 322
    Kasteel Keukenhof 216
    Muiderslot 146
    Utrecht road trip 165
    Waag 110
cathedrals, see churches &
    cathedrals
caves & tunnels 11
    Maastricht
        Underground 298
cemeteries
    Erebegraafplaats
        Bloemendaal 131
Centraal Station 187
Central Netherlands 258-
    77, **260**
    accommodations 277
    festivals 261
    itineraries 261
    shopping 275
    travel within Central
        Netherlands 267, 274
    travel seasons 261
Centrum 176, 185
children, travel with, see
    family travel
churches & cathedrals
    Co-kathedrale Basiliek van
        de Heilige Nicolaas 53
    De Papegaai 61
    Domkerk 154
    Eusebiuskerk 265
    Grote Kerk van
        St Bavo 128
    Kapucijnenkerk 293
    Nieuwe Kerk 53, 128, 211
    Oude Kerk 60
    Westerkerk 66
climate 30-1
clothes 32
costs 304
    travel 303
country calling code 315
coworking stays 305
credit & debit cards 304
culture 107, 185, 195, 309,
    324-5, 330-2, 333-5, 336-7,
    338-9

Map Pages **000**

cycling 37-9, 40-1, 43, 303
  Arnhem 265
  Bike Totaal Rodenburg 232
  De Boshalte 103
  Guill van de Ven 291
  tours 72-3, 254

D

De Pijp 98-103, **99**
accommodation 121
drinking 100
food 102-3
travel within De Pijp 98
Delfshaven 180-1
Delft 25, 211, 212
Den Bosch 282-9, **285**
  drinking 283
  food 286-7
  transport 282, 290
Den Haag 23, 28, 199-210,
  200-1
  activities 206
  entertainment & nightlife 210
  food 202, 206
  history 202, 207
  itineraries 204
  shopping 208
  travel within Den Haag
    199, 211
  walking tour 204, **204**
Den Helder 138
Deventer 275
disabilities, travellers with 313
doctors & pharmacies 307
DOMunder 320
Drenthe 26, 252-6, **253**
drinking 308, see also
  individual locations
Dutch language 33, 316-17
Dutch Pride 312

E

Eastern Islands 114
Edam 142, 143
Efteling 290
Eindhoven 294
electricity 315
emergency numbers 315
Enkhuizen 142, 145-6, 149
entertainment & nightlife
  83, 308
  Amare 206
  B'Femme 84
  Blend XL 84
  Bostheater 103
  Cinetol 100
  Concertgebouw 93
  De Hallen 97
  De Ridammerhoeve 103
  Forum 242

Groningen 248
  Haarlemmerbuurt 70
  Leidseplein 84
  Lellebel 85
  Melkweg 85
  Montmartre 85
  Movies, The 71
  Museumplein 87
  NedPhO-Koepel 105
  Noorderkerk 71
  Paradiso 85
  Philips Stadium 294
  Reguliersdwarsstraat 84
  Rembrandtplein 84
  Rialto 100
  Vrijhof 295
  Westergas 76
  WORM 184
etiquette 32
Euromast 323
events, see festivals & events

F

family travel 41, 132, 145, 306
  Efteling 290
  Elfstedenhal 226
festivals & events 30-1, 35, 234
  Amsterdam Dance Event
    31, 85
  Amsterdam Light Festival
    30
  Breda Jazz Festival 292
  Carnaval 31, 297
  Elfstedentocht (ice skating
    race) 226
  Groningen 243
  Holland Festival 31
  Johan Cruijff ArenA 107
  King's Day 31
  Museumplein 87
  National Tulip Day 31
  North Sea Jazz Festival
    31, 189
  North Sea Round Town
    fringe festival 189
  Oerol Festival 31, 231
  Kwaku 106
  Tulipmania 77
films 33
food 34-6, 308, see also
  individual locations
  cheese 197
  Edam 142, 143
  Gouda 196, 197
forts, see castles & forts
Franeker (Frjentsjer) 228
Friesland (Fryslân) 218-37, **220**
  accommodations 237
  itineraries 221, 236
  travel seasons 221
  walking tour 236, **236**
Frisian Lakes 27, 232-6, **233**

G

galleries, see art galleries &
  installations, museums
gardens, see national parks,
  parks & gardens
gay & lesbian travellers 312,
  330-2
Giethoorn & Weerribben-
  Wieden National Park 27,
  271-3, **272**
Gouda 25, 29, 196, 197
Groesbeek 269
Groningen 26, 242-8, **245**
  activities 246
  drinking 243
  festivals 243
  food 246, 248
  travel within Groningen 242

H

Haarlem 22, 28, 122-49, **124, 127**
  accommodation 149
  activities 125, 130, 134, 143
  drinking 130
  festivals & events 125
  food 128-9, 143
  itineraries 125
  navigation 124
  shopping 128
  transport 126, 131, 142
  travel seasons 125
  travel within Haarlem 124
Harlingen 229
He Hua Temple 58
health 307
highlights 6-7, 8-19, 67-9
Hindeloopen 233
historic buildings & sites
  Begijnhof Kapel 56
  Binnenhof 202
  Blokhuispoort 225
  Engelse Kerk 56
  Gemeenlandshuis van
    Delfland 212
  Hollandsche
    Schouwburg 112
  Houten Huis 56
  Huize Frankendael 107
  hunebedden 252, 320
  Jachthuis Sint Hubertus 322
  Kamp Westerbork 255
  Markt 211
  Oude Kerk Oosterbeek 266
  Posthoornkerk 70
  Proeflokaal de Ooievaar 62
  Pyramide van Austerlitz 167
  Radio Kootwijk 268
  St Servaasbasiliek 297
  Stadhuis 132
history 12-13, 102, 163, 320-3

Alkmaar 133
Amersfoort 166
Corrie ten Boom Huis 129
Den Haag 202
Fryslân 225
Giethoorn 273
Groningen's former Jewish
  Quarter 248
Hofjes 130
hunebedden 252, 320
LGBTIQ+ 330-2
Napoleonic wars at
  Naarden 147
Nieuwmarkt's Jewish
  Quarter 115
Operation Market
  Garden 264
Red Light District 59
Rotterdam art heist 184
Rotterdam Blitz 190
Stadsarchief 83
Utrecht 155
Zaanse Schans 141
Hoge Veluwe National Park
  267, 268
Hoorn 145
hostels 305
hotels 305
Hunebed Highway 252
hunebedden 320

I

innovation & inventions 338-9
  Afsluitdijk 229
  Phillips 294
insurance 307
itineraries 22-9, see also
  individual locations

J

Johan Cruijff ArenA 107

K

Kampen 274
Kasteel de Haar 164
Kinderdijk 23, 29, 197

L

lakes & dams 326
  Dam 52
  Gasselterveld 256
  Het Wed 131
  Strand Oosterpas 131
language 33, 224, 316-17

Lauwersmeer National
Park 249
Leeuwarden (Ljouwert)
222-6, **223**
drinking 226
food 222, 224
itineraries 222
travel within Leeuwarden
(Ljouwert) 227
Leiden 214
Lelystad 148
LGBTIQ+ travellers 312,
330-2
Lisse 24, 216

Maastricht 295-8, **296**
Marken 143, 144
markets
Albert Cuypmarkt 98
Antiekmarkt 213
Antique Market 129
Boerenmarkt 71
Botermarkt 129
Christmas Market 129
Den Bosch's Markt 287
Grote Markt 129, 210
Kaasmarkt 132
Landmarkt 119
Lindengracht Markt 74
Noordermarkt 74
Ten Katemarkt 97
Vondelparl markets 93
Westerstraat Markt 74
Markthal 191
Mauritshuis 209
Medieval Centre 52-62
drinking 58, 59, 61
food 56
money 304
monuments
Brandaris Lighthouse 231
De Schreeuw 106
Haarlemmerpoort 71
Hoofdtoren 145
Nationaal Monument 52
Nationaal Monument
Kamp Vught 289
National Slavery
Monument 106
Spreeksteen 106
statue of Bosch 283
Waterpoort 232
World Peace Flame 205
Muiden 146, 147
museums, see also art
galleries & installations
Airborne at the Bridge 262
Airborne Museum
Hartenstein 266, 322
Allard Pierson Museum 56

Amsterdam Tulip
Museum 71
Arnhem War Museum 263
Bunker Museum 231
Castellum Hoge
Woerd 163
De Pont Museum 291
Drents Museum 255
Edams Museum 142
Electrische Museumtramli-
jn Amsterdam 97
Eye Filmmuseum 118
Fenix 195
Fotomuseum Den
Haag 207
Fries Museum 224
Fries Scheepvaart
Museum 232
Grachtenmuseum
Amsterdam 70
Groninger Museum 246
Henry Willig's The Story of
Edam Cheese 142
Het Fries
Verzetmuseum 224
Het Natuurhistorisch
Museum 185
Het Scheepvaartmuseum
110, 323
Hollands
Kaasmuseum 132
Houseboat Museum 74
Joods Museum 115
Jopie Huisman
Museum 235
Kaap Skil Museum 137
Kattenkabinet 83
Keramiek Museum
Princessehof 225
Kröller-Müller Museum 267
Kunstmuseum Den
Haag 207
Levend Paarden
Museum 97
Marine Museum 138
Marker Museum 144
Moco Museum 93
Mondriaanhuis 166
Museum
Catharijneconvent 160
Museum De Dageraad 100
Museum de Zwarte
Tulp 216
Museum Giethoorn 't Olde
Maat Uus 273
Museum Gouda 196
Museum Ons' Lieve Heer
op Solder 61
Museum
Rembrandthuis 108
Museum Rotterdam 189
Museum Speelklok 160
Museum van de Twintigste
Eeuw 145

Museum Van Loon 78
Museum Villa 76
Museum Willet-
Holthuysen 79, 321
Museumplein 87
Museumwinkel Albert
Heijn 141
Nationaal Biermuseum 132
Nationaal Fietsmuseum
Velorama 270
Nationaal Jenevermuseum
Schiedam 190
National Prison
Museum 256
Nederlands
Openluchtmuseum 264
NEMO Science
Museum 111
Next Nature 294
Nijntje Museum 160
NXT Museum 119
Philips Museum 294
Railway Museum 159
Rijksmuseum 90-1
Rijksmuseum de
Gevangenpoort 206
Sonnenborgh Museum &
Observatory 160
Stadsarchief 83
Stedelijk Museum 92
Storyworld 242
Teylers Museum 129
Valkhof Museum 270
Van Gogh Museum 94-5
Van Kleef 207
Verzetsmuseum 113
Volendam Museum 144
Wereldmuseum
Amsterdam 104, 322
Wereldmuseum
Rotterdam 183
Westfries Museum 145
Yi Jun Peace Museum 210
Zaans Museum 141
music 33

Naarden 147
Nationaal Park De Alde
Feanen 227
National Holocaust
Museum 113
national parks, see also
parks & gardens
Biesbosch National Park
29, 198
De Noordsvaarder 231
Drenthe 256
Duinen van Texel National
Park 135
Dwingelderveld National
Park 253

Haagse Bos 199
Hoge Veluwe National
Park 267
Koekamp 199
Lauwersmeer National
Park 249
Weerribben-Wieden
National Park 273
Zuid-Kennemerland
National Park 28, 131
Nieuwmarkt 108-15, **109**
accommodation 121
activities 111
drinking 111
eating 110
entertainment 112
itineraries 114
travel within
Nieuwmarkt 108
walking tour 114, **114**
nightlife see entertainment
& nightlife
Nijmegen 269
North Holland 22, 28, 122-49,
126-30, **124, 127**
accommodation 149
activities 125, 130, 134, 143
drinking 130
festivals & events 125
food 128-9, 143
itineraries 125
navigation 124
shopping 128
transport 126, 131, 142
travel seasons 125
travel within North
Holland 124
Northeastern Netherlands
238-57, **240**
accommodations 257
cycling tours 254
entertainment 248
itineraries 241, 247, 254
travel within Northeastern
Netherlands 249
travel seasons 241
walking tour 247, **247**

Olympisch Stadion
Amsterdam 101
Oosterpark 104-7, **105**
accommodation 121
opening hours 315
Oude Kerk 60, 321
Oudewater 167

palaces
  Paleis Lofen 155
  Paleis Noordeinde 208
  Royal Palace 57
parks & gardens, *see also individual locations*
  Amstelpark 101
  Amsterdamse Bos 102
  Begijnhof 56
  Het Park 186
  Hortus Botanicus 112, 214
  Keukenhof Gardens 22, 216
  Koekamp 199
  Noorderpark 118
  Oosterpark 106
  Open Tuinen Dagen 79
  Park Frankendael 107
  Sarphatipark 100
  Vondelpark 86
  Vroesenpark 190
  WH Vliegenbos 119
people 324-5, 333-5
planning 32-3
population 315, 324-5
prescriptions 307
public holidays 315
public toilets 315
public transport 303, *see also individual locations*

Randstad, The 336-7
Red Light District 52-62, **54-5**
  accommodation 120
  food 60
  highlights 57, 60
  shopping 59
  travel within the Red Light District 52
religion 324-5
responsible travel 310
Rijksmuseum 90-1
Rotterdam 23, 29, 170-217, **172-3, 178-9**
  accommodations 217
  activities 192
  entertainment & nightlife 195
  family travel 198
  festivals & events 174
  food 190
  history 190
  itineraries 174-5, 188
  transport 196
  travel seasons 174-5
  walking tour 188, **188**
Royal Palace 57

safe travel 307
Sassenpoort 321
Scheveningen 203
Schiermonnikoog 250
Schokland 148
shopping 59
  Concerto 79
  De Bijenkorf 52
  De Hallen 97
  De Pijp 103
  Den Haag 208
  Haarlem 128
  Haarlemmerbuurt 70
  Hoogkamp Antiquariaat 84
  Kalverpassage 61
  Kalverstraat 61
  Nam Kee 58
  Negen Straatjes 63
  Spiegelkwartier 84
  sustainable 314
  Utrecht 159
  Vondelpark 96
  Zwolle & Deventer 275
SIM cards 302
smoking 315
South Holland 170-217, **172-3**
  accommodations 217
  family travel 198
  transport 196
  travel seasons 174-5
  festivals 174, 205
  itineraries 174-5
  transport 196
travel seasons 174-5
Southeastern Netherlands 278-99, **280**
  accommodation 299
  itineraries 281
  travel seasons 281
Southern Canal Ring 78-85, **80-1**
  accommodation 120
  food 82-3
  travel within the Southern Canal Ring 78
sustainable travel 310
  shopping 314
  swim safety 307

tap water 307
temples
  He Hua Temple 58
Terschelling 231
Texel 135-8, **136**
Tilburg 291
time zone 315
tipping 304
train travel 303

transport 303, *see also individual locations*
  I amsterdam City Card 56
  Tourist Day Ticket 194
  watertaxi 192
travel seasons 30-1, *see also individual locations*
travel to/from The Netherlands 302
travel within
  The Netherlands 303
tulips 216
  Amsterdam Tulip Museum 71
  Tulipmania 77
Twente 276

UNESCO World Heritage sites
  Kinderdijk 197
  Nieuwe Hollandse Waterlinie 328
  Rietveld Schröderhuis 159
  Stelling van Amsterdam 328
  Van Nelle Fabriek 189
  Veenhuizen 256
  Woudagemaal 235
Urk 148
Utrecht City 154-63, **156-7**
Utrecht Province 22, 150-69, **152**
  accommodation 169
  activities 158
  drinking 160-1
  entertainment & nightlife 158, 160-1
  food 163, 164
  festivals & events 153
  history 155
  itineraries 153, 162, 165
  road trips 165
  seasonal travel 153
  travel within Utrecht 164
  walking tours 162, 168, **162, 168**

Valkhofpark 321
Van Gogh Museum 94-5
Van Gogh 268
Veluwezoom National Park 269
viewpoints 10
  A'DAM Tower 116
  Bornrif Lighthouse 228
  Domtoren 154
  Eierland Lighthouse 137
  Eusebiuskerk 265
  Forum 242
  Haagse Toren 206
  Kempentoren 291

Kopje van Bloemendaal 131
  Onze Lieve Vrouwe Toren 168
visas 302
Vlieland 230
Volendam 143
Vondelpark 86-97, 323, **88-9**
  accommodation 120
  drinking 93
  festivals & events 87
  food 87, 92, 96
  highlights 90-1, 94-5
  shopping 96
  travel within Vondelpark 86

Wadden Islands 27
Waddinxveen 197
walking 42-3, 251
walking tours, *see also individual places*
  Centrum 188
  Den Haag 204
  Friesland (Fryslân) 236
  Groningen 247
watertaxis, 192 *see also boat travel*
weather 30-1
Weerribben-Wieden National Park, *see Giethoorn & Weerribben-Wieden National Park*
Westen 186, 189
Western Canal Ring 63-77, **64-5, 73, 75**
  accommodation 120
  drinking 71
  food 70, 77-8
  itineraries 72-3, 75
  shopping 76
  transport 63
  walking tour 75, **75**
wi-fi 302
windmills
  De Gooyer 112
  De Molen Adriaan 130
  De Riekermolen 101
  Zaanse Schans' windmills 141
Workum 234
WWII 320

Zaanse Schans 139, **140**
Zuid 101
Zuiden 190, 192
Zuid-Kennemerland National Park 131-2, 133
Zwolle 27, 275

"Hoge Veluwe National Park (p267) is nothing like the postcard Netherlands. It's a forested ridge, a knobby backbone running through the Central Netherlands."

"Zipping around Rotterdam (p176) in a watertaxi, the captain showboating for my daughter, speeding up, crashing into waves - it's a blast."

All rights reserved. No part of this publication may be copied, stored in a retrieval system, or transmitted in any form by any means, electronic, mechanical, recording or otherwise, except brief extracts for the purpose of review, and no part of this publication may be sold or hired, without the written permission of the publisher. Lonely Planet and the Lonely Planet logo are trademarks of Lonely Planet and are registered in the US Patent and Trademark Office and in other countries. Lonely Planet does not allow its name or logo to be appropriated by commercial establishments, such as retailers, restaurants or hotels. Please let us know of any misuses: lonelyplanet.com/legal/intellectual-property.

Mapping data sources: © Lonely Planet© OpenStreetMap http://openstreetmap.org/copyright

THIS BOOK

This 10th edition of Lonely Planet's The Netherlands guidebook was researched and written by Barbara Woolsey, Abigail Blasi, Mark Elliott, Catherine Le Nevez & Sara van Geloven. The previous edition was also written by them. This guidebook was produced by

Destination Editor
Daniel Bolger

Coordinating Editor
Lauren Keith

Cartographer
Corey Hutchison

Production Editor
Lucy Jones

Image Researcher
Megan Cassidy

Cover Researcher
Rhianydd Hylton

Thanks Sofie Andersen, Fergal Condon, Gwen Cotter, Kate James, Sandie Kestell, Anne Mulvaney

Paper in this book is certified against the Forest Stewardship Council™ standards. FSC™ promotes environmentally responsible, socially beneficial and economically viable management of the world's forests.

Published by Lonely Planet Global Limited
CRN 554153
10th edition - Jun 2026
ISBN 978 1 83869 969 7
© Lonely Planet 2026 Photographs © as indicated 2026
10 9 8 7 6 5 4 3 2 1
Printed in China

PROM LEFT: LUNYI AL/PEARLS/SHUTTERSTOCK, KIRILL UMRIKHIN/SHUTTERSTOCK